T0319929

Stuck with Tourism

Stuck with Tourism

SPACE, POWER, AND LABOR IN
CONTEMPORARY YUCATÁN

Matilde Córdoba Azcárate

UNIVERSITY OF CALIFORNIA PRESS

University of California Press
Oakland, California

© 2020 by Matilde Córdoba Azcárate

Cataloging-in-Publication Data is one file at the Library of Congress

ISBN 978-0-520-34448-8 (cloth : alk. paper)
ISBN 978-0-520-34449-5 (pbk : alk. paper)
ISBN 978-0-520-97555-2 (ebook)

Manufactured in the United States of America

28 27 26 25 24 23 22 21 20
10 9 8 7 6 5 4 3 2 1

Para mi familia, de aquí y de allá

CONTENTS

CONTENTS

ILLUSTRATIONS

MAPS

FIGURES

ACKNOWLEDGMENTS

In hindsight, this book started in 1994, a convoluted year in Mexican history marked by the start of the North American Free Trade Agreement, better known as NAFTA, the Zapatista movement, the assassination of the candidate to the presidency for the Institutional Revolutionary Party (PRI), Luis Donaldo Colosio Murrieta, and civic unrest. It was also the year that, just out of high school, I first visited the Yucatán Peninsula in the southern part of the country. Little did I know then the deep impact this trip would have on my near future.

It was not until 2002 that I came back to the Yucatán Peninsula, this time, to start ethnographic research for a PhD in sociocultural anthropology at the Universidad Complutense de Madrid. The coexistence of radically different social, cultural, and built environments, the perceived stability of tourism sites in the face of national unrest, and the invisible yet utter dependence of tourist cities upon labor from rural areas that I observed in 1994 had animated my anthropological curiosity regarding development. As part of my PhD, I did a binational comparison between two state initiatives that promoted alternative tourism as a rural development strategy: Celestún, in the Gulf of Mexico coast of Yucatán, and Taramundi, Asturias, in the north of Spain. I traced shared dynamics and struggles between tourists and those working for tourism in these places. But by the early 2000, the changes stemming from tourism in the Yucatán Peninsula were too intense and too broad to comprehend as part of a binational comparison. Celestún had morphed into an urban area and tourists had vertiginously multiplied. In my postdoctoral research, I decided to tackle tourism-related changes in the region by following the connections between tourist sites that appeared in Celestún's tourists' narratives as well as in service workers' movements in the region.

This book is the result of this long-term effort. It is the product of many collaborations, each of which has shaped its content and form during a period of over twelve years. I am indebted to the generosity, care, and friendship of many in Yucatán, most of them not part of any academic circles. Including all the people who shared their time and their stories with me, I am especially grateful to the Fuentes family: Ana Garcia and Pedro, Lupe and Atahualpa, Ximena, Peter and Cecilia, Javiera and Joaquin, Daniel, Nicolás, Camila and Mau. Thanks for your friendship, your hospitality and making me one of the family during these many years. Traveling to Yucatán always feels like coming back home and this is thanks to you. I am grateful to Ynnel Cruz and Pato Medina for showing me around the different layers of Yucatán's social life. Thank you to Marco Gutiérrez for always having a spare room for me, and to your family for our conversations, openness, and frankness in addressing Celestún's social aspects. Dreyde and all the craftswomen at the ria and the beach at Celestún, thank you for your frankness and laughter; Carlos, Manuel, and César, thank you for your time and your friendship. Geanny and Giselle, I cherish the bond that staying still yet moving at the beach enabled us to craft. I am thankful to Gabriela Fierro for our shared Temozón Sur fieldwork experience and to the managers and workers at Hacienda Temozón Sur and Hacienda Xcanatún with whom I spoke, interviewed, and walked so many times. Manuel, I would not have learnt about Tekit without you. I am thankful for your teachings as well as those of Don Ben, Doña Ucha, Ana, and your extended family. The pitayas at Don Ben's always made me feel at home with you. *Dios bo'otik.* I am most grateful to Mary Carmen, Leo, and Lidia for opening up your homes and for your patience in showing me the specifics of sewing. Thank you for your friendship, for your time, for sharing your knowledge, and for guiding me so many times when I felt lost.

At different moments and places, Maria Esther Ayala Arciprestre, Idalina Baptista, and Lillyadi Briceño made fieldwork in Yucatán a genuinely enriching experience by opening up doors, walking difficult paths together and sharing good ones, and listening nonstop. How nice to see how geographers, urban planners, communication scholars, and anthropologists can come together to create beautiful things in the most unexpected ways.

Numerous colleagues have shaped this book over the years, at various stages and in many different ways with their intellectual engagement, collegiality, and friendship. None is responsible for the arguments made here and yet without them this book would have been something different. It has been through conversations and discussions with them that many of the central tenants of the book got argued over, strengthened, tied up, and enunciated in written form. María Cátedra, Marie Jose Devillard, Susana Castillo, and Adela Franzé at the Anthropology Department, Universidad Complutense de Madrid, have been a constant reminder that even in times of crisis colleagues remain colleagues and stand for each other. I am grateful for your teachings and mentoring in the earlier stages of my anthropological journey and ever since. Patrick Anderson, Boatema Boateng, Javier Caletrio Garcerá, Maria Dolores Cervera Pacheco, Paloma Checa Gismero, Brian Goldfarb, Amanda Datnow, Jaume Franquesa, Maria Luisa Hernández, Samuel Gaffney, Cindy de la Garza, Lilly Irani, Sofía Lana, Densy Peláez, Paula Santa Rosa Siqueiros, Michaela D. Walsh, and Ameeth Vijay offered continuous camaraderie during my fieldwork, writing, and/or revision phases. I am grateful to have been surrounded by such an amazing group of people.

I owe special thanks to those who read drafts of the book proposal and/or specific chapters. Sarah Buck Kachaluba, Virginia R. Domínguez, Rosaleen Duffy, Ben Fallaw, Alex Fattal, Kimberly Guinta, Angelo Haidaris, Vernadette Vicuña Gonzalez, Grant Leuning, Suzanna Narotzky, Gavin Smith, Rupert Stasch, and Marik Sthern, thank you for engaging each argument with such delicate detail. Catherine Ramírez, Jim and Renata Fernández, Gary Fields, Kathy Kopinak, Valerie Hartouni, Robert Horowitz, and David Serlin, thanks for your support, for our conversations, for your readings and for forcing me to get the story right. Juan Córdoba Ordóñez and Amy Wok, what would have I done without your cartographic knowledge? Sarah Becklake, Bianet Castellanos, Margaret Chowning, Fernando Domínguez Rubio, Kerry Keith, Mimi Sheller, Christo Sims, Daniel Ramírez, and Matt Vitz read the entire manuscript and commented on the line level. Your suggestions and insights refined and enriched many arguments. I am deeply grateful for your time and your generosity.

Chandra Mukerji, Nancy Postero, and Elana Zilberg read and discussed not just one or two, but many iterations of the manuscript. In these last three years, we talked through and rewrote some of its central ideas—and then talked and rewrote again—over coffee, at the beach, at home, and in the office. I can't thank you enough. I am grateful for your trust in my ideas and the ways you showed me that writing is never accomplished alone. Thank you for our friendship, for your understanding, and for your enormous support. I am indebted to José Luis García García, Setha Low, John Urry, and Neil Smith, all of them very present in this work, because at different moments each one "saw the book"—in a very early draft, over an atlas map, in a conversation—

even before I could see it. This book would not have been possible without your intellectual enthusiasm, your uttermost generous attention, and your fearless scholarship.

Research, fieldwork, and writing were made possible by funding from several institutions. I am grateful for the support granted to different parts of this research by the National Predoctoral Fellowship Program of the Spanish Ministerio de Educación y Ciencia; the Department of Social Anthropology at the Universidad Complutense de Madrid; the National Development and Innovation Research Plans of the Spanish Ministerio de Ciencia e Innovación (SEJ2005–05650; CSO2008–04941; CSO2011–26527; CSO2016–75722); the Fulbright Postdoctoral Fellowship Program, and the Oxford Programme for the Future of Cities, University of Oxford. At my home university, the University of California San Diego, I am most grateful to the Unit-18 Non-Senate Faculty Awards as well as to the Senate Faculty Awards and the Academic Senate General Grants, which supported my travel to scholarly meetings and helped me cover the costs associated with two images and the index of this book. The Institute of Arts and Humanities' Early Career Manuscript Fellowship at the University of California San Diego supported me to complete the manuscript in its last stages and its flexibility enabled the fine editing of Amanda Pearson. I am most grateful to my home department, the Department of Communication, for making the book possible, not only by enabling research and time for writing, but also, by pushing me to follow every critical interdisciplinary thread with the reassurance that there is always room for it.

Many other universities and research centers helped this book come together by providing physical space to write, access to libraries, and the opportunity to do formal presentations of research, give talks and classes, or sit in on seminars. These events have uniquely contributed to make this book what it is. I am thankful to the Sociology Department at the University of Lancaster, United Kingdom; the Department of Human Ecology at the Center for Research and Advanced Studies of the National Polytechnic Institute, Mérida, Yucatán (CINVESTAV); the Centre of Latin American Studies at Cambridge University, United Kingdom; and the Earth and Environmental Sciences Program and the Center for Place, Culture and Politics at the Graduate Center, City University of New York (CUNY). I am especially thankful to John Urry, Ana García, Federico Dickinson, Julia Fraga, Julie Coimbra, Yehuda Klein, and David Harvey, who made these arrangements possible by accepting me as an international scholar during different stages of research. I am also grateful to Stanley Brandes and Paolo Favero for granting me access to library resources and seminars at the University of California Berkeley and the University College of London at a time when reading for research was all I needed to do, and to the 940614 UCM research team Territorio, Cultura y Desarrollo for providing a long-standing venue of geographical thinking.

At the University of California San Diego, I am especially thankful to the Center for US-Mexican Studies and in particular, to Greg Mallinger and Melissa Floca, who have seen this book grow with the uttermost interest. In a period of intense teaching responsibilities, it was thanks to you that I found a renewed impulse to keep writing, a much-needed room of my own, and the collegiality of other Mexicanist fellows on campus. I am thankful to the International Institute, whose support for the faculty and graduate research groups Nature, Space and Politics and Indigenous Resource Governance in the Américas over the last three years has been a scholarly anchorage that allowed me to write and revise in the most nourishing intellectual company. The 2019 Mellon Foundation Sawyer Seminar on Cities also provided a stimulating year of revisions and above all, an incredible, generous group of interdisciplinary scholars with whom to read, think, and debate. I am especially thankful to its coprincipal investigators, Nancy Postero, Nancy Kwak, Pamela Radclift, and Sharon Rose. Your support has built an invaluable and much-needed, solid network of care in academia and beyond. Institutionally, I am also very grateful to Pronatura Yucatán and in particular, to Eduardo Galicia for hosting me at the NGO's station during the initial steps of a challenging fieldwork in Celestún.

Over the years, I have shared parts of this book in workshops and sessions at professional meetings. Conversations and discussions born from sharing research in progress have pushed me to finish readable drafts and helped to shape initial thoughts and intuitions into proper arguments. Thanks to all that made this possible either by inviting me to present research, by participating in collective efforts to push disciplinary boundaries, or by joining in conversation. I am especially grateful to Manuela Ivone Cunha for inviting me to organize the 2007 Young Scholars Plenary Session at the European Association of Social Anthropologists on the topic of mobilities; to Naomi Leite, Maria Garvari Barbas, Nelson Graburn, Amir Gohar, and the participants of the 2011 Tourism Imaginaries Workshop and the 2018 Tourism Governance book project at the University of California Berkeley for enabling me to connect to a large network of tourism scholars in the United

States; to the 2011–2012 Public Space Research Group at the Graduate Center at CUNY and their participants; to Fabio Mattioli for inviting me to participate in an urban financialization session at the 2015 American Anthropological Association and to Smoki Musaraj for pushing us to think together about the historicity and spatiality of finance; to Suzanne Scheld and Jayne Howell's efforts to relocate kinship and care to the forefront of my research in Tekit at the 2016 American Anthropological Association meeting and for their constant support for my research; to Claudia Zamorano Villareal for organizing both one of the most productive talks at the Centro de Investigaciones y Estudios Superiores en Antropología Social (CIESAS), México D.F, and a fun co-organized session at the American Geographers Association when we were both about to move out from New York; to Mary Mostafanezhad and Roger Norum for, among many other things, a thought-provoking 2013 American Anthropological session on informality and a double session on the Geopolitics of Tourism at the 2017 American Geographers Association meeting, with particular thanks to Mary for our ongoing efforts to make the proceeds of this meeting into a larger collaboration; to Heather Hindman, Jennie German Molz, Tim Edensor, and Quetzil Castañeda for thought-provoking discussions of research in progress at many of these venues; to the organizers and participants at the Department of Anthropology Monday Seminar at the University of Chicago for a rewarding venue to share a first draft in 2018; and to Gabriela Vargas Cetina, Steffan Igor Ayala, and the 2019 Anthropology Without Limits Conference organizers at the Universidad Autónoma de Yucatán for opening up the door to an amazing network of anthropologists without borders. I am most grateful too to the Seminario Permamente de Turismo at the CINVESTAV and CIESAS, coordinated first by Ana García and Gustavo Marín Guardado, and later by Samuel Joualt from the Universidad Autónoma de Yucatán (UADY). Our seminars and fieldwork stays proved to be a challenging and rewarding forum of regional experts with whom to share fieldnotes and first ideas. I am grateful to all the researchers and students who participated in this seminar and commented on my research, in particular, to the recently formed CO'Ox Mayab network which, as is critical with tourism development, is always on the lookout for initiatives that work.

Kate Marshall, Enrique Ochoa-Kaup, and their team at the University of California Press have been the most supportive, understanding, and attentive editors that I could have imagined. Thank you to Caroline Knapp and Cindy Fulton for walking the manuscript to the end in the most daring circumstances and with such enthusiasm. And thank you all for making this project a reality. It has been a real pleasure working together.

On the more personal journey that this book has been, I am grateful—for the constant support in asking how I was doing—to *mi madrina*, my cousin Susana Vegas, my aunt Isa Azcárate and so many of you that it would take me a page to elaborate! My sisters Inés and Elena have challenged me to make this the book I wanted it to be, even when that meant, most of the time, having less and less time together and traveling further and further away. *Gracias hermanas.* My parents, Mati and Juan, and also Bibo Fer, and my in-laws, Fernando and Rosi, made research and writing manageable after I became a mother and during many summers and winter breaks when I had to carve out silent time to think and write. *Gracias. Siempre pensé que vosotros estabais haciendo el verdadero trabajo.* Mamá, thanks for your almost daily encouragement. You kept me sane and looking at the bright side even at a distance. Papá, thank you for your contagious love for field research and so much more. *Gracias padres por estar ahí siempre.* My children have known this book for their entire lives. They have accompanied me in different moments in the field, making research challenging and gratifying in ways I did not imagine could co-exist. Mateo, thanks for your smiles and encourage-ment over so many international moves and adjustments to new places, lan-guages, routines, and peoples. *Gracias por ponerme café cuando estaba tan cansada de escribir.* Olivia, thanks for your singing and drawing by my side, night and day, no matter where we were. *Gracias por nuestras siestas para pensar mejor.* You two made this book possible too. And Fernan, my loving support, my academic accomplice and partner in life, thank you for granting me sanity over ups and downs, for your intellectual bounteousness, and for your trust in me. This book that you know so well is part of the ecology that we have crafted together, which we now know, with all its beams and cracks, works through different weathers, metaphysical imbroglios, emotional melt-downs, illness, parenthood, cities, peripheries, and everything in between.

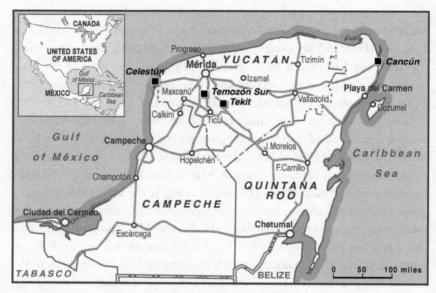

MAP 1. The Yucatán Peninsula and the four sites of this ethnography: Cancún, Celestún, Temozón Sur, and Tekit. Map by author.

Introduction

PREDATORY AND STICKY TOURISM GEOGRAPHIES

IMAGINE A LARGE SCREEN SUSPENDED in front of a manual slide projector. Every time the projector changes slides, the distinct sound of a click is followed by total silence. Then, a buzzing sound.

Click. Silence. Buzz. Slide 1. Cancún. A beach resort city in the Mexican Caribbean. Ata, a thirty-nine-year-old Pemex worker from Veracruz, sits in the kitchen of his small prefabricated house.[1] His wife, Ana, prepares dinner. He recalls his experience of Hurricane Wilma in the city where, in 2005, he had just migrated to work at a large national construction firm. His face is tense, his teeth grind, his hands clench in fists on the table. During the storm he had no choice, he says, but to leave several workers from the villages locked in a small industrial warehouse with just a portable radio and an insufficient supply of water. His supervisor ordered him to lock them up despite knowing that there were only a few gallons of water on hand. Feeling responsible for their well-being, Ata recalls disobeying orders and returning in his van to pick up the workers in the eye of the storm. He mutters, "I remember the silence. The lampposts and trees all over the street.... I remember their faces when I opened up the doors. They were terrified. The storm was not over yet. They had never experienced a hurricane before." Ata's disobedience got him fired. What struck him most was that only two days after the hurricane, those same workers were queuing up among many others hoping to be recruited by tourist resorts to clean the algae and debris from the beach. As Ata put it, "It is as if they were hungry for tourism to come back." For the next two months, the laborers worked to beautify "paradise" in a city built, purposely, to exclude them.

Click. Silence. Buzz. Slide 2. Celestún. A fishing town trapped inside a protected natural area. At the estuary of the UNESCO Ria Celestún

Biosphere Reserve, near the Gulf of Mexico coast, only five hours away from Cancún by car. The ocean breeze. The penetrating chirp of birds emanating from nearby mangrove forests. At intervals, a strong, noxious smell of putrefactive fish, garbage, and salt. Aboard a rudimentary boat, a group of eight middle-aged German tourists observe in silence with their orange life vests on and cameras in hand. They watch two fishermen shout insults and exchange punches over who will give them a ride to observe the pink flamingos at the estuary. For the tourists, this is an unexpected scene. They later tell me how they were taken aback by the violence, which was in stark contrast to the "pristine natural oasis" and "natural sanctuary" featured in the brochures they had received from their hotels. For the fishermen involved in the fight, as well as for both Lalo, a biologist working for a national conservationist NGO in the estuary, and myself, violence had become "the new normal." Fights seemed to be the way to win a spot in the estuary in order to access fish and, more importantly, to get physically close to ecotourism's dollars.

Click. Silence. Buzz. Slide 3. Temozón Sur. Inside an old hacienda's *casa principal* transformed into a luxury hotel in inland, rural Yucatán. It is midday. Intense tropical heat. Insects buzzing. And silence. Stasis. Patricia, a middle-aged Maya indigenous woman dressed in a traditional white *terno* sits in a wooden chair fighting sleep. There are "important guests" at the hotel and she is on call waiting for them to decide if they want body massages. She won't be able to go home that night to care for her sick mother and attend to her three children. When this happens, she says she feels "captive," "treated like a prisoner." Besides, she suffers because she cannot explain to others in the village that the massages she offers inside the gates of the hotel are not sexual, or that the *terno,* the traditional festive attire of Maya women, she wears to work is not meant to seduce guests. But at least, she says, the hacienda hotel gave her "a house to live in, small but a house after all," and she does not have to commute to work or migrate to the coast or the United States, like many other local villagers. She says she is "grateful" to the hotel's owner, whom she refers to as the "new patron."

Click. Silence. Buzz. Slide 4. Tekit. At home at another inland town. It is dusk already. Electrical lines crisscross from house to house. The lamppost lights just went on. A *cumbia* song plays loudly on a portable radio. It is muffled and interrupted by mechanical noises. On and off, short and slow, without pause. Inside a one-room cement house, Luis and Lucía, a young married Maya couple, are sewing on Singer machines. Their heads are bent over, their backs slightly curved toward the machines. Their eyes, watery and red, are intently focused on the needles. One hand on the needle, one hand on the fabric. Their feet, in flip-flops, are on the pedals. Behind them there is a king-size bed with a white embroidered quilt, a wooden wardrobe, a large plasma TV and radio with speakers, and a small altar with all its figurines covered with blue sheets. They tell me that these sheets protect their belongings "from cotton pollution." Like most in town, they are assembling the regional shirt, the guayabera, coveted as a textile souvenir and ubiquitous as uniforms in the hospitality industry. They have become financially indebted and beholden to Lucía's uncle who brings them the cloth to sew. They claim that assembling the shirts is a "true, true job." But it generates cataracts in their eyes, asthma in their lungs, and financial and moral debts. And yet, this work is the only way for them "to have a good life," to save money for the village's fiesta, to stay together as a family, and to care for the land as their ancestors did.

. . .

During my ethnographic fieldwork in the Yucatán Peninsula in southern Mexico, from 2002 to 2016, I documented the region's dramatic transformation through state-planned tourism development. The vignettes above situate the four ethnographic chapters of this book, in which I explore the livelihoods, contradictions, and sacrifices, the invisible and partial relations, the labor and sensorial landscapes that have created and sustained this region as a global tourist space since the mid-1970s. These moments illustrate how tourism pervades the region's landscape, transforming social relations and household dynamics by erasing potentialities and displacing habitual ways of doing, living, and imagining. But simultaneously, they show how tourism opens up unexpected collaborations, spaces of hope, and opportunities for well-being that previously did not exist.

The goals of this book are to make empirical sense of the tension between how tourism destroys and how it creates, and to understand how the Yucatán's inhabitants "get stuck to tourism" as their only route for making a "good life." I do this through an ethnographic exploration of how people like Ata, Patricia, Lalo, Luis, and Lucía maneuver within what has become an inescapable tourism reality. Their experiences, and the buildings and landscapes they inhabit, constitute a contemporary geography of late capitalism whose importance has been underestimated.

The everyday scenes and contradictions captured in the vignettes above belong to Yucatán, but they could easily describe other everyday lives in the many places around the world where tourism has become an inescapable component of contemporary life.

Tourism is a major force in the shift to a service economy, one that organizes the circulation of people, goods, capital, and images around the world. Services and commodities created for tourists shape quotidian and intimate acts in consumer societies, from how we make sense of and move around our cities, to how we daydream about escaping from the grind of work and everyday pressures, to how we construct personal identities. Although as tourists we rarely notice, the people who provide these services and produce those commodities are also transformed by them.

Chances are that you have been a tourist, traveling to experience new things, to learn from others, to encounter new landscapes and emotions, to give back, or to rediscover your inner self. Souvenirs from those trips might decorate your home. Chances are that you have experienced tourism, both its pleasures and its prices, crowds, and pollution. You might even have worked for the hospitality industry, as a bartender, a volunteer, a guide, or maybe you have shared your couch or rented your house to tourists.

The powerful effects of tourism are a relatively recent phenomenon. Barely a century ago, tourism was a privileged activity within the reach of the affluent alone. It was only after the Second World War, with the expansion of the consumption society and the emergence of the leisured middle classes, that tourism began to consolidate itself as an industry that has since morphed into a pervasive reality. This process began between the mid-1950s and the 1970s, when states and governments in the First World started to promote mass tourism through modernization discourses that emphasized technological and infrastructural development and economic growth as a way to help societies with "comparative advantages" in their march toward Western ideals of mass consumerism and progress (Mowforth and Munt 2015; Britton 1991). The expansion of the tourist industry accelerated in the 1980s and 1990s as part of neoliberal agendas set by states and international organizations across the world and meant to develop emergent ideas of socially equitable and green economic growth (Rojek and Urry 1997). For many countries, especially poorer countries in the so-called Third World, tourism was seen as a path that could integrate them symbolically and practically into the world community

(Enloe 2000, 3). Since the 2000s, amid ecological and financial crises, tourism has continued to grow. Governments have fostered this expansion through discourses of poverty alleviation, pro-poor development, heritage preservation, and community participation as ways of "contributing," "giving back," and "empowering" through "guilt-free" ethical spending and mindful travel.[2] The UN proclamation of 2017 as the International Year of Sustainable Tourism for Development reflects the contemporary belief that tourism is a catalyst for effective development because it enhances natural conservation and "resource efficiency," reverses colonial inequalities, empowers marginalized indigenous people, and builds cross-cultural "corporate empathy" and "global prosperity."[3]

Today, it is difficult to find a country that has not promoted itself as a tourist destination or that has not used tourism as a major economic sector and an integral part of its growth policies (Telfer and Sharpley 2015). This has made tourism the fourth-largest export sector in the world after fuels, chemicals, and automotive products. In 2019, tourism generated US$8.9 trillion (10.3 percent of global GDP) and 330 million jobs, the equivalent of one in ten jobs in the global economy (World Travel and Tourism Council 2019). Tourism is also one of the largest catalysts of global human mobility, similar in force and manner, some authors claim, to military mobility and empire building (Baranowski et al. 2015). International tourism has been growing at an annual rate of 3–5 percent over the last ten years, outpacing the growth of international trade and other sectors of the economy (World Travel and Tourism Council 2019; UNWTO 2019b). And these numbers show no sign of abating. The World Travel and Tourism Council (2019) forecasts that tourism will grow 4 percent annually until 2030. In less developed countries, "tourism acts as an engine for development through foreign exchange earnings and the creation of direct and indirect employment" (World Travel and Tourism Council 2019). Tourism is the highest or second-highest source of export earnings in twenty out of the forty-seven world's least developed countries (UNWTO 2017b). For many of these countries, "tourism *is* development," as Mexico's 2001–2006 National Development Plan bluntly put it.[4]

Tourism's centrality to the organization of contemporary life makes it a force that extends well beyond the economic realm. Tourism also pervades the sociocultural, political, and ecological arenas. The tourist industry is one of the leading producers of global imaginaries.[5] It is a powerful form of meaning-making: narratives of the self and other, conceptions of the past and the future, and dreams of natural and cultural encounters are produced by tourism through desire, anticipation, and memorabilia (MacCannell 2011; Gravari-Barbas and Graburn 2016; Salazar and Graburn 2016).Over the last decades, the tourist industry has massively reorganized and repurposed the physicality of places to fit those dreams and imaginaries, recreating the untouched tropical island, the primitive native village, the pristine natural reserve, the authentic past. It has done so through specially curated built environments and infrastructures that aim to foster consumption—the oceanfront all-inclusive resort, the restored colonial building, the scenic highway, the theme park—and through discourses of contemplation, cultural encounter, heritage preservation, cultural remediation, indigenous empowerment, civic engagement, or sustainable participation (Sorkin 1992; Dávila 2016; Vogel 2016).[6]

Tourism has also become a generalized practice of statecraft. Across the Pacific and the Caribbean, tourism has been propelled by governments and tourist stakeholders as the "new sugar" (Sheller 2003; Pattullo 2005; Gonzalez 2013) and in the Americas, as well as in Chinese and Arab regions, tourism has manufactured leisure cities from scratch. This is the case with Cancún in the Yucatán Peninsula (chapter 1), Las Vegas, Atlantic City, Thames Town, and Dubai, among others. These themed cities follow the same modernist ideals that Holston (1989) described in his anthropological critique of Brasília, Brazil's manufactured capital city in the 1960s. In Europe, Canada, and North America, urban planning is almost inseparable from tourism, and cities such as Barcelona, Palma de Majorca, Skopje, Vancouver, and San Francisco are pushed toward creating monumental architecture and cultural and natural heritage designations, and advancing gentrification in the name of tourism growth (e.g., Franquesa 2013; Mattioli 2014; Shoval 2018).

The importance of tourism is also visible in how it produces ideas and captivates hopes about collective and individual class and gender identities, ethnicities, and sense of belonging. At a collective level, international tourism is widely promoted by states, governments, and international agencies as an effective tool for dialogue and cultural exchange capable of building bridges across seemingly insurmountable political and cultural differences. As the UN World Tourism Organization put it, tourism promotes "cultural wellbeing, environmental restoration, peace and mutual understanding" (UNWTO 1980, 2017a). At an individual level, tourism is about having fun or getting jobs. Tourism also fosters dreams and defines values for the modern and postmodern selves. Tourism, as MacCannell (2011, 53) puts it, epitomizes the imperative social command to "Enjoy!" But tourism and traveling are also epitomes of freedom, social distinction, and upward class and social mobility for the working, middle, and upper classes. Consumption societies legitimize traveling and spending as civic practices that foster national, regional, local or household socioeconomic good. The mantra "shop, fly, and spend," popularized post-9/11 in the United States, exemplifies these experiences to the extent that moving around the world as a tourist has been internalized as part of what it means to be an exemplary global citizen (Brown 2016).[7]

Tourism is so integral to the tapestry of contemporary life that it is almost elevated to the rank of a human right. In fact, the UN World Tourism Organization's 1980 Manila Declaration on World Tourism reads: "the right to access to holidays and to freedom of travel and tourism, a natural consequence of the right to work, is recognized as an aspect of the fulfillment of the human being by the Universal Declaration of Human Rights." It should not come as a surprise, therefore, that the Manila Declaration continues, "tourism is considered an activity essential to the life of nations, its development is linked to the social and economic development of nations and can only be possible if man . . . has access to creative rest and holidays and enjoys freedom to travel" (UNWTO 1980, 1). Five years later, the UN World Tourism Organization Tourism Bill of Rights and Tourism Code asserted that "the exercise of this right constitutes a factor of social balance and enhancement of national and universal awareness" (UNWTO 1985). In 1997, the UN Global Code of Ethics for Tourism (GCET) stated that the "right to tourism" should be seen as "a right equally open to all the world's inhabitants," encouraging all, and in particular public authorities, to support and warrant the liberty of tourist movements (UNWTO 2007). In 2019, the GCET is still not legally binding but it has been signed by hundreds of private stakeholders and adopted as a corporate tourism governance model.[8]

Crucially, the transformation of tourism into a central feature of contemporary social life has not been smooth. The tourist-host relationship has always been an ambivalent one, fraught with tension and deception. Conflict often stems from the industry's selective interpretations of history as heritage and from uneven land appropriation, both of which directly contribute to environmental degradation and rapid acculturation.[9] Like traveling and travel writing, tourism engages in, and reproduces, colonial, celebratory narratives of European or North American superiority (Pratt 2007; Nixon 2017; Sheller 2003). In the Global South, tourism has acted as a form of imperialism through symbolic, embodied, and material violence (Nash 1977; Kincaid 1988; Nixon 2017).[10] Tourism, like war, can reinforce prevailing ideas of empire as well as forms of gendered and racial domination (Lisle 2016; Gonzalez 2013; Kincaid 1988; Enloe 2000). In the Caribbean for example, myths and metaphors of paradise are formed around the plantation (Nixon 2017). And while contemporary dreams of delight are necessarily reconfigured versions of privilege, so too has tourism become one of the world's most contested political arenas.

The importance of tourism for local, national, and global economies and the generalized and intense circulation of tourism imaginaries and identities have transformed tourism into a powerful geopolitical anchorage that informs, contests, and coproduces contemporary politics at international, national, regional, local, urban, and household scales. On the one hand, and in the name of securing international tourism, tourist cities and regions have become favorite grounds for the privatization of public space and for militarization.[11] Historic battlefields, concentration camps, bases, even nuclear plants have become landscapes of tourism expansion (Lisle 2016; Klein 2008; Enloe 2000; Sheller 2003; Gonzalez 2013). In these sites, tourism is used as a political technology and a weapon to advance nationalist ambitions and ethnic assimilation projects. On the other hand, tourism destinations and attractions, like beaches, religious monuments, and parks refashioned for tourism, have become sites where people gather to claim their rights and to protest political decisions and assaults on citizenship (Low, Taplin, and Scheld 2005; Edensor 1998).

In some places, local populations have attacked tourists or fenced themselves off as ways to cope with contradictions (Boissevain 1996). Among fishing communities in the Gulf of Mexico coast, ecotourism resulted in an uptick in violence, as Lalo and I could observe, as a way to control the few jobs it provides (chapter 2). In other locations, people have exploited cultural stereotypes (Cohen 1987; Chambers 2009; Vainikka 2015) or invented and reappropriated rituals, such as festivals, for nationalist projects (Hobsbawm and Ranger 1992; Rowen 2016; Picard and Robinson 2006). In other instances, tourism's meanings and practices cohabitate with entrenched local ways of organizing, creating novel contradictions and struggles for the control of resources, cultural meanings, and physical space (Edensor 1998, 2005; Wynn 2011). Among indigenous peoples in Latin America, for example, tourism development begets new forms of servitude but also old forms of labor activism and resistance (chapter 3). In many European cities where locals have become outnumbered by tourists, like Venice, Lisbon, and Barcelona, antitourism and tourism-phobic social movements are gaining new political leverage in the larger fight for affordable housing and access to public space.[12] In these places, citizens unite to fight "overtourism," or too much tourism, asking for better regulations and strict limitations on tourism, not in order to demand the end of tourism but in order to regain housing affordability, public space, and quality of city life.[13]

At the same time, tourist sites and infrastructures created for tourism—such as hotels, scenic drives, museums, fairs and festivals, markets, malls, trains, or airports—have become at risk for violent attacks due to their iconic status as global symbols of Western excess and uneven capital accumulation (see Clayton and Korstanje 2012). The terrorist attacks in Barcelona's popular Ramblas, Berlin's Christmas market, and iconic tourist areas in London, Paris, Manchester, and Brussels are examples of this growing global phenomenon.[14]

In addition to its economic, social, and geopolitical significance, tourism has also become an important variable in the precarious ecological balance of the planet. In the Anthropocene, or more accurately the Capitalocene (Moore 2015), tourism is a driver of climate change.[15] Tourists fly, drive, or navigate to their destinations using carbon-intensive means of transportation. Skiing, water activities, recreational hunting and fishing, mountain hiking, biking on trails, sightseeing, shopping, and eating out are tourism-related activities that contribute to environmental pollution and gas emissions. Between 2009 and 2013, the practices of traveling, shopping, and eating associated with tourism were responsible for 8 percent of global greenhouse gas emissions (Lenzen et al. 2018). Tourism-led urbanization, infrastructure development, beach development projects, and food and souvenirs commodity chains, to name just a few, also affect soil, flora, fauna, air, and water in forests, deserts, and oceans across the globe.

All these economic, political, sociocultural, and ecological variables together make tourism one of the most powerful orderings of the geographies of contemporary capitalism.

TOURISM AS AN ORDERING OF
LATE CAPITALIST GEOGRAPHIES

Arguing that tourism is an ordering implies that it is an active social and geographical force that carves up the landscape and permanently recasts values and identities, as well as sociocultural, political, and ecological life.[16] Tourism spaces are not already there, waiting for us to visit them. Rather, they are spaces that need to be systematically imagined, narrated, planned, designed, constructed, performed, sustained, and secured, in both imagination and physical form, *as* tourist spaces *under* the tourist gaze.[17] This is a process of production that takes place through the labor of government officials, planners, real estate agents, architects and designers, conservationist experts, development volunteers, and service workers alike (Urry 2011, 2007; Sheller and Urry 2004; Gonzalez 2013).

Tourism orderings work in practice by *re-spatializing* and *scaling-up* territory, nature, and sociocultural life for global consumption. By re-spatializing I mean creating new sociocultural relations and ecological processes through their relocation in social and geographical space (Low 2016); and by scaling-up I mean amplifying—both in discourse and practice—particular ideas about space, nature, and culture.[18] These processes of tourism re-spatialization and scaling-up occur simultaneously across geographical scales at material, symbolic, ecological, and political levels.

On a material level, tourism scales up places and peoples, ecosystems and habitats as productive forces in the pursuit of profit-making. In this sense, tourism has become one of the most powerful terraforming activities in late capitalist societies. Governments and corporations engineer forests, mountains, beaches, deserts, islands, wetlands, and material infrastructures such as roads, streets, houses, hotels, pools, parks, and museums, designing them to shape new relations of people, capital, labor, and resources (Hannam, Sheller, and Urry 2006). Tourism landscapes and infrastructure require not only new modes of circulation, but also new forms of stasis, immobility, and mooring, as well as forms of being and acting in the world (Bissell and Fuller 2013). Tourism reworks bodies and creates subservient classes of workers, especially among ethnic and indigenous minorities. Tourism landscapes and infrastructure reorient action to and through consumption; in order to enlarge the presence of markets, they promote flexible labor and intensify the extraction of land as well as natural and cultural resources for the enjoyment of a few.[19]

On a symbolic level, tourism creates and stabilizes iconic infrastructures and modernist architectures through which the world is apprehended and ordered according to Western cultural imaginaries of escape and encounter. These modernist infrastructures and architectures colonize imaginations of the past, the present, and the future, and manufacture neoliberal consent around embodied dispositions to serve and/or to consume.[20] In so doing, tourism secures territories in a sedentarist Western metric of progress, civilization, and cultural domination. For this reason, tourism's symbolic orderings are also a pervasive lens through which people view the world and each other, and through which the very idea of the other is constituted and consumed. This tourist gaze, as John Urry calls it, has become one of the most powerful orderings, defining and reifying patterns of inclusion and exclusion, gender and racial ideologies, and understandings about nature, culture, and society at large. In many parts of the world, tourism oversimplifies indigenous bodies, politics, and places by promoting a kind of primitivism and pastoral exoticism used to reveal or conceal larger national market goals.[21]

On an ecological level, tourism orders and regulates physical environments by mobilizing and consuming natural resources like water, sand, and air for leisure and consumption, by scripting the natural world according to modern aesthetics of contemplation, management, and spectacle, and by reorganizing regionally and locally specific ecological relations between inland and coastal ecosystems alongside largely international tourist flows and desires (Urry 1995; Igoe 2017; Haldrup and Larsen 2009; Sheller 2003). Since the advent of industrial capitalism, tourism has read the landscape and exploited it for profit (Urry 1995; Macnaghten and Urry 1998). From pioneer seaside resorts such as Blackpool in Lancashire, to the largest mass resorts of the Caribbean, to Dubai's engineered Palm Islands, to incursions in the Antarctic, tourism involves material interventions in the physical landscape accomplished through recurrent shortsightedness in planning, and the enclosure of land and resources. Moreover, these tourist infrastructures—such as oceanfront hotels, malls, roads, and boardwalks—rely on activities that have irreversible ecological consequences, such as aluminum mining and smelting (Sheller 2014), or sand dredging to refill beaches and aid construction.

On a political level, tourism orderings are meaningful and powerful forces whose influence spans geographic scales. The grand tours of the seventeenth through nineteenth centuries, facilitated by the advent of large-scale rail transportation, moved British nobility to France and Italy in search of the roots of Western civilization. Having taken such journeys could grant them influential political positions, marriage into a higher social class, and increased social mobility after their return home (Urry 2011). In the centuries that followed, rail and steamship travel became more accessible and travel in general became more democratized. The mantra "tourism *is* development," mentioned earlier, has more recently led to tourism informing a vast array of the relations between North and South, rich and poor, developed and underdeveloped countries. Moreover, as noted earlier, contemporary tourism orders geographical relations—urban and rural, coastal and inland—through political ideologies of consumption that enunciate, in a classist, racialized, and gendered manner, who can move, to where, and how. Tourism and traveling are practices of statesmanship and nation building, generating new centers and pleasurable peripheries (Hall 2017; Lew 2001). They animate and legitimize discourses and practices of territorial ambition and control. Tourism imaginaries, often restrictive and stereotypical, inform a great deal of the formation of contemporary political affects, including fears about and hopes for the future (Mostafanezhad, Córdoba Azcárate, and Norum, forthcoming 2021).[22]

It is important to understand tourism today not simply to learn about the particularities of the industry or the dynamics of host-guest encounters. Equally important is that tourism, like religion, family, the market, and the state, has become a key variable of contemporary patterns of sociopolitical and cultural life, racial and gender discrimination, sovereignty disputes, militarization, ecological deterioration, the circulation of commodities, the organization of labor, and uneven geographical capital accumulation. Tourism matters, in other words, because it is a powerful socio-material, semiotic, and political vector shaping how we read, move through, dwell and work in, carve out, and *interpellate* the world.

My account of tourism as an active ordering of the geographies of late capitalism is concerned with the question of *how all of this happens in practice:* How does tourism work as an agent in the production of space? Who is doing this labor? And at what costs? To respond to these questions, I have followed the perspectives and experiences of those who design, organize, manage, study, and govern tourism destinations as well as of those who work for the industry, who live in, visit, and consume tourism places and attractions.

The main finding that I develop in this book is that the contemporary re-spatializing and scaling-up of tourism orderings is creating a new type of geography of capitalist production and consumption, what I call a *predatory and sticky tourism geography.* This is a geography that naturalizes processes of extraction—of land, resources, labor, and culture—and that entraps people in contradictory situations in which predation is the only way forward.

PREDATION, TOURISM, AND EXTRACTION

My research in Yucatán shows that tourism generates a predatory geography because it operates in an extractive way. Throughout this book I show how tourism works according to a typical extractive logic, by which it invades, plunders, and exhausts places, bodies, and resources in order to satisfy short-term consumer demands at the expense of long-term considerations for their renewal.[23]

Like other extractive industries, such as mining, oil, or gas, tourism is predicated upon coordinated orderings of spatial, social, and ecological life that demand long-term, costly, and capital-intensive infrastructure development. Its logistics are multiscalar. That is, tourism orderings are simultaneously governed by actors and institutions across local, regional, national, and international scales.[24] Their logic is predatory because tourism works by generating an institutionalized consensus across scales and actors to govern the world through extraction—of human labor, natural and cultural resources, local wealth, and memories—for both profit and the enjoyment of those with the discretionary capital and time for leisure. As such, tourism is a coordinated form of capitalist power that, like large dams and coal or lithium mines, is reengineering the Earth in dramatic and most probably, irreversible ways.

Tourism's extractive logic is premised on territorial enclaves.[25] Much in the same way that oil, gas, and mining industries require offshore platforms, large pipes, and large pits in order to operate, tourism engineers and stages—materially and symbolically—landscapes to transform things into how they "should be." In the process, there is erasure, cancellation, and the destruction of other possible worlds.[26] This is clearly visible in Yucatán's coastal and inland areas. The region's coasts have been reorganized by tourism as transnational global enclaves that cater to cosmopolitan imaginaries of escape and encounter with nature, while inland areas have been transformed to cater to nostalgic imaginaries of ancient Maya culture and indigeneity (chapter 4). Following this reorganization, places like Cancún are made to appear "global" and connected through recognizable symbols of cosmopolitanism, such as high-rise glass "starchitecture" (chapter 1), internationalized environmental brands (chapter 2), or gourmet culinary experiences offered in indigenous hacienda hotels (chapter 3).[27] Other locations, such as Tekit, must respond to a rhetoric of locality and tradition, and offer exotic displays of cultural Otherness as primitivism (chapter 4). As a constitutive form of extractive capitalism, or *extractivismo* as it is called in Latin America, tourism development reorganizes social life and its material expression in such a way that it enables and normalizes resource extraction. And like other extractive enclaves, tourism enclaves, their infrastructures, architectures, and built environments also reduce life to capitalist resource conversion (Gómez-Barris 2017; Svampa 2015; Sawyer and Gómez 2012).[28]

Once ordered under the tourist gaze as locations one can escape to and/or where one can encounter nature or other cultures, places and people become in practice "positional goods": goods whose value derives from their spatial position in socioeconomic fields of meaning and practice (Hirsch 1976; Redclift 2006). Maintaining this position requires reflexive inquiry (Stasch 2009; Bruner 2004), that is, an active recognition of how tourism's imaginaries and spatialities are at work. It also requires the stability of touristic representations in time and physical space, which demands, in turn, the stability of material infrastructure for tourist circulation and consumption, and of the forms of labor and power subtending them.

Like other extractive industries, tourism relies on cheap labor (Patel and Moore 2017). We are familiar with some of its most common and visible expressions, like the hotel maid, the bellboy, the restaurant server, the cook, or the tour guide. Yet, as this book shows, there are a myriad of other less visible forms of labor and forms of labor (im)mobility acting in the shadows of the tourist stages. For example, there is the stasis and intensive family labor involved in creating souvenirs from home (chapter 4), or the stillness and fist fights that locals engage in to get proximate to tourists at UNESCO-protected natural areas (chapter 2), or the place-based re-patronages and modern forms of indigenous labor subordination at reconstructed hacienda hotels (chapter 3). Some forms of cheap labor, such as the ones that exist in hacienda hotels, find their genealogy in colonial forms of domination. Other forms of cheap labor, such as the ones that keep afloat mass beach resorts (chapter 1) or the ones that transform houses, villages, and livelihoods into factories for the hospitality industry (chapter 4), respond to contemporary forms of predatory financial capitalism.

At the same time, maintaining the position of tourist sites in the global market also requires constantly carving out and scaling-up new assets for global consumption. Just as oil and gas extraction industries seek new oil fields and gas deposits, the tourism industry constantly searches for new spaces, resources, and experiences that it can incorporate into the extractive logic of global consumption. Crucially, however, and in contrast with other extractive industries, the assets that can be incorporated into this tourist extractive logic are virtually endless. Almost anything, anywhere, can become a resource for the tourism industry: a place, a tradition, a ritual, a plant, an animal, food, bodies, emotions, solidarity, revolution, even health, birth, death, or environmental disasters (Bunten 2008; Greenwood 1989).[29] Tourism is, in this sense, one of the most efficient capitalist technologies, thanks to its almost unmatched capacity to advance production and consumption through the seemingly endless creation of new zones of commodification (Moore 2015).[30]

Tourism geographies are also predatory because tourism is carving up the planet for consumption in environmentally unsustainable ways. As noted earlier, tourism directly contributes to climate change. In addition to the environmental footprint required to sustain the massive system of mobilities organized around the tourist industry, maintaining touristic representations of destinations requires extensive natural resources. Tourism consumes places, and, like other extractive industries, it produces controversial "ecological amputations" (Gudynas 2015, 25). Tourism development might not advance through the exercise of direct, physical violence, or state and military repression, but tourism also acts in a violent manner.[31] Its orchestrated inscriptions in the material and symbolic forms of social, cultural, and ecological life in order to render lands and peoples extractable have become so naturalized, so normalized, that they might be preventing the imagination of worlds outside of capitalism.[32]

While many scholars have studied the commodification and circulation of natural and cultural elements for tourism consumption, the associated extractive processes of *maintaining* a space as a tourist space have been less scrutinized (Sheller and Urry 2004). As I detail in chapter 1, maintaining the white and powdery sands that sustain the image of the idealized Caribbean beach in Cancún requires nested processes of land and resource enclosure as well as constant dredging to remove sand from protected coral reefs. Enclosing and dredging are pervasive social and ecological practices that privatize common areas and contribute to the deterioration of the reefs and to coastal erosion, accelerating inequalities and reducing the natural barriers that coastal cities need to protect themselves from storm surges and winds. Likewise, maintaining a nostalgic representation of the past in inland Yucatán requires producing and sustaining European-inspired built environments, architectures, and forms of landscaping and taste that not only privatize local communal resources, like cenotes, and basic services like water provision, but also introduce invasive species that threaten local ecosystems and keep a colonial past (chapter 2 and chapter 3). And as I show in chapters 1, 2, and 3, tourism contributes to and benefits from ecological disasters, which the tourism industry views as propitious opportunities to maintain and expand its extractive logics. In Yucatán, such practices are evident in the aftermath of hurricanes, when state and local governments, real estate agencies, and nonprofit organizations lead reconstruction processes that further the extractive nature of tourism through land and resource enclosure.

Tourism, therefore, is predatory because it opens up territories for consumption and profit. It does so by surrendering land and its future uses to financial whims, by prioritizing transnational corporate rule, and by dispossessing younger generations from the possibilities of making a living from their lands in the long term. Yucatán is an example of such a fragile and vulnerable landscape, where, as I show, state-planned tourism development has short-circuited citizenship by debilitating social networks of care and belonging (chapter 1), and has reorganized family life and households by entrapping them in financial debt and the cycles of the industry's seasonality (chapter 4), resulting in ecological and social conflicts across the region.

And yet, describing tourism orderings as predatory offers only a partial picture of how tourism works in practice. Tourism simultaneously invites and constrains, provides and weakens. This is evident in Ata's account of the Cancún workers' hunger to rebuild a place created to exclude them, or in Luis and Lucía's account of assembling guayaberas from home, a "true, true job" that despite compromising their health has enabled them to stay together as a family, to care for land and valued traditions, and to provide a better existence for themselves. This is the paradox that makes tourism landscapes "sticky."

TOURISM AND STICKINESS-AS-ENTRAPMENT

I describe tourism orderings of land and of ecological and sociocultural life as *sticky* because they work as forms of entrapment. They trap, capture, and entangle everyday rhythms, and with them, people's livelihoods and imaginaries. Tourism holds people in place and places in time.[33] People *get stuck* in and with tourism's predatory orderings because tourism enables, even if only in the short term, the amelioration of otherwise precarious conditions of living.[34]

During my ethnographic fieldwork over the years, service workers, governmental officials, urban planners, scientists and common people expressed to me how they felt that they and others in the region were "stuck with tourism" (*engrapados al turismo*). They always used the expression in a bittersweet tone that indicated both the widespread, visible, material footprints of tourism's infrastructure in the landscape and also the impossibility of escaping them. But the phrase was not only about the present.

Tourism's stickiness established a relation with time. Often, particularly among indigenous peoples working at beach resorts or luxury hacienda hotels, it was used to conjure up a centuries-long, thriving monocrop agro-industrial landscape that had turned to ruins, leaving people devoid of economic alternatives by the 1970s, but which people "had grown used to." Being stuck with tourism, then, also established a comparison with the way things were in the past. It evoked evoked acceptance of the lasting and potentially pervasive dynamics expected from the state-led turn towards as yet another monocrop economy tourism. Stickiness served to make sense of this present by recourse to the past. As an expression, "stuck with tourism" reminded people that state-led tourism was a long-term response to another economic and social crisis.

Since the mid-1970s, the territories and resources scaled-up for and by state-planned tourism development have become the new centers of economic, sociocultural, and political life. Tourism has become the lens through which life is apprehended and the terrain wherein life unfolds. For example, it is the roads and Cancún's international airport, both created to support international tourism, that organize the distribution of bodies, labor, food, capital, and supplies. It is physical proximity to tourism's stereotypical representations of indigenous Maya Otherness that grants some the ability to provide for their families and stay put, while condemning others to migrate (chapters 3 and 4). It is tourism's seasonality that marks the rhythms of air pollution, ocean acidification, and waste production in the region's subterranean water networks, as well as the quality of the sand, the duration of fishing bans, the presence of the military, or the migratory and feeding cycles of endangered animal species, like the pink flamingo (chapter 2).

The geographies produced by tourism orderings are not only sticky in a material, physical way or in reference to a present that echoes a past of economic dependence. In Yucatán, to be stuck with tourism is to be rooted in place, immobilized, or forced to move, hyperconnected to the global and sutured to the spaces and temporalities created by the industry's whims. Importantly, it is also about being trapped or entangled within *contradictory moral regimes*. I call these moral regimes contradictory because, as I show, they get people stuck in situations of ambivalence. While tourism's predatory ways are generally acknowledged as oppressive in Yucatán, they have become accepted and reproduced as necessary, inevitable, effective, or even good, as means to access a better life.

Acknowledging that this tourist reality is inescapable, people in Yucatán engage in strategic entanglements with the past, with family and kin organization, with former forms of labor and political activism in order to make sense of, maneuver through, and sometimes temporarily avoid or contest just-in-time and flexible modes of labor which they acknowledge they are unable to fully disengage from.[35] As Castellanos (2010a) notes, for example, indigenous peoples from inland Yucatán often describe Cancún as the *xtabay*, a siren who entraps wayward men and consumes them. Cancún is a place of allure and opportunity, a magnet that *is also* a place of vice. For low-wage service and construction workers like the ones Ata worked with, for city planners, or for government officials in the city, participating in tourism's predatory ways becomes a necessary condition to make a living, to govern, and to open up individual and collective spaces of hope. For example, I detail how local researchers working to mitigate receding beaches along the Caribbean have to strategically channel international funds to ameliorate urban planning provisions for coastal cities, all the while knowing that politicians and the tourist industry will use their maps and predictions to further enclose public spaces and natural resources for tourism, depriving local populations from using them (chapter 1). I also show how, for those working for tourism in inland Yucatán, playing the stereotypical Maya, like Patricia, traps them within colonial representations and old exploitative labor regimes, at the same time that it provides them with the ability to keep their families together, to upgrade their houses, and to maintain their indigenous values in place in a context of economic crisis and migration, as it did for Luis and Lucía and many others sewing from home (chapters 3 and 4).

This paradox of acknowledging loss while willingly participating in predatory practices is what makes tourism geographies sticky. In regions like the Yucatán Peninsula, which have become economically dependent on the tourist industry, this stickiness ensnares people and puts into place *sacrificial logics*.[36] According to these logics, participation in the predatory ways of the industry is seen as necessary even when it is done at the cost of endangering one's own health, or education, or memories of the past, or even when it risks the long-term sustainability of local ecosystems, or suspends everyday moral values about the environment, equality, or social justice. Within these sacrificial logics, enclosing public beaches for tourism, like destroying mangrove forests for new hotels and rehearsed indigeneities, "makes sense" because beach resorts, green spaces, and anachronic representations of indigenous alterity generate jobs and these are the landscapes that keep tourists coming back.

People in Yucatán often ask, If not tourism, then what? When I posed this question to Ata, Patricia, Luis, Lucía, and many others like them, they said that it is "thanks to tourism" that people in the region do not have to "jump to the other side" and migrate to the United States (chapter 4). For Luis and Lucía, it is "thanks to tourism" that Maya peoples are able to live according to valued, inherited sociocultural ideologies, family practices, and religious beliefs. It is "thanks to tourism" that peasants can keep "the milpa alive" and intergenerational extended families together.[37] Tourism, many like them say, has brought "progress." By progress some, like the fishermen in Celestún (chapter 2), mean access to food, shelter, electricity, or potable water. For others, like Ata, progress means having a seasonal job, higher education, housing, and modern services. For many, tourism is the possibility, the only possibility, of participating in and belonging to a global consumer community through access to wage labor, material commodities, or conspicuous consumption while staying at home in a place they know and feel they belong to, with people they care about.

Radically reorganized by state-planned tourism development and economically dependent on the activity, the Yucatán Peninsula is an opportune site to illuminate the agency of tourism in patterns of spatial production in late capitalism for at least four reasons. First, tourism was not an important variable in the region's economy prior to 1974, when the Mexican state founded Cancún as a master-planned tourist city. Second, since then, tourism has been systematically legitimated and sanctioned as a development tool by governments, international bodies, corporate actors, and NGOs from international to local levels through discourses of land improvement, sustainability, and indigenous empowerment. Third, Yucatán has become a favorite testing ground for the most widespread worldwide tourism models—that is, mass tourism, cultural tourism, and natural tourism—as well as for the laboring practices, infrastructures, and backstage socio-spatial dynamics required to sustain the positions of these tourist places in the global market. Fourth, and as a direct result of these orchestrated interventions in the landscape, tourism has materially and symbolically reorganized the Yucatán Peninsula into a unique tourist geography, or "a world to escape to" that is still observable in the making. In what follows, I show that this predatory and sticky tourist geography, while new, is not a total rupture with the region's past. In fact, tourism in Yucatán must be understood as the latest episode in a series of historical, political, economic, and sociocultural transformations that are characteristic of the way capitalism works at large.

A WORLD APART

Historians and anthropologists in the mid- to late twentieth century described the Yucatán Peninsula as a place "where Mexico dies," as "another Mexico," a "marginal periphery," a "periphery within the periphery," or "a world apart" (Redfield 1968; Re Cruz 1996; Moseley and Terry 1980; Wells and Joseph 1996).

Several geographical, sociopolitical, and economic factors inform these definitions. The Yucatán Peninsula is relatively isolated from the rest of the Mexican geography. The region lies between the Gulf of Mexico coast to the west and north and the Caribbean Sea to the east. It encompasses close to 125,000 square kilometers and includes the Mexican states of Yucatán, Campeche, and Quintana Roo, as well as the northern parts of Belize and Guatemala. Geologically, the region features unique physiographic conditions, including an almost entirely flat karst (limestone) terrain—the highest point, the Cerro Benito Juárez, rises a meager 210 meters above sea level— and an absence of rivers. These unique geological conditions provide little drainage, which causes considerable subterranean erosion, which has in turn produced the region's unique caverns and sinkholes, called cenotes. Cenotes are both sacred places in the Maya cosmology and one of the must-see natural tourist attractions of the region (chapter 2).

The Yucatán Peninsula is also considered a unique place in global history and culture. In the northern part of Yucatán, close to the port of Progreso, is the Chicxulub crater, created around sixty-six million years ago by the meteorite that marked the end of the dinosaur age. And it is a central node of the Mesoamerican culture and one of the six "cradles of civilization," according to archeologists.

But geography and culture are not the only reasons for Yucatán's reputation as a world apart. Physical mobilities and embodied politics have also played important roles. Like many other Caribbean and North American regions, the Yucatán Peninsula has been historically forged by migration for the purposes of the circulation of resources, labor, plants, food, visual images, and venture capital (see Sheller 2003). The region has always held a difficult position in the Mexican nation-building project, and it is still often referred to as the "free and independent republic of Yucatán." Yucatán declared its independence from Mexico twice, in 1841 and in 1846, and it remained neutral in the 1846–47 Mexican–American War that followed the United States' annexation of Texas. Importantly, the region was ravaged for more than five decades by the Caste Wars (1847–1901), an indigenous rebellion against heavy tax burdens, poor working conditions, and land usurpation (Stephens 2018; Reed 2001).[38] The Caste Wars were ultimately ended by Porfirio Díaz's "land re-conquests," but they delayed the start of the Mexican Revolution in the region until 1915 (it began elsewhere in 1910), and with it, the agrarian reforms that regulated communal lands through the creation of the *ejido* system (1915–35).[39]

The other major element informing descriptions of Yucatán as "a world apart" was the agroindustry of the henequen (sisal), which ruled economic, social, political, and ecological life in the region for most of the nineteenth and twentieth centuries. Known as Yucatán's "green gold," henequen fiber harvesting, production, and distribution provided the region with relative economic sovereignty. In the context of nation building, henequen acted as a centrifugal force, connecting the Yucatán Peninsula to global markets and international circuits of commodity exchange while only tenuously linking the region to the nation's fate (Brannon and Baklanoff 1987; Baklanoff and Moseley 2008; Baños Ramírez 2003, 2014).[40]

Crucially, henequen production carved out an uneven and divided social landscape, characterized by a deep divide between rural and urban spaces, and among white, mestizo, and indigenous communities. Throughout the henequen times, urban centers, like Mérida, renamed "the White City," were symbols of urbanity, cosmopolitanism, fashion, and capital connected to Europe, while rural areas were inland peripheries filled with cheap labor and cheap land from which crops were harvested for export. Henequen haciendas, and in particular their main buildings or *casas grandes,* acted as symbolic and material inscriptions in the landscape of this uneven and racialized sociopolitical and economic organization (see chapter 3).

This world collapsed in the late 1960s when nylon replaced henequen in global markets, plunging the region into a devastating crisis. The shift in the raw materials market led to the abrupt dismantling of the henequen agro-industry and it was tourism that, as locals generally point out, "placed Yucatán back in the international map." The Mexican state considered the region's Caribbean coast an ideal location to jumpstart tourism as an experimental model for national economic growth. It created Cancún in 1974 as a master-planned tourist city and as Mexico's first integrally planned tourism center for development. The creation of this new tourism center was a direct response to major events at regional, national, and international levels: the henequen crisis, the Mexican debt crisis, and the international oil crisis. For many in the region and beyond, it was the rise of Cancún that "saved them" and gave them hope and enabled progress at a time when hunger and desolation ruled.

Tourism was not an important topic for Mexico's national governance until the mid-1960s. At that moment, the tourism and travel industries increased exponentially at an international level and states started to adopt tourism as the favorite tool both for planned economic growth and, concomitantly, for sociocultural and environmental thriving (Berger, 2006). Responding to the development theories of the late 1960s and 1970s, the state creation of Cancún as a master-planned tourist city (chapter 1) followed modernization ideals and theories of comparative advantage that viewed tourism as an ideal way to reconnect both the region and the nation's economies to global markets by developing infrastructural poles that could act as engines for economic growth through foreign investment.

The experiment was successful, at least if judged by the raw numbers. In less than four decades, Cancún grew from less than one hundred inhabitants to a city of more than half a million. Since the 1990s, the city has been one of the world's leading tourist destinations. By 1995, barely two decades after its creation, 1.7 million tourists visited Cancún annually. In 2017, that number reached 5 million tourists per year—more than Cuba and the Dominican Republic combined. As a result of state-planned tourism development, Cancún has one of the busiest international airports in Latin America, which services over two thousand flights daily and over 23 million passengers annually.[41] Today, Cancún is responsible for almost 30 percent of Mexico's tourism income (OECD 2017) and it is difficult to overstress the importance that the creation of this planned tourist city has had at a regional scale.

Yet, even before Cancún was created, Yucatán was a region with a deep history of being used as a commodity supply zone through natural resource extraction and indigenous labor (Forero and Redclift 2006). The arrival of tourism, in this sense, did not disrupt this model. If anything, it signaled a continuity in the practices that had mobilized and captured the region's coasts and inland areas, indigenous populations, and natural and cultural goods as resources for extraction. The ideological, discursive, and pragmatic coupling of *tourism as development* that occupies this book takes place against the backdrop of Mexico's authoritarian corporatist state using the region as a laboratory for its economic policies (Fallaw 1995; Fallaw and Rugeley 2012; Osten 2018). State-led, top-down approaches to development have propelled tourism in an effort to attract foreign financial capital in order to achieve economic growth. The region has become home to all sorts of tourism interventions, which have followed historical forms of extraction that have used the region's lands, peoples, and ways of life as resources for consumption.

Traditional expressions of Yucatán as "a world apart" have now been taken up by the Mexican state, local and regional governments, and transnational travel corporations to brand the region as a unique world "to escape to." Over the last decades, this language has been strategically appropriated by the state and local governments to brand Yucatán as a "safe place," detached from Mexico's drug war and violence.

Today, not only does the Yucatán Peninsula have the leading beach destination in Mexico and the Caribbean, but also it is popular worldwide as "the land of the Maya." Well over two million tourists annually have visited the archeological remains of Chichén Itzá since it was named one of the "new Seven Wonders of the World" in 2007.[42] New attractions continue to pop up, like Cancún's underwater museum (chapter 1), or Maya indigenous luxury hotels and spas (chapter 3). In 2017, travelers voted the "shabby chic" city of Tulum, a few kilometers south of Cancún, as Mexico's hottest culinary destination and eco-resorts there are multiplying fueled by social media travel influencers' desire for the ultimate vacation.[43] Cozumel, just north of Cancún, has become the leading cruise ship destination in the world, with over three million arrivals annually (Martínez 2012).

The result of these transformations has been the organization of Yucatán around a unique tourist geography, "a world to escape to" that has left its people, as they often say *engrapados al turismo* (stuck to tourism): their lands, fates, and futures sutured—sometimes willingly, sometimes forcefully—to the vicissitudes of this industry and its predatory orderings of time, space, labor, and sociocultural life.

ETHNOGRAPHY IN A "WORLD TO ESCAPE TO"

My research follows a long tradition of political economy studies of the Yucatán Peninsula that are preoccupied with the historical articulation of land, labor, and capital (Brannon and Joseph 2002; Moseley and Terry 1980) as "seen from below" (Fallaw and Rugeley 2012; Terry 2010, 256). Most of these historical approaches, however, with important exceptions aside (Eiss 2010), end their narratives in the 1970s, precisely when Cancún was created, thus leaving an enormous gap in attention to the region's contemporary changes.[44]

This book builds on and contributes to contemporary ethnographies and scholarly travel essays focused on the region by offering a comparative and historically informed ethnography of the relations between tourism, space, and capitalism. It does so by starting in the present, looking at the specifics of everyday livelihoods and their architectural milieus in the areas—coastal and inland, rural and urban—where people like Ata, Lalo, Patricia, Luis, and Lucía live and work, then putting them together as the introductory slides did, through a consideration of the regional scale.[45]

The regional scale is an important analytical lens for three main reasons. First, tourism representations of the Yucatán Peninsula as "a world to escape to" are produced by mobilizing geographical imaginations of the region as a container of unique and well-differentiated attractions and staged places. Contemporary inhabitants of the peninsula, researchers, and tourists all operate and move within the territory informed by these relatively new but overarching representations of the Yucatán Peninsula for global consumption. Through infrastructure provision, architectural restorations, tourism signs and symbols, and people's routinized movements to and from those attractions, these tourist representations become material realities that are, in turn, generative of social practices, meanings, and values, as well as political action and new forms of inequality.

Second, despite the pervasiveness of tourism transformations, and despite their salient territorial manifestations in villages, towns, and cities across the region's geography since the mid-1970s, there has not yet been a comprehensive ethnographic account looking at how Yucatán's coasts, inland areas, cities, and rural areas have been differently scaled-up and re-spatialized for tourism consumption *at a regional level*. Nor has there been any ethnographic account addressing the ways that common people experience, make sense of, and appropriate these spatial changes *across the region*, or the consequences of putting contrasting tourism modalities at work *simultaneously* in space and time.[46] As a matter of fact, since Robert Redfield's (1968) *The Folk Culture of Yucatán*, there has not been any anthropological attempt to address the Yucatán Peninsula's socioeconomic transformations using a comparative regional ethnographic perspective and without losing sight of the specificities of the practices of everyday life.[47] *Stuck with Tourism* aims to do so.

Third, in my ethnography the importance of the regional scale transcends that of area studies. Many interpretations of tourism ignore the regional scale as an ethnographic device and instead promote an understanding of the industry at a global, macroeconomic scale, or study its effects on destinations through area-specific, local micro-ethnographies of face-to-face, host-guest encounters (Smith 1977). The result is an understanding of tourism as an agent of globalization under reductionist accounts of global-local relations, impacts, and motivations. In Yucatán, however, the rapid emergence of a new regional cartography of infrastructures, architectures, social practices, mobilities, and temporalities created by tourism post-1974—what I have called a "world to escape to"—demands simultaneous ethnographic attention to seemingly disconnected practices as they happen in place while also creating space.[48]

The work of feminist geographers and political ecology scholars has informed fundamental aspects of my ethnography, in particular their emphasis on the gendered nature of political-economic and ecological processes as well as the centrality of both social reproduction and the body in the theorization of capitalism (Meehan and Strauss 2015; Harcourt and Nelson 2015; Rocheleau, Thomas-Slayter, and Wangari 1996). I approach this aspect of my ethnography by following, thinking from, and theorizing local interpretations and native categories, giving them agentic capacities capable of transforming and rearranging local relations in ways that can pose challenges to the established regional, national, and global dynamics created by tourism (Meehan and Strauss 2015, 14–15). To do so, I have used elements of three methodologies that have typically remained separate: multisited research (Marcus 1995), global ethnography (Burawoy et al. 2000), and mobile methods (Sheller and Urry 2004; Büscher, Urry, and Witchger 2010). From multisited research I take the ethnographer's combined attention to sites, connections among sites, and sites' imaginaries. From global ethnography, I use the politics of scale and the attention to historical processes; from the mobilities paradigm, I borrow the idea of ordering practices as socially generative practices.[49] By combining these three methodological approaches I am able to historicize and ethnographically account for patterns of spatial production outside the constraints of area studies, powerful "global" discourses, and "local" vicarious agencies.

In this book, I compare and contrast the built environment, labor, and everyday experiences of workers, urban planners, visitors, government officials, and inhabitants in Cancún, a city transformed into a beach resort (chapter 1); in Celestún, a fishing town reimagined as a UN-defined natural enclave (chapter 2); in Temozón Sur's historic buildings recreated as luxury hotels (chapter 3); and in Tekit, a henequen town morphed into a factory for souvenir production (chapter 4). I do so through an ethnography conducted over twelve years in these four different sites, each representative cases of the planned use of tourism as a state development tool in the region and beyond. I examined mass tourism development in Cancún, on the Caribbean coast; ecotourism development in the Biosphere Reserve Ria Celestún on the Gulf of Mexico coast; indigenous luxury tourism in the inland municipality of Temozón Sur; and the domestic production of uniforms and souvenirs for the hospitality industry in the inland town of Tekit. The first three places are among the most visited and emblematic sites of the region's, and the world's, mainstream and alternative tourism models: beach resort tourism, nature tourism, and cultural tourism. Along with the archeological site of Chichén Itzá and the region's cenotes and convents, these are the sites that mass tourists, backpackers, and travelers are invited to visit when they come to the region. My ethnography about the fourth site, Tekit, illuminates the livelihoods of textile factory workers in towns where hotel uniforms and tourist souvenirs are created.

I chose these four sites for my ethnography because each case is representative of a major historical and political inflexion point in how the tourism industry has been articulated as a development strategy in the international arena (in the mid-1970s for Cancún, the mid-1990s for Celestún, and the early 2000s for Temozón Sur), and because in each site, the transformations directly associated with tourism are palpable even when tourists are not physically present (as in Tekit since the late 1990s). While many anthropologists have explored archeological tourism in the region (e.g., Castañeda 1996; Clifford 1997; Breglia 2005, 2006), less attention has been paid to the development and realities of other kinds of planned tourism, which I address in this book.

To be sure, there are other important tourist ventures in the region that I do not cover, among them archeological tourism, the fishing eco-reserves along the Gulf of Mexico, the thriving cruise industry and second residence tourism in Progreso, the emergent solidarity tourism network in inland Maya areas, the booming New Age tourism at cenotes in Valladolid and eco-resorts in Tulum, and the exclusive organic culinary and healing experiences offered in and around Mérida and the Caribbean coast. In this sense, I do not claim to offer a comprehensive account of all tourism developments taking place in the Yucatán Peninsula. But my argument is that the four case studies in this book offer a representative sample of the labor, material, and symbolic sociospatial transformations that predatory tourism has produced in the Yucatán.

Put together, each of the four cases provides an entry point to explore how the internationally, nationally, and regionally acclaimed dyad of "tourism *as* development" has intimately changed the region's spatial, social, and ecological relations. Each case reveals how the Mexican state anchored and legitimated tourism ventures through international and national development discourses of modernization (Cancún), environmental sustainability (Celestún), and community participation and indigenous empowerment (Temozón Sur and Tekit). Each case shows how state, regional, and local institutions implement heterogeneous tourism ventures as market-driven, engineered projects for profit. Giving ethnographic attention to how the region's inhabitants work for, experience, and make sense of a variety of tourism models and then bringing them into dialogue with each other enables me to show how tourism development works *across scales* to produce and sustain the Yucatán as a "world to escape to." Together, these cases show how tourism development has generated a predatory regional tourism geography that sticks people like Ata, Lalo, Patricia, Luis, and Lucía with an uneven relational set of labor mobilities, immobilities, and moorings, ones that simultaneously exhaust landscapes, resources, and bodies, and open up spaces of connection, possibility, and hope. These intersecting mobilities produce embodied spaces riven with moral contradictions because tourism's land hunger and predatory nature affect the health and future of local populations, who sacrifice daily to work for an industry that has monopolized opportunities to carve out a good life.

In the conclusion, I reflect on the inherent contradictions of sustainable tourism and capitalist consumption in the face of climate change. I build on Train Maya, a new tourism infrastructure project that Mexico's newly elected president, Andrés Manuel López Obrador, launched in 2019 to connect the Mexican southeast. I use Train Maya to highlight the contemporary fixation, which has populated the imaginations of those on the left and the right in Mexico and beyond, on using tourism as a development strategy. I then zoom out of the Yucatán Peninsula to show how the dyad of predation and entrapment might also explain tourism's orderings of space and social life beyond the region. In doing so, I call for a disciplinary retooling that aims to reorient the academic and institutional imagination of tourism as encounter toward a consideration of tourism's agentive force in patterns of spatial production.

ONE

Beach Enclosures

MANUFACTURING A CARIBBEAN PARADISE

A DESTINATION UNDER THE WEATHER

George is a middle-aged Canadian national who works for a well-established real estate agency in Cancún. The day we first met, in October 2010, he was wearing designer glasses and the typical work attire of the regional tourist industry: a guayabera, slacks, and polished shoes. He had been working in Cancún for just a month after being transferred from Mexico City. His work routine consisted of showing luxury apartments in two new twenty-story oceanfront towers and managing the online presence and marketing of the project.

Seated in an air-conditioned glass office right at the gate of the towers, and obviously bored, George promptly accepted my request to visit an apartment on a higher floor, so I could take some aerial pictures of the beach. We took one of the two elevators and went up to the thirteenth floor. To my surprise, the elevator did not open into a lobby but right into the apartment's American-style kitchen. Perhaps sensing my surprise as a sign that I could be a potential buyer, or simply wanting to rehearse his seller's pitch, George took the opportunity to give me a full tour of the model apartment. Always talking to me in English, he began by proudly pointing at the all-glass walls, which afforded a mesmerizing view of the blue Caribbean Sea blending into an even bluer sky. He then escorted me room by room, enthusiastically elaborating on the construction materials used in the carvings on the door's frames, the selection of designer furniture from Brazil, and the modern bathroom tiles.

After touring the interior, we moved to the balcony. Before opening the sliding doors, George warned me to leave my bag inside and to grab the camera firmly with one hand while holding the balcony's rail with the other.

Outside, the wind gusted strongly. Securing the door against the wind with the weight of his body, George pointed at the Jacuzzi in the corner of the balcony and smiled. As our gazes crossed paths, he realized that I was not looking at the Jacuzzi but at the shantytown down below, sitting next to the luxury towers. Perhaps interpreting my look as a sign of concern, George exclaimed, "Don't worry about the shantytown over there! The next storm will move the water towards them. People will be relocated. We'll have a nicer view, extended golf courses, and one more swimming pool over there." The noise from the wind was so strong that he was almost shouting.

George's comments are an example of the predatory tourist geographies that shape everyday encounters in Cancún. His words, like many others that echo them on a daily basis, are the result of historical practices of exclusion that have shaped the urban development of the city since the Mexican government created it, almost from scratch, in 1974 as Mexico's first integrally planned tourism center for development.

The creation of Cancún was a watershed moment for the Yucatán Peninsula. As people often say in the region, "There is a before and an after Cancún." As home to more than half a million residents and host to five million tourists in 2017, Cancún's centrality for the regional and national economies is captured in colloquial expressions that describe the city as "the engine," "the goose that lays the golden eggs," or a "money-making machine." These expressions reflect the speed, efficiency, and brute mechanical force with which planned tourism development has dominated nature, the built environment, and those that dwell in it. It is this blatant force that explains sales pitches like George's: it is assumed that the economic growth created by tourism necessitates social displacement, and that the destruction caused by storms will bring opportunities to develop larger and fancier tourist spaces that will in turn sustain the city as a competitive Caribbean beach destination in the global tourist market.

This reality became painfully evident right after my visit with George. The blue sky of the morning had turned gray by afternoon, and it had started to rain hard. The afternoon rain and the morning's wind gusts, which had forced George and me to grip the balcony rail, foreshadowed the arrival of Hurricane Paula. The Category 3 hurricane reached landfall in Cancún on October 12, 2010, just two days after our meeting. Evacuations were mandatory for Isla Holbox and Isla Cantoy, two islands located a few kilometers north of Cancún. All sea transportation and hundreds of national and international flights were cancelled later that day.

In the days following Hurricane Paula, many of the city's central streets and surrounding areas were flooded. There was stagnant water everywhere. The local radio reminded the population to stay safe, to look out for hidden electricity cables, and to be vigilant to avoid consuming potentially contaminated water or being bit by mosquitoes, which can carry the dengue virus. Days passed and the stagnant water began to mingle with sewage from broken septic tanks. Mosquitoes multiplied and so did foul smells. Many areas of the city remained without electricity for weeks. Broken trees and debris accumulated on the streets and were only occasionally picked up by drivers on their commutes. Access to potable water was scarce and when available, it was expensive. Everywhere I went there was an eerie sense of waiting, of silence and inaction—aside from big stores' private security patrols, which were placed at the entrances to banks and supermarkets, such as Walmart and Superama, in downtown Cancún.

The scenario was radically different in the city's tourist zone, the so-called Hotel Zone. Gardeners, sanitation workers, electrical maintenance personnel, and other uniformed workers were visible everywhere. Tourist police—a branch of the local police exclusively devoted to ensure law and order in the tourist area—established checkpoints at the entrance of the Hotel Zone. In front of all-inclusive hotels, crews of brown-skinned indigenous men trimmed palm trees and bushes, cleaned debris from sewer drains, and fumigated against mosquitoes. Others picked up the red gulfweed (*sargazo*) that now covered the tourist area of the beach and put it in trucks. Most of them were seasonal migrant workers from inland villages in Yucatán who, as one of them told me as he waited in line at the gates of a well-known resort in order to get a job, had come as soon as they learned the storm was hitting Cancún, to "help clean the hotels and the beach." They were protected from head to toe, wearing handmade breathing masks made out of old t-shirts and scarfs. No algae was collected from public areas of the beach. In those places, the sand was hardly visible, buried under *sargazo* where sand fleas thrived.

The ocean remained green and blackish for the rest of the week. The tourists who ventured into the water had to jump over slippery cement blocks covered in black plastic that had been erected to hold the beaches in place after the storm. They complained in my interviews with them about the "difficulties of getting into the sea," their lack of desire to have a fall "while on vacation" and of "feeling the sand was like mud." Claudia, a middle-aged Canadian tourist who was trying to climb over the black blocks for an early morning swim when I met her, put it this way: "This is so disgusting and dangerous! You don't pay to come that far to not find the Caribbean but a hole of mud that resembles the river in my town instead." Peter, a middle-aged tourist from London, posted a similar complaint in an online review about encountering "the horrible brown/grey you get on the English coast and definitely not something you'd expect from the Caribbean Sea."[1]

Such comments were repeated by many of the tourists whom I interviewed that month. Months and years later, these comments abound, albeit for short times only, on influential travel websites such as TripAdvisor, where they are joined by comments about the friction visitors experience between the imagined Caribbean they expected from tourism brochures and marketing and the reality they encounter. This friction is a new normal for Cancún. Its location in a hurricane-prone area in the age of climate change has rendered Cancún vulnerable to rising sea levels and to increasingly recurrent and virulent tropical storms and hurricanes. And yet, despite the friction between reality and representation, despite the evident deterioration of its infrastructure and beaches, Cancún continues to thrive as a leading Caribbean beach resort destination.[2] In this chapter I ask how a destination that is so "under the weather" has managed to keep its leading position as a Caribbean beach paradise in the tourism market. What is the labor involved in producing and securing this position? Who is doing this labor? What are the socioeconomic, political, and environmental effects of maintaining this tourist destination? And at what cost is all of this done?

In asking these questions, I want to explore what it takes to create and maintain the idealized tourist imaginary of the Caribbean beach paradise in Cancún. I begin by exploring Cancún's 1974 master plan and analyzing how it was used by the Mexican state and international development institutions to strategically scale up the city for global consumption. Second, I describe how, in practice, this has been achieved by implementing predatory planned tourist development that privatizes land and resources. This development method follows the enclosure model, whereby the leisure industry carves out separate spaces for tourism consumption in cities around the world (Bianchi 2003; Britton 1982, 1991; Telfer and Sharpley 2015; Duffy and Smith 2003).[3] I argue that in Cancún this planned tourism development model has generated a system of *enclosures within enclosures,* or nested instruments of flexible privatization, materialized in what I call architectures of escape, like the all-inclusive resorts and high-rise condominiums that populate the city's tourist zone. I show how these enclosures within enclosures are a direct result of postdisaster opportunism following Hurricanes Gilbert (1989) and Wilma

(2005).[4] Third, I examine how these enclosures within enclosures rely on processes of disciplining and civilizing institutions and bodies that are similar to those observable in both colonial Yucatán and in modern, flexible, just-in-time labor regimes such as the maquiladoras on both sides of the US–Mexico border.[5] I discuss how Cancún's predatory tourism development entraps people in a ghettoized geography of global consumption. Cancún's inhabitants, governments, and expert knowledge are stuck in a *sacrificial logic* that naturalizes and legitimates land enclosures as well as the extraction of resources and labor (not to mention class, racial, and gender inequalities) in order to promote the city's reputation as a global tourist destination.

Finally, in the conclusion, I reflect on the sustainability of Cancún's tourism development in the face of anthropogenic climate change pressures. I show how Cancún's absolute dependency on enclosed spaces of global consumption has created a distinctive marketization of urban governance that focuses on securing the short-term survival of the city's destination as a Caribbean beach resort while systematically disregarding the long-term social and ecological threats that permanently afflict this under-the-weather destination.[6]

THE MANUFACTURE OF PARADISE AND THE RISE OF A TOURIST GHETTO

Planning a Beach Paradise

The creation of Cancún began in the early 1970s with the Cancún Project, also known as the Cancún Master Plan (1970–95). The plan was historically informed by a broader development strategy pursued by the Mexican state during the presidency of Miguel Alemán Velasco (1946–52) that sought to use tourism as a key element in the development of the nation's productive areas. The 1946 development plan marks the beginning of tourism policy in Mexico, but it was not until the mid-1960s that the First National Tourism Plan (1962) pointed to tourism, and particularly to the creation of new tourism destinations, as a direct incentive for foreign investment. This effort focused on the country's coasts, and particularly on Acapulco, Puerto Vallarta, and Cozumel, "sea, sand and sun destinations" (Castro Alvarez 2007; Guerrero Rodriguez 2012). By the mid-1970s, the Mexican state focused on diversifying its tourist offerings by developing its "virgin" coastal areas (Talledos Sánchez 2012, 124). This state-planned development strategy, known as the Planned Tourism Destination Policy, created five *centros integralmente planeados* (CIP) across the nation, for which Cancún was to be the pilot case.[7]

The attention to tourism as a planned development strategy by the Mexican federal government did not take place in a void. By the late 1960s, countries in the Caribbean region like Jamaica, Barbados, and the Bahamas had created and consolidated the first mass tourism resort economies. Such countries found in tourism a viable path of modernization and economic sovereignty in the nascent global order (Pattullo 2005; Wong 2015; Telfer and Sharpley 2015). Moreover, in the context of the import substitution industrialization strategies of the 1970s, tourism emerged in many states in the Caribbean as an "industry without chimneys" that could create economic growth by inviting leisure-seeking visitors to escape to "Third World pleasurable peripheries" within the comfort, safety, and risk-free bubble of the familiar (Turner and Ash 1975). The invitation was preceded by large public and private investments guided by the interventionist role of the state in development and its role, ever since, as entrepreneur and banker in the creation of tourism infrastructure side by side with the business community (Berger 2006; Clancy 2001) It is against this background that Mexico turned to and secured tourism as a national development strategy.

Under the direction of Antonio Enríquez Savignac, a Harvard economist, former employee of the Inter-American Development Bank, and later head of the World Tourism Organization, each Mexican CIP had to meet three economic goals: the generation of foreign currency; the creation of a new source of employment; and the stimulation of an economic multiplier effect within the regions where the planned tourism center would be constructed (FONATUR 1982). Each tourism center, moreover, had to be located in a geographical area that could meet three main criteria. First, the location should allow the CIP to have manageable implementation costs. Second, the area should contain exceptional natural assets. And third, it should be economically disadvantaged, with a low rate of economic development or, as they put it, "severe backwardness and marginality" (Clancy 2001).

In the early 1970s, the Caribbean coast of the Yucatán Peninsula, fully immersed in the henequen crisis, met all three criteria. In an interview commemorating the thirty-five years since the creation of Cancún, Fernandez Hurtado, one of the bankers and main visionaries behind the development, explained the selection of the area as follows: "The country of rum [Cuba] was closed to the world, tourists from the East Coast in USA left Cuban beaches, Mexico could conquer all those travelers because Cancún also had the correct location . . . and Yucatán's (people) needed work" (Vega Campos 2010, 28).

Cancún not only provided a convenient location to host US tourists in search of alternatives to Cuba, but it also offered the opportunity to control what the Mexican state had long perceived as "a double periphery": a land of untapped resources and the rebel *indios* of the Caste Wars (Pi-Sunyer and Thomas 1997). Fears of regional indigenous uprisings, the rise of a leftist movement in neighboring Guatemala, and also the availability of "an army of underemployed or irregularly employed workers" (Redclift 2006, 171) were among the main reasons for selecting Cancún as a pioneer location.[8]

Historically, as I discuss in the introduction, the Mexican state had struggled to control the Yucatán Peninsula and turn it into a productive region for the national economy. The Cancún Project can thus be seen as a classical example of a "frontier enclave development" (Redclift 2006) that, in a context of liberal policies, targeted an underdeveloped, economically peripheral area for national growth through foreign investment. In practice, the implementation of the plan followed the model of industrialization through maquiladoras that had been taking place since the 1960s in the north of Mexico. The idea was straightforward: to integrate Mexico's economy into the world economy through state-planned tourism poles that could revitalize regional economies through a trickle-down effect while directly contributing to the national economy by using international capital and technical assistance to boost infrastructure development. Cancún was thus a real-life experiment to test two propositions. First, that tourism could be deployed as a modernization strategy by developing, from scratch, a city that would maximize investment returns through value-added oceanfront real estate development in order to extract foreign currency from international markets.[9] Second, that the state could use the tourist industry as a strategy of state control by incorporating indigenous forces into the market economy—while keeping them, as I will show, at a controlled distance—and also by rooting tourism in historically informed development narratives regarding indigenous modernization, aka assimilation (Castellanos 2010b). Daniel Ortiz Caso, one of the first engineers of Cancún, summarized this as follows: "How to justify the creation of a golf camp in the middle of a mangrove, the modification of beaches and rivers, and the presence of prostitutes in the middle of construction work areas? . . . The objective was to bring foreign currency to the country, and that seemed to justify it all" (Vega Campos 2010, 53). Construction started in 1974, and Sigfrido Paz Paredes, another Mexican-educated Harvard economist and member of the UN Secretary of Communication and Transport, was in charge of executing Cancún's master plan. That same year, the federal government created the state of Quintana Roo on the Caribbean coast of the peninsula and designated it as a free trade zone (Martí 1998) with reduced regulations and tariffs, in order to pave the way for what the Mexican state called "the modernization of the periphery" through coastal resort tourism (Clancy 2001).

The plan was implemented through a pioneering multiscalar effort involving national actors such as the Mexican federal government, the Bank of Mexico, and the newly created National Fund for Tourism Promotion (FONATUR), as well as international actors, like the World Bank and the Inter-American Development Bank.[10] The mission of this multiscalar alliance was to generate economic and social development by transforming remote tropical lagoons and mangroves in a socially and economically backward region into an elite "sea, sun, and sand" international resort destination. Beaches were the strategic asset for scaling up the region for global tourism. Fernando Martí, one of Cancún's most well-known visionaries and chroniclers, explains, "We concentrated on the coasts, because previously conducted surveys showed that the beach was the principal attraction the foreign tourist was looking for" (Martí 1998).

The main idea behind the plan was to create a resort that could appeal to the Western imaginary of a Caribbean paradise of white sandy beaches, palm trees, and turquoise waters (Baldacchino 2012; Sheller 2003). This was also a paradise to be filled with colonially inspired, sexualized, racialized, and gendered spaces, objects, bodies, and desires (Nixon 2017). In order to create and secure this idealized tropical imaginary, Cancún was designed around a radical socio-spatial segregation that divided the city into two distinct zones: one for tourists and one for locals. In what follows, I discuss the government policies, architecture, and labor used to produce this segregation and secure the ideal Caribbean beach as an enclosed, productive tourism stage for capital accumulation.

Building Paradise: Segregation by Design

Cancún's master plan designed a city that encompassed 12.7 hectares, 80 percent of which were part of the Nichupte lacunar system (García de Fuentes 1979). This area was divided into two spatially and functionally segregated zones: Cancún Island and Cancún City.

Cancún Island, or the Hotel Zone (Zona Hotelera), was conceived as a self-contained "leisure/tourism zone" built upon the narrow seventeen-mile barrier island that separates the Caribbean Sea from the Nichupte Lagoon. The Hotel Zone was built in three phases, each characterized by segmentation into big blocks divided by large avenues. The Mexican state remains in control of Cancún Island through FONATUR, managing the sale and distribution of land and the regulation of land uses.

Cancún City (Ciudad Modelo or Ciudad Cancún) was built inland and was originally conceived as "the workers' city" and a backdoor service area for Cancún Island. Mostly marketed towards middle-class Mexicans and comprising a series of large blocks (*super manzanas*), ironically the workers' city did not initially include housing for its working classes. To this day, most tourism brochures and maps equate Cancún with the Hotel Zone; Cancún City is notably absent from these descriptions and depictions.

Along with these two zones, the 1974 plan also included building Cancún's International Airport, which was connected to Cancún City and the Hotel Zone through two different routes in order to separate the circulation of tourists from that of workers and goods. One of the reasons for this radical segregation was to avoid the problems facing other Mexican coastal tourist sites in the 1970s, in particular Acapulco, which were struggling to attract international tourism flows (García de Fuentes 1979). As described in the master plan, the intention with Cancún was to avoid "polluting the tourist landscape" with "visible shanty towns" by creating "an exclusive, small-scale luxury destination" serviced, at a prudent distance, by a veiled, small, middle-class city designed as a tropical variation of British garden cities (Vega Campos 2010).

Cancún experienced explosive growth right from the start in both of its halves. In the Hotel Zone, the first hotel opened for business in September 1974. By the end of 1975, Cancún had fifteen hotels comprising 1,322 rooms, and it had hosted 99,500 tourists (FONATUR 2006). Two decades later, by the mid-1990s, there were over seventeen thousand rooms, most of which were in all-inclusive resorts. In 2000, the city had already received over two million visitors; in 2017, it had almost nine hundred hotels and well over thirty thousand rooms (Caribbean Tourism Organization 2015; fieldwork 2010; Datatour 2018).

Cancún City grew apace. In the early 1970s, the area where Cancún was to be located had only a small fishing village of less than a hundred inhabitants. In 1980, Cancún City already had 33,000 inhabitants, and ten years later the

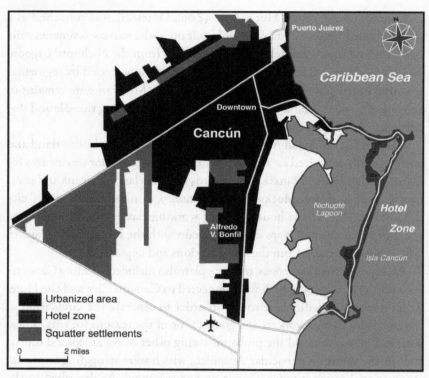

MAP 2. Cancún's urban development and segregated planning. Map by author.

population had risen to 167,730. Since 1990 the population of Cancún City has grown rapidly, from 300,000 in the late 1990s to 630,000 in 2010, to an estimated 725,000 in 2018 (INEGI 2019). As a result of this meteoric growth, the original model city planned by FONATUR was soon overwhelmed. Since the mid-1990s, Cancún City has been expanding as a collection of irregular settlements, locally known as *colonias,* which have been characterized by Fernando Martí (1998) as Cancún's "lost city" and which are mostly seasonally inhabited by indigenous peoples from inland Yucatán as well as from other Mexican states. According to local estimates, 20 percent of Cancún's population live in *colonias,* and new irregular settlements or shantytowns have been created every month since 2008 (IMPLAN 2009).

Regional, national, and global factors all explain Cancún's explosive tourist and urban growth. At the regional level, the henequen crisis fueled a vast migratory movement from inland Yucatán to the coast in search of economic alternatives. Employment in the construction and service sectors associated with the newly created tourism industry in Cancún became particularly attractive work options, and often the only ones, for impoverished peasant and indigenous families and low-paid workers fleeing the *ejido* crisis in the neighboring states of Campeche and Yucatán, which had by then become self-subsistent and faced increased pressure from population growth.[11] Consequently, many of Cancún's city dwellers were from the start indigenous men and women from inland rural Yucatán and, over the years, also migrant workers from other parts of Mexico and Central America who arrived at the city with varied conceptions and expectations of land, housing, and what a city should be. At the national level, tourism became a central national strategy for economic development during the 1970s and 1980s. During the presidency of Lopez Portillo (1976–82), the importance of tourism grew as a direct response to both the global energy crisis, which signaled a need to develop viable alternatives to oil, and the global financial crisis, which increased Mexico's vulnerability as the second-most indebted nation in Latin America (Pastor 1989). The 1982 debt crisis and President Miguel de la Madrid's (1982–88) subsequent turn to neoliberal policies had a radical effect on the way tourism was articulated as a hegemonic economic sector for Mexico. Madrid stressed the increasing centrality of tourism "for economic and social development" in his first government report, dated September 1, 1983, in which he mentioned tourism's importance for the national economy thanks to its "capacity to generate productive jobs, to contribute to a balanced regional development, to stimulate the other economic sectors and to strengthen the cultural identity of our 'pueblo.'" The equation of tourism with development crystallized for the first time in the 1983 National Development Plan, which asserted tourism as "an ideal industry to foster a modern aesthetics of progress and marketization . . . to get out of the crisis; to recover economic growth capacity; and to initiate the qualitative changes in economic, political and social structures together with the moral renovation of society."[12]

For the Mexican state, as well as for many economists and politicians, Cancún has empirically validated the use of tourism as a viable modernization strategy. In less than four decades, the Cancún experiment radically shifted the centuries-old regional sociodemographic and economic organization of the Yucatán Peninsula. Indeed, this experiment moved populations, labor, resources, capital, and infrastructure from inland areas (where henequen haciendas were located) to the Caribbean coast (once the land for chicle extraction and a hiding place for Caste War rebels). The tourist booms of Riviera Maya, Playa del Carmen, Cozumel, Isla Mujeres, Tulum, Majahual, and more

FIGURE 1. Cancún, aerial perspective, circa 1970. Source: Aclarando,
https://aclarando.wordpress.com/.

recently, Holbox and Costa Maya, along the Caribbean coast attest to Cancún
having generated the desired triggering effect in economic and urban growth
(Guardado 2015). The result of this transformation is that while in the early
1980s, the tertiary sector (service and tourism) in Quintana Roo represented
less than 35 percent of the economy and the primary sector (agriculture) represented almost 54 percent, by 1990, the tertiary sector represented almost 65
percent and the primary sector had regressed to less than 20 percent. In 2010,
the tertiary sector accounted for over 85 percent of the economy, while the
primary sector represented less than 1 percent (INEGI 2010).

But the questions that tourism-as-development advocates often overlook
are: At what cost has this development taken place? How has it taken form
and shape over time? Cancún is a textbook example of why development
is not necessarily coupled with more economic growth or better infrastructure. In fact, as critics show, the shift to tourism in Cancún has not been
accompanied by either socially inclusive development or environmental sustainability (Torres and Momsen 2005a, 2005b; Clancy 2001; Castellanos
2010b).

Cancún's transformation into a Caribbean paradise has permanently
reorganized the city into a predatory geography that extracts nature, labor,
and resources for global consumption. This predatory geography has materialized through the creation of enclosures within enclosures in which land,
resources, and infrastructure within already enclosed spaces are cordoned off
and commoditized. These enclosures within enclosures operate as nested

FIGURE 2. Cancún, aerial perspective, 2019. Source: Juan Carlos Hernández Hernández, iStock Photos.

instruments of flexible privatization whereby resources are appropriated, commoditized, and incorporated into global chains of capital circulation. The rest of this chapter shows how this predatory tourism geography has evolved in Cancún through "disaster capitalism," which occurs in particular in the aftermath of natural disasters, like hurricanes. Disaster capitalism takes advantage of natural disasters as opportunities to further enclose tourist spaces such as the beach, and subordinate public services, resources, labor, and land management to market imperatives.[13]

PARADISE ENCLOSED AND DISASTER OPPORTUNISM

The absence of large, high-intensity hurricanes (Categories 4 and 5) prior to 1988, together with the unavailability of data prior to 1970, helped to foster an optimistic belief among Cancún's inhabitants, city planners, and the federal government that the city was somehow immune to natural disasters.[14] This belief was shattered on September 14, 1988, when the massive and virulent Hurricane Gilbert struck the city. Known in Mexico as the "hurricane of the twentieth century," Gilbert caused over two hundred deaths in Mexico, forty of them in Cancún. More than half a million people were displaced and material losses were estimated at over US$300 million (Aguirre 1989, 33). The hurricane's rapid growth in less than forty-eight hours, together with its erratic path, caught Cancún largely unprepared, and it razed both the Hotel Zone and Cancún City. As one local authority put it in an interview with me, "In 1988, with Gilbert, people in this city experienced a hurricane for the first time and it surprised them all. . . . Just imagine how little thought was given to this [issue], that it occurred to no one [to plan for] hurricanes when inventing Cancún." Hurricane Gilbert was just the first of many to reach Cancún. Since its creation, Cancún has been hit by two of the most virulent hurricanes to strike Mexico on record—Hurricane Gilbert (1988) and Hurricane Wilma (2005)—as well as countless strong tropical storms that have destroyed the city's main tourist infrastructure several times.

One could reasonably assume that the recurrence of hurricanes and storms would challenge the stability of the destination as an idealized Caribbean beach in the global tourist market. But this has not been the case. As a matter of fact, the opposite is true. In the aftermath of Hurricane Wilma in 2005, for example, a huge banner reading "Cancún is back again, stronger" was boldly draped from one hotel. One might wonder, perhaps naively, whether "stronger" means that these extreme weather events have provided the city with opportunities to address the vulnerability of its citizens and to redress the racial, social, and spatial imbalances that have characterized the city since its inception. But that has not happened. Instead, federal and municipal governments as well as tourism corporations have viewed hurricane destruction as a creative occasion to accumulate capital (Harvey 2007). The resulting enclosures within enclosures have helped hotel and real estate investors— enabled by state, regional, and municipal authorities—to further privatize and commodify Cancún's land and public resources, especially the beach, for the exclusive use of the global tourism industry and those able to exercise their right to play or take vacations. The outcome has been the transformation of the Hotel Zone into a "city of walls" (Caldeira 2000). It is a segregated space, a "fortified enclave . . . privatized, enclosed, and monitored space for residence, consumption, leisure and work" and a "socially homogenous environment . . . turned inward and not to the street" (Caldeira 1996, 308). This transformation has produced an environmentally unsustainable, exclusionary social and material space, as well as conflictive moral choices for urban planners, governments, and inhabitants.

The development of this system of enclosures within enclosures has taken place in Cancún through specific reconstruction dynamics and tourism infrastructure developments that took hold following Hurricane Gilbert in 1988 and Hurricane Wilma in 2005.

All-Inclusive Resorts after Hurricane Gilbert (1989)

Hurricane Gilbert hit Cancún in September 1988, just over ten years after the city's creation. No evacuation plan was in place for either tourists or the general population, and the results were predictably disastrous. In her 1988 report of the hurricane, a *St. Petersburg Times* journalist described the chaos of the situation: "Three wide-eyed Los Angeles teachers get out at a beach-front resort but are immediately herded onto a bus bound for one of the downtown hotels. Clearly, people are beginning to get worried, but there is no sign of an organized evacuation. No police directing traffic. No public works crews setting up barricades. No Red Cross trucks bringing in emergency supplies. Hundreds of laborers mill about hotel construction sites waiting—as we later learn—for rides that never materialize. In some cases, their employers have simply left them to ride out the storm as best they can."[15] According to field observations made in the week following the hurricane by a team from the US Committee on Natural Disasters of the National Academy of Sciences and the National Academy of Engineering, 60 percent of Cancún's two hundred thousand inhabitants lived in irregular settlements surrounding downtown when Gilbert struck (Aguirre 1989, 34). Gilbert either completely destroyed or severely damaged these makeshift houses, leaving them without roofs and walls or any kind of service (34). Nearly every kilometer of the coast's beaches was reshaped or eroded, and the beach's slope was left "too acute for recreation" (Clifton 1991, 340).[16] Most hotels in the Hotel Zone suffered some kind of structural damage, and over four thousand hotel rooms were severely damaged. In the three months following the hurricane, the state finances of Quintana Roo declined by 65 percent due to the loss of an estimated US$87 million in tourism revenue (Aguirre 1989, 33).

And yet, despite the devastating effects of the hurricane, Cancún soon reemerged as the premier tourism destination of the Caribbean. By mid-December 1988, just three months after Gilbert, 80 percent of the hotel rooms were back in service. Record levels of new construction in the area resulted in twenty-one new hotels that opened within two years of the storm (Clifton 1991, 340). In seven years, the room capacity of the Hotel Zone almost doubled, from less than twelve thousand rooms in 1988 to almost twenty thousand in 1995, which represented 12 percent of all the available rooms in Mexico (Hiernaux Nicolás 1989).

How did this rapid reconstruction process happen?

Two months after the hurricane, Mexican President Carlos Salinas declared Cancún a "space of exception" and prioritized the rapid reconstruction of Cancún's Hotel Zone, highlighting the centrality of the city as "an engine for the national economy." The investment required for the reconstruction of tourism infrastructure—over US$4.5 million, according to an estimate by the Inter-American Development Bank (Aguirre 1989)—was well beyond the resources of the state of Quintana Roo. The federal government, through FONATUR, started the most aggressive privatization strategy in its short history as a way of shouldering reconstruction costs. To facilitate access to international loans for disaster reconstruction and the influx of foreign capital, the federal government also undertook an unprecedented national restructuring of foreign investment laws. By permission of Salinas's 1989–1994 National Development Plan, which aimed to achieve growth through denationalization and deregulation, Cancún became one of the first cities in Mexico to privatize its water and electricity services (Pradilla Cobos 1997).[17] Recovering from Hurricane Gilbert became an opportunity to implement those wider reforms in Cancún, with an emphasis on capturing international capital inflow through tourism activities. In practice, this strategy entailed selling land, as well as renting or selling those "existing enterprises with any operational costs" to foreign and private capital (SECTUR 1996, 201). By letting go of those enterprises with operational costs, FONATUR started looking for "operational and financial efficiency in [its] investments through changing operators and concessions to private investors" (201). Urban reconstruction efforts were put in place with the goal of re-establishing tourism and capital flows to the regional and national economies. In practice, this strategy allowed the Mexican state to sell large tracts of the Hotel Zone's public land to tourism multinational corporations and real estate investors. By the mid-1990s, at least one half of the city's luxury grand tourism and five-star hotels were regulated by foreign franchise agreements, while transnational Mexican corporations controlled the majority of the other hotels (Torres and Momsen 2005a; Castellanos 2010b).

The increasing delegation of power and responsibility from the Mexican state to private transnational capital in Cancún's Hotel Zone was done at the cost of poor or nonexistent urban development plans for the rest of the city. Leon, a pioneer inhabitant in Cancún who used to fish for a living until

Gilbert hit, reminisced in an interview with me about the post-Gilbert era: "No credits for new boats or motors. No equipment. Just cardboard sheets ... Why, if hotels received millions of *pesos*? Why did fishermen not receive some help? This is indeed what I call a governmental stunted [*atrofiada*] attention." The initial socio-spatial segregation impetus of the 1974 master plan was not only kept in place but expanded thanks to the advent of a particular kind of tourism infrastructure: the all-inclusive resort.

All-inclusive resorts consist of self-contained spaces offering full board, accommodation, drinks, and entertainment activities for a flat rate that is paid in advance to tour operators. In many cases, the flat rate also includes airport transfers, special sports activities (e.g., golf, scuba diving, horseback riding), and spa treatments (Issa and Jayawardena 2003, 168). All-inclusive resorts differ from traditional resorts in that they require larger amounts of land for in situ recreational infrastructure. Moreover, their philosophy of seclusion also varies from that of traditional hotels. All-inclusive hotels explicitly aim to detach tourists from local indigenous culture and spaces through the creation of a racialized geography that reorganizes the mobilities of people, labor, capital, and resources.

Prior to Gilbert, low-density luxury hotels were the dominant business model in the Hotel Zone. During the 1990s, the mass tourism all-inclusive resort, enabled by the privatization processes after Gilbert, transformed Cancún from an elite and low-density tourist destination into the mass-tourism vacation destination that it is today. An urban planning expert working in Cancún commented to me on the predatory capacity of these hotels, saying, "What did the government do in Cancún? They changed debt for investments, they sold debt and hotel corporations, Spanish ones in particular came to invest.... Hotels started to generate such an attraction that they sucked everything. Restaurants ... jewelry shops and other shops started to die [because] people just didn't go outside." The advent of all-inclusive resorts reorganized the relationships between the Hotel Zone and Cancún City, deepening the division between these two areas. Before the hurricane, and despite the spatially segregated nature of the destination, there were everyday economic and social interactions between Cancún City and the Hotel Zone. In the early stages of the tourism enclave, for example, tourists who lodged at the Hotel Zone often visited the main markets in downtown Cancún City to buy souvenirs or to eat at local restaurants. Hotel managers who lived in downtown Cancún City traveled daily to the Hotel Zone. Local and regional produce such as tortillas, tomatoes, and chiles was offered at hotel restaurants.

Gilbert, and the advent of the all-inclusive resorts that followed, disrupted these relationships of exchange and interdependency. As production from local and regional markets could not meet the demands of the growing number of tourists, the Hotel Zone developed connections to international supply chains that bypassed Cancún City, the region, and the national scales. Pro-Poor Tourism Partnership highlighted, for example, that in 2015 "only 4.5% of fruit, 3.4% of vegetables, and 1% of meat consumed by hotels is supplied by producers in Quintana Roo" (Torres and Momsen 2004, 306).

As spatial enclosures nested within the wider enclosure of the Hotel Zone and predicated upon exclusion, all-inclusive resorts functioned as self-contained habitats for private consumption secured through the regimentation of people, capital, and objects within tightly controlled spatial circuits. Like visitors to a theme park, tourists have little incentive to leave the premises and experience life outside the walls of the resort. Tourists are typically picked up from the airport and transplanted into the hotel lounge. According to local estimates, about 85 percent of tourists never step outside the enclosed space of their all-inclusive hotels to eat, walk, or take pictures (Grupo Ciudad 2007). The remaining 15 percent usually travel outside the hotels in prepackaged tours previously arranged by hotels to archaeological sites or for nature excursions.

The advent of the all-inclusive resort has entailed a de facto privatization of public spaces, like the beach, which has been cordoned off through an intricate set of physical and immaterial boundaries. One of the most prominent material boundaries is architecture. Most all-inclusive resorts are built on the narrow oceanfront corridor, which is limited on one side by the beach and on the other by the Boulevard Kukulcán. The hotels are immediately adjacent to each other, thus allowing little space for accessing the beach. The walls, fences, and gates that secure the resorts create a massive barrier that has blocked both physical and visual access to the beach which, it is important to note, is a public space under Mexican federal law. On a bus ride with Maria, an indigenous Yucatec Maya worker at one of the all-inclusive hotels, she explained, "when the hotels came, we could no longer see the sea. . . . and each new one is bigger and thicker [than the others]."

In addition to these tangible physical barriers, the process of creating enclosures within enclosures after Gilbert also relied on a number of immaterial, but equally effective, boundaries traced by socioeconomic status, race, and constant surveillance.[18] The conspicuous difference between the affluent and typically white-skinned North American and European tourists and the

FIGURE 3. All-inclusive resort encroaching upon the public beach, 2013. Photo by author.

indigenous and brown-skinned locals often still acts as an insurmountable barrier for the latter. These barriers are constantly at play when walking the beach, when trying to access an all-inclusive hotel either from the beach or from the entrance gates, and also when deciding where to go shopping. I will come back to these practices later in the chapter but for now I want to highlight that the surveillance that started with the development of all-inclusive hotels is, in many ways, an act of profiling based on race and socioeconomic status. In a July 2012 interview with me, the son of one of the first residents of Cancún synthesized what has become a recurrent feeling about how the enclosure of the Hotel Zone works: "After Gilbert, free movement in Cancún came to an end. It is maybe even possible to think about what apartheid is in South Africa to think about what the Hotel Zone is for [the city] inhabitants. . . . Credentials are needed to get in, sometimes it is not an ID, it is the color of your skin. . . . Interiorized segregation is what makes them [the local population] even more vulnerable. They just don't feel entitled to enter that zone of the city, to go to the beach." The fear of the public embarrassment that would result from being stopped while walking on the beach is an effective deterrent to non-guests trying to access the beach. It is through this set of intangible and tangible boundaries that the beach has been effectively cut off from public space and public use and incorporated into the hotels as a naturalized extension of their swimming pools. As a result, the once public beach has thus split into a series of "hotel beaches," each recognized by the name of the hotel that fronts it, with access restricted to hotel guests.

The development of enclosures within enclosures in the form of all-inclusive resorts in the Hotel Zone after Hurricane Gilbert illustrates the process whereby tourism advances a predatory geography that appropriates, commodifies, and incorporates public spaces into global chains of consumption and capital circulation. It also illustrates the splintered nature of these predatory tourist geographies (Graham and Marvin 2001). While both the Hotel Zone and the city of workers are active nodes in the larger predatory geography of tourist and financial global networks, not all areas of Cancún do it in the same way or with the same intensity. Some areas, such as the Hotel Zone and very specific enclosed spaces within it, matter more than others. In Cancún, the ability to access and participate in these enclosed spaces and the global networks to which they are connected becomes the discriminating factor in the allocation of economic and political resources.

This system of enclosures within enclosures created in Cancún a new urban, political, and economic cartography organized around new boundaries. This system has deepened the divide between the serviced enclosures connected to global circuits and the remaining areas, which are excluded from its benefits but which are nonetheless dependent on them for their survival. The absolute dependency of the city, and the rest of the region, on these enclosed spaces of global consumption increases the dependency and vulnerability of the region to the fluctuation of global tourist markets as well as to natural disasters. This became evident in 2005, when Hurricane Wilma brought Cancún, once again, to its knees.

High-Rises, Time-Shares, and Displacing Responsibility after Hurricane Wilma

Hurricane Wilma is the most intense hurricane on record in the North Atlantic region and it is one of the twenty strongest storms ever recorded worldwide. It stayed over Cancún for forty-eight hours straight, on October 20 and 21, 2005. While there were no human casualties directed related to the storm, the hurricane tore the Hotel Zone to pieces and devastated entire sections of Cancún City. Nearly all of the city's residential areas experienced intense flooding and structural damage, and over three hundred thousand residents of Cancún City lost their homes. More than 80 percent of rooms in the Hotel Zone suffered severe damage, while the beaches were obliterated, causing not only an estimated daily loss of US$1.5 million in hotel revenue but also irreversible environmental damage.[19] As one local official put it, after the hurricane, the Hotel Zone "was full of sand. All the palm trees were on the ground. . . . The beautiful [sea] color we have [had turned] black, such devastation. I thought, 'Cancún is over. There won't be Cancún ever again.'" The strategic relevance of Cancún's Hotel Zone to the Mexican economy became apparent once again in the prompt but selective posthurricane response by the federal government. On the first evening after the storm, a contingent of 240 military personnel landed in Cancún to protect the Hotel Zone and certain commercial areas and banks in the city's downtown area. Reconstructing tourism infrastructure for "the public good" was the main rhetoric. In an attempt to speed postdisaster recovery in time for the December peak season, Mexican President Fox declared a "state of national emergency" and pledged nearly US$2 billion in assistance, half of which was designated for the reconstruction of hotels, restaurants, and other tourism-related facilities at the Hotel Zone. The other half was used to fund a temporary employment program for tourism workers affected by the hurricane—an innovation since Hurricane Gilbert. In addition to these federal funds, reconstruction efforts were also funded with loan assistance from the Inter-American Development Bank and the World Bank, although the amounts of these loans were never publicly disclosed (Alvarez 2015).

This massive investment of funds delivered prompt results. Within two weeks, water and electricity were restored. The infrastructure connecting the Hotel Zone to the airport was fully restored. New palm trees were brought in and planted to beautify the main tourist boulevard. The beaches, which shrank drastically as a result of the storm, were fully replenished in three months thanks to a massive engineering effort to dredge sand that cost over US$20 million, paid for by a consortium led by hotels and the federal government (SEDESOL 2010). As a result of these multiscalar efforts, 80 percent of Cancún's hotels were opened to the public five months after Wilma, a figure that reached 90 percent a year later. Perhaps even more surprising, in less than three years, Cancún surpassed its pre-Wilma room capacity, adding 21,300 new rooms in real estate development projects. In practice, this meant that by 2008 the Hotel Zone had exceeded the thirty-thousand-room capacity legally established in the original master plan.

The source of the phenomenal tourist growth post-Wilma is to be found, once again, in the strategic use of a postdisaster scenario for capital accumulation. If post-Gilbert recovery entailed exceptional measures to restore Cancún, including the massive privatization of public lands that facilitated the expansion of all-inclusive resorts in the Hotel Zone, the recovery strategy post-Wilma was to minimize investment risk by transferring it to tourists.[20]

This risk transfer was accomplished through a legal loophole. Under the provisions of the 1993 Cancún Urban Development Plan, there was a land use category—"areas for special recreational tourist services"—which had remained largely underused as it was meant to regulate parking (one parking lot per hundred square meters of built area). Interestingly, this regulation did not specify anything about *not* building in these areas, as was the case for the other land use designations, which had severe restrictions about construction, including a prohibition on erecting buildings over four stories high. Tapping into this largely unregulated land use category, real estate consortiums and hotel corporations—with the acquiescence of local authorities—began to buy tracts of land categorized under this use in order to invest in a new business model: the time-share resort, comprising mixed tourism and residential units (villas) and high-rise condominiums (towers) such as the one in which George and I met.

The time-share resort was an attractive option for investors for a number of reasons. One of them was that, like other well-established tourist destinations, many of Cancún's hotels were caught in a cycle in which the need to cut prices to remain competitive generally implied the gradual downgrading of hotel infrastructure (Warnken and Guilding 2009). Crucially, for many hotel corporations in the Hotel Zone, the all-inclusive model proved too inflexible and costly after natural disasters of the likes of Wilma. This model required resort owners to make major investments in order to sustain a steady flow of tourists as well as to access large and costly global supply chains. As a result, the typical cycle of investment recovery for resort businesses spanned over a decade. The dramatic rise in insurance premiums after Wilma further extended this cycle of investment recovery for the all-inclusive business model. The tourism industry thus started to perceive the all-inclusive model as a high-risk investment in a hurricane-prone area like Cancún. As a result, hotel companies began looking for business models with shorter cycles of investment recovery.

Spurred by the large cash flows for insurance premium payments after the hurricane, various hotel corporations replaced damaged all-inclusive hotels with high-rise condos. This was the case with Allotment 18, an eighteen-hectare seafront property that shifted from a small-scale hotel to an all-inclusive resort after Hurricane Gilbert, then to a high-rise time-share resort after Wilma. The trajectory of Allotment 18 became common. As a result of this shift toward high-rise condominiums, the room capacity of the Hotel Zone increased by nearly two thousand rooms by 2010, only five years after Wilma, with eleven low-density tourist areas changing zoning to the "special recreational tourist services" category (SEDESOL 2010). That year there were twenty-five thousand units within high-rise condominiums and residential villas, nearly the same room capacity within hotels.[21]

FONATUR's leading manager in 2010 explained the transition in an interview for this research, "Wilma was the costliest hurricane ever. [The Cancún government said,] we need money to recover. [President] Fox, without coming, without evaluating [in situ], said: 'There, you have it.' . . . Reconstruction was not done by the government. . . . It was done by financial capital. . . . [The Mexican state] just wanted to keep money moving [and] they built rooms and more rooms. They never thought about vulnerability. They just knew land was cheap and governments decided to open to business to grow." As enclosed architectures, high-rise time-share condominiums share similarities with all-inclusive resorts. Both offer gated access and specific amenities like pools, golf camps, fitness centers, the de facto privatization of the beach, and 24/7 security patrols. There are, however, some critical differences with regard to ownership legislation, investment incentives, and long-term maintenance of the buildings. In all-inclusive resorts, a single legal entity (e.g., the property owner, the management company, the divestment group, or the hotel chain) is responsible for property development, management, maintenance, and marketing. In most cases, resorts have a business plan that includes funds for renovations, sales, demolition, and reconstruction. They also have contingency plans in case of hurricanes to evacuate their guests.

High-rise condominiums generally entail a form of multiownership and shared responsibility for the property, which is distributed across myriad agents with divergent interests in the building. First, there are the many apartment owners. As George explained to me, most owners of time-share condos are not residents in Cancún, but wealthy individuals who use the condos as investments. Second, there is the "body corporate," which represents all owners in order to avoid conflict and administer repairs and maintenance of the buildings. Body corporates are generally created to ensure standardized governance and equitable rights among all owners, but in Mexico they are still a relatively gray legal area whose implementation depends on state governmental regulation, the owners themselves, and real estate interests.

While the primary goal of body corporates is to ensure compliance with governmental regulations, owners who live in the apartments and owners who lease their units to visitors have divergent investment interests. In general, owners as private investors are not year-round residents in these units. In fact, they might have never set foot in them. These private investors see high-rise condo units as long-term investment assets that are similar to owning shares in the market (Warnken and Guilding 2009). This tends to generate a high turnover in ownership and a detachment from everyday management and care, tasks that get displaced to current residents and dysfunctional body corporates. In this multiownership regime, entrepreneurs, developers, and landowners aim to keep building costs low to attract buyers; body corporates aim at complying with governmental regulations and keeping fees low to attract investors; and individual owners seek to maximize their particular form of investment.

High-rise condos also bring new actors into the tourist arena, for example, real estate agents, like George, and other intermediaries. Real estate agents are involved in sales and management of the facilities and are becoming increasingly instrumental in this tourism model due to the high turnover in ownership. The more broadly a high-rise condo can publicize its development to a global market, the easier and faster its units will be sold. In this sense, the shift to time-shares points at the further entrenchment of the internationalization of Cancún through tourism. Whereas the hotel industry was mostly in the hands of North American, Spanish, and Mexican hotel chains, the move to time-shares has meant the scattering of ownership across a global scale, further cementing Cancún's global orientation.

This multiownership regime poses serious problems for an ecologically vulnerable and hurricane-prone area like Cancún, since it facilitates the predatory displacement of risk and responsibility in potential reconstruction processes. In the high-rise condo model, investors recover their investments in a shorter timespan than they do in the hotel time-share model. Real estate agents and investors dissociate from the property as soon as all apartments are sold. In other words, touristic high-rise condominiums allow a material and legal reorganization of responsibility that enables investors to externalize some of the risk and costs associated with maintenance or postdisaster reconstruction processes to individual property owners. Moreover, investors have little vested interest in, for example, contributing to future beach recovery efforts. In the event that a natural disaster destroys apartment units, insurance and reconstruction costs will be directly imputed to individual property owners, the federal government, and the municipality.

Fearful of the potential long-term effects of condominiums, the Hotel Association in Cancún is trying to regulate their construction. And yet, as they themselves acknowledge, there is little room to maneuver. As one of the association's leaders recognized in an interview with me, "Trying to regulate condominiums is hard. It is like fighting with lions. They are terrible for Cancún. When people buy them, they don't generate jobs, they don't generate money, they just come a few days a year. The rest of the time they rent it and they don't pay taxes like hotels [which] pay the 11 percent of VAT, plus 3 percent of the cost of the room to the promotion of the destination. These people don't care about Cancún . . . they only take advantage of its consolidated place in the tourism market." One evening after Hurricane Paula, I was talking to Armando, one of the oldest people working at Protección Civil in Cancún, the city council branch in charge of coordinating responses to natural disasters. He was concerned about the rapid proliferation of high-rise condos, and exclaimed, "Condominiums are invading us. . . . They are everywhere . . . fifteen, twenty-stories high. . . . Do you know how many people can live there? Do you know what this means if a three-meter wave hits the coast? The sea would just need to show its tongue and they will be gone." While in principle, Cancún's Master Plan "guaranteed public access to beaches" and the "preservation of the five-mile zone separating the tourist zone from [the] mainland" (Aguirre 1989, 32), in October 2010, unrestricted public access to the beach was possible at only nine sites on the twenty-five kilometers of Boulevard Kukulcán. In 2016, this number decreased to five. On a bus traveling through the Hotel Zone, Maria further elaborated on how high-rise condos had contributed to privatizing not only access to the beach, but also the sensorial experience of the beach. Pointing through the bus window at a large tower at the entrance of the Hotel Zone, she said with resignation, "high-rise condos are like Oxxos [the Mexican chain of convenience stores with a widespread presence in the region]: we cannot even get the ocean's breeze."

This logic of enclosure within enclosures is not unique to Cancún. Land enclosure and privatization of natural resources constitute two of the main processes through which the tourism industry predatorily carves out spaces for tourism consumption in cities around the world (Telfer and Sharpley 2015; Duffy and Smith 2003). As in Cancún, this process is intensified in the aftermath of disasters. This is what has happened in places like Sri Lanka after the 2004 tsunami, or New Orleans after Hurricane Katrina in 2005, where natural disasters have helped governments in the process of neoliberalization (Johnson 2011).[22]

Something that is remarkable in the case of Cancún, though, is the general lack of resistance or manifest opposition to these orchestrated predatory practices of capital accumulation, land acquisition, and ecological neglect. As many inhabitants put it, enclosing the beach for tourism is necessary to keep "the engine" working as a productive global tourist space, as an idealized Caribbean beach resort. As Castellanos (2010b) already noted in her ethnography of Cancún, tourism is the source of low-skilled jobs and short-term contract positions that residents depend upon for their livelihoods.[23] It is this dependency that makes these predatory tourist geographies sticky: people get trapped and stuck in them. This kind of stickiness shows how tourism has reorganized not only physical space and ecological life but also social life by creating a sacrificial logic whereby actively participating in, or acquiescing to, the production of enclosures, the privatization of public spaces, or the restriction of one's own freedom is accepted as a necessary cost of keeping the tourism engine working.

PARADISE DISENGAGEMENTS
AND SHARED SACRIFICES

As noted at the outset of this chapter, the success of Cancún as a leading tourist destination in the global market depends to a great extent on minimizing the potential contradictions between tourists' lived experiences of Cancún and its brand image in the tourist market, which conditions tourists' expectations.

Minimizing this friction between reality and representation requires daily toil. For example, inside the gates of hotels, workers are trained in what to say and what to do to keep tourists captive and to respond to marketed imaginaries of escape. Tourists are offered the official tourism map of Cancún, which does not contain any visual or narrative reference to Cancún City. At some resorts, maids, waiters, bartenders, cleaners, and staff other than those working at the front desk are instructed not to share information about the city's services beyond the resort. In these face-to-face encounters, hotel workers emphasize that it might be unsafe if guests were to venture outside of the hotel property. These representations and interactions secure the Caribbean imaginary of a self-contained leisure island "out of place" by preventing tourists from venturing and circulating outside enclosed spaces of tourism consumption. As a North American young woman and health professional who regularly visits Cancún's resorts put it in an interview for this research, "When I come to Cancún I want to feel in paradise. I don't want to be bothered with poverty or suffering. I just want people smiling around me, I want happiness."

I interviewed several tourists during my fieldwork, like Monica and Javier, a couple visiting Cancún from Guadalajara, Spain, for their honeymoon, who did not know that Cancún was part of Mexico. When they learned this, they became concerned about their safety and tried to book their day-trips to Chichén Itzá and the nearby Biosphere Reserve Sian Ka'an through international providers based in Spain. Their experience is far from unique and reflects larger efforts by the federal government to disassociate Cancún from Mexico in branding campaigns.

One of the key sites to secure the continuity between imagined and lived reality of the tropical paradise at all-inclusive resorts and high-rise condominiums is the beach, which has to be kept as close as possible to the paradisiacal image advertised in brochures. "Beach guards" play an important role in upholding this image; they usually stand at the border between one resort and the next, keeping unwanted visitors out of the enclosed beach perimeter. They constantly surveil people walking along the beach, verifying whether they are wearing the hotel's identifying bracelet, either by visual identification from a distance or by conducting "stop-and-probe" interviews of passersby. Guards also keep pedestrian vendors away from guests lounging on the hotel's beach hammocks and under its hut-like umbrellas, restricting vendors' circulation closer to the water (as this is still public, federal land).[24]

These practices re-create, through repeated performance, the boundaries of a predatory tourist geography organized around racial and socioeconomic profiling. As pointed out earlier, for many locals and tourists, the fear of the public embarrassment of being stopped while walking on the beach effectively deters them from using public areas, which are de facto privatized. However, while these practices of profiling and monitoring are acknowledged as wrong and unjust, they are generally accepted as necessary sacrifices in exchange for gaining access to the benefits of the tourist industry and enjoying its possibilities. Leonardo, a thirty-five-year-old interior designer from Guadalajara and regular visitor to Cancún's beaches, elaborated in an interview about being stopped at the fence of the resort where he was staying: "I am used to being stopped. I am just used to it. I am brown and the people working in the hotels just think I do not belong. . . . They ask for my wrist-band and identification and then they let me in. . . . They never apologize. . . . I do not think they are racists or something. They just do what they are told to do and I just come the same way!" His words are an example of how tour-ism has advanced through a sacrificial logic that becomes accepted and inter-nalized as part of daily life. This same logic is reproduced within the hotels by the workers.

Cancún's all-inclusive resorts function as archetypal neoliberal corpora-tions. Hotels operate within an established hierarchy of managers at the top and manual workers at the bottom. The managers, who have their own hier-archies and ranks, rotate across the company's hotels within a given destina-tion and around the world, generally every week and every two years, respec-tively. Foreign managers do not necessarily need to speak the local language, while floor managers are regularly recruited locally or, if not, are conversant in the local language. Manual workers, also heterogeneous as a collective, are mostly indigenous and are recruited locally on a seasonal basis and generally have precarious, low-wage jobs. In Cancún, tourist resorts exercise a strict gendered disciplining of workers and rely deeply on emotional labor.[25] Women are typically employed in the realm of the private, that is, indoors, to attend to classic domestic tasks, such as working as maids, receptionists, or cleaners. The lighter their skin, the more visible and public and the less demanding are their jobs. The darker their skin, the more traditionally they are dressed and the less visible they are in common hotel areas.[26] Men are employed in visible, outdoor spaces, serving as beach and swimming pool waiters, security guards, and clerks. In their case as well, the darker the skin the more mechanical and manual the work and the lower the wage. Workers like Ixchel, a receptionist in a large, upscale resort, are fully aware of these racial practices and like other inland indigenous Maya service workers, she uses her indigeneity to access labor and labor spaces.

One not-too-busy morning at the hotel reception area, after having exchanged random conversation, I asked Ixchel about her natal village and things that were similar and different in Cancún. She responded,

> At home I don't use as much makeup as in my town, or hair gel. . . . I don't wear the *terno* to work . . . or my gold. . . . Tourists like it here, they want to learn about the Maya. . . . The manager insists we look Maya, like in the pic-tures in the magazines, like the *Yucatán Today*. . . . It is easy to do if you are *morenita* [have brown skin]. . . . You just wear more hair lotion and makeup and the *aretes* [earrings], you smile and you got it!

FIGURE 4. Workers picking up seaweed in front of an all-inclusive resort, 2019. Photo by author.

In addition to these gendered and racialized practices, workers are subjected to other forms of disciplining and surveillance. Like factory workers, in Cancún, hotel workers move in and out of the Hotel Zone in their hotel uniforms at designated times. Public transportation or hotel vans bring them in and pick them up at certain times and locations in the city. With a six-day work week, workers are regularly scheduled in such a way that their weeks, days, and hours never look the same. In one of my fieldwork stays in Cancún, I talked with Emilio while he was embellishing sand ashtrays with the hotel logo along the pool. When we talked, he explained that he had been working for the hotel for three months and that he started helping out cleaning algae from the beach, but he never knew what he was going to do until he arrived at the hotel. He had been working in embellishing the sand ashtrays for the last week and he said he enjoyed being able to see the tourists around. We talked for only ten minutes before a security guard came to ask me if everything was fine. Every time a tourist engages in a conversation with a worker, the same routine applies.

For many workers like Emilio, working at beach resorts is an opportunity that comes with sacrifices, such as losing one's freedom to talk and move independently without being controlled and monitored.[27] Many resorts also conduct weekly urine and blood tests on workers to ensure that they are "clean" of drugs and alcohol in their interactions with tourists. Workers like Miguel, a bartender at a large resort when I met him, adjust to these monitoring practices, modifying their labor tactics according to the hotel's rules and regulations. As he told me, "If I know I am still drunk it is better not to show up to work, otherwise they put you on a list and hotels share that information, so it is difficult to find another job."

Corporate social responsibility hospitality programs also provide some workers with cell phones. In her ethnography of indigenous migrant workers in Cancún, Castellanos (2010b) shows how these digital devices in some cases empower indigenous workers in their experience of the city by enabling them to have more contact with home and also, to escape the boredom of routines that require long waits via internet access and online gaming. At the same time, in the context of economic informality cell phones also serve to extend the control of corporations over individual lives, as Castellanos points out, rendering workers accountable beyond the workspace.

An extreme example of this accountability is the requirement that workers live on a hotel's grounds while on shift. In some instances, especially along the Riviera Maya, resorts have built twin cities, or worker villages, across the highway from the actual resorts. This is the case with both the water park Xel-Ha and the Palladium Resort. These worker villages include accommodations, one meal per day, and laundry facilities. Housing buildings are coed but are segregated by gender: women live in the top floors of the building and men in the lower ones. Married couples are not allowed to live together. Another extreme case of accountability—and in this case also ethnic labor segmentation—is the practice of some hotels of targeting entire Maya villages as their labor source, providing busing to and from the village to the hotels and making the village itself dependent on one hotel for their livelihood.[28] Backstage villages and captive workers in Cancún's all-inclusive resorts reflect the larger reality of tourist spaces becoming factory-like spaces where the totality of a worker's life—work and leisure time, production and reproduction—becomes entrapped in asymmetric power relations in which they are controlled and regulated to maximize profits.

Workers face the process of becoming entrapped in these relations with resignation and ambivalence. While they acknowledge these practices as discriminatory and abusive, they also recognize that it is thanks to them that they have access to cash and the possibility of sending money to their hometowns, which otherwise would be impossible unless they were to migrate internationally. Itxel elaborated on this form of entrapment, explaining how it was stickier for indigenous women like herself. With five younger sisters still living with their parents in Sotuta, an inland community marked by migration to Cancún, twenty-one-year-old Itxel said that she came to the city to work in the hotels as a way to provide "enough and fast money" to keep her sisters studying. "I can go to visit them sometimes and when my father [who is also in Cancún] comes back, he helps my mother [meaning he takes the money back home]. . . . This way we don't have to cross [to the USA], we are closer even though we are far . . . I am still with them." Many workers praised the small-scale twin cities during my interviews, especially one case in which the tourist resort built a pedestrian bridge over the highway in order to prevent workers from risking their lives when coming to work.

This ambivalence between giving and taking, enabling and constraining, proximity and distance sits at the heart of the sacrificial logic that tourism has nurtured in Cancún. Crucially, this sacrificial logic has done more than entrap individuals into ambivalent moral regimes. It has also shaped the moral fabric of the city by weakening social bonds and creating a generalized sense of detachment and disengagement. This was best reflected in an interview with Ata, whom I mention in the book's introduction, and Ana, his wife. They are a young married couple from Veracruz and Mérida, respectively, whom I had met a few years ago in Mérida. Both survived Hurricane Wilma in Cancún, having just moved there from Mérida as newlyweds, and they experienced firsthand the discrepancy in how tourists and locals were treated in evacuation efforts and the aftermath. Ata explained with a certain resignation what he endured after Wilma:

> The first thing [for the municipal and federal government] was restoring business of course, they just care about the business. A week after the hurricane, with the news reporting water shortages for most areas of the city, you could see [official] trucks with imported palm trees going towards the tourist area. Everything there was clean just a week after [the hurricane]. . . . At hotels there were lines of people asking for jobs. . . . For them, rebuilding the hotels is a priority even when their houses might have no roof, electricity or water. . . . We stayed without electricity for weeks and we had water to drink because I bought all the containers from a truck when I went to rescue the workers at my work. . . . It was painful to see your neighbors looting and feeling alone. . . . The fear of a lack of community put us off as much as wanting to leave the city immediately after the hurricane.

This experience meant that when Hurricane Paula hit five years later, they decided to leave the city as soon as they learned tourists were evacuating. As Ata said, "In a city made of migrants, where no one belongs and that you do not consider your own, who cares?" To which Ana added, "But hurricanes also help tourism. . . . [They] make the city nicer, you know, they help to build the city as the paradise that tourists want, so [afterwards] it is always nice [*bonito*] and new tourists want to come."

The tension between their words resonated with me for months. For those living in Cancún working and feeding the tourism machine, disengagement and the strategic use of the city is what defines their relationship to it. As Ana put it, Cancún is a city that fosters, and functions through, instrumental relationships: "[Living in Cancún] I learned not to ask many questions to my neighbors. . . . You know everybody comes and goes. . . . You do not work in social relations with your neighbors because they are not going to last. . . . People come to Cancún as we did: to sacrifice a few years of your life to make money faster and then move out and start your life and your family in a nicer place." As Ana's words reflect, the continuous demand for a flexible workforce to meet the ever-growing tourist demand has transformed Cancún into "a come-and-go city" *(una ciudad de paso)*, characterized by transient relations and a pervasive sense of "rootlessness" *(desarraigo)*. As another longtime resident put it in a local newspaper, "Cancún is populated by people who reinvent themselves upon arriving in a community inhabited by strangers. . . . This phenomenon has generated family dynamics of great loneliness and little emotional attachment to the land that takes them in."

The result of this dynamic is that, after almost five decades of existence, Cancún still lacks a strong civic and political network to organize against labor abuses, ecological crimes, or racial discrimination.[29] This absence does not stem from a lack of consciousness or awareness about tourism's predatory logics and its effects on the environment and peoples' lives. Rather, it stems from how tourism entraps people into a sacrificial logic. Workers have become so dependent upon tourism, their everyday work and living spaces so monopolized by the industry's designs, that they have become stuck to its inequitable ways and have normalized its predatory relations. As it is stressed, time and again, among Cancún's inhabitants, the Hotel Zone is "the goose that lays the golden eggs": it is an area to be protected and respected as a restricted space for tourist consumption so that people in Yucatán can have jobs and enjoy "progress."

Tourism has indeed generated jobs, roads, and infrastructure. It has also allowed indigenous migrant workers to become homeowners, even as it has encroached on their rights over land (Castellanos 2020). Tourism's affordances work at the cost of entrapping natural and social life within renovated forms of extraction and racialized servitude. According to oral accounts from workers during my fieldwork in Cancún, an average waiter and maid in 2015 earned US$5–7 a day. Renting a one-bedroom apartment in the city center costs an average of US$278 a month, and US$130 outside of the city center. Basic electricity, water, and garbage services for a 915 square foot apartment are close to US$70. A carton of milk in a supermarket costs US$3.15 dollars and a 10 oz. bottle of water almost US$1.[30] Official data from 2015 reveals that the portion of the population living in poverty has increased to almost 36 percent. In 2017, an estimated 43 percent of Cancún's population had wages below minimal well-being standards (CONEVAL 2019b).

As in other tourist cities across the world, workers see no options but to take on more risks, debt, and sacrifices regarding family life to be able to participate in tourism and "get ahead." This endless cycle has led sociologist David Karjanen (2016), studying tourism in San Diego, to argue that service-oriented cities become "servant class cities," with highly polarized labor markets, low-wage and low-benefit jobs, few upward career paths, and predatory and exploitive financial services. This is certainly the case in Cancún, where tourism is a vehicle for reproducing long-lasting economic, sociocultural, and spatial inequalities based on class, race, and origin. And yet, as Ana put it, "Cancún is worth it if you know how to be in the city." Or as Ixchel said, "because of work in Cancún I have a solitary week, I am mostly alone, but I get to see my sisters and if my work is good I might also get them in [to jobs at the hotel]."

CONCLUSION: SECURING PARADISE IN THE FACE OF CLIMATE CHANGE

Cancún is a city designed and planned for tourism. It exists because of tourism, and it functions by forcing the disengagement of its own inhabitants, who sacrifice, in the name of tourism, their own claims to public space, improved social relations, and leisure time. It is a city that works by naturalizing the predatory logic of enclosure and the extraction of land, ocean, sand, and labor so that paradise can keep going as a productive space for the regional and national economies as much as for global corporate capital. It is also a city in which, ironically, the very practices and infrastructure designed to preserve this image are contributing to its erosion.

Research shows that the tourist infrastructure that keeps Cancún up and running causes increased beach erosion, a result of prolonged exposure to intense ocean currents which is due to, among other things, the accelerated loss of ecosystem protection and the death of coral reefs from untreated sewage water that is discharged into the ocean (Escudero-Castillo et al. 2018; Goreau and Hilbertz 2005). In a personal communication with Thomas J. Goreau, a biogeochemist, marine biologist, UN secretary of sustainable development, and president of the Global Coral Reef Alliance, he pointed out that Cancún's 1974 master plan had envisioned sewage treatment for a population of two hundred thousand people but that the sewage system had not been updated since then. As a consequence, "everything that surpasses this number goes directly into the ocean" (Thomas J. Goreau, personal communication with author, March, 2019). According to his research, 80 percent of the sewage in Cancún is untreated, and the 20 percent that is treated is not treated at levels that are healthy for marine species such as coral reefs. As a result, sewage resulting from tourism has increased the growth of the sea grass and algae that forms at the bottom of coral reefs, killing the reefs at a faster pace than anywhere else in the world (Goreau and Hilbertz 2005).

Most of the attempts to mitigate these damaging ecological effects have been directed at preventing beach erosion. This is not surprising since the beach is, after all, the main asset Cancún has to compete in the global tourist market. The most aggressive plan for beach maintenance started after Wilma through a cooperation between FONATUR, some of Cancún's hotels, and a large corporate geosynthetics multinational, to "bring Cancún's beaches back to life."[31] A multinational company specializing in textile and chemical technology "for the protection of people and their living and working environments" was hired, as its own press release asserted, to develop a geotube shoreline protection system so that "millions of dollars of property and tourism [could be] restored and permanently protected." The plan consisted of installing 1.24 miles of geotube units designed to hold sand in place when a storm arrives, dredging sand from the Gulf and pumping it onto the shoreline, and rebuilding the sandbar through the submersion of a breakwater construction. As a result of these engineering efforts, the company claimed, "The breathtaking beaches are back. And so is Cancún as Mexico's top international tourist destination. One that's much better prepared for hurricane seasons to come."

In light of my ethnography, these efforts reveal a different reality: one that points, again, at selective planned infrastructural interventions and the emergence of a new system of segregation. The protection of the beach only

FIGURE 5. Geotextile tubes exposed after Hurricane Paula, Cancún Hotel Zone, 2010.
Photo by author.

occurs in front of the hotels that have paid for these interventions and in front of the city's most valuable and profitable land. The state, the regional and local governments, and environmental institutions turn a blind eye to these projects, in one more example of tourism's predation and stickiness in practice, so that tourists can keep coming.

The geotextile tubes project is just the most recent episode in a forty-year history of attempts to maintain a fragile, exiguous, and hurricane-stricken sand barrier as a beach paradise for global consumption. "Cancún spends millions of dollars a year pumping sand onto the beach," a visibly angry Thomas J. Goreau told me, "and it all washes away since there is no living reef to protect it. Since they don't sieve [the sand dredged from the corals], it is full of sharp shell fragments after the fine material washes away, so you can't walk on the beach barefoot anymore."

Lisa, from Shanghai, learned about this the hard way when she stayed in an upscale resort in the Hotel Zone in the summer of 2015. Marketing had promised a sensory paradise in a "resort inspired by a yin-yang philosophy," that, as she told me, would invite her "to relax and connect with nature." "The beaches were paradise," she recalled, in talking about the hotel's promotion, "solitary, quiet, inviting ... so beautiful and peaceful." A prepaid van was waiting for her and other guests at the airport to transport them nonstop to the resort. This was a must for Lisa's mother who had expressed concerns about her daughter's security in a third world country. Upon arrival at the hotel, her room was ready and "looking exactly as in the pictures." On her first morning at the resort, Lisa went to the beach ready for a run and the ocean swim she had been envisioning for a long time. Then, as she put it, "paradise collapsed."

Not only was the beach narrower than in the marketing images but the sand was "shellish and hurtful to her feet." Jogging was "too painful" and swimming in the ocean soon proved a total ordeal. During her first dip, the water felt "muddy." Then, as she vividly remembered, when the water reached only her knees she suddenly found a big hidden slope which, combined with a strong wave, toppled her over and rolled her back to the shore. "It was so embarrassing" and "uncomfortable," she recalled. During the rest of her vacation she did not step back onto the beach, and spent her time alternating between her room and the hotel's pool, "feeling sort of trapped ... not being able to connect with nature at all" and "disappointed" with the experience in general.[32]

Lisa's experience matters because since Hurricane Wilma in 2005, climate change challenges have pushed Cancún and, in particular its beaches, to newer and more extensive ecological struggles—ones that do not go unnoticed by tourists. Periodic macro blooms of sargassum triggered by increased ocean temperatures, permanent beach erosion, continual sand extraction, and sewage pollution leading to the death of coral reefs are critical in a destination whose success in the global tourist market depends precisely on keeping the city stable as an imagined Caribbean beach paradise. And rather than halting these ecological threats, geotextile tubes such as the ones installed after Wilma are furthering them.[33]

The outcomes of this logic affect not only Cancún. They have larger political and socio-ecological consequences that transcend the city and the Yucatán Peninsula and point at the role of tourism in creating unsustainable patterns of ecological degradation and neglect. Alarmed by the destructive effects of Hurricane Ivan in the Caribbean in 2004, the UN International Office for Disaster and Risk Reduction (UNISDR) pressed the Mexican government as well as other Caribbean nations to put in place monitoring systems for their coasts. Local governments were urged to conduct coastal assessment reports. In Cancún, there have been four risk assessment reports and disaster mapping initiatives created under the auspices of the United Nations and funded by state support, national and regional public research centers, universities, and Cancún's hotel's association. However, the findings from these reports have been systematically disregarded.[34] This disregard is, again, far from accidental. In a tourist city that grew out of orchestrated segregation, efforts to point out flood-prone areas or other dangers in the Hotel Zone could lead to international environmental protections that would hamper the ability of the local and federal governments and corporations to incorporate land into tourism ventures. Proponents of maintaining Cancún in its popular geopolitical imagination—a Caribbean beach paradise for the leisure classes—are bound to minimize the scientific evidence about potential risks or unsustainable practices so the city can continue to be flexible enough to reinvent itself when needed.

At the time of the writing of this book, in 2019, Cancún still lacks an operative disaster prevention strategy. Ironically, the city council largely relies on Armando's local knowledge at Protección Civil for what to do. Sand dredging has become a new normal for tourists at the beach, where cranes, tow trucks, geotextile tubes, and pipes as well as "a surreal smell of oil"—as Eileen, a British tourist told me—"pollute" the idealized Caribbean, while the "tourist machine" keeps building new golf courses, artificial marinas, resorts, and condominiums. "I will think more than twice before coming back to Cancún," Lisa gravely commented to me, "and yet ... prices are so competitive!"

It is unsettling and ironic that Cancún has recently become a hub for international summits on climate change, including the 2010 UN Climate Change Conference, the 2016 Cancún Climate Change Conference (UNFCCC COP 16), and the 2017 UN Global Platform for Disaster Risk

Reduction (GP2017), gathering experts in oceanfront resorts with sinking shorelines to discuss climate change. If these absurdities were not enough, in 2009, an underwater contemporary museum of art, MUSA, opened in the Marine Protected Area of Cozumel, just in front of Cancún, making anthropogenic ecological degradation the latest tourist must-see by attracting thousands of tourists to an artificial coral reef made of submerged life-sized sculptures representing iconic consumerist moments such as watching TV, driving a car, or creating waste.[35] Confronting tourists with their own consumption practices, according to the museum, urges them to reflect about carbon economies, warming seas, and ocean acidification. The museum redirects tourists' movements from the endangered reefs at the Mesoamerican Barrier, and yet, the copyrighted nature of the experience and the fact that access to the protected area is not controlled ends up creating another predatory tourist attraction.

Besides, Cancún is still a major referent in tourism development, in particular for the small islands in the Caribbean and the Pacific, which look at tourism and ventures such as MUSA as an avenue for regional development: "They all want to be Cancún, because Cancún is the world's biggest example of the capitalization of nature and coral reefs for profit," said Goreau, airing his frustration in a Skype conversation with me after a laudatory presentation of MUSA as an example to follow at the 2018 UN Small Island State Conference that he was attending in Samoa. "It is a classic example of bad science manipulated for political reasons, resulting in disastrous environmental policy." Over the years, beach resort tourism à la Cancún has been amply criticized by experts and tourists alike as a low-cost, environmentally unfriendly, culturally unaware, and deeply commodified form of travel (Vainikka 2013). It is out of these reflexive critiques that a host of new models of tourism began to emerge and materialize worldwide in the 1990s. Looking at nature and the environment, some of these alternatives, such as ecotourism, promised to develop a more "sustainable," "inclusive," and "responsible" form of tourism. In the decades to follow, the Yucatán Peninsula became, once again, a real-life experiment in putting these alternatives to mass tourism into practice. Alongside the Caribbean beaches, new spaces and species, such as the pink flamingo, became globalized icons beckoning travelers to the Yucatán. The next chapter moves to the Gulf of Mexico coast, where a decade after Cancún's creation and in direct opposition to it, the Mexican state promoted ecotourism as an environmentally friendly development strategy.

TWO

Wild Hotspots

CONTESTED NATURES ON THE MAYA COAST

ALL IN FOR THE PINK FLAMINGOS

I vividly remember the first time I visited Celestún, a fishing town along the Gulf of Mexico coast. It was a hot day in August 1994. I had taken an early-morning bus from downtown Mérida with a small group of local biology and anthropology students. The purpose of our trip was to observe the pink flamingos that nested in the estuary of the town, Ria Celestún. We arrived at Celestún's main plaza about three hours later, after a rugged and suffocating ride in an old bus repurposed from Madrid's public municipal transport system.

In 1994, Celestún was still outside the region's tourist circuits, which were dominated by Cancún, Chichén Itzá, and the then-emerging large beach resorts along the Riviera Maya. I recall how, once we arrived there, we got lost trying to reach the *ria,* or estuary. There were no tourist signposts or billboards. There was nobody around to ask for directions. We walked to what looked like a restaurant next to the beach and asked where we could see the pink flamingos. A man offered us a ride. We jumped in the back of his truck and drove to the entrance of the estuary, backtracking the bus route for about three kilometers. Once there, and after we had waited for a while under a makeshift palm-roofed hut *(palapa),* another man took us in a motorboat. He explained that he was a fisherman and did these tours *(paseos)* on his free time to earn some extra money.

The boat took us along leafy wetlands. It stopped at an open-air cenote (sinkhole) in the middle of a dense mangrove forest, where we spotted a crocodile. After an hour or so, we arrived where the flamingos were. There were hundreds of them. The boatman stopped the motor and asked if we would like to get closer to the birds. We nodded silently and prepared our cameras. Then, he moved slowly toward the birds and when we were almost within a hand's reach, he started the motor again. The engine's noise made all the flamingos take flight, briefly surrounding our boat in a dense pink cloud pierced by loud and sharp noises.

This rehearsed provocation was meant to provide us with a spectacular and authentic encounter with nature as wilderness. Something "unique from Celestún," as the boatman put it. Yet this was not the only element that made the visit to Celestún unique. The absence of other tourists, as well as the spontaneity of the arrangements, made this trip starkly different than the visits I had made a few days earlier to the archeological sites of Uxmal and Chichén Itzá. There, tourist crowds, buses, turnstiles, tickets, bathrooms, and signposts are omnipresent. English is the language spoken, and the encounters between tourists and locals follows scripted rituals that have little space for ambiguity, contradiction, or random mingling.[1]

It was not until 2002 that I returned to Celestún, this time to start ethnographic fieldwork on tourism development for my PhD in social anthropology. Just as I had done in 1994, I took a bus from downtown Mérida. Unlike the almost empty and battered bus I recalled, the bus I embarked on this time had air conditioning and was full of people and packages. There were about fifteen locals who seemed to be going to Celestún for business. Some carried large black plastic bags with textiles, others wooden trays filled with handmade desserts. Most were traveling alone. There were also a young Canadian couple and a French guy traveling as backpackers and carrying the usual gear as well as a battery of local snacks and water bottles.

As the bus entered Celestún, a couple of hours later, it soon became clear that this was not the laid-back, off-the-beaten-path community that I remembered. Billboards and tourist signs in English and Spanish lined the entrance of the estuary announcing our arrival to the Biosphere Reserve Ria Celestún with large depictions of stylized pink flamingos flying over the estuary at sunset. In addition to these official promotional billboards, both sides of the road were peppered by large Corona and Coca-Cola ads, inviting the viewer to relax with a well-known series of Westernized and gendered allusions to leisure-time activities—mostly half-naked white women in bikinis having drinks while reclining on the white and powdery sand of deserted beaches. The trunks of the palm trees along the main avenue toward the plaza were painted bright pink. *Tendejones* (small street shops) selling all sorts of merchandise, from diapers to Sabritas chips and prepackaged tortillas, were ubiquitous.

FIGURE 6. Official tourist banner and pink flamingo metal sculptures at the entrance to Celestún, 2015. Photo by author.

The magnitude of the changes that had occurred in Celestún since my last visit was confirmed upon entering the main plaza. The semideserted plaza of my memory was now buzzing with activity and packed with seven chartered tourist buses. As soon as I descended from the bus, three men on bicycles approached me and the three backpackers. Gesturing with arms and hands, they wanted us to follow them. They talked loudly in broken English and repeated that they had "the real" and "authentic flamingo tour." Getting closer, they reached out for our hands and arms, grabbing us, trying to pull us to walk with them toward the beach. They were frantic, and verbally expressed their frustration when we refused, leaving on their bikes while blowing into plastic whistles hanging from their necks. In my fieldwork notebook that night, I annotated: "tourism has definitively arrived in Celestún."

But what, exactly, had happened between 1994 and 2002?

To find an answer to this question we need to go back to the year 2000, when Mexico formally declared a biosphere reserve in the land where Celestún is located. This was also the year when the state began an aggressive push to develop ecotourism by promoting Celestún, and the newly inaugurated Biosphere Reserve Ria Celestún, as a "sustainable" and "natural" alternative to Cancún and the Riviera Maya's beach resorts, which were increasingly saturated as tourism destinations.

The changes that occurred in Celestún as a result of the creation of the biosphere reserve and the state-led push for ecotourism could not have been more dramatic. In just a couple of years, Celestún rapidly morphed from a town that was outside the radar of packaged tourism to one of the most visited ecotourism destinations in Mexico, regularly featured in official national tourism marketing campaigns as "a world biodiversity niche," a "pristine natural oasis," or as "the natural stop" to contemplate pink flamingos in their "wild" habitat. The results of this branding strategy were nothing short of spectacular. In 2000, more than twenty thousand tourists visited the estuary of Celestún (SEMARNAT 2000). Only four years later, in 2004, that number climbed to fifty thousand tourists per year, with over a hundred officially permitted boats circulating at the estuary daily (Pinkus Rendón and Pinkus Rendón 2015) and many thousands more doing so as part of under-the-radar in situ arrangements with fishermen, as I later observed myself. By 2017, the number of tourists visiting Celestún had reached eighty thousand (Datatur 2018), which effectively meant that the town had quadrupled its tourist flow in less than two decades. Absorbing such growth had other cascading effects in the community, and in particular, it meant the advent of new social and ecological conflicts. Here, unlike in Cancún, the growth of tourist infrastructure had not quite matched the numbers of arriving tourists. Notwithstanding, Celestún would not become another Cancún, and international conservation and environmental regulations were in place—at least on paper—to avoid such an outcome.

During the first months of fieldwork in Celestún, I soon realized that behind the official stories of sustainable tourism success and the glossy ecotourism brochures, there was a very different, and difficult, reality. I learned, for example, that in addition to gaining fame as a new ecotourist resort, Celestún had also gained notoriety as the "Afghanistan of the Maya coast," with regional and national news regularly reporting on violence and social conflicts in the community. Eduardo, a senior local researcher from Mérida's Center for Research and Advanced Studies told me, half joking and half serious, how everyone at the institution talked not about *Celestún* but about *Afghanistún*. Not only was this view, I gradually realized, echoed by many locals, like Andrés, a fisherman native to Celestún who described it as a "lawless village" *(un pueblo sin ley)*, but it was also reflected by a heightened military presence. Celestún had become a new frontier best characterized, as I will show, by lawlessness and ongoing labor conflicts.[2]

In my conversations with Celestún's residents, it soon became clear that, for them, the pink flamingos were the source of the conflict, as they were the element that had propelled the estuary conservation and the economic growth of the community through tourism. Miguel, the owner of the town's only youth hostel, where I worked in exchange for a bed, elaborated on this. He pointed at the contradictory nature of ecotourism, which capitalized on the pink flamingos to increase economic activity while at the same time promoting the preservation of the species and its habitat. This, he told me, had produced an "overregulation" of the area that frustrated people. One day, sitting in the lobby of the youth hostel, he said that ecotourism had transformed the town into a "wild place." He did not mean the romanticized sense of wild, as a place that results from untamed yet enriching spiritual journeys. He meant wild in the sense of a difficult place that encouraged what he called "the roughness of its people." I would encounter this roughness many times during my fieldwork. Repeatedly, people joked about this roughness by pointing at a huge hole in the tower of the city council building, where the clock should be located. To them, the missing clock in such a distinctive building and in such a public space should be proof enough of the seriousness of the conflicts at the heart of the town.

In this chapter I explore the paradoxical effects that the arrival of ecotourism has had on Celestún's inhabitants and how it has altered their spatial and everyday dynamics. I show how ecotourism has scaled up Celestún and transformed it into yet another global tourist stage ruled by internationally legitimized discourses around sustainable development and global environmental conservation. My argument is that, as in Cancún, this scaling-up process has resulted in a new, predatory, and sticky geography. Despite the discourse on species and habitat preservation, ecotourism in Celestún is organized according to the extraction of nature—understood as natural resources, and in particular, access to pink flamingos—for global leisure consumption, which has created a community riven with social and ecological conflict.

The chapter begins by situating Celestún within the larger transformations that took place in the late 1980s and early 1990s at a global scale, when, coinciding with the global environmental movement, the so-called alternative tourisms, like ecotourism, began to emerge as alternatives to "sea, sun, and sand" mass tourism models. By then, enough evidence had accumulated to show that, in practice, mass tourism exacerbated social differences and environmental deterioration almost everywhere in the world (Pattullo 2005; Brockington, Duffy, and Igoe 2008). In the case of Celestún, the international, state, and regional pushes toward ecotourism development took place within the global impulse to turn natural protected areas into productive segments of the economy by adopting a managerial approach to nature conservation. The practical translation of these pushes in Celestún has been to produce a particular tourist model organized around the contemplation of the pink flamingo at the estuary of the Biosphere Reserve Ria Celestún— what locals call "the pink tourism." As a result, Celestún is stuck socially, politically, and ecologically around two hotspots, the estuary and the beach, the two physical locations of the pink tourism model that have been scaled up in predatory fashion for both ecotourism and conservation.

The second part of the chapter focuses on how these hotspots have become overregulated and militarized territories where local populations fight to stay still in order to be physically proximate to tourists and extract economic benefits from ecotourism. I focus on the workers and new stakeholders that ecotourism has created, in particular, the so-called boatmen *(lancheros)* in charge of showing the pink flamingo, and the shell craftswomen *(artesanas de conchas)*. I discuss the struggles, everyday labor, and spatial (im)mobilities of these collectives in their claims to maintain control over the scaled-up territories of the estuary and the beach. I show how these collectives exercise both their right to space and their power over local resources. They do so by deploying different forms of physical mobility and stillness and by strategically using ecotourist and global conservation vocabularies and imaginaries—like environmental preservation and biodiversity—to mediate and resolve domestic or local conflicts.[3] The third part of the chapter elaborates on the violent nature of this new predatory tourist geography. Ecotourism, despite optimistic discourses and glossy brochures, has in fact contributed to normalizing violence in the community. Although it does not have the gates, walls, and tourist police that Cancún uses to enforce the spatial segregation that creates social and racial disparities, ecotourism in Celestún has likewise gone too far (Duffy 2002). Ecotourism hotspots work like extractive pits for global leisure, in which nature, labor, and local wealth are extracted for tourism consumption. In the fourth and final part of the chapter, I elaborate on the Celestún that exists beyond the pink tourism model. I do so by examining the displaced leisure practices of *vacacionistas* and other regional holidaymakers as well as the tentative and precarious economies that have emerged to cater to them. By focusing on these displaced spaces, the criminalization of particular local practices in regards to the environment, and the need to make visible other social collectives, I want to foreground the silenced heterogeneity and the constraints of a real alternative tourist place that has also become stuck in official discourses, representations, and practices produced by and for (eco)tourism.

IN THE NAME OF NATURE: CONSERVATION, ZONING, PROHIBITIONS, AND THE LANDING OF EXPERTS

The international emergence of alternative tourism in the late 1980s and 1990s can be seen as the combined result of two different developments. The first of these developments was internal to the tourist industry and had to do with its need to cater to and create alternatives for tourists looking for adventure "in nature" and/or "cultural" authenticity, and who, increasingly, were dissatisfied with the "sea, sand, and sun" mass resort tourism model represented by the Costa Bravas, the Daytona Strips, the Atlantic Cities, the Blackpools, and the Cancúns of the world (Butler 1990). The second development was the global consolidation of the environmental and heritage preservation movements, based on sustainability claims in international development policies. Against this background, alternative tourisms offered the promise of a sustainable development model that could reconcile seemingly irreconcilable economic and ecological imperatives while at the same time empowering local populations (Mowforth and Munt 2015; Sharpley 2009).

One of the main alternatives to mass tourism that emerged in this context was ecotourism, which was defined in 1990 by the International Ecotourism Society as "responsible travel to natural areas that conserves the environment and improves the well-being of local people" (TIES 1990). The emergence and institutionalization of sustainability discourses around ecotourism, was particularly important for Latin America and the Caribbean region, where state governments began to view ecotourism as a viable way to develop small-scale, low-density, environmentally sensitive, and socially responsible alternatives to extractive industries such as coal and oil mining that had dominated much of their economies (Weaver and Lawton 2007). Ecotourism, so mainstream institutional discourses went, offered an alternative growth model that not only cared for natural resource renewal and community development but also educated tourists about the natural environment (Butler 1990; Pattullo 2005; Duffy 2002).

It is within this particular context that "off-the-beaten-path places," as the industry started to brand them, began to emerge as strategic sites for global tourism consumption. One of those places is Celestún, which the Mexican National Tourism Secretary (SECTUR) defined as an ideal place to implement and test ecotourism as a planned development tool with a low environmental impact factor *(turismo de bajo impacto)*.

However, and as various authors have pointed out, the reality of ecotourism as a sustainable development tool has rarely matched its original promise. Acknowledging that there is no single nature but many natures (Macnaghten and Urry 1998) helps to make clear that ecotourism is essentially a Western-centric concept that burgeoned as a "one size fits all" alternative alongside Western-centric conservationist approaches and tourists' exercises of class and social distinction back at home (Cater 2006; Mowforth and Munt 2015; Munt 1994). As a result and in practice, ecotourism has often been coupled with an aggressive faith in market solutions to environmental problems, giving rise to a new era of extraction and environmental managerialism dressed in the language of sustainability and participation (Mowforth and Munt 2015; Brockington, Duffy, and Igoe 2008; Büscher and Davidov 2013). This is especially evident in biosphere reserves located in developing countries, where state-planned ecotourism is promoted as "responsible travel that conserves the environment and improves the well-being of local people" yet is accomplished through top–down, extra-local governance alliances, as well as through the commodification and spectacle of wildlife and/or selected natural resources to attract a global flux of capital, labor, and tourists. Examples abound, from Latin America to Africa, Asia, Europe and North America (see Weaver and Lawton 2007; Fletcher 2014; Brockington, Duffy, and Igoe 2008; Jamal and Stronza 2009).

The Biosphere Reserve Ria Celestún offers a good example of how this international attempt to conserve while consuming nature has created extractive logics by reducing nature to particular resources and habitats of international relevance that are profitable for the national economy. Enrique, a biologist from Mexico City residing in Celestún at the time of my fieldwork, elaborated on how this happened in Celestún's case: "What they did in Celestún comes from the historical development of environmental law in Mexico . . . they just tried to see biosphere reserves as businesses . . . for profit . . . extracting [*sacándoles*] natural resources with a business mentality and hence, they just started to promote them as tourism destinations." Enrique's words could not have been more accurate. For the Mexican state, ecotourism has been explicitly and unapologetically coupled with a planned technocratic strategy to generate "sustainable, responsible, distributive, and profitable" growth (CONANP 2018, 6). The National Plan for the Development of the Tourist Sector as well as the Alliance for Tourism, both created under President Zedillo de León (1994–2000) were unambiguous about this, establishing plans to "cut regulations in order to ease development of resort areas, make foreign investment in the tourist areas easier, improve infrastructure, and promote ecotourism" (SEDESMA 1996, 12). In the Yucatán Peninsula this meant using ecotourism to diversify the region's economy and diminish its dependence on Cancún by deploying alternatives to sun, sand, and sea tourism along the Gulf of Mexico coast. This was achieved through the strategic use of international conservation policies and, in particular, the designation of natural protected areas such as the Biosphere Reserve Ria Celestún.

The declaration of the Biosphere Reserve Ria Celestún in 2000 was the culmination of a process that began in 1979, when the Mexican federal government designated Celestún's estuary as a "wildlife refuge for the greater flamingos." In 1979, Celestún was a town of two thousand inhabitants, the majority of whom were nonindigenous and made a living through fishing, and through processing and distributing fish meal and salt for animal and human consumption across the region. In 1988, Hurricane Gilbert severely damaged the four fish meal ovens located at the town's beach, dismantling this livelihood. In 1989, coinciding with the international surge of the environmental movement, the area was reclassified, also by the Mexican federal government, as a "special biosphere reserve." This updated status was intended to emphasize the existence of ecosystems with endemic species of fauna or flora, in this case the pink flamingo, which in theory "had not been affected by humans." Lalo, a biologist working in Celestún with one of the leading conservationist NGOs at the time of my research emphasized how this designation was based on the protection of "single animal species and not their entire ecosystem" or the cultural practices surrounding them. Then in 2000, the Mexican state started conversations with the United Nations to reclassify the area as a "biosphere reserve." This last change was particularly important, since it responded to international demands led by the UN World Heritage Committee to shift conservation discourses and actions from individual species to their habitats, as well as from universal understandings of nature to culturally specific ways to act in nature. In Celestún, what this meant in practical terms was the expansion of conservation zones and species well beyond the estuary and the pink flamingos.[4]

Since 2000, the biosphere reserve has legally covered an area of 181,482 hectares, which includes mangrove forests and wetlands, coastal dunes, habitats for sea turtles and a myriad of birds, and vegetation of international significance. Together with El Palmar State Reserve and the Biosphere Reserve of Los Petenes, the Biosphere Reserve Ria Celestún is part of a World Wildlife Fund ecoregion—a marine protected area containing one of the world's most preserved coastal wetlands.[5] The protected area spreads between the states of Campeche and Yucatán and, crucially, it includes two different population centers: Celestún, in Yucatán, with over five thousand inhabitants in the year 2000, and Isla Arena, in Campeche, with approximately three hundred inhabitants.

The declaration of the biosphere reserve, therefore, brought not only a change of name but also a radically different spatial logic of preservation that, as I show in this chapter, has had critical effects for the population. One day, as I discussed the effect of these new inclusions with Lalo, he argued that, while many of these "protections were wet paper [*papel mojado*]" since they were never implemented in practice, they were all the same extremely important because "they had generated conflict." Many in the town concurred with Lalo. They thought that the extended protection of the area, which also included severe limits on fishing, especially on the Yucatán side, had turned Isla Arena and Celestún against each other. Sara, a native of Celestún and owner of a small store downtown, lamented this situation since, as she put it, "before the flamingos, the people of Isla Arena and Celestún were one.... We were united, good neighbors. But now this has ended, and we all fight for fishing.... [People from Isla Area] they think we have more fish, more resources, because we also have tourism . . . but you have seen this is not true!"

Lalo's and Sara's words must be understood against the backdrop of the state-led conservation initiatives that reorganized Celestún's urban and ecological space and governance starting in 2000. In 2003, the Ramsar

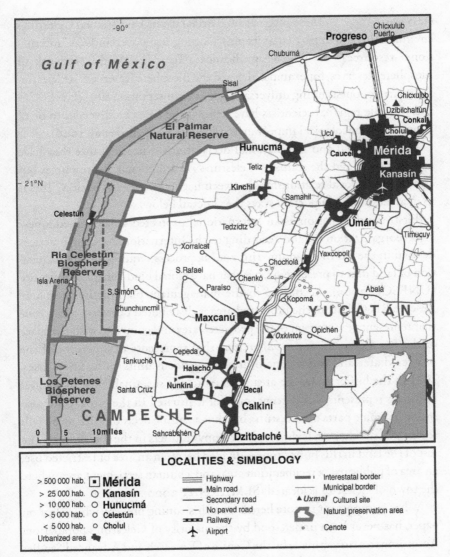

LOCALITIES & SIMBOLOGY

> 500 000 hab.	◼ **Mérida**	Highway	Interestatal border
> 25 000 hab.	○ **Kanasín**	Main road	Municipal border
> 10 000 hab.	○ **Hunucmá**	Secondary road	▲ *Uxmal* Cultural site
> 5 000 hab.	○ **Celestún**	– – No paved road	Natural preservation area
< 5 000 hab.	○ **Cholul**	Railway	Cenote
Urbanized area		✈ Airport	

MAP 3. Celestún and the Biosphere Reserve Ria Celestún. Map by author.

Convention, also known as the Wetlands Convention, declared the Biosphere Reserve Ria Celestún a "wetland of International importance" (Ramsar Convention 2004). A year later, in 2004, the reserve was included in the UN Man and the Biosphere Program (MAB), an international intergovernmental scientific program, created in 1971, that by 2017 had come to manage over six hundred biosphere reserves in one hundred and twenty countries

(UNESCO 2017).[6] These international declarations have framed Celestún's environment, and in particular its pink flamingos and wetlands, as "international resources" of "global significance." The UN World Network of Biosphere Reserves, for example, defined the Biosphere Reserve Ria Celestún as "an area of outstanding universal value as a conservation site" (UNESCO 2009), while regional scientists have defined the area's biodiversity to be of "macrocosmic ecological importance" (Batllori Sampedro et al. 2006).

These national and international declarations matter because they have not only redefined the status of Celestún's *ria* and its natural resources but also reworked local relationships between nature, space, and society. This is so in at least three important ways that I detail below.

First, the designation as an international protected area entailed a new legal reorganization of land according to the international zoning practices defined in the MAB program. This zoning process requires the reorganization of land uses to preserve species that have global biodiversity significance (UNESCO 2009). According to the management plan of the Biosphere Reserve Ria Celestún, the protected area is distributed between: a *core zone* that represents 37.2 percent of the protected area and coincides with the space of the Ria Celestún; and a *buffer zone* that represents 62.8 percent of the protected area and is distributed in heterogeneous units with various uses. Within the buffer zone, the area devoted to the sustainable use of natural resources represents 82.3 percent, most of it situated in the estuary but also including some parts of Celestún's beach—a zoning decision that, as we will see later in the chapter, is the source of many conflicts in the community. The rest of the land in this buffer zone is divided between an area of restricted use, an area of public use, a recuperation area, and a human settlement area, where the town of Celestún is located (SEMARNAT 2000).

What is important to note here is that this zoning process, while clear on paper, has never been understood by the majority of Celestún's population. According to a survey made by the Centre of Research and Advanced Studies of Mérida (CINVESTAV) in 2004, 90 percent of the community did not know that they lived in a protected area. The 10 percent of the population who were aware of this fact misidentified the protected area as being confined to the estuary and the pink flamingos themselves (Méndez-Contreras, Dickinson, and Castillo-Burguete 2008). I have been able to confirm this data over the years during my fieldwork in Celestún. Whenever I have asked someone about the biosphere reserve, they have always referred to the pink flamingos and directed me to the estuary. As I demonstrate in the next section, this apparent lack of knowledge stems in part from the specific spatiality produced by the state-planned implementation of ecotourism.

Second, the international and state-sanctioned protection of the area as a biosphere reserve meant the arrival of a new system of conservationist regulations that severely restricted productive community activities in Celestún, especially fishing at the estuary. Fishing prohibitions include international, national, and state regulations aimed at sustainability, and they have focused on species like the octopus, sea cucumber, and pink shrimp, all three highly valued in the local, regional, and international fishing and tourism economies. These prohibitions are officially justified as a response to the alleged overexploitation of fishing resources caused by "massive, irresponsible, and unsustainable catches in a protected area" (SEMARNAT 2000). Official discourses and the media routinely represent local populations as "environmental criminals" "in need of" environmental education, or as "predators [*depredadores*] of the sea and its resources." Here it is important to note that since the closure of the fish meal processing factories, fishing—for sustenance and for petty sale in regional markets and to tourist restaurants—has become the main livelihood for many residents and inland immigrants in both Isla Arena and Celestún. For example, in the year 2003, a few years after the implementation of the Biosphere Reserve, fishing for pink shrimp at the estuary affected 90 percent of families in the community (Batllori Sampedro et al. 2006). In 2015, the number of families directly and indirectly involved in fishing at the estuary and making a living from fishing at the estuary was still 90 percent (Guerrero and Pelcastre 2017). Most of the species caught, like pink shrimp, are later served as ceviche in Celestún's, Hunucma's, and Mérida's cantinas as well as in Celestún's beach restaurants. The work of processing the fish for ceviche is conducted mostly by women in their homes, and it generates a relatively stable source of provisional income for many families.

Ironically, the importance of fishing for Celestún is the byproduct of development policies that the Yucatán state government implemented in response to the henequen crisis of the late 1970s. Inspired by national policies like "La Marcha al Mar" in the 1950s, the state promoted fishing as an economic alternative for inland rural populations after the collapse of the henequen haciendas.[7] The fishing industry received massive state support in the form of infrastructure development, equipment, and tools, which brought thousands of indigenous peasants from inland Yucatán to a new life in the coastal towns of the Gulf of Mexico (Fraga and Cervera 2004). As in Cancún (chapter 1), most of this labor migration was unplanned and was met at a local level by an absolute lack of service provision. Moreover, it brought into a coastal environment groups of indigenous peasants unaccustomed to the sea, sharpening the cultural and racially informed differences between inland Maya populations accustomed to living from *el campo* (the land) and those coastal Maya native to Celestún, who were accustomed to living from *el mar* (the sea). It was also this state-led shift toward fishing that enabled the formation and growth of an economic patronage system in Celestún. In this patronage system, a single patron—or *cacique,* as they call him locally—Don Solís, a fisherman native to Celestún, has been able to control most of the formal and irregular fishing activities in town. From production to distribution, Don Solís nearly monopolized the reception of state support for the processing of fish meal during the 1980s and later on, he controlled state support for fishing in the form of boats and equipment as well as infrastructure subsidies. In 2019, Don Solís remained the owner of the two fish warehouses in Celestún, and hence the only one with the capability to conserve fish fresh for regional distribution and export.

The result of these regional development efforts was that, by the late 1980s, precisely when national and international policies were turning to nature conservation, regional development policies were fueling the massive labor migration of inland populations to coastal municipalities like Celestún, a place undergoing its own economic and ecological crisis after Hurricane Gilbert. Inland labor immigration to the community increased by 88.7 percent between 1980 and 1990 (INEGI 2005), creating one of the most dramatic population shifts in the state of Yucatán. While the demographic growth rate of the state as a whole was 2.6 from 1980 to 1990, the growth rate of Celestún was 6.1; it grew from 2,520 to 4,506 inhabitants in those ten years. From 1990 to 1995, the state demographic growth rates were 2.4 and 1.5, respectively, while Celestún's demographic growth rates were 2.7 and 3.5, respectively, reaching a population of over 5,500 inhabitants in 1995, 7836 in 2015, and close to 10,000 inhabitants in 2018 (INEGI 2015b).[8]

This intense labor immigration shifted the official statistical classification of Celestún from a rural community (fewer than 2,500 inhabitants) to a largely urban one (INEGI 2000). This is a meaningful change that is largely overlooked in conservation efforts and development initiatives and is intentionally silenced in ecotourism promotion. It matters because it is in this context of simultaneous intense and racially marked population growth and environmental conservation that many of the social conflicts would be created. Local authorities estimate that since the early 1990s, about one thou-

FIGURE 7. Irregular housing settlements built upon rubbish-filled lagoon, Celestún, 2005. Photo by author.

sand indigenous migrant workers, along with their extended families, have come to Celestún during the fishing season (August–April) to make use of the estuary for fishing pink shrimp. As Don Leon, a fisherman native to Celestún, explains, "People from the villages [*los pueblitos*] don't dare to fish in the sea.... They are afraid of the sea.... They are confined to fish at the estuary." This culturally informed spatial confinement of labor migrants to the space of the estuary, and the fact that urbanization has taken place in an uneven, unplanned fashion and has been principally limited to the swamps has not only exacerbated ecological problems at the estuary, but has also heated social relations in the town as well as with neighbors in Isla Arena. As Hanson (2016, 467) has noted in her research, in no time Celestún became "one more example of how urban disasters and biodiversity conservation are disproportionately located in tropical low-lying coastal areas," topics to which I will return later in this chapter.

The third way in which the creation of the Biosphere Reserve has reworked the relations between nature and society in Celestún has been through the arrival of a plethora of technocrats, scientists, NGO workers, and government officials. Locals refer to these social collectives as "the technicians" *(los técnicos)* and "the government people" *(los del gobierno)*, and typically perceive them as one and the same. There are, however, some elements that differentiate the labor of these collectives on the ground.

Since the mid-1990s, a variety of research institutions have developed programs, activities, and stations in Celestún including, among others, the World Wildlife Fund (WWF), the Japanese International Cooperation Agency (JICA), Ducks Unlimited México AC (DUMAC), Pronatura Yucatán (PPY), the regional nongovernmental organization Niños y Crías, the Center of Research and Advanced Studies (CINVESTAV), the Yucatán Scientific Research Center (CICY), and the Yucatán Autonomous University (UADY). Exceptions aside, the research of these institutions has been almost exclusively focused on the physical environment and the well-being of the pink flamingos rather than on people and their uses of natural resources. One of the anthropologists working in the town put it this way in one of my interviews with her, "my colleagues here . . . they totally forget that nature is a cultural category. If they don't include people in their studies, there is nothing to expect from sustainability actions." When these scientists visit the community, they are easy to identify because of the institutional logos on both their clothes and on the vans and cars they drive. They act as the guarantors of the endangered natural resources of the area, which are seen as threatened by what official discourses describe as the "unsustainable practices of the community" (SEMARNAT 2000). Generally, they are not welcomed.

In addition to these research institutions, the Mexican state operates in the area through four different governmental agencies: the Comisión Nacional de Áreas Naturales Protegidas (CONANP); the Procuraduría Federal de Protección al Ambiente (PROFEPA); the Secretaría de Medio Ambiente y Recursos Naturales (SEMARNAT), in charge of supervising municipalities' compliance with environmental laws; and the Patronato de las Unidades Culturales y Turísticas del Estado de Yucatán (CULTUR), a regional agency in charge of administering tourist attractions in Yucatán, including controlling the official ecotours offered in Celestún.

Unlike researchers, state officials do not have offices *(estaciones de trabajo)* in Celestún, but they regularly visit it. These visits have often ended with locals attacking them over disputes about using mangrove wood to heat and cook in homes, and mostly, about regulating fishing resources at the estuary. This violence has been reported in international conservationist research sites, like *Parks Watch* at the Center for Tropical Conservation at Duke University, which cited Celestún as an example of the conflictive social relations that can arise when local populations are not included in the management of natural protected areas. As one of the biosphere reserve directors explained to me, "the biosphere reserve is an initiative of the federal government in which local authorities do not have a role to play.... What could one expect if they were never consulted? If no plan was ever showed to them?"[9]

These tensions were evident during my fieldwork in Celestún, especially during my first stay in the community when I lived for a couple of months at a local NGO office. When I first shared my intentions to live in town, local researchers had recommended instead coming back to Mérida every night, arguing that Celestún "was not a safe place for a foreigner, or for anyone wearing a uniform." A local conservationist NGO offered me a place to stay in Celestún for the first months, and while this housing arrangement helped me arrive in the community and to live at no cost, as well as to meet most scientists with projects in the area, I had to work hard to explain to locals that I was neither a "nature expert" nor a "technician," and that I was interested in people's experiences, accounts, and perceptions of their everyday lives. It was only after I had repeatedly come back to the community over several years, provisionally worked for the youth hostel, and helped craftswomen daily at the beach in their interactions with tourists that locals finally set aside the "nature expert label" for me and instead started to introduce me by saying, "This one is not interested in the flamingos but in people." Those words, together with keeping a calculated distance from other experts and government officials in town, worked to open up the town to me in ways that had not been possible before.

It is against the background of this tension between locals, experts, and government officials, created by the region's historically informed labor migration and the simultaneous international and national implementation of the biosphere reserve protections, that we must situate the arrival of ecotourism at Celestún. Given the restrictions imposed on traditional activities like fishing, ecotourism was introduced in Celestún as a viable development strategy that could both help "to diversify economic opportunities for the population" and, in so doing, serve as "an opportunity to minimize conflicts between [the] local population and conservation authorities" (SEMARNAT 2000). Paradoxically, ecotourism in Celestún was to be developed in the very same spaces and with the same resources that conservationist legislations and practices sought to protect: the pink flamingo and their habitat in the estuary. How this paradox was negotiated in practice is what I explore next.

In the 1995–2001 Yucatán state plan, created under the governorship of Victor Cervera Pacheco (1984–88 and 1995–2001), ecotourism was described as "the real way to travel to Yucatán" and institutional attention and resources began to be channeled toward its promotion. In Celestún, the main aim of these campaigns has been to insert the town as a "nature stop" in the regional circuits of prepackaged tourists coming from the all-inclusive resorts in Cancún and the Riviera Maya, by promoting it in travel brochures and maps—alongside Maya archeological sites and tropical beaches—as a "natural treasure," a "fragile ecosystem," or a "refuge for wildlife." The main asset for this promotion has been the pink flamingo, which has been transformed into a flagship species *(especie bandera)* and icon of an alternative Mexico worldwide. Travel agencies like México Desconocido (Unknown Mexico), part of Grupo MundoMex, for example, highlight and promote Celestún as "one of the national natural must-sees," while travel magazines and blogs like the *Yucatán Times* and *México Premiere* urge readers to "think pink" and highlight "the American Flamingo as Celestún's signature bird and feathered attraction."[10] During my research, I have spotted pink flamingos from Celestún printed in public buses and subway stations in Madrid, London, and Mexico City as well as in AeroMéxico, Mexicana, and Volaris airplane magazines, in *Condé Nast Traveler* magazine and in a myriad of other popular texts. In all these, flamingos mingle with restored luxury colonial architecture as examples of an authentic "escape to nature in a sleepy, slightly seedy beach."

In these tourist representations, Celestún appears as an accessible conservation area with no clear culture or place attached to it, an island-like paradise of global biodiversity that is all the same close enough to the region's international airports of Mérida and Cancún. "I want the real nature" said Violeta, manager of an eco-hotel in Celestún, while showing me the hotel, "and I know tourists are tired of the artificiality of Cancún and the theme parks there, so I invested here . . . far away from Cancún, in a still unspoiled area to offer the real nature experience to them."

These representations of Celestún are no different from those operating in other natural protected areas around the world, where nature has been commodified through its reduction to charismatic species and their subsequent spectacularization for consumption (Igoe 2017). In the case of Celestún, its particular geographical location has helped to produce and sustain this curated image of a real and pristine nature. Celestún is located fifty kilometers away from the next inhabited community, the town of Hunucmá, to which it has been connected by road only since the 1980s, thanks to the construction of a two-kilometer bridge over the estuary. In between the two towns, there is a large tropical jungle mostly used as a giant illegal garbage dump by people from both Celestún and Hunucmá.

Since tourism activity in the area takes place within a protected zone, Celestún's official tourist infrastructure amounts to a single official *parador* at the estuary—a thatched big building with turnstiles, bathrooms, and a small souvenir and refreshments store—and a few local hotels and restaurants at the beach. This tourist infrastructure is not only very small considering the tourism flows that the community hosts, it also has the peculiarity of being concentrated in two very limited spaces: the estuary at the outskirts of the town and a stretch of beach less than one kilometer long (marked in black in map 4).

There are several reasons why this tourist infrastructure is concentrated in these two locations. In the case of the estuary the explanation is obvious: the estuary is where flamingos nest and eat. In the case of the beach, the explanation is a little bit more complicated and has to do with historical networks of regulations that have been imposed over the area and the effects they have had in the displacement of human populations over time. On its east side, the beach borders a protected coastal dune in which no human activities can take place because protected marine sea turtles lay their eggs there (SEMARNAT 2000). The biosphere reserve, NGOs, and scientific institutions tightly control and monitor this area, together with the estuary. The western side of the beach contains the old and abandoned warehouses and factories that were once used to process fish meal, and that were devastated after Hurricane Gilbert in 1988 and forced to close (Fraga and Doyon 2008; Uc Espadas 2007). Today this side of the beach borders the majority of the irregular settlements that house the community's immigrant population, including that of Debra and her family, who live in a makeshift house built on a foundation of the plastic bottles and garbage that they collect early in the mornings.

Houses such as Debra's are part of larger irregular settlements in the swamps, built upon rubbish-filled areas that create strong smells that keep away tourists, locals, and, paradoxically, development institutions too. Despite their visibility and prominence, these precarious makeshift human settlements and the everyday practices of Debra and other Maya indigenous women like her are not part of any urban plan or conservationist representation of the biosphere reserve, let alone any tourist brochure. Their institutional invisibility, along with the development programs that prioritize sustainable fishing or ecotourism, directly contribute to problems in managing waste disposal and sanitation, in turn fueling ecological neglect within an already vulnerable area (see Hanson 2016, 2017). This invisibility also normalizes informal habitation practices and subjects indigenous labor migrants to extreme levels of marginality and discrimination.

Yet the official tourist representation and spectacularization of Celestún routinely depict the estuary and beach as symbols of this small picturesque community, a peaceful ecotourism resort and unique conservationist sanctuary for pink flamingos. This image of place is reproduced and performed through ecotours to see the flamingos. The trajectory of the ecotours is always the same: tourist buses park at the entrance of the estuary in the infrastructure built by the federal government, the *parador* of the estuary. Here, tourists board the boats that take them into the estuary to contemplate flamingos just as I did in 1994. Afterward, the buses drive the visitors to Celestún's main plaza, next to the protected stretch of beach, where they walk directly to a beach restaurant for a prebooked lunch. After two hours, they go back to their buses and depart. It is important to note that these tours take place within the core and buffer zones of the biosphere reserve, that is, in conservation spaces where human activities are supposed to be kept to a minimum and to be closely monitored in the name of global conservation and sustainable development.

The ritual circulation of ecotours to and from the estuary and the one-kilometer stretch of beach bypasses the rest of the community. Leon, who owns a small *tendejon* in the middle of Celestún's main avenue and whose house is built upon a rubbish-filled area close to the estuary, said to me one day, while looking at the tourist buses pass by, "I see the buses pass by, the nice cars drive to the beach . . . none stops here . . . They say ecotourism has helped . . . but just look around . . . The benefits must be somewhere else."

The geography of Celestún is, in many ways, an example of what Mimi Sheller (2013) calls the *islanding effect* of uneven tourism mobilities. It is the estuary and the beach, and no other sites in the community, that have been put to work by tourism development as open-air extractive pits. To be outside the estuary and the beach means to be disconnected from that world and its benefits. To be within them means to have the power to benefit from, and sometimes reorder, the global resources of work and capital that flow through them. Miguel, the owner of the youth hostel in town, echoed Sheller's idea in one interview with me, when he argued that ever since ecotourism started at

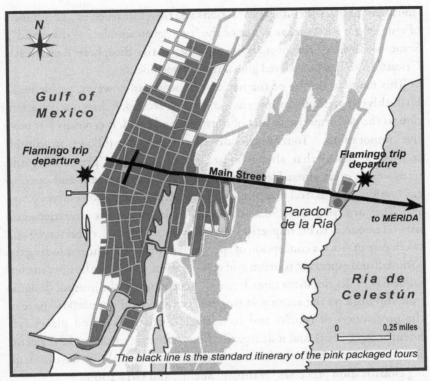

Gulf of
Mexico

Flamingo trip
departure

Flamingo trip
departure

Main Street

Parador
de la Ría

to MÉRIDA

Ría de
Celestún

0   0.25 miles

The black line is the standard itinerary of the pink packaged tours

MAP 4. Boat tour departure points and itinerary of pink packaged tours, Celestún. Map by author.

the estuary, "Celestún is an island ... nobody cares about waste or drugs or education.... Those in the government just care about the *ria* because it gives profits and these profits escape us."

The result of this islanding effect is that the estuary and the beach have become *hotspots* where all want to be, but to which only some have access. The concept of hotspots has been widely used in academic disciplines including biology, human ecology, geography, sociology, and communication studies to define particular spaces where a number of elements, resources, or practices are concentrated in a more than usual way. In mainstream conservation and tourism policy-planning, terms such as "biodiversity hotspot" or "tourist hotspot" have become common currency. For example, biosphere reserves are considered to be major biodiversity hotspots due to the terrestrial concentration of species richness, threat, and endemism (Norman 2003) and tourist places are conceived of as major tourist hotspots when they can offer "must-see" natural or cultural attractions and therefore receive large numbers of visitors (for instance, as at one of the "new seven wonders of the world"). Some biodiversity hotspots, as in the case of the Biosphere Reserve Ria Celestún, are also considered global tourist hotspots.

This mainstream use of the notion of hotspot is, however, problematic. First, this use presupposes space as a container; second, it does not pay attention to the performative nature of hotspots; and third, it typically has positive connotations.[11] Tourist or biodiversity hotspots, it follows, are considered to be spaces that already exist, as fixed entities, "pre-existing and immoveable grids amenable to standardization measurement and open to calculation ... cadastral mapping and engineering practices" (Harvey 2005, 121). They are taken as self-contained loci enclosing tourist attractions and natural resources to be, respectively, consumed and enjoyed, or preserved and taken care of. Such a conception of space severely restricts understanding the sociocultural aspects of tourism and conservation, as well as the uneven consequences of development (Smith 2008). Acceptance of the hotspot designation also neglects the active role that tourists and local populations have in the production of tourist and conservation experiences and places (see Edensor 1998, 2001), and it disregards the constitutive role that the dialectic, asymmetric, and situated relations of mobility and immobility have in shaping globalization processes (Hannam, Sheller, and Urry 2006).

Contrary to this conception, I define hotspots here as highly contested sites articulated by uneven (im)mobilities in which global flows (of people, capital, work, and ideas) are condensed and in which locals fight to stay still. These hotspots can be considered as privileged sites to study the paradoxical nature of global processes (such as tourism and conservation) that depend for their success on the immobilization of people, the concentration of resources, and the appropriation of space. These contentious hotspots can be considered as "heated" spaces where social and ecological temperatures rise.

This is evident in Celestún, where development and conservation institutions, NGOs, governments, and, above all, the local population fight vigorously to appropriate and immobilize themselves in the estuary and on the beach. In the next section, I describe the new socio-spatial system of (im)mobilities that ecotourism hotspots have generated. Physical closeness to and distance from these hotspots, as well as the tourists themselves, has emerged as the new sociopolitical organizing principle in Celestún. Attending to social practices in these hotspots shows the predatory ways in which the tourism industry physically transforms local environments and livelihoods for global consumption on an everyday basis, but also, the sticky and sacrificial logic through which local populations maneuver to advance their interests while being stuck within ecotourism representations and discourses.

CONTENTIOUS ECOLOGICAL HOTSPOTS AND LABOR IMMOBILITIES

The sensory landscape of Celestún is complex and contradictory. At times, the ocean breeze fills the town with a much-needed refreshing cool draft that combats the suffocating tropical heat. At other times, the breeze is almost nonexistent. In these times, a nauseous smell of putrefied fish, rubbish, and salt impregnates it all. On those occasions, the town feels stagnant, abandoned, and pestilent.

Some pink-packaged tourists are shocked by the combination, as if alarmed by the fact that nature smells. And, often, it smells bad. This is, they say, not what they expected from glossy brochure images of a natural paradise and a biodiversity heaven. Maria Isabel, a tourist from Madrid who had joined a packaged tour from Mérida to Celestún and whom I interviewed in 2002 after her tour as she ate at the beach, was still shocked with her experience, "The experience was not great. . . . The foul smells, smells of rotten fish, I would say, are everywhere in the estuary and they come and go. . . . I mean I know this is a natural reserve but still it should not smell like rubbish! . . . Nature is all about freshness and here we are almost unable to breathe normally!" For many, the shock does not end with smells. Nor even with mosquitoes, nor with the town's open-air garbage piles and large population of street dogs with scabies. Fistfights and insults, and boats set on fire in plain daylight, are every now and then included in their ecotourist experience.

To understand the origin of these conflicts we must remember that, as an activity developed within a preservationist area, ecotourism in Celestún is a highly restricted productive activity. The bulk of this activity is carried about by a group of ex-fishermen called *los lancheros,* or boatmen. This is a group of eighty-six natives of the town, all men, who, in a growing community of almost ten thousand people, are the only ones legally authorized to take tourists to the flamingos.

Lancheros are part of a very small network of families native to Celestún linked with fish meal production in the 1980s. Along with Don Solis, the economic patron, they were able to own their own boats and/or fishing equipment. *Lancheros* have been organized into "societies of social solidarity" since the mid-1990s, when the initial state-led impulse toward natural and cultural tourism alternatives to Cancún required that municipalities make their civic organizations visible as a condition for receiving funds for recreation activities. In Celestún, seven of these societies were originally created to offer "environmentally responsible ecotours," four of which were based at the estuary and three at the beach, from where it was possible to access the estuary and the pink flamingos via a longer route.

At the time, the members of these societies had no training in tourism and hardly anyone in them spoke English. Most of these *lancheros* had their own boats but some of them rented them from the local cacique, who has held a monopoly on fishing activities in town since the late 1980s. For him, as many put it in town, tourism was not initially a business, so the fact that other fishermen put their boats to work to show flamingos to tourists was not an issue as long as they did not interrupt his networks of power over fishing. Besides, there was at the time no tourist infrastructure in the town, apart from one beach restaurant and two family-owned hotels. During these initial years, tourism was largely irregular and fragmented, relying on a few fishermen like the one who took us to the estuary in his truck and the one who gave us the tour that I described at the opening of this chapter. Tourism data is not available before the year 2000 and locals who were there at the time recall the number of international visitors being relatively small, "maybe one couple or two in a month" as Miguel's mother, Conchita, owner of the oldest hotel in Celestún, said looking through her client books.

In 1996, Lalo, then a master's student in biology collaborating with a federal conservationist NGO that had close ties to the Mexican political party Partido Revolucionario Institucional (PRI), spotted not only the first negative impacts of boat tours on flamingo habitats but also the willingness of many visitors to pay a fee to enter the reserve. He wrote an internal report detailing both and his document "ended up," as he says, "in the wrong hands in the government." In light of Lalo's report, and through this NGO's networks in the regional and the federal government, the latter decided to reorganize tourism activities in the town so as "to make them more profitable," as Lalo told me. They fused all societies of *lancheros* into a single collective, the Federacion de Lancheros Unidos de Celestún, and two years later, in 1998, they built the two major tourist infrastructures, locally referred to as *paradores,* one at the estuary and one at the beach, that would centralize the tours and provide basic services for tourists through the state secretary of tourism, CULTUR.

As Lalo explained to me, with a tone of helplessness,

> It all started with my study of the impact of tour boats on flamingos . . . My NGO was interested in learning what the economic benefits of tours at the estuary were. They wanted to learn if the flamingo tours were leaving economic benefits in the community, if any. I created a questionnaire to ask if people would pay a fee to come to see the flamingo and almost 90 percent said yes. . . . I used this information to demand federal funds for some infrastructure for these tours at the estuary and then we [the NGO] lost control of it all. . . . When we realized the federal government had taken over, they sent a guy from SEMARNAT and CULTUR and imposed the reorganization of *lancheros,* they started construction for tourist infrastructure and aggressively started to publicize the place. . . . We got out of the picture, like that! In that tricky way [*gachamente*]! And more people just started to arrive!"

From that point on, any *lanchero* wishing to receive institutional funds or subsidies for fuel, boat repairs, life vests, or training had to be part of the Federación, had to use the infrastructure provided by the federal government, and had to comply with newly created regulations on itineraries and times. The federal government installed turnstiles to count the number of people accessing the *paradores,* and they put a CULTUR office in charge of controlling tickets to access the reserve. They regulated that a maximum of six tourists could ride on one boat, and life vests became mandatory. Finally, they designed two different tours to see the flamingos, a one-hour tour and a two-hour tour. *Lancheros* were obligated to offer the boat tours for the flat rate of 1,500 Mexican pesos (around US$85), of which they earned only 20 percent since the rest was meant to go back to "the Reserve," as they refer to CULTUR, in order to enforce conservation and provide cleaning services for tourist areas (e.g., toilets, changing stations, and common shaded areas). The federal government also regulated, for the first time, the distances to be maintained between boats and pink flamingos. Lalo's NGO started to train a group of *lancheros,* called Los Peregrinos, in nature tourism activities. Tourists could now buy the services of a regular *lanchero* boatman or get the services of a trained *lanchero* boatman who was also a nature guide. At a local level, this training is accepted as a sacrifice that one must undergo in order to receive funding for tourism and be able to make an income outside fishing. As Miguel, one of Los Peregrinos, said to me in an interview, "the government asks you to organize in cooperatives, so you just do, you give your name, you accept. . . . There is a price to pay because they can come after you if you don't do things as they said. . . . But you have to do it to be able to work. . . . There is no other way." These new regulations and organization did not sit well with most. For fishermen native to Celestún, like Leon and his sons, who were excluded from participating in tours, this was just another example of a de facto expropriation of the communal spaces of the *ria*, the sea, and their natural resources, which had been the basis of the community. As Leon bitterly put it one day, seeing a group of *lancheros* pass by his *tendejon,* "here the flamingo tours are for them, for 'the favorites'. . . . For the rest of us, just problems."

But for *lancheros,* who saw tours as opportunities to make some extra money, these regulations by the federal and state governments were also perceived as problems, as direct intrusions into a space they claimed as their own. Divisions among *lancheros* started to arise and the Federacion split into two main collectives, the so-called *lancheros de la ria* (boatmen from the estuary) and *lancheros de la playa* (boatmen from the beach). In practice, these divisions were less a direct response to the new top-down organization and more an expression of the perceived sacrifices and unevenness in the daily organization of their activity. For one, both groups of *lancheros* have to be present all day at either the estuary or the beach, waiting for tours to come. Through this waiting, a new form of stickiness began to emerge and, with it, new conflicts.

The *lancheros* working at the beach were also particularly unhappy with the location of their *parador,* which was two blocks away from the main plaza and hence two blocks away from where tourists disembark. "It was too far from tourists," Angel, a *lanchero* from the beach explains. "Buses get here on a short schedule, they park at the plaza and they just stay in that area of the beach. . . . Tourists were not going to walk to here. . . . We had to be there, for them to see us." Oscar also referred to this spatial injustice when he said, "We were never consulted about where to put the *parador* . . . If they had asked, we would have said here and not there . . . It makes a difference . . . from over there you don't see the buses coming; when you finally see them, you don't have enough time to get to them before they go into the restaurant." With these words in mind, it should not come as a surprise that just a few months after the *parador* was completed it was set on fire and destroyed.

Since the fire, the beach *parador* has not been reconstructed. The dead infrastructure is used as a provisional and precarious platform from which to sell fried fish during the summer and Easter holidays, and as a refuge for

FIGURE 8. *Lancheros* waiting at the *ria* for the arrival of tourist buses, Celestún, 2007. Photo by author.

alcohol and drug consumption during the rest of the year. The *lancheros de la playa* have built their own makeshift stand to receive tourists and distribute tours at the main entrance of the beach, right between the restaurants and the main plaza. They were the ones I encountered in my trip in 2002, frantically cycling, whistling, and grabbing me and the other backpackers for the "real flamingo tours." Their work remains unpredictable and depends on overflow from the *parador* at the estuary. Flamingo tours at the beach are organized outside of institutional regulations, controls, and itineraries, at least until they enter the estuary at which point, they need to comply with the biosphere reserve navigation rules. Boats departing from the beach are not counted in official tourist statistics, and *lancheros* are not offered any training or financial help to develop their activities. During tourist seasons, boat rides from the beach are the only option to see the flamingos for those tourists arriving on their own in rented cars since the allocation of boats at the estuary is normally saturated. These independent tourists are not provided with life vests for the rides and prices shift according to a tourist's appearance. As Lalo explained "they are ignored by the government as if making them invisible was a punishment for the fire of the *parador*. . . . They won't recognize them if they do not comply with the use of the *parador* and since they are not going to do it, they ignore them."

The *lancheros de la ria*, with fifty-seven members, also showed their discontent with the institutional reorganization of the activity by the government by claiming the space their own. They erected a precarious kiosk with makeshift benches and hammocks right in front of CULTUR's main office at the estuary's *parador*. Like the boatmen from the beach, they organized a more flexible and irregular system of shifts to extend their control of tourism beyond institutional quotas and CULTUR's regulations and monitoring. This requires them to be physically present at the *parador*, and to be remain stuck to it in order to avoid losing their shifts. It is by being physically there, stuck to this hotspot, that *lancheros* from the estuary ensure their monopoly over tourism's benefits. They survey and deny access to the estuary to the other licensed tourist boatmen, who are effectively forced to operate from the beach and to find other ways into the estuary. They also short-circuit the participation of other trained nature guides in tours because "they always take the best tips." They also control the number of tourists who get into each boat and the length of the tours depending on the season and fishing activities. During fishing seasons, they illegally subcontract their tours to *martillos* (hammers), persons in the community who conduct the tours for them for a few pesos while they enjoy a beer at a cantina or attend to other business.

Given their physical proximity to CULTUR's office, their everyday labor at the *parador*, and their hanging around biologists and natural scientists, boatmen at the estuary, along with their families, are perceived in the community as the "wealthy ones" and the "privileged," while the rest of the community, including boatmen at the beach, are seen as excluded from ecotourism's benefits. However, for many of these "privileged" men, the rapid access to dollars and the tediousness of waiting has also meant greater levels of alcoholism.

In contrast with the stillness of *lancheros* at the estuary, those working at the beach have to be in constant movement, continually walking and biking to and from the estuary while staying confined within a very well defined one-kilometer stretch of the beach. If they want to earn some dollars, they have to be quick to lure the tourists coming to Celestún in rental cars and buses to the beach before they go back to the estuary. Their success depends on their ability to control this proximal space and make sure that no other boatmen recruit tourists for their rides.

The system of labor (im)mobilities in which *lancheros* are trapped is also evident in the new stakeholders who have emerged associated to these tourist

FIGURE 9. Craftswomen setting up their stalls at the beach on a windy day, Celestún, 2015. Photo by author.

hotspots, among them the *artesanas,* or craftswomen. The *artesanas* are a group of twenty-five women native to Celestún, in most cases wives and relatives of boatmen from the beach. Along with the boatmen, they have become the gatekeepers of ecotourism activities in this space by gradually occupying the beach and claiming it as their own. To do so, they have erected twenty precarious and illegal stalls from which they sell handmade souvenirs. This spatial appropriation helps them both to gain access to tourists from the pink packages and to control the access of other collectives, especially other sellers attempting to access the beach.

During the main tourist seasons, such as the Easter and summer holidays, these women spend the whole day at the beach. Every morning at about five o'clock they ride to the beach on their bicycles, which are packed with all their handmade crafts, tables, and sunshades. Once on the beach, they carefully pin all the crafts to boards so that the wind doesn't blow them away. While they wait for tourists, they thoroughly survey the beach in search of any unwelcome vendors. If any such vendors are detected, these women, with the help of the *lancheros,* expel them from the beach. They conduct this kind of surveillance throughout the working day. After the tourists leave, at about six or seven o'clock in the evening, the craftswomen dismantle their stalls and ride home again where they spend the night making more goods to sell.

Many of the beach craftswomen refer to their work routines as *sufridas* (painful) and they say they do not enjoy being *atadas* (tied) to the beach all day. The strong winds from the ocean are not healthy and often give their kids, who normally are with them all day, earaches. Besides, they cannot eat a proper warm meal and instead have to eat prepackaged food, which is expensive. Yet, knowing that being there is necessary in order to get closer to tourists' dollars, and knowing that benefits from fishing are increasingly unpredictable, they say this is "a sacrifice" they are eager to make, a "pain" they are ready to endure to contribute to their families' otherwise precarious incomes.

The spatial practices, labor (im)mobilities, and sacrifices of the *lancheros* and the *artesanas* are examples of the kind of spatial stickiness and entrapments created by tourism's predatory orderings of space and nature for consumption. Scaling up the estuary and the *ria* as hotspots, ecotourism not only has redefined social relations in Celestún, creating a new hierarchy of power and stakeholders, but also has created new ways of being, dwelling, and relating to nature and space. These collectives know that in order to reap the benefits from these tourist hotspots they have to remain stuck to them, a situation which has created what Adela, one of the leaders of the craftswomen, defined as a "war on space and resources." This war means not only strategically appropriating a geographical space, but also getting stuck to and maneuvering global discourses and representations about environmental conservation, sustainability, and biodiversity.

In the next section, I turn my attention to how this is done, by focusing on how these discourses are strategically used and reappropriated to defend local interests related to fishing, which have resulted in further heated conflicts.

A WAR ON SPACE AND RESOURCES

Conflicts emerging from the contradictory web of interests created by ecotourism, environmental protections, and bare survival are constant in Celestún. In these conflicts, boatmen, craftswomen, and local authorities regularly use conservationist and ecotourism discourses about land and natural resource management to resolve their competing interests. They do so through place-based interventions at the estuary and the beach, the hotspots that the tourism industry has scaled up and respatialized for consumption, where these claims can gain traction and be used to advance local politics and articulate demands to access land and control natural resources. Their struggles show that conflicts related to ecotourism and resource extraction are always also about identity and territory (Büscher and Davidov 2013; Sawyer 2004).

One example of such conflict took place on the beach in 2005 while I was doing fieldwork. The conflict emerged around craftswomen attempting to control the space of the beach. Despite the flow of tourists at the beach, craft sales are normally very poor, rarely exceeding one hundred pesos (about US$7) per woman on a good day. This situation has generated among craftswomen a strong sense of competition and confrontation with possible competitors. One of those competitors was a group of immigrant craftswomen from Chiapas, whom Adela, one of the local craftswomen, described as "direct competitors for the few pesos we earn." It was Adela, along with her sister, who expelled these women from the beach and brought them, together with their small children, to the city council.

In front of an impromptu audience in the plaza, the mayor argued that, in a natural protected area like Celestún, beach vending was not allowed. The women, whom he dismissively called "the Chiapanecas," were ordered to leave the town on the next bus to Merida. Episodes like this are not rare. When they occur, craftswomen leverage their familiarity with the experts and volunteers with whom their husbands and brothers work. Local authorities are aware of both the close links between the *artesanas* and the *lancheros,* and the international and financial support that the *lancheros* receive through ecotourism. This is why they generally opt to turn their backs on outsiders, which in turn empowers the local craftswomen and their families to take control of tourist flows to the beach and beyond and reap its benefits.

It is not uncommon in Celestún that the conflicts generated by attempts to control these hotspots and the resources that circulate in them are articulated at a larger scale. One of the conflicts that is most vividly remembered—and recounted by fishermen, craftswomen, and NGO personnel—took place in 2002. The conflict received ample coverage in the national and regional press. The Mexican Navy arrested a group of fishermen native to Celestún at the estuary, took them to the Kobén prison in Campeche, and accused them of illegally fishing for pink shrimp inside a natural protected area. The imprisonment of the fishermen triggered demonstrations led by *lancheros* demanding the liberation of the detained fishermen. They claimed that fishing for pink shrimp was part of the community's "practices and customs" and blamed the incident on the director of the biosphere reserve.

Since there was no response to their demands, demonstrators blocked the entrance to the biosphere reserve. *Lancheros* argued that "if the *ria* is closed for fishing it is closed for tourism too." After a few days of growing tension, with the biosphere closed and a navy ship stationed at the estuary to monitor fishing, the conflict exploded when *lancheros* and fishermen native to Celestún stormed the navy ship and kidnapped three marines. *Lancheros* and fishermen from Celestún then accused the marines of "irresponsible behavior that endangers pink flamingo conservation." According to the *lancheros,* the marines were sailing very close to the animals, frightening them, and prompting them to fly away, which, they argued, would "decrease the number of tourists coming to the *ria.*" The *lancheros* and fishermen offered to free the three marines in exchange for the liberation of the fishermen who were still at Kobén. The federal government responded by storming Celestún, mobilizing three sections of the Marine Corps and several helicopters and sending more than five hundred federal and state policemen to the area.[12]

After heated discussions, the federal government released the fishermen without charges. Tourist activities returned to normal. Soon after, the navy ship disappeared from the estuary, *lancheros* recovered control over ecotours, and though still illegal on paper, the local fisherman resumed fishing pink shrimp with hardly any monitoring.

The militarized federal response to a local fishing conflict indicates the global importance of the estuary and its resources (fish, flamingos, and tourists) as a tourist hotspot. The conflict is also a good example of how local populations, like the *lancheros,* strategically skip regional and national scales and instead appeal directly to international interlocutors, global expert discourses, and tourism imaginaries that portray Celestún as a biodiversity paradise and a sustainable ecotourism destination in order to advance their interests and secure control over these hotspots and their resources.[13]

These types of conflicts and strategies have become more frequent in Celestún over the last decade, and while tourism continues unabated, locals have leveraged such conflicts to their advantage. Protests like setting boats on fire in plain daylight, as happened in 2013, 2015, and 2017, have become a way to call attention to their interests and show discontent with what they consider to be "outside interference" in the management of resources, in particular those related to fishing and the control of land for tourism.

FIGURE 10. Armed forces patrolling the beach in Celestún during the Easter holidays, 2007. Photo by author.

Lancheros, craftswomen, and fishermen have recently started to organize in order to fight not only attempts to privatize the shoreline with oceanfront developments but also the illegal fishing of protected species, both of which they see as threats to their daily survival. They have mobilized large groups of supporters in front of the city council building, and orchestrated violent clashes and attacks against the federal police and conservationist NGOs. Perhaps one of the more revealing conflicts was the one that erupted in the summer of 2017, when Celestún's mayor and his family had to flee the community amid teargas, escorted by federal police.[14] A regional news media headline read: "Celestún has changed its pink color for the color of ants" (*Celestún se vuelve color de hormiga*).[15] The immediate cause of this conflict took place in July 2017, when a group of fishermen accused the mayor of Celestún of illegally appropriating federally protected coastal land titles and selling them to a construction company with several housing projects in Merida, Cancún, and Cozumel. The practice of appropriating land while serving on the city council was nothing new and has been accepted by the population with a mixture of resignation and tolerance. This time, however, "it was too much" as many put it. "We saw them working, fencing off the beach right in front of his house and this was enough," a fisherman told the press. That night over two hundred people marched toward the city council, stormed it, set a beach *palapa* on fire, and destroyed two federal police cars. "They wanted to lynch me," the mayor said to a local newspaper. In the national press, *La Jornada* wrote about the incident as a case of "illegal appropriation of land" and "civic resistance." The fishermen accused the mayor of trying to keep the land for himself in order to subsequently sell it to a Canadian company that was already building a hotel on an adjacent property—all within the buffer zone of the reserve. The mayor said he had sold the land because tourism was a source of income for the population of Celestún.

At the root of these tensions is the predatory logic of land appropriation and privatization that ecotourism has brought to Celestún.[16] Since Celestún gained traction as a natural must-see, Don Solis has opened two large beach-front restaurants and a hotel and has co-opted both the potable water distribution in town and the collection of used plastics for resale. The expansion of his patronage from fishing to tourism, while contested by native fishermen, is tolerated on the basis of reciprocity since it is "thanks to Don Solis" that most in town have a job, or a boat to fish in. However along with Don Solis's expansion into tourism businesses, other tourist developments like the Eco-Hotel Xixim and the large Canadian beach resort hotel, Playa Maya Resorts, have started operations on the west side of the beach, where most *ejido,* or communal, land is. Since 2002, these hotels have been expanding their services to include vacation rentals, spas, and a variety of leisure activities in what they define as "the invigorating freshness of an unspoiled natural area" (Playa Maya) or "the perfect space of peace; a place to find your balance again; to discover harmony with nature together with those you love."[17]

These existing and projected large corporate tourist establishments increase the demand for public land, which creates novel frictions and conflicts like the one involving the mayor. And not only that. They also contribute to another form of social exclusion by increasing the competition felt by the family-owned hotels, hostels, and restaurants in the community that cater to tourists not included in the pink packaged tours.

In the next section I turn my attention to these other forms of tourism and other spaces, ones that do not fit into the typical representations of Celestún as an ecotourist paradise, yet that also inform its contemporary physical and social geographies.

Though they are unacknowledged by official discourses and representations of Celestún as a wildlife sanctuary for ecotourism, Celestún is also frequented by "other tourists" *(los otros)* who travel to Celestún independent of the pink package tours. These tourists—many of whom began visiting Celestún years before ecotourism gained traction—typically come from other cities, towns, and villages in the states of Yucatán and neighboring Campeche. They come in families and groups, in cars, rented minibuses, or crammed and dilapidated vans. They typically stay for weekends and religious holidays. For some of them, Celestún is the first place where they encounter the sea. For others, it is just a regular beach town in which to enjoy fresh fish on a Sunday while drinking beverages, relaxing under sunshades, and sitting in chairs or on blankets listening to music.

One of the groups included in these *otros turistas* (other tourists) are those locally called *turistas de la playa y restaurants*, tourists of the beach and restaurants. They are typically part of Mérida's middle class, and for them being tourists on the Caribbean coast is too expensive. Celestún's beaches emerged in the 1990s as a convenient and affordable alternative where they could be tourists, eat fish, and get boat rides to admire the flamingos. These tourists and their practices shape a less patterned and more exceptional Celestún—one that can be consumed regardless of its categorization as a biodiversity hotspot—where they arrange unofficial boat rides, eat protected fish "under the counter," and get discounted meals at the restaurants. Alberto and Estefania, a young couple from Mérida visiting Celestún with a group of friends, compared the town to Cancún: "We can't afford going to Cancún or Tulum anymore as we used to do.... Celestún also has the ocean and although its beaches are not as nice you get to spend the day at the beach and drink beer and eat fish." Still, these tourists increasingly feel the pressure that the pink-packaged ecotours place on Celestún. Maria, a native of Mérida whom I interviewed as she ate fried fish at the beach, told me, "*Restauranteros* have told us they have to cater for Italians and other gringos [foreigners].... We cannot eat at the restaurants even if we can pay for it.... We cannot use the restrooms.... I know that when I come but I have come here since I was a kid and this is not going to stop me." Don Renato, owner of a beach restaurant, acknowledged the situation, lamenting that he could not do much as his business was trapped by the pink-package logic: "I have agreements with these tours and I cannot let others use the tables that they have booked. . . . Even if they pay I cannot provide for them because if when the bus arrives I do not have the tables ready then they [the packaged tours] will not come again."

Another important group among these other tourists are those the locals call *turistas de los pueblitos*, the tourists of the villages. Comprised mostly of poor indigenous families, this collective is different from both the pink-packaged tourists and the *turistas de la playa y restaurantes*. They typically flood the municipality during religious festivities. Since they cannot afford the high prices of the restaurants, nor even the illegal boat rides to admire the flamingos, these families bring their own food and beverages on their trips and assemble their tents to spend the whole day at the beach. The city council, in association with national beer corporations like Corona, provides entertainment for this collective of indigenous holidaymakers, in the form of beer festivals that feature alcohol, loud music, and young women in bikinis who dance on pop-up stages. The *turistas de los pueblitos* place most of their shade structures, tents, and plastic chairs on the west side of the beach. Here, however, the development of new condos has begun a familiar story of displacement. The west side of the beach is now monitored by private security guards, who regularly dismantle the families' tents and force them to move further into the protected area of the coastal dune.

A whole precarious and provisional local economy has risen to cater to the needs of these other tourists, including disposing of their waste. Groups like the *pepenadoras* (women who collect plastic to sell in the black market) have appeared in town. These women, among them Debra, whom I introduced earlier, are seasonal indigenous migrant women who come to Celestún with their children and husbands during the fishing seasons. They live in rubbish-filled areas along the estuary. While their husbands are fishing, they collect garbage and plastic bottles from the beach to sell either to other immigrants who use them to support and fortify the makeshift foundations of their houses, or to the city's cacique, who sells them in Mérida. In addition to the *pepenadoras,* a whole tentative and precarious economy has emerged to service the vacationers, setting up everything from portable toilets to small carts that sell fish or beer. Darlene, for example, buys fish from the fishermen at the port, fries it in a gas stove that she installs in the burnt *parador,* and sells the fried fish at a discounted rate to vacationers.

These groups and their practices are absent from both the official tourist brochures and the conservation discourses about sustainability and biodiversity promoted by the international organizations working in Celestún. They are also missing from most of the statistics and from local and federal urban development plans. On the rare occasions in which they appear in the official discourses of these institutions, they are described as "environmental criminals" and are blamed for the rubbish they leave behind or the insalubrity of their practices. The official erasure of these collectives, their practices, and spaces is far from accidental. Making visible these social conflicts would endanger not only the sleek arrival of buses and pink packaged tours but also the flow of international funds for ecotourism activities or beautification projects to keep the "natural paradise" "unpolluted." Their disappearance is a necessary sacrifice to preserve and promote the area as a sustainable ecotourist resort.

CONCLUSION: THE FLAMINGO COAST

The case of Celestún offers another example of the predatory and sticky geographies created by state-planned tourism development. This alternative tourism model touts its sustainability and operates under the guise of nature preservation, with nature being imagined and acted upon as something beyond human practice. The result of this disassociation of nature from human practice—or of nature and the built environment as Vogel (2016) puts it—has been not only an environmental failure, but also losses for most. By paying attention to tourism practices, its labor-related (im)mobilities, and the built environment, I show how ecotourism and conservation practices in Celestún have transformed a large fishing community into a must-see nature stop trapped inside a UNESCO natural protected area. This transformation has taken place by scaling up—in the name of global conservation and leisure contemplation—the estuary and the beach as tourist hotspots where pink flamingos and their habitat are akin to raw materials in open extractive pits. Positioned as an alternative to Cancún on the opposite coast of the region's geography, Celestún's planned turn to nature has been a top-down strategy to keep the Yucatán Peninsula under the global tourist gaze and hence, profitable for the national and regional economies. But ecotourism has not emanated from the community, nor has it involved an even distribution of labor and resources. Quite the contrary. Rather than delivering the promised sustainable and inclusive economic growth for the local population, this scaling-up has produced in Celestún an unequal geography of capitalist accumulation that has profoundly reshaped the spatial and social fabric of the community, benefited only a few, and fueled social and ecological conflicts.

Today, after more than twenty years of nature conservation practices and more than ten years of ecotourism, tourism has failed to provide most of the community in Celestún with any real development. Only those spaces (i.e., the estuary and the beach) that have been scaled up for global tourist consumption and nature conservation have become magnets for labor, capital, and resources in which newly empowered local collectives like boatmen, fishermen, and craftswomen fight to control and monopolize tourism's benefits. The result has been an increasingly militarized area, trapped in a violent logic that excludes most inhabitants and other forms of tourism from both the economic benefits of the activity and the enjoyment of the beach and the estuary as leisure spaces. In 2015, more than 40 percent of the economically active population in Celestún earned less than the minimum wage (US$3.5 per day); 45 percent of households still cooked with either wood or charcoal and only 32.6 percent had a refrigerator. Only 5.2 percent of Celestún residents had access to medical care, and only 7.2 percent had achieved secondary or higher levels of education (INEGI 2015b). The town lacks both a high school and a hospital. Those who want to pursue high school or graduate education must commute to schools in either Hunucmá (fifty kilometers away) or Mérida (more than two hours commute by bus). Celestún has neither a doctor who is on call nor an ambulance and it does not have prenatal or birth services. Rates of alcoholism and gender violence are comparable to larger urban centers in Mexico, and children die from preventable respiratory and digestive illnesses, a nurse told me.[18] Moreover, the town still lacks an urban development plan to assess the impact of tourism activities, and as a result both the informal urban growth and the solid waste generated by fishing and tourism multiplies.

According to recent state governmental data, 60 percent of homes in Celestún are built on permeable soils, on the edges of wetlands in annual flood zones, or in generally muddy areas. The town also generates an excessive amount of garbage compared with its population, with nearly five tons produced daily (SEMARNAT 2009). According to my field observations, much of this trash is left behind by beach tourists of many sorts.[19] Rather than providing a sustainable future for young girls like María and Ximena, whose mothers are beach craftswomen, ecotourism has stuck them in a precarious everlasting present that traps them at the beach where they work to bring home pesos. In my last visits to the town in 2019 I learned that María was pregnant and Ximena had quit school, complaining that "there was nothing to do."

Yet, contrary to the acquiescence found in Cancún (chapter 1), where state-led tourism development and transnational infrastructure expansion has hardly been fought by residents, ecotourism development in Celestún has generated heated confrontations. Tourism planners have not found the docility and acquiescence that they encounter from the migrant workers in Cancún. Instead, fishermen native to the town—who existed prior to tourism development—have been active in strategically using expert categories (such as "biodiversity" or "sustainability") from conservation and tourism discourses to articulate and demand pragmatic solutions to fishing prohibitions and ecotourism restrictions. Tourism planners have also encountered a group of local researchers, mostly biologists and an anthropologist, who are involved with the community, like Enrique and Lalo. The tensions that I highlight in this chapter do not show any sign of abating, as the tourist industry continues to advance its predatory logic along the Gulf of Mexico, where garbage accumulates and local health deteriorates while governmental attention is still directed to the protection of internationally recognized species.[20]

As a result of the receding beaches of the Caribbean coast and the rise in insurance premiums after Hurricane Wilma in 2005, transnational hotel corporations have been eyeing the Gulf of Mexico coast, now rebranded in official and private tourism marketing as "the Pink Coast," for their condos and luxury hotels. Some are already in full operation, like Playa Maya Resorts, advertised as a resort "in the heart of a Natural Protected Area," which "radiate[s] with the invigorating freshness of an unspoiled natural area." Others are already underway, like The Reserve, designed as a series of ocean-front luxury condos for Canadian expatriates. What the future holds for these initiatives is uncertain, but research shows that if social relations and environmental pressures continue to be ignored, the Gulf of Mexico shores run risks similar to those already observed in the Caribbean coast.

The next two chapters move to inland Yucatán, to some of the in-between spaces and more intimate practices that connect the touristy coasts of the region. Tourism in the towns of Temozón Sur and Tekit focuses on appealing to the cultural authenticity of this area of the Yucatán. Focusing on the precarious, racialized, and gendered nature of service labor at hacienda hotels and the domestic production of souvenirs and uniforms for the hospitality industry, these chapters highlight the centrality of social reproduction in processes of capital accumulation informed by tourism.

THREE

Colonial Enclaves

SITE-SPECIFIC INDIGENEITY FOR LUXURY TOURISM

IN A "BUNKER HACIENDA HOTEL"

March 2007. Presidents Felipe Calderón and George W. Bush met for their first Mexico-US presidential summit at Hacienda Temozón Sur, in inland Yucatán, the first of five historical haciendas restored as indigenous luxury hotels in the region. In February 1999, three years prior to its opening to the public, the hacienda hotel had hosted Presidents Ernesto Zedillo and Bill Clinton. A private heliport was built for the occasion. In 2007, in preparation for the presidential summit, the electricity network and paved roads were extended in the village of Temozón, where the hacienda hotel is located. Additionally, six Maya vernacular huts were refurbished and painted bright red and white to match the hacienda hotel's walls, creating an idyllic indigenous village that formed a polished corridor leading to the hacienda's gates. At the doorsteps of every hut, as the dignitaries arrived, Maya women worked on handicrafts. They were dressed in impeccable embroidered white *ternos,* the traditional attire of the region, and also one of the touristic symbols of Mayaness in contemporary Yucatán.

Photographs of the officials shaking hands, smiling at the camera, posing with their wives, were circulated widely in local, regional, national, and international media. These images are hallmarks of binational dialogue and they have consolidated haciendas as pivotal architectures in contemporary narrations of the Mexican nation that emphasize historical heritage, indigenous culture, and tradition.

This romanticized staging of political dialogue, history, and Maya indigeneity stands in stark contrast with journalists' reports describing the hacienda hotel as "a bunker hotel" and a "narco-hacienda," and its surroundings as quasi-militarized areas:

> On the eve of their meeting, Hacienda Temozón Sur where Mexican and US presidents Calderón and George W. Bush are meeting has become a bunker. Two weeks ago, the peace of the almost 200 inhabitants that live in the hacienda's *casco* has been transformed. Military checkpoints have been created 1 kilometer away and the North American Secret Service police scrutinize the population as well as the villages most proximate to the hacienda. Military checkpoints annotate the car plates of all those that enter and leave the village and employees from the hotel have even been banished from returning to their homes at night. They cannot move without going through the checkpoints.[1]

> The hotel zone of Mérida and the town of Temozón Sur are today "under siege" by more than 3,000 US and Mexican soldiers and police officers. . . . Residents of these places are blocked from walking in their own neighborhoods. Demonstrators are kept walled out miles away. The corporate media will—if past is prologue—withhold the uncomfortable facts from the public about the narco hacienda where the presidents will meet but it will, no doubt, quote the presidents as they praise each other's heroism in the so-called fight against drug trafficking. . . . The parties and logos change but the story remains the same. . . . In a hacienda in the Mexican southeast, it is déjà vu all over again.[2]

Talking to the people of Temozón during my fieldwork, it soon became clear that the militarized atmosphere conveyed in these journalists' accounts is far from exceptional. This is what happens each time the hacienda hotel receives "important guests": not only presidents and politicians, but also pop stars, film and television idols, and families from the Mexican and Yucatec elites. These guests book the hacienda hotel to record albums and film telenovelas, or to celebrate weddings, *quinceaños,* and other special events.

On these occasions, hacienda hotel workers like Patricia, a Maya massage therapist, and Juan, a Maya gardener, have to wait inside the hacienda's gates. When these "important guests" are around, "the town is under siege," and as Patricia told me, one "is trapped in the hotel" and "treated almost like a criminal." They are on call twenty-four hours a day to respond to the guests' desires and needs. Often, as Juan and Patricia put it, they are treated "like servants" just as they were years ago, when the hacienda hotel was not a tourist space but a productive agro-industrial site devoted to henequen extraction.

FIGURE 11. Riot police block confront a protest during by the visit of US President George W. Bush, near Uxmal, Mexico, 2007. Photo by Israel Leal, courtesy of Associated Press Images.

One evening in 2012, sitting at the doorway of her house, Patricia elaborated on the presidential summits and her current work at "the hotel," as they call it in town. She used words of gratitude to describe her experience in a place that has provided her with a house and an income that has allowed her to stay in her village and not migrate. But she also spoke with defeat and resignation about how the workplace has resuscitated old forms of racialized and gendered labor servitude.

[When presidential summits happen] it is like we become the center of the world.... Here in this forgotten place ... helicopters, the military everywhere ... checkpoints! ... Without being able to use our telephones and go home.... When there are important guests it is almost the same but not that big.... We become trapped [*atrapados*].... You need to put up with this [*aguantar*] to work for them [the hacienda hotel]. With the henequen, men came to the hacienda to work all day until the sun was too hot. We [women] stayed at home. Now, some of us, we come to clean as maids or massage therapists [*sobadoras*]. We sit there and wait, and fight sleep when there is no work.... When guests are in, I can't go home and check on my mother or cook the meals for the children. I need to ask my sister to do it.... I can't use my cellular phone to communicate.... I have to be ready for whenever they [guests] are ready.... I do as the manager tells me.... It is *esclavo* [a slave job]. Still I prefer this because I do not need to travel to Mérida or Cancún to work. . . . I am grateful [*agradecida*] because they gave me a house . . . because there is work in the village so I can be close to my mother. . . . She does not understand what I do and I don't explain. I know I am questioned [in the village] but I do not care because I have a house and a job, and I can stay put.

Patricia's words point to the invisible but vivid lines that connect the tourism-driven contemporary re-spatialization of Yucatán's coasts with the extractive, racialized historical geographies of indigenous labor in inland Yucatán. This connection takes place simultaneously across space and time through an alliance among the tourist industry, cultural heritage preservation, and disaster opportunism. This chapter explores how luxury indigenous tourism has forged this alliance, and it also explores the repercussions it has had on both indigenous life and livelihood strategies for people like Patricia and Juan.

To explore this dynamic, the chapter first contextualizes how luxury tourism has emerged in Yucatán, and how it fits alongside the other models of tourism that we have explored so far in this book, like mass tourism along the Caribbean Coast (chapter 1) and ecotourism in the Gulf Coast (chapter 2).

Luxury indigenous tourism in Yucatán is synonymous with The Haciendas, a private-public partnership among the state, the private sector, and the non-profit sector united in a rhetoric of heritage preservation, as well as indigenous empowerment and social responsibility—a partnership that burgeoned in inland Yucatán after Hurricane Isidore in 2002. The Haciendas, of which Hacienda Temozón Sur is the flagship property, are a group of five repurposed ex-henequen haciendas owned by businessman Roberto Hernández, former owner and president of Mexico's largest national bank (Banamex, currently Citibank), and one of the wealthiest men in the world, according to Forbes.[3] The Haciendas are managed by the Luxury Collection, a branch of Marriot Hotels and Resorts since 2018, that curates "rare finds" and "authentic treasures" in an "unsurpassed collection."[4] The Haciendas are also part of one of Mexico's most ambitious organizations of "entrepreneurial social responsibility," the Fundación Haciendas del Mundo Maya (FHMM). Created and directed by Hernández's wife and daughter, FHMM aims at "alleviating poverty and devastation in Maya indigenous communities." As stated on their website, its mission is "strengthening identity in order to produce sustainable development. Generate actions that promote local identity, recognition, and recovery of the Mayan cultural expressions, overcoming extreme poverty by furthering education, health, and sustainable development opportunities while involving the local population as promoters of their own social development."[5]

They aim to achieve this goal by repurposing historical buildings with "indigenous flair" and converting them into luxury tourism destinations. In terms of branding and marketing, The Haciendas cater to a different type of tourist than those who frequent Cancun's resorts (i.e., the "beach seekers" and the "spring breakers"). They aim to provide an alternative tourist experience that is tailored to travelers who are interested in other cultures. The preceding chapter examined this move away from standardized tourist experiences, such as beach resorts or more passive ways of being a tourist, and toward alternative modes of traveling "in nature," such as ecotourism. It explored how alternative forms of tourism in the region were initially fostered through natural heritage preservation and conservation of land and resources along the Gulf of Mexico coast during the late 1980s and 1990s. In no time, as I show in chapter 2, pink flamingos became like Caribbean beaches and archeological remains: one more checkmark on tourists' bucket lists when visiting the region. This chapter and the next are situated as examples of the simultaneous efforts to put an economic value on culture through the state mobilization of tourism as development.

In practice, this process of engineering culture for profit has been accomplished by anchoring nostalgic representations of Maya culture to those areas with an existing and documented history of Western archeological excavation—such as Chichén Itzá, Tulum, and Uxmal. This last site, which UNESCO added to its World Heritage list in 1997, is part of the Ruta Puuc, a forty-one-kilometer network of secondary roads into the Mexican Maya Puuc heritage area. While these cultural sites have become agglomerated and packed with the same "passive hordes" as beach resorts, it is semi-industrial buildings, such as haciendas, repurposed as colonial architectures that have taken the lead (Breglia 2009; Loewe 2010; Córdoba Azcárate 2014). This is a process that has been done though "imperial eyes" (Pratt 2007)—specifically, through internationally sanctioned Western discourses on cultural heritage and historical preservation as well as through public-private orchestrated responses to an increasingly global awareness about the rights of indigenous peoples. Indeed, indigenous luxury tourism has colonized the imaginary geographies of the region's henequen agro-industrial past by transforming these haciendas into privileged elements for statecraft, as sites of global economic value, culture, and labor extraction.[6] It has done so by recreating the hacienda owners' lifestyles through selective architectural, landscaping, and social practices. These practices, along with the creation of nostalgic, seden-tarist, and politically charged representations of indigeneity have resulted in the privatization of land, natural resources, and indigenous cultural prac-tices, and have contributed to trapping indigenous workers like Patricia and Juan within new labor servitudes and novel patronages at former workplaces and sites of production.[7]

Hacienda hotels are an example of larger trends in both philanthropic capi-talism, according to which capitalism can be philanthropic in and of itself, and elite casino capitalism, in which the mobile lifestyles of the superrich or the "global elite" dictate what is imagined as well as the parameters of developments that are later replicated and mimicked around the world (Elliott and Urry 2010, 82; Sinn 2012). In this case, tourism development capitalizes on the promise to deliver heritage as something old and monumental, rescued with "good taste" (Kirshenblatt-Gimblett 1998) and not accessible, price-wise, to all pockets. And yet, their repurposing for tourism is also an example of the production of pal-impsest architectures, where lands and buildings used for one purpose in the past are subsequently reused for another (Schwenkel 2014). Some of those past uses, including the memories and phantoms they might evoke, are more evident than others in present designs. Their cracks and layouts enable intricate and often contested embodied experiences of place. In the case of the hacienda hotels, this repurposing of landscape and architecture has relied on the produc-tion and commodification of *site-specific forms of being indigenous,* that is, forms of being indigenous that exist and unfold within a particular geographical loca-tion, architectural milieu, and fabricated sedentarist historical dimension.

Looking at the logics of production in luxury hacienda tourism shows how tourism preys on the past for profit, entrapping sociocultural and labor dynamics in an aestheticized present that is inattentive to local and regional histories of racial, gender, and labor discrimination. Yet, as this chapter will show, tourism has not only oppressed and silenced. It has also awakened a revolutionary past in the form of silent yet conscious resistance against the hacienda hotel as a contemporary labor site. This conscious resistance, which include *forms of collective forgetfulness,* signals tourism's ambivalent ordering of space, time, and social life in inland Yucatán. It shows a form of contem-porary *strategic entanglement* (Bonilla 2015) within a predatory tourist geog-raphy from which people cannot fully disentangle. It illustrates how tourism takes away while also giving life to new forms of social action through which workers make use of past forms of political action to maneuver within, and figure out, this contradictory reality.

In what follows, I first contextualize the history of the haciendas to situate their current position in the popular geopolitical tourism imaginary of Yucatán as "a world to escape to." To do so, I explore the role of haciendas and their architecture during the henequen era. I elaborate on their role as status-conscious architectures that served to inscribe the power of hacendados over indigenous populations in the territory. Yet these haciendas were also sites of revolution where indigenous contestations of oppressive land management and labor practices were performed, and later, also repressed. Second, I show how architectural and landscape renovations for tourism reinscribe the racialized and spatially segregated built environment of the henequen hacienda as a productive space for global consumption. I show how tourism extracts monetary value, cultural resources, and labor from inland Yucatán both through creating nostalgic spaces—similar to the region's touristy archeological sites—and through spatially fixing a racialized and gendered indigeneity whose production has been however, emptied of political meaning.[8] Following the theory of heritage as a new mode of cultural production that creates a second life for dying modes of living (Kirshenblatt-Gimblett 1998, 1995), or that keeps while selling (Franquesa 2013), I show how catering to elites also takes place by creating a "taste for luxury." This "taste for luxury" revitalizes traditional Maya cultural practices—in particular, those dealing with healing, cooking, and eating—fixing them in an invented past with market value. Consequently, Temozón village and its inhabitants have become stuck to a selective, elite-driven, and site-specific re-creation of the lifestyles of the haciendas' patrons (patrones). This form of tourism silences and erases the village's revolutionary past as well as its present. In reality, this marginalized and impoverished indigenous community is *also* a geographical space of buildings with monumental façades in which binational dialogues about Mexico's war on drugs take place.

The chapter then shows how these selective restoration practices are contested and have benefited from the necessity of rebuilding in the aftermath of Hurricane Isidore in 2002. Making use of disaster opportunism, transnational corporations and elite bankers have become the new *patrones* for a collective of former hacienda workers (peones) who have been "placed back" on the hacienda's grounds (Breglia 2009, 262). I show the ambivalences and sacrifices that these interventions—largely made in the name of indigenous empowerment and community development through tourism—have created for workers like Patricia, who perceive the hacienda as both a *space of danger* (due to both its past as a henequen production factory and its present as a host to narco-elites) and a *space of hope* (due to its status as a source of income in times of necessity). I elaborate on this by focusing on how the hacienda hotels' position as a luxury tourist experience has awakened old forms of labor struggle and collective action, and how workers use these strategies to accommodate and/or resist tourism's transformations in the everyday.

In the conclusion, I describe the limits and incongruities of using indigenous luxury tourism as a community development tool in inland Yucatán.

A PLACE IN HISTORY: HENEQUEN EXTRACTION, ELITE FORMATION, AND REVOLUTION

Haciendas are not just one more kind of building in the Yucatán Peninsula. They exist in the regional collective imagination as the epitome of the henequen agro-industrial boom, bust, and decay over the nineteenth and twentieth centuries—rather than as remnants of a bygone golden age, as tourism narratives routinely assert. For many, particularly for indigenous rural peasants from inland Yucatán, haciendas represent an epoch of slavery and debt peonage, and they are architectural reminders of the region's unequal accumulation of wealth.

To understand this particular imagination, it is important to examine the history of haciendas and the role they played in the region's economy and social organization. Haciendas in Yucatán fit the classical definition of a Latin American plantation provided by Wolf and Mintz (1957): "an agricultural estate operated by a dominant landowner ... and a dependent labor force, organized to supply a small-scale market by means of scarce capital in which the factors of production are employed not only for capital accumulation but also to support the status aspirations of the owner" (380). In Yucatán, however, the "small-scale market" became a large international market through the commercialization of henequen, the "green gold" that was the region's monocrop from the last quarter of the nineteenth century until the mid-twentieth century. As historian Sterling David Evans (2013) has noted, henequen from Yucatán provided the best binder twine for agricultural work before the invention of the combine as a harvesting technology in 1835. In 1875 the invention of the McCormick binder would only increase the demand for twine and, as a consequence, a long-lasting economic dependency between Yucatán and the Great Plains of the United States and Canada emerged.[9]

This dependency on henequen generated and engendered other ecological, social, and political changes in each of these regions, none of which can be understood without attention to their interlocking nature. Of special interest to this discussion is the almost uninterrupted local elite control of land management, plants, and cultivation techniques since the nineteenth century, which I will come back to later in the chapter.[10]

The henequen boom years, from 1880 to 1920, indelibly shaped the organization of land, labor, and social relations in Yucatán. In 1916, Yucatán had eleven hundred haciendas exclusively devoted to henequen processing. There were nearly 213,000 hectares under cultivation, producing and exporting over two hundred thousand tons of henequen a year, mainly to the United States (Fox 1961, 225; Mukul 1990, 53). By 1920, henequen comprised more than 95 percent of the region's exports (Brannon and Baklanoff 1987; Wells 1985). At that time, Hacienda Temozón Sur, owned first by Carlos Peón and then his son Humberto Peón Suárez, both of them liberals, had one of the largest shares of henequen industrial equipment in the region, and it was one of the most important productive landholdings in Mexico, with 6,600 hectares and 640 workers.[11]

Haciendas not only structured the economic life of Yucatán. They also articulated its social organization and cultural dynamics. Henequen haciendas enforced a highly structured social system through racism, paternalism, and coercion (Mattiace and Nonnenmacher 2014). As Van Young (2006) put it, haciendas epitomize "a theoretical anomaly but a manifest historical reality," that of "a commercial economic organization and feudal/paternalist social organization" (xxiii). Haciendas in Yucatán were paradigmatic examples of how land ownership is intertwined with elite status in Mexico. Their social organization was comprised of the hacendados, or landowners, who were mainly creoles (persons born and naturalized in Yucatán but of European origin), and the peones, or land workers, mainly indigenous Maya and for some time also migrant workers from Korea and other parts of Mexico, mostly Yaqui *indígenas* from Sonora.

Neither hacendados nor peones were homogeneous social groups; they varied greatly according to their origins, cultural and racial backgrounds, commercial interests, and ideologies. Yet, both collectives shared several characteristics that make it possible to conceive of them as distinctive social groups (Ancona Riestra 1996). First, hacendados shared what Wells (1991) defines as the "hacendado elite mentality" guided by the principle that "no expense is too great." The result of this mentality was sumptuous material consumption, including ostentatious homes, ornate carriages, grandiose parties for *la gente decente de Mérida* (literally "decent people" from Mérida), and frequent trips to Europe (Wells 1991, 134–35). Second, hacendados had total control over the processes of production and distribution of the henequen. Third, they exercised severe political and repressive power over the peones; and fourth, peones were subjected to what has been defined as helpless peonage or regimes of semislavery (Alston, Mattiace, and Nonnenmacher 2009; Katz 1974).

Each hacienda had its own currency, payment system, financial operations, and norms of social conduct, all of which were unilaterally established by hacendados. Haciendas were organized around a debt-peonage labor system. Hacendados paid peones a daily or weekly wage in either the hacienda's own currency or company vouchers *(vales)*. These vouchers were valid only at the hacienda's store, the *tienda de raya,* which supplied basic goods and necessities within each hacienda to peones and their families (Ancona Riestra 1996). Besides, haciendas also used a system of hereditary debts and loans aimed at controlling labor—mostly through marriage, housing, and job incentives—to discourage Maya workers from fleeing (Mattiace and Nonnenmacher 2014, 367). These coercive methods were crucial in establishing a dependent relationship that tethered peones to particular *hacendados,* who were themselves tied to regional political elites (Nickel 1997).

Haciendas' architecture was an important contributor to organizing, sustaining, and reinforcing this uneven social organization. Buildings and infrastructures featured spatially segmented and architecturally distinct population settlements and domestic units, and they were designed to maximize productivity and inscribe hacendados' power (Peniche Rivero 1999). Although their composition varied across the region, the architectural design of haciendas included many similarities: la *casa principal,* or *casa grande,* usually the largest building, where the hacendado and his family kept their living quarters and in which most of the administration took place; Maya vernacular houses, where resident peones lived; and other major constructions under hacendados' administration and control. Among the latter were the aforementioned *tienda de raya;* the *casa de maquinas* or machine room, where the henequen processing took place; la *casa del mayordomo,* where the foreman lived and where the administration took place when the hacendado was away; and a *capilla* or chapel, which stressed the importance of the hacienda as a population center.

This collection of spaces is known as the *casco* of the hacienda. In addition to the *casco,* the hacienda also included the fields where henequen was planted and harvested, as well as the population settlements and the workers' living quarters.

Casas grandes were built upon elevated basements, and they did not respond to local architectural styles of the time. Generally, they included an eclectic mix of highly decorative European styles, which varied from baroque and rococo to neoclassical, Arabic, and even Asian-inspired designs (Witynski and Carr 2008). As Wells (1982) put it, "looking to the far-off capitals of the Western world for inspiration and design, the prosperous *henequeneros* built ornate palaces with marble pillars, intricately carved facades, and ostentatious stained-glass enclosed porticoes" (224). *Casas grandes* were then new buildings commissioned by hacendados generally in colonial styles in order to look wealthy and to connect themselves both to a wealthy past and to international, mostly European and North American, lifestyles. They punctuated the landscape, epitomizing the particular elite lifestyle and mentality of the hacendados. And now they have become the targeted buildings in The Haciendas' selective renewal, as indigenous luxury hotels.

At every hacienda, the *casa grande* contrasts with vernacular Maya houses, which are highly functional and totally dependent in their design on climate conditions (Rodriguez Viqueira and Fuentes Freixanet 2006). In contrast to the extravagant styles and imported materials used to construct *casas grandes,* vernacular houses have an elliptical structure with walls made of mud (adobe) or limestone and roofs covered with wooden poles and palm tree leaves. The architectural contrast between ostentation and austerity was deliberate and obvious during the henequen era. It materially reinforced the social, racial, and economic distance between hacendados and Maya indigenous people employed as peones. This is a distance that, as I show, luxury tourism aims to re-create.[12]

Several factors contributed to making some haciendas, like Temozón Sur, sites of ethnic and labor contestation: the asymmetrical power relationship between hacendados and peones, the poor living and working conditions of most of the latter, and the material ostentation in the landscape (Castellanos 2010a; Fallaw 1995). In fact, one of the most violent revolutionary episodes in the agrarian postrevolutionary history of the region occurred in Temozón Sur. I am referring to the assassination at Hacienda Temozón Sur in January 1937 of two of the most well-known revolutionary peasants, Ignacio de Mena and Alberto de Sosa, who fought for land reform. The men were shot dead before the visit of one of Mexico's most important agrarian revolutionary leaders, Lázaro Cárdenas. Their assassination led revolutionary peasants to attempt to rename the hacienda as "Hacienda Temozón Sur de Mena y Sosa."

The violent deaths of Mena and Sosa positioned Hacienda Temozón Sur at the epicenter of the region's agrarian reform. It was at Hacienda Temozón Sur that "the ceremonial kickoff of land reform" (Fallow 2001) was staged by hacienda workers. And it was here that Cárdenas started the region's well-known "Cruzada del Mayab" to introduce *ejidos*—autonomous and collectively held land taken by the state and redistributed to peasants—in 1937. During Cárdenas's visit to Temozón, and for the first time in the region, the Partido Nacional Revolucionario (PNR) bused in thousands of Maya laborers in an attempt to force the government to address labor conditions in the hacienda (Fallow 2001, 89).[13] Cárdenas's public support after the murders of Mena and Sosa empowered peasants around Yucatán state to organize a six-month strike among workers at haciendas *henequeneras*. These events also informed the creation of a Liga Femenina de Acción Social in Temozón—a women's civic organization typical of the Mexican Revolution and part of a larger national network to organize rural women in order to reclaim their labor rights (Ramírez and Torres Alonso 2016; Buck Kachaluba 2018).[14]

Cárdenas's statue, historically placed in a central location in the village of Temozón Sur, commemorates the revolutionary agrarian victories in the village. But as I will show in the next section, the inauguration of the hacienda hotel silenced this revolutionary legacy by relegating the statue to an unfrequented and less visible spot (Buck Kachaluba 2018), and by omitting any reference to social and labor activism or support for the Mexican agrarian revolution.

The henequen world remained in place until the 1970s when the advent of synthetic fibers, like nylon, rendered henequen, and with it the haciendas, obsolete. By the 1970s, most haciendas in Yucatán were completely abandoned. Hacienda Temozón Sur, however, remained an active manufacturing and distribution center of sisal until 1987, when its shredder plant (*planta desfibradora*) finally closed production. By that time, Yucatán's elites had been drastically reconfigured. The Yucatec elites who had been organized around the haciendas disintegrated and became part of a global, heterogeneous group connected with transnational corporations.[15] It is within this context that we can situate the birth of The Haciendas, the tourism venture.

According to both the official story and local accounts from researchers in
the region, in the late 1990s Roberto Hernández (owner of Mexico's largest
bank, CitiBanamex) and Alejandro Patrón Laviada (brother of the former
National Action Party [PAN] Yucatán governor Patricio Patrón Laviada)
acquired a series of abandoned henequen haciendas in the Yucatán Peninsula.
Their intention was to turn their *casas grandes* into upscale luxury hotels, and
to do so they created a real estate business group, Grupo Plan, directed by a
well-known Mexican architect, Luis Bosoms (Roberto Hernández's son-in-
law), and they formed a partnership with the US company Starwood Hotels
and Resorts through one of their leading brands, the Luxury Collection
(bought by Marriott Hotels in 2018). After this, Hacienda Temozón Sur,
together with four other haciendas in inland Yucatán bought by the banker,
were restored under the auspices of Fomento Cultural Banamex, a nonprofit
branch of Banamex (now CitiBanamex) that was created in the late 1970s in
response to the 1972 UN World Heritage Convention, which recognized the
need to address the historical and cultural forms in which people interact
with nature as fundamental for preservation.[16]

This last point reminds us that The Haciendas' tourism venture must be
understood within the global impulse that arose in the late 1980s and 1990s
to foster an economically productive relationship between cultural heritage
and cultural tourism (Baud and Ypeij 2009; Kirshenblatt-Gimblett 1998). As
an industry itself, heritage, as Barbara Kirshemblatt-Gimblet (1995, 369-372)
reminds us, is "a mode of cultural production in the present that has recourse
to the past"; it is a "value-added industry that produces the local for export
through tourism," which is symptomatic of "the problematic relationship of
heritage objects to its instruments." In Yucatán, the alliance between heritage
and tourism followed Cancún's creation in the mid 1970s, but it strengthened in 1987, when Chichén Itzá was included in the World Heritage list,
which exponentially increased the number of visitors to the region.[17] Since
then, the Mexican government and private investors have sought to extend
heritage protection to a wide range of other sites in order to enhance tourism,
knowing that UNESCO's designation has a multiplying effect on the
number of tourists visiting such destinations.[18]

Since the mid-1990s, the archeological sites of Uxmal (1996) and Mayapan
(1997) in the Ruta Puuc have been declared UNESCO World Heritage sites.

In this context of cultural protection, two processes help to situate the interest in ex-henequen haciendas for luxury tourism. First, at a time when Cancún and the Riviera Maya had become increasingly touristified and agglomerated, inland areas fascinated those travelers who were interested in cultural authenticity. The state began to promote the region's haciendas during the 1990s, as the "other" Maya heritage of Yucatán, one that "exists under erasure . . . overshadowed by Yucatán's monumental archeological heritage," such as Chichén Itzá, and one that claims to be "more authentic" and to foster a real and more spiritual connection with living indigenous peoples and practices.[19] Second, and related, was the inauguration, state promotion, and rapid consolidation of the archeological Ruta Puuc, described by the BBC travel section in 2011 as "a string of five well-preserved Maya archeological sites just a day trip from Mérida . . . where visitors can connect with the spirit and pathos of the Mayan people with an intimacy and immediacy that is lost in the bigger and more-trafficked Maya sites of the region like Chichén Itzá and Tulum" (Benchwick 2011).[20]

For tourists like Alex, a Spanish backpacker whom I interviewed at Uxmal, just a few kilometers from Temozón Sur, inland Yucatán represented a "more authentic" and "real experience of Maya culture." "Cancún," Alex said, standing at the top of Uxmal's pyramid and looking at the low tropical forest below, "is like Disneyworld, all brands, all North American . . . nothing real. . . . I used the airport and then came to these routes and forests where you still can find pieces of real and more authentic culture that is not just for tourists . . . It is just how people lived."

The Haciendas emerged in this context as the latest expression of the efforts to grow and secure tourism in Yucatán, now rebranded as the "land of the authentic Maya." The Haciendas are promoted as part of larger nationalist heritage preservation discourses that narrate and spatially fix indigeneity as a collection of material artifacts of contemplation (Craib 2004, 38) by mobilizing architectures along the nearby UNESCO World Heritage site of Uxmal and Mayapan, and, more recently, also Izamal, which has been in the UNESCO tentative list for World Heritage nominations since 2008.[21]

Yet, what is distinctive about The Haciendas' tourism venture is not simply the mobilization of heritage or indigenous culture for tourism consumption, but its use of the term "indigenous *luxury*." The main idea behind hacienda hotels is that luxury is an economic resource that can be deployed to foster economic development by linking locality, history, and the material

FIGURE 12. Abandoned henequen hacienda near Temozón Sur, 2012. Photo by author.

FIGURE 13. A guest enjoys a swim in a pool once used for animal husbandry, Hacienda Temozón Sur, 2007. Photo by author.

expression of indigenous cultures with conspicuous consumption and tourism development.

The idea that luxury can be mobilized for economic development is an old adage. David Hume (Hume 1985; Cunningham 2005) and Adam Smith (1976) underlined the crucial role that a taste for luxury consumption played in economic development in eighteenth-century Europe (see Brewer 1998).[22] In the tourism industry, luxury has been often considered as an economic resource that creates consumption and therefore contributes to economic development (Rojek and Urry 1997, 2). Yet, as Page (2009) argues, luxury tourism is a form of "extravagant conspicuous consumption" that emphasizes "the inequality between those with the means to consume such experiences and those unable to consume them" (149). And this, we know, is a class issue.

Unlike other tourists and travelers, luxury tourists do not merely aim to consume and spend. They intend to consume and spend with taste. When native or indigenous peoples are added to the mix, then this taste often reproduces and reinscribes historically informed practices of domination. Taste and luxury have been closely articulated with ideas about the authenticity of peoples, places, and objects (Picard and Wood 1997; MacCannell 1973; Bruner 2001, 2004), and with the exclusivity of experiences (Chronis and Hampton 2008; Kirshenblatt-Gimblett 1998).[23] In Yucatán, luxury tourism has been specifically articulated to cater to the tastes of Western tourists who are eager for social distinction and historical reconciliation by restoring and addressing the abuses of colonialism over indigenous populations.[24] These indigenous populations are always, however, imagined through imperial eyes (Pratt 2007), that is, through the eyes of foreign travel books and European conceptions of indigenous others as "closer to nature," as well of expert archeological knowledge—and they are hardly ever seen on their own terms.

Hacienda hotels are specifically marketed to provide a form of social distinction through "ethical luxury consumption" that is in direct opposition to these other forms of being a tourist and traveling in the region, which are considered too vulgar, crowded, and "without purpose beyond oneself," as one of the hacienda guests told me. The hacienda hotels are promoted as being culturally aware, sustainable tourist alternatives for elite tourists: people who look for hotels that "curate the destination experience . . . who seek the invisible deal and who escape with the right credit card believing in the power of marketing and more importantly, in the power of people."[25] In this milieu, Hacienda Temozón Sur in particular claims to be "a distinct and cherished expression of its location; a portal to the destination's indigenous charms and treasures." It is advertised as a distinctive place where one can live as "in the 19th century, but still receiving high-end luxury" treatment, in "a superb residence in the heart of the Yucatán Peninsula which recreates the Belle Époque of the Mexican southeast," and which "creates opportunities for locals who would never have had the chance . . . to earn a living in rural Yucatán" after the henequen crisis.[26] As part of this niche market, hacienda hotels are an example of what Zizek (2009) calls the ideology of ethical consumerism, in which citizens redeem their consumer guilt through charity or "responsible spending" but never leave the consumption cycle that animates contemporary capitalism.[27]

But what has this historical restoration—done for the sake of luxury tourism—meant in practice? How has it been achieved? And what does it tell us about the predatory and sticky nature of tourism as a particular spatial ordering of contemporary capitalism? In practice, the repurposing of former henequen haciendas into luxury hotels has taken place through the manufacturing of a themed colonial utopia in a contained enclave.[28] Luxury tourism in Yucatán has produced a romanticized scenario that coincides with nostalgic representations of place and indigenous otherness while binding native populations and local landscapes to resuscitated sociospatial and labor inequalities. At Hacienda Temozón Sur, this has implied the re-creation of the hacendado lifestyle through a series of selective architectural arrangements, landscaping practices, and a repertoire of staged and professionalized indigenous labor practices devoted to pampering tourists' senses. These processes have detached the hacienda hotel from its ambivalent past (Breglia 2009) and have materially anchored it to a romanticized and essentialist one that has little resemblance to the inegalitarian socioeconomic system of production it was.

The Casa Grande: *Erecting Gates and Celebrating Material Culture*

The refunctionalization of the architectures of the hacienda's *cascos* and the aesthetic display of objects linked to the hacendado's elite lifestyle are central in the performative power of hacienda hotels as luxury spaces. These are material practices that aim to instantiate and objectify tourists' desires by enacting an imagined, and otherwise completely anachronistic, colonial aesthetic for contemporary luxury tourism consumption.

In practice, this process of restoration has re-created the hacienda as a coherent and romanticized tourism stage in which tourists' experiences and imaginaries are unambiguously equated to those of the hacendado during the golden years of the henequen boom. This romanticized stage is achieved through three interrelated material operations: first, a gated and staged entrance that accentuates seclusion and provides a crafted vision of an aseptic indigenous labor force; second, a focus on the *casa grande* as the site of the hacienda hotel, intentionally overlooking the other spaces of the hacienda; and, third, the conversion of the hacendado's everyday objects into museum-like artifacts. Let me explore them in detail.

Gating and staging. To get to Temozón Sur Hacienda Hotel one must cross gates and provide proof of reservation, or declare the intention of one's visit, to a designated staff member who controls the access of cars and people to the hotel grounds. As at most resorts in Cancún (chapter 1), the gated entrance stands for privilege and marks exclusivity. But at the hacienda hotel, the luxury experience is intended to begin before entering the gates. Branding strategies emphasize Hacienda Temozón's "small-town charm" and its setting "deep in the Yucatán and not too far from the fabled Mayan site, Chichén Itzá." The imagination of the hacienda as within a small indigenous community that is directly connected to an ancient culture creates a spatial continuum in the tourist's imagination of the region as a "world to escape to" where tourists can glide from place to place, from present to past without disruption.

To create and secure this image, Grupo Plan rebuilt the former hacienda walls and gates, originally built not only to create a sense of isolation but also to prevent workers from fleeing (Ancona Riestra 1996), and they replaced the old layout of streets and houses close to the *casa grande* with an idyllic row of traditional Maya vernacular huts at the hacienda's main entrance. This staged scenario, which I address later in the chapter, provides tourists with a first impression of a homogenous and organized harmonious community working for and alongside the hacienda hotel. This vision fosters an imagination of a contained and sanitized indigenous Otherness that is free of conflict.

The gated entrance and staged enactment help to maintain the hacienda's present reality as a culturally aware and thematic "superb oasis of luxury and relaxation" detached from its immediate social context.[29] The pristine vernacular huts stand in stark contrast with the landscape of poverty and the lack of opportunity that characterize Temozón Sur and its surrounding villages and towns. Outside the narrowly staged space at the hacienda's gates, the 180 houses in the village and the more than 1,700 in the neighboring town of Abalá (INEGI 2015b) offer the typical contemporary rural landscape of Yucatán: a mixture of poorly built Maya huts, concrete houses, and makeshift housing peppered with global brands and regional political propaganda, and lacking any infrastructure to supply potable drinking water or waste collection to its residents.

The transformation and selective enactment of Temozón created by the arrival of luxury tourism has been far reaching. Sarah, a North American scholar and frequent traveler to the region, who visited Temozón in 2000 and in 2014, recalls her impressions on her two trips:

> I arrived in Temozón de Mena y Sosa for the first time on May 18, 2000.... The plaza was really more of an open space or park; there were no buildings lining it as was the norm in other communities. The town was very quiet; I didn't see anyone. Instead of finding a central government institution, such as a municipal palace, ejidal commissary, or even a church, I found an elegant hacienda which I soon discovered was being converted into a luxury hotel. Although the hacienda was beautiful, I didn't feel comfortable there; on the contrary, the space scared me. I had visited old haciendas that had been converted into active cooperatives or museums, but this reminded me more of an abandoned slave plantation, occupied only by spirits of the past ... A statue of Lázaro Cárdenas stood in front of the hacienda and the abandoned and empty central "plaza." Both the statue and the plaza seemed lost and alone, as if they had been randomly and meaninglessly placed there ... When I returned to Temozón in 2014, the hotel had been completely restored and was fully operational ... I didn't feel the same discomfort or fear that I had felt in 2000.... I had to walk to the end of the road along the hacienda perimeter walls in order to find community members' houses, hidden behind the hotel. I also had to ask for the monument to Cárdenas, because I didn't see it. Instead of appearing in the open, as it had in 2000, it was blocked by a building with an artisanal workshop sponsored by the "Banamex Foundation," where I found women making table and bed linens for sale. They told me how to get to the monument, which required walking around the building and wading through weeds up to my knees.[30]

Temozón's inhabitants who have lived through this process corroborate the vivid transformation that Sarah describes. Maria, the owner of a small store in the plaza, describes how the new houses block her view of the fields and prevent people from gathering in the shade under the central ceiba tree in front of the store to chat. "I do not see *borrachitos* [alcoholic men] anymore," she said one evening, "but I do not see other people either as I used to.... The workshops [*talleres*] bring tourists but they come in cars, park, buy, and go. . . . Nobody stops to stay."

Most of the FHMM projects involve infrastructure and the material transformation of the built environment. Most projects entail a top-down approach to building housing and roads. But instead of receiving input from the community, FHMM consults with technicians and experts and uses multiscalar agreements. These are elements that have been essential in the embellishment and functionality of the hacienda hotel as a distinctive tourist place. After Hurricane Isidore, for example, FHMM donated construction materials, in particular cement blocks, adobe, and thatches for roofs to rebuild houses near the hacienda hotel. While these materials provided shelter for many families in Temozón, they also served the purpose of intentionally building houses that were aesthetically similar to Western nostalgic representations of what a Maya dwelling settlement should look like: a collection of isolated hutches of palm and adobe along unpaved streets.

For the inhabitants of Temozón, mostly Maya and mestizo peasants, adobe stands for austerity and lack of progress, especially when compared with the sumptuous style of the hacienda's *casa grande* just a few meters away. Cement, while a symbol of progress, also confines these inhabitants to standardized housing structures that are totally decontextualized from local and regional needs. As Juan explains, "cement blocks are solid but they don't let the air in, they suffocate you. . . . In this climate you need the air to come and go. . . . The cement blocks that they give us are only enough to build one little room, a door, and a window and that is it." What is more, haciendas' original architectural styles for workers' housing were already designed to maximize surveillance and to make sure workers turned out to work upon the first bell ringing and were not intoxicated. The stone walls around these house plots were lower than in the village to maximize surveillance over peones and hacienda hotel reconstruction reproduces this logic (see Ancona Riestra 1996).

Paving roads, providing housing, and installing electricity have improved Temozón Sur inhabitants' commutes and everyday lives, but these amenities are also pertinacious reminders of Hernández and his family as the new *patrones*. As such, his desires and needs dictate how these improvements can be used. As Pedro, who works for the hacienda hotel, puts it, when guests come to the hotel "you know you have to stay indoors if they ask you to. . . . We do not complain because while they are not around, we get to use the roads and commute faster."

I will come back to these moral dilemmas later in the chapter. But what is important to highlight here is how tourism has emerged as a legitimate actor in the ways that many inland towns operate. Tasks that used to belong to the state and municipal governments, such as designing urban spaces and providing housing and jobs, are now granted by tourism corporations and hence, planned with profit in mind.

Inside the Gates

The selective enactment of the past continues inside the hacienda, which has been designed, as one of the promotional tourist brochures states, "to restore original designs, like paintings, decorations, furniture *but drawing a line* [emphasis mine] where the historical part ends and the luxury experience begins." This line has been erected by erasing all references to the productive spaces within the hacienda and focusing reconstruction efforts on the *casa grande,* transforming it into a twenty-eight-room luxury retreat. The building has been carefully painted in its traditional colors. Original materials, like iron, stone, and wood have been maintained for major visible structures, while the furniture and decorations in both common areas and rooms re-create the European Renaissance style of the hacienda's former owners (Ancona Riestra 1996). To achieve this effect, old pieces of furniture such as pharmaceutical cabinets have been transformed into new necessities such as minibars or bookshelves in the tourists' accommodations. Additionally, the interior design for all the rooms includes imported European furniture and Renaissance-style paintings.

In the henequen era, the *casas grandes* at haciendas like Temozón Sur were used by hacendados as *casas de recreo* (vacation houses) for the weekends and holidays and their European artifacts represented luxury and social hierarchy. These artifacts were also intended to create the extra-ordinary experience of inhabiting a European palace in the middle of tropical Yucatán. Today, the arrangement of colors and selection of furniture and paintings are crucial ways to mark nostalgic continuity with colonial times and the hacendado's European aspirations. As The Haciendas puts it in its promotional brochures: "The property's high-elevated ceilings, and the exquisite ambiance of its 28 guest rooms and suites, evoke the splendor of the colonial times when these premises were built."[31]

The rest of the buildings within the Hacienda have been retrofitted to serve tourism consumption purposes. The old machine house, for example, has been converted into a museum space in which restored everyday objects are exhibited together with a collection of black-and-white images from the hacendado's private albums. The objects and images that are on display almost exclusively portray the everyday luxurious lifestyle of the hacendado and his family, eliding the hard work of the peones or the slavery-like conditions in which they were forced to live. Instead, the images showcase family celebrations such as weddings and christenings, the hacendado dealing with paperwork in his office, his frequent travels to Europe or the United States, and gentlemen holding meetings at the *casa grande*. In all of these pictures, the hacendado and those around him wear European-style clothing and accessories. The objects on display (e.g., bicycles, lady's umbrellas, children's toys) reflect the luxuries of the hacendado's life—there are no references to the hacienda as being a highly inegalitarian socioeconomic system. The spaces that were used for drying, dyeing, and storing henequen have been transformed into tennis courts, jogging tracks, swimming pools, and conference rooms.

This selective link to Yucatán's past is thus manufactured by re-creating the *casa grande* and its immediacies as stages for tourist consumption. The result is a conflict-free bucolic image of the past that is detached from current local and regional realities. It is precisely this detachment from the present and the reattachment to an imagined past that enables tourists to have a guilt-free experience at the hacienda hotel—much as hacendados did. Some tourists, like Ana, a woman from Canada whom I met at Temozón Sur in 2008 while she was having a swim at the pool, find some irony in the sheer unevenness of the form of tourism they engage in, and yet they find a way to justify it through the hacienda hotel's restoration achievements. Ana reflexively commented on this:

> At The Haciendas, the idea is to create a nice village, with little shops painted and women dressed with typical costumes. I see it is not real. This is part of the tourist attraction they sell. I have walked around and the real village is just behind this façade and it has very little to do with this. . . . Still, the building is real, you know, it was used and meant a lot for the economy of the region. . . . Tourism rescued it from abandonment and I feel this is something good.

The staged entrance and the selective attention to material culture in restoration practices for tourism purposes are not unique to Temozón or the hacienda hotels. They are in fact an example of a larger trend in heritage management practices to objectify places by focusing on architecture and objects and attributing inherent cultural values and significance to these things (Smith 2006; Prats 2004; Mármol, Frigolé, and Narotzky 2010). They illustrate how "culture is substantialized and abstracted from its uses becoming something material available to conservation" (Byrne 2014, 154) and contemplation: a building, a carriage, a kitchen tool. And how, in addition, heritage preservation and the tourism industry work together to fabricate, enact, and extract value by transforming the past into an imaginary geography, romanticized and free of conflict.

However, these imagined geographies are not simply evoked or contained within architectures and objects, they are also embodied by the workers so the place can live up to those imaginations. At Hacienda Temozón Sur this is done through gardening and the cultivation of the senses.

Versailles in the Tropics

As sociologist Chandra Mukerji (1997) argues, gardens are privileged tools of the modern imagination and privileged "laboratories of power." Gardens have been used for pedagogy: to enact narratives about the present and the past, to represent particular world views, and to legitimate power relations of domination (Rottenberg 1995). The gardens at Hacienda Temozón Sur fit many of these uses. Hotel corporations use gardens as "laboratories for and demonstrations of [their] capacities to use the countryside as a political resource" (Mukerji 1997, 2) as well as sites of capital accumulation.

At Hacienda Temozón Sur, the use of the countryside as political and economic resource has been achieved by transforming the hacienda's thirty-seven-hectare gardens into an imitation of the formal gardens or "gardens of order" of the Palace of Versailles. The intention is clear: to shape tropical natural features in inland Yucatán according to the region's reimagined consanguinity with Europe in order to create a particular vantage of the past and the present. Panoramic vistas from the *casa grande* over adjacent buildings are secured by respecting the original elevated structure of this building as well as by the delineation of symmetric paved pathways that have the *casa grande* as their center of reference. The elevated location of the *casa grande* and the meticulous layout of the pathways clearly confirms the centralized power of the hacendado over peones, much as it once confirmed the power of kings over their populations. The elevated structure of the *casa* from which the hacendado once controlled all of the hacienda's spaces and activities, now allows managers and tourists visual control over the movements of those who cater to them, while enjoying the views of a domesticated forest that maintains the exotic exuberance of the tropics without all its annoyances.

Domesticating the tropics is not an easy task. Every day, ten gardeners are responsible for collecting leaves and other organic debris, caring for birds and their cages, tending to exotic plants in flowerpots, and fumigating for tropical insects. Guests can linger in carefully planned shaded spaces surrounding the gardens, where they are soothed by the rhythmic sounds of water fountains and artificial pools. There is also a carefully curated botanical garden, in which clients can read, in English and Maya, labels that describe several of the most important medicinal plants, curated by Grupo Plan. Here, indigenous medicine matters as yet another signifier of Maya-ness and tradition. These plants are also sold at the local workshops and The Haciendas' boutique stores as "folk plants" by indigenous women working for the Fundación.

The intensive landscaping and gardening at Hacienda Temozón Sur contrasts with the landscapes of ecological neglect that lie right outside the hacienda's gates. These are landscapes made of hectares upon hectares of abandoned henequen fields, where deforestation and their associated problems of erosion and desertification are evident. While some of the abandoned henequen land is reverting to forest, and most serves as open landfills for waste, as in the immediate surroundings of Temozón, in other areas local farmers are returning to practice subsistence agriculture, repurposing the lands for milpa production by using the environmentally controversial technique of slash-and-burn (*roza, tumba, quema*). According to the Yucatán Urban Development and Environment Secretary, Yucatán lost more than one million hectares of forestland between 1976 and 2000 (see Lutz, Prieto, and Sanderson 2000).

At Temozón Sur, it is not possible to use henequen lands for subsistence, Hernández having bought them for tourist development. The result is that these lands have become illegal open-air dumps that have created serious health problems in Temozón Sur, where dengue and diarrheic diseases are, according to municipal data, far more prevalent than in nearby towns and villages. Although The Haciendas' tourism venture is not responsible for these otherwise common problems of rural Yucatán, it does fuel ecological neglect by ignoring their existence and by inhibiting the provisional use of land for subsistence. Ironically, the FHMM, while neglecting "nature" outside of the hacienda's gates, has recently adopted international discourses on environmentalism and conservation to promote hacienda hotels "as sites for conservation . . . and . . . environmental education."

Creating a cocooned, European-inspired microclimate lends material support to discourses about sustainability so that tourists can enjoy a guilt-free experience. But physical and material seclusion is not the only thing required to create a taste for luxury at the haciendas. A sensory engagement with a stereotypical yet professionalized Maya indigenous Other is also part of the tourist package.

Indigenous Flair and Flavor

Hacienda Temozón Sur provides its guests with a taste of the affluent lifestyle by pampering clients' senses through personalized attention and unique adaptations of local cuisine, as well as services such as therapeutic body massages. These practices involve adapting and adjusting workers' bodies and spatial movements to guests' requirements. These adjustments are based on the disciplining of indigenous bodies and their performance within a highly choreographed space in which, as Edensor (1998, 106) puts it, "bodies are tutored in 'appropriate' ways." This tutoring demands professionalized indigenous workers, as well as their performance of ritualized and deeply racialized host-guest encounters in staged atmospheres.

In our conversations over the years, managers at Hacienda Temozón Sur have taken pride in affirming that most of the hotel workers at the hacienda hotel are indigenous and native to Abalá and Temozón Sur, and that many of them, or members of their families, had been previously employed as peones in the henequen hacienda. These managers believe there is intrinsic value in employing indigenous workers who have a historical relationship to the place, and they present the hacienda hotel as a tourist venture that honors a lifetime of indigenous work.

This narrative is part of a performative ritual, orchestrated during face-to-face first encounters with the guests at the hacienda's main porch. Hotel managers organize these first encounters around a well-known battery of colonial relations of domination, and they normally unfold as follows.

After going through security at the hacienda gates, guests are greeted on the porch by an indigenous waiter, always male, impeccably dressed in a white uniform with a golden tag with his name on it. He carries a tray with cold *agua de Jamaica* (hibiscus tea) and hot towels for the guests to wipe away the tropical heat from their hands and faces. Normally through gestures, guests are invited to sit and wait for the manager before checking in. Shortly after, the manager—always white, always male, generally a foreigner—shows up dressed in formal guayabera attire. Embodying the old foreman's role, he greets his guests, apologizing for any inconvenience on the trip. Then, he introduces the hacienda hotel personnel. On cue, the personnel come up to the porch and line up, hands behind their backs, smiling and greeting the guests. The manager introduces the staff, emphasizing that they are indigenous Maya who either worked at the hacienda themselves or have family members who did. The manager offers his guests the possibility of special personalized services, which can include having the person of their choosing attend to their needs or arrange their itineraries for lunches, dinners, and activities.

English-speaking, indigenous Maya waiters and maids interact with clients during their stay at the hacienda. Those who do not speak English, who are the majority, stay out of sight and address guests only through gestures and servile mannerisms, bending the body, lowering their eyes, and respecting an established and rehearsed physical distance. Women are dressed in impeccable *ternos* while men are dressed in plain brown guayabera uniforms. All of them, around forty people, are supervised by the manager, who is an employee of the Luxury Collection. This manager is referred to by the hacienda hotel workers as *el manager* or *el gerente* (the manager), just as the hacendado's foreman was decades earlier.

The disciplining of the bodies of those who cater to guests and the development and organization of etiquette is most visible at the hacienda's restaurant. Waiters have been trained in how and when to address clients: they carefully observe corporeal distances, control their voices and gestures, refrain from talking excessively, and practice great care when filling glasses, lighting cigarettes, or escorting guests to their tables. Both the waiters and the maître d' are under the constant surveillance of the manager who, playing the role of the foreman and host, observes, controls, and constantly corrects their interactions with guests. Guests, on their part, expect careful attention and demand it, sometimes with just a look, if the service is not up to their standards.

One summer day at the hacienda's restaurant, waiting for an interview with the manager, I observed a situation that illustrates this last point. I describe it in my fieldwork notes as follows:

A couple of middle-aged Mexican visitors complained about an overcooked steak to a uniformed indigenous young man. Three other uniformed men observe their gesticulations at a distance. Their bodies rest against the wall. A manager appears. He moves fast. The steak is taken away and a few minutes later, a complimentary bottle of European imported red wine is served. Away from the table, he says to me, "Unacceptable behavior. I never get used to these people's lack of etiquette. It is one of my daily chores here ... to make sure they fold the toilet paper the right way, to make sure they keep their distances and look in the eyes of clients, that they lay the table correctly. Details matter. Details matter when counting what is luxury and what is not. But how to communicate this with them if they don't even have a toilet to clean at home?

Situations like the above are common at Hacienda Temozón Sur. They happen with a sense of normalcy that naturalizes the presentation of an indigenous self as uniformed and trained to serve. These situations also reveal the constant valuation process that is at play in every interaction and that signals who can be decent, be clean, and know luxury—as well as the urge to educate others in these standards when opportunity arises.

Bodies are not the only thing that matter in the staged production of indigenous luxury. Taste also plays a crucial role in how tourists are invited to escape to the past. The production and presentation of unique flavors has become a dominant leitmotif in differentiating haciendas from other forms of cultural tourism in Yucatán. Hacienda hotels have turned to fusion cuisine as a way to achieve distinction. The most popular Maya dishes and traditional ingredients are cooked at hacienda hotels by an internationally recognized Mexican chef listed as one of thirty Mexican celebrity chefs and trained by Ferran Adriá of El Bulli restaurant in Spain.[32]

At the haciendas, meat is served with imported wine, fish is cooked with European herbs, spices, and condiments, chocolate and orange desserts take the place of spicy fruit salads, and fresh bread is served alongside corn tortillas. Nothing could be further from contemporary diets in inland Yucatán, which have undergone what Leatherman and Goodman (2005) have termed the "coca-colonization of the Yucatec Mayan diet." This "coca-colonization" refers to the increased consumption of highly processed, calorie-dense, and nutrient-poor foods and sweetened beverages in inland Maya communities. This widespread diet is closely associated with two of the region's major health problems: diabetes and obesity. According to data from the Instituto Mexicano del Seguro Social (IMSS), the state of Yucatán has the highest prevalence of type 2 diabetes in the nation; in Mexico as a whole it is the second leading cause of death, after cardiovascular illnesses (INEGI 2018).[33]

As a way of creating an elite tourist experience of the past, "ancient," "traditional," and "holistic mystical" treatments promise to put guests in touch with "ancient Maya culture." These treatments typically consist of therapeutic body massages that are promoted as ways to revitalize, energize, and purify the self, and as spiritual encounters with an indigenous Other. As the hacienda hotel puts it in its promotional brochures, "the 37 hectares covered by the site, a large pool, the cenotes, wonderful paths, and a spa offering treatments inherited from the Mayan culture merge so that guests take a deep plunge into relaxation and comfort."

Massages and spa rituals take place in the recently renamed Hol-Be Spa, or the "cave spa," in the village's cenote. Providing such services in the cenote is controversial in the eyes of workers and the larger population of Temozón.[34] Maya communities revere cenotes for their religious, spiritual, and social importance. They are communal spaces, used for ritual practices and, more recently, for family recreation (Guardado 2012, 2008; Stone 2010; Ruz 2006).

The Hacienda Temozón Sur has cordoned off and privatized the cenote as a self-contained enclave in order to create an "authentic" and "natural" space where tourists can enjoy a ritual Maya massage, *sobadas*. The spa has trained native women from Temozón, like Patricia, to perform these *sobadas*. Performing *sobadas* as massages has also required resignifying the meaning of the still-active work of rural indigenous midwives *(parteras)*, healers *(sobadoras)*, and shamans *(chamanes)* for tourism consumption. Inside the hotel, *sobadas* have lost their meaning and symbolism as a practice still performed by old women to help other women in labor and by male shamans to heal the sick body. At the hotel, the *sobadas* are self-indulgent practices similar to those provided in Western spas and seaside resorts. Following trends of spiritual and religious tourism in Latin America, and particularly in neighboring Chiapas and Guatemala, the hacienda hotel has also recently added an on-site shaman, originally from Switzerland, who specializes, as promotions put it, "in mystical medicine, Mayan rituals, and traditions."

In many ways, indigenous foods and *sobadas* are examples of the contradictions inherent in a tourism model that is predicated upon a cultural encounter with the Other, but that is in fact practiced in isolation. At the hacienda's restaurant and spa, tourists are enveloped in a timeless, luxurious microclimate from which the endemic poverty and lack of opportunities affecting the most proximate rural Yucatán are veiled. In so doing, The Haciendas' tourism venture extracts value from living cultural traditions and communal spaces, as it entangles inland Yucatán's indigenous population in former productive spaces and refashioned labor servitudes. This appropriation and resignification for tourism of meaningful living traditions has stuck many to new sociocultural, labor, and familial struggles. The rest of the chapter looks at some of these struggles in detail.

After the original henequen hacienda in Temozón closed its export processing factory in 1987, the majority of the active population in Temozón Sur and Abalá migrated to Cancún, Mérida, or the United States. Today, many men work provisionally at a large pig factory in Kekén, to which they commute daily in search of work, or they work in construction in Mérida. Some young women work a few kilometers away from Abalá at PoliMérida, a maquiladora specializing in manufacturing bags, and the rest of them are either too young to migrate or have family responsibilities that require them to stay in order to care for children and elders. Although Hurricane Isidore disrupted these labor dynamics, closing down the factories for months, it is still this latter collective of women and elders that the hacienda hotel relies on as a permanent source of labor. To do so, FHMM has organized them into civic societies of social responsibility, or cooperatives of *sobadoras* and craftswomen. Through loans for these cooperatives, the FHMM channels resources for community development initiatives from international and national agencies and the state while providing human capital and resources to the hotel.

Drawing on social responsibility models as a form of sanctioned civic associationism or community cooperativism, "development" through the strategic use of culture and the privatization of land and resources is a winning strategy.[35] Whereas in communities along the Gulf of Mexico coast, like Celestún, populations have maneuvered state-led demands of cooperativism by means of informal networks of power that have empowered local groups such as boatmen and craftswomen in the effective control of the commons (see chapter 2), in inland Yucatán, state-led community cooperativism has become entangled in practices of dispossession. On the one hand, this form of community cooperativism has resurrected the organization of labor—as well as the struggles around labor and credit—that characterized the Mexican Revolution and the times of Cárdenas and the Partido Socialista del Sureste (PSS), as well as the Porfiriato and the henequen period, when national institutions such as the Banco Nacional de Comercio Exterior (BNCE) controlled *ejidatarios* through credit and when patrons exercised control over workers through debt-peonage and loans. On the other hand, it has also helped the extended neoliberal push for planned cooperative management as a way to fully appropriate indigenous commons.

At Temozón Sur, this is evident in the case of the *sobadoras* working in the cenote and the craftswomen working in the huts outside the hacienda. The *sobadoras* are a group of six indigenous women native to the town, like Patricia, who work for the hacienda hotel as "ancient Maya healers" in the cenote. They have been trained as professional massage therapists in an effort to "bring Maya wisdom and tradition" to the hacienda's guests while "helping Maya families in their daily sustainability."[36] However, as they told me in interviews in 2012, *sobadoras* barely reach the daily minimum wage of sixty Mexican pesos because the hacienda hotel requires that they rent the spaces at the cenote and the spa room, but they only get paid when there are clients who require their services. Patricia explained to me how they work: "We are fifteen women in the cooperative: six from Temozón, four in Santa Rosa, three in San Jose, and two in Uayamon. I do not know the others or how they work but here in Temozón we charge US$200 for the *sobada* but we hardly get 35 percent of it. . . . we need to pay rent for the spa and cannot make alternative wages because we commit from 7 a.m. to 7 p.m. for work days . . . even if there are no guests we cannot get to our houses." Patricia must be on site and on call when the hotel receives "important guests." Then, as she said, she sits and waits and fights sleep because she must be on call twenty-four hours a day.

Craftswomen have been also organized into a cooperative by the FHMM, and then subcontracted by the hacienda hotel to create handicrafts (e.g., henequen fiber products, embroidery, soaps, candles, and sculpted silver jewelry) to sell at the hotel's boutique stores. These women, around ten of them, rent the huts that are in the staged Maya village at the entrance to the hotel. Although they pay to use these spaces, they are not entitled to live there nor are they permitted to use them for any other activities. When there are guests around, craftswomen put their children and animals behind the huts, and "real life" as Leona, put it to me, happens there, "hidden" and "out of sight." Although these women are organized as legal autonomous community cooperatives, they have very little decision-making power with regard to managing the business. The craftswomen work for two Mexican design brands created by FHMM, one for artisanal products (Taller Maya) and another one for gourmet food products (Traspatio Maya). These women sell their products at any of the five restored hacienda hotels' boutique stores and give a share of their sales to FHMM. FHMM buys and distributes the materials with which the crafts are made. It also establishes the final price and makes all decisions regarding distribution. Risks, on the other hand, rest solely on the women's shoulders. As Leona said, "we are told off by the FHMM if products are not in good shape or have flaws. . . . If they tell us to work on a design and it does not sell then it is all our fault."

The FHMM artisanal brands—and the organization's brand itself—have recently become part of world fair trade organizations and are in compliance with the World Fair Trade Organization Trade Principles (2018). Rebranded in 2018 as *Design* Artisanal Brands, their products promote the hacienda hotels by using images of Maya indigenous women, such as close-up photographs of their hands and faces, or of the women wearing their crafts and smiling, showing their golden teeth, a symbol of prosperity in Yucatán.[37] This form of representation of indigenous alterity promotes The Haciendas' brand as a sustainable tourism destination that is attentive to cultural Otherness and that gives back to rural Yucatán communities. In practice, however, these activities do not provide these women with long-term financial or business autonomy. At least not for now. On the contrary, they entrap them in economic dependency and even cultural and economic alienation, since they do not decide what counts as Maya and how, nor are they owners of their labor or the products of their labor. This form of representation entraps them within a nostalgic past in which indigenous peoples were not wage laborers, peasants, or revolutionaries, but part of peaceful, docile, self-sufficient communities that worked the land with their brown hands. This conflict-free form of representation is the one currently used to rebrand indigenous women in particular, not just as objects of visual consumption, but as agents, designers, and entrepreneurs of their own futures.[38]

The smooth, conflict-free consumption that emerges from these depictions and practices stands in stark contrast with the hacienda's past as a revolutionary site and with its present as a place of social and ecological neglect. Still, this is an erasure that many in Temozón Sur and elsewhere perceive to be worthwhile, since it allows them to make a living in a landscape that is otherwise depleted of alternatives. "All in all," a regional researcher told me in a conversation about the hacienda, "with all the privatization and misinterpretation of indigenous culture, the hacienda is a hotel and it provides for jobs where there are none." I address this paradox in the next section.

APPRECIATION, SHARED SACRIFICES, AND CONSCIOUS RESISTANCES

In 2012, at a small conference in a regional university, a local anthropologist critical of The Haciendas' tourism development claimed that "[Hernández and his family] bought the *cascos* and the lands. . . . They restored the buildings but left the lands to die. . . . They basically put an end to [*compraron*] the future of generations." These critical words are echoed by workers at the hacienda and the population in Temozón. However, among workers and Temozón Sur's population it is common to find a different inflection in these words. While questioning the hacienda hotel's practices, hotel workers and village inhabitants also see in tourism an opportunity to make a better living in a precarious present. The workers and local community are, they say, "grateful to" (*agradecidos*) the patrons at the hacienda hotel, but they also need to "beware of" (*tiene que cuidarse uno*) them. These dual perceptions of hope and dread, gratefulness and foreboding, are informed by the fact that it has been the FHMM and Hernández, not the state or the local government, who have attended to their needs. Juan, for example, feels grateful to have a job that allows him to stay in his natal village without commuting or migrating, but he complains sometimes that the work is too demanding for his age and too unpredictable. In a walk through the hacienda hotel's botanical gardens, Juan elaborated on this unpredictability and how hard it was to sustain the manicured tropical stage that he maintains in order to meet guests' expectations: "These plants and fishes are not from here, they brought them here and some are not used to the heat, others are invasive. You have to learn to deal with them and care for them because the guests like them. . . . We have to always have fresh roses for the women to cut and place in rooms. It is not easy, it is not easy."

As in old times, Juan knows how to take care of himself. If his workday has been too demanding and the pay did not reflect the extra hours, or if he was paid late, he does not show up to work for a few days until the hotel manager sends someone to look for him. When I asked him why he would not show up for work, he explained, "This is the way we showed discontent during the henequen. . . . If they did not pay us, we would not show up to work the next day." Aware that he is valuable to both the hotel managers and the tourists as a former hacienda peon, and also conscious of the hacienda's shortage of labor, Juan strategically uses his absence as a way to make his claims heard while avoiding direct confrontation.

These labor practices are deeply rooted in the history of the hacienda as one of the sites where the storm of the Mexican Revolution (1910) gathered after summers of discontent dating back to 1876 (Wells and Joseph 1996). The chronic labor shortages at the hacienda hotels also reveal connections with this revolutionary yet suffocated past. Neus, an FHMM employee, blamed the need to hire personnel from outside Temozón on women's short-term perspectives and lack of understanding of what working for luxury tourism meant. One evening in 2010, after a poorly attended community workshop to recruit craftswomen for the hotel, she argued, "There is a lot of apathy . . . a lack of commitment. . . . They want benefits in the short term. . . . They see tourism as easy money . . . and they do not realize that they have to work as a team. . . . Teamwork does not give them anything back [*no les reporta nada*]. . . . They are heavily influenced by consumerism and they just want more and more superfluous things." But there is more than apathy and consumerism at work here. Not working for the hacienda hotel, or working on and off, is an old tactic from the henequen era, exercised by Temozón's inhabitants to protect themselves and their families against potentially abusive managerial labor practices.

The manager, much like the old foreman, regulates and controls their movements inside the hacienda, dictating which spaces they are in and when. Villagers resent these management practices, and they are dissatisfied that they cannot rely on the hacienda as a source of employment when needed. But these management practices also generate confusion among workers at the hacienda, who do not entirely know who is ultimately responsible for what or whom. "When a problem comes," as one of the gardeners told me, "they pass the ball among one another until one gets tired and does not complain anymore."

Elder workers like Juan, eighty-seven years old, work daily at the gardens in eight-hour shifts from either 7 A.M. to 3 P.M. or 3 P.M. to 11 P.M. Like most of the gardeners, he is paid every fifteen days and he is not a member of any cooperative. When there are guests, their shifts vary because they have a "100 percent no noise rule," so they are not allowed to run their machines or move around the garden as usual and "tasks accumulate." When this happens, timetables become unpredictable and salaries suffer because as he says, "the patrons do not count the extra hours. . . . They just see there is work to recover that was not done."

Workers also know how to orchestrate subtle yet organized and effective confrontations with the manager. These confrontations take the form of labor practices that were typical during the henequen era, when workers had to earn the patron or foremen's trust to gain his favor. "If you get close to the manager," Pedro, a receptionist at the hotel when I met him, said "you can earn his favor and he can help you if you get in trouble." Knowing that the workers' desire to get closer to them is mostly instrumental, Hilario, a manager I interviewed at the end of his two years working at Temozón, complained about his "solitude" and "the impossibility of making true friendships because I know I am being used."

Discussing the labor practices at the hacienda hotel during his two years of service, Hilario told me how he could see that workers were unhappy about particular events, elaborating on how they engaged in forms of "organized collective forgetfulness":

> It is not like they are going to tell you if something is bothering them.... They just start not doing their jobs here and there.... They forget to do things all at the same time! ... It is by putting these pieces together during the day that I realize they want me to address something or that there is a problem.... For example women do not arrange fresh flowers in the room or they let them die without changing them.... The gardeners are late in lighting candles in the evening or servers are particularly slow in serving the food.

For workers like Juan, Pedro, and Patricia, this collective forgetfulness is performed amid a mixture of gratitude and defeat. This is also the case for Elena and Mónica. Elena, for example, is a thirty-five-year-old widow and mother of two small children. She is one of the youngest *sobadoras* at the Hacienda. When I talked to her, she had been working for the hacienda for five years after her husband passed away in a construction accident in Mérida. She lives in a modest cement house in Temozón Sur with hardly any furniture, and she cooks meals over an open fire. In addition to caring for her children, she is also in charge of caring for her elderly mother and her husband's parents, since both of her brothers commute weekly to Mérida to work in the construction sector and her husband was an only child. Like Patricia, she sees working at the hacienda hotel as a "sacrifice that helps bring money to the family." She does not plan to remain working at the hotel for much longer because "it is a slave job" *(es esclavo)*. But she says she is grateful for the possibility of having a job that allows her to stay in the village and not have to commute. She is grateful *(agradecida)* she says, because the hacienda hotel has brought electricity to the town, and for her and her family also "a better house ... small, but better" after Hurricane Isidore.

Elena elaborated on the hacienda's tense labor relations and the forms of everyday resistance workers exercised, such as slowing down the pace at which they completed their tasks. In doing so, she established a nostalgic comparison with the henequen era.

> It is ugly now [*esta feo*]. Before [in henequen times] it was better. Men worked at the hacienda and everybody earned the same ... it was an easy and peaceful life.... Now with the hotel everything is ugly.... The managers of the spa and the hotel do not get along and workers are pitched against each other

to please them. . . . Sometimes with the other women we show we are angry [*molestas*]. We don't do things as fast [*vivamente*] as we could . . . we take time. . . . This makes them angry! . . . But all they care about is to sell, to sell, to sell. . . . They all earn commissions if they sell and they do not care about labor conditions. . . . I do not plan to stay for much longer, I want to save for my daughter's *quinceaños* and then I am done!

Elena, Patricia, and two other elderly *sobadoras* from Temozón vividly recall an incident in 2004 when one of them was blamed for a client's bad reaction to a bee-sting while receiving a massage at the cenote. The client asked for the *sobadora*'s resignation and the hotel manager complied. Upon learning that the woman had been fired, none of the other women showed up for work until the manager allowed the dismissed worker back on the hacienda's grounds. Although they never explicitly complained to the managers or to the FHMM personnel, their position, which they repeated time after time in our talks, was clear. They made sacrifices working in the cenote. They got bee stings and mosquito bites almost daily. The humid, cold air of the cenote made them sick. And just because a guest got stung once, it was not a reason for the *sobadora* to lose her job. It was not their fault and it was not fair, since the cenote should have not been turned into a labor space on the first place.

Like Elena, Mónica, was about to turn thirty-five when I met her. She had been working for the hotel since it opened in 2002. Mónica began work at the hotel provisionally and seasonally as a maid. Now she is one of the supervisors of the laundry, the public areas, and the maids; she is also the person whom the hacienda hotel relies on the most to talk to journalists and researchers. Mónica sees working at the hotel as a "good sacrifice." Her job benefits her family, but it also binds her to "play being Maya for guests." She says she is grateful for the hacienda. Thanks to the FHMM, she completed both elementary and secondary school, and both her husband and younger sister found employment at the hacienda hotel as a gardener and a maid, respectively. Mónica has two kids and an established work schedule from 7 A.M. to 4 P.M. When there are no clients, she can have three days of rest. She appreciates her regular schedule because she is also in charge of caring for her husband's father, whose family migrated to Cancún.

Mónica values the work of the hacienda hotel for the village, and mostly, that it provides a source of income without having to commute. "People come and they do not like the work. . . . They do not like that you cannot get out of the hacienda and they leave. But then they end up coming back because it is better here. . . . You do not have to pay for the bus and you do not have to

FIGURE 14. Gardeners manicure the surroundings of the *casa principal*, Hacienda Temozón Sur, 2012. Photo by author.

pay for lunches. . . . And if you work well and show interest, the Fundación helps you with your studies." For her, the hacienda hotel is "an opportunity to get things done for *el pueblo* [the village]. . . . To organize ourselves on the margins of the city council and have as we have now, electricity and waste collection." After Hurricane Isidore, it was not the state but Roberto Hernández, *el patron*, who brought construction materials to Temozón's inhabitants, and it was the hacienda that offered shelter and temporary jobs to those who lost everything. And even if the services the hotel provides are partial and not reliable, it is thanks to the hotel that rubbish is collected in town. It is "thanks to the hotel," as many like Mónica put it, that some of Temozón's women and elders have been able to earn an income, improve their basic education, stay put, and make the village more livable for those who do not migrate.

In many ways, Mónica and Elena's perspectives reveal the triumph of utilitarianism brought about by tourism. On the one hand, this system has revived old patronage labor relations and uneven labor conditions, but it has also ameliorated otherwise precarious existences. In a rural setting such as Temozón Sur, desolated after the henequen demise, depleted by migration, and where women have limited opportunities in strongly patriarchal societies, the hacienda hotel offers a source of income to some. But such employment comes at great cost. Neither Elena nor Mónica find it easy to work at the hacienda hotel, not least because the space is still perceived with suspicion by the village elders and those who have never been inside its remodeled gates. The exclusivity of the hacienda hotel and the fact that the hacienda hotel's enclosure has eliminated access to otherwise communal and public spaces like the church and the cenote fuel local perceptions of the hotel as a space of danger.

When it comes to indigenous women's labor, the hacienda hotel is also considered by many indigenous elders as a "site of promiscuity," where Maya women are indebted to the patrons, or guests, just as they once were to the hacendados. *Sobadas* at the cenote often demand a gendered intimacy and indigenous women's hands on foreign bodies, and women like Patricia, Elena, and Mónica are required to wear the mestizo *terno* dress for work. They are conflicted about doing so, since *ternos* are an embroidered and delicate dress customarily reserved for special occasions such as religious festivities and *vaquerias* (regional festivals). Since other women wear *hipiles* to work (the traditional work attire for indigenous and mestiza women), the fact that hotel workers wear *ternos* is perceived by their peers in the village as an expression of vanity and pride. Besides, there is a general confusion about what sort of hotel the hacienda is. Elena, for example, has yet to explain to her mother, her children, or her brothers what kind of work she does. She lives "with fear" of rumors that her work is "impure" and she has lost friendships because of it. "How to explain what a massage in a spa is? Or that I touch the bodies of the guests? Or why I wear the *terno* to work?" she says.[39]

Similarly, Mónica did not tell her husband that she was working at the hacienda hotel because she thought he would be jealous. She only told him when her work schedule started to be demanding and her role in the FHMM became more visible to the community. Her husband accepted her work at the hacienda hotel, but only when they employed him, too, so that he could oversee her.

Similar struggles arise for indigenous men working at the hacienda. Pedro Ku, for example, has been working for the hotel for eight years. He has obtained his secondary degree with the help of the FHMM and learned basic English to communicate with guests over the phone and in person. When he is not working for the hacienda hotel, he lives with his father and grandfather, both former milpa workers, in a medium-sized humble cement house in Abalá. He is the youngest of seven siblings, the rest of whom work in the construction industry in Mérida, as meat dispatchers in Kekén, and as hostesses in Cancún. Like the other hotel workers, Pedro also has a difficult time explaining his job to his father and extended family. Well into our conversations, Pedro one day explained, "My father does not know what is inside of here [the hacienda]. . . . They think this is just one more hotel but they do not understand the work I do . . . or the importance of the hotel in the world."

Pedro has been accused several times of engaging in prostitution at the hotel. Still, he says he likes his job because "I have learned to be more educated . . . to respect distances and not talk over people." He also likes it because, unlike his brothers and sisters, he has money and time to go out and *pasear* (go for a walk for the joy of it) in Mérida. And yet the hotel, he says, is not his future. Like other workers at the hacienda hotel, Pedro anticipates the end of the hacienda hotel "just as henequen ended." He uses his time advantageously to acquire as much knowledge and as many connections as he can, so he will be able to make a living by migrating to Cancún, ideally, he says, to work for an upscale beach resort, "where people are not as closed-minded as here."

Pedro's experiences and aspirations speak to how tourism not only orders social relations but also shapes imaginations. Hacienda hotels in inland Yucatán create a continuum of possibilities in which someone like Pedro can imagine himself jumping from tourist site to tourist site. It is a career in tourism that gets regularly imaged as a future. Like Elena and Mónica, Pedro acknowledges that the hacienda hotel has brought educational opportunities and infrastructure (electricity, better-paved roads, and transportation) to their village.

And yet, like them, he does not think this tourism venue is a viable option for future generations. The re-creation of stereotypical indigeneity in host-guest encounters, and the way they get stuck in subcontracting labor practices and unpredictable timetables, in order to attend to those who travel in customized vacations, fix these workers in an old labor space that re-creates a past in which they had no agency in shaping their own futures.

CONCLUSION: SCALING UP INDIGENOUS CULTURE

If the previous chapter showed how ecotourism development in natural protected areas resulted in the reduction and commodification of nature to a single animal species, The Haciendas' luxury tourism venture is an example of how culture and history are extracted and scaled up for tourism consumption. Hacienda hotels materialize, visualize, narrate, and project inland Yucatán as a pleasing prospect for investors by both reviving European consanguinity and proximity with global elites, and maintaining distance from regional beach resort tourism "a la Cancún." They do so in the name of historical and cultural heritage preservation and indigenous empowerment. And they execute their vision through commercialization and privatization, which have had an impact on inland Yucatán. As Low, Taplin, and Sheld (2005) put it in their study of recreational parks in New York, the use of historical landscapes for recreation is a contested process, even though this contestation does not always play out in plain sight.

Marketed as jewels of Mexican cultural heritage, the stories and imaginaries of domination that hacienda hotels illustrate depoliticize a past of labor struggle and revolution as well as a present of social and ecological neglect. They invite tourists to jump from golden era to golden era while turning a blind eye to local and regional current realities. The articulation of luxury tourism at restored historical buildings as a community development strategy at local, national, and global scales legitimizes these spatial and temporal jumps. Restored haciendas for luxury tourism, like Temozón Sur, illustrate how inland Yucatán and indigenous Maya populations are being incorporated into the contemporary landscape of the region as "a world to escape to." Scaled up for global consumption as spaces for the global rich, haciendas emplace new desires and trace new travel routes that bring to inland Yucatán global personalities, Mexican elites, and cultural travelers who want to escape Cancún and all that it represents—standardized mass consumption, Westernization, environmental neglect. This is an escape that, as I show in this chapter, is organized around discourses of cultural encounter, but that advances through the material transformation of Yucatán's past into a privatized space open for extraction through the creation of secluded, guilt-free atmospheres for tourism's predatory accumulation strategies. The Haciendas show how particular tourist interventions anchor space, nature, and socio-cultural life to global patterns of elite capital accumulation by reinventing the region's past while sticking indigenous bodies and identities into productive spaces ruled by old labor servitudes and segregated spatialities.

The result is a collection of practices and built environments that are not that different from the agro-extractive logic that once ruled inland Yucatán. If during the henequen era sisal was the raw material produced and distributed for export, in luxury hacienda tourism it is the bodies, labor, and nostalgic imagination of the lived spaces of the past and an indigenous Other that get extracted and commodified for profit. This form of production entraps indigenous bodies into a past of semislavery, re-created in historically

FIGURE 15. A child playing in a random street a few blocks away from Hacienda Temozón Sur, 2018. Photo by author.

meaningful, local built environments according to the interests of elite global financial capital. In this refashioned reality, they "belong" to the space of the haciendas as particular enclaves designed and ruled by global tourism fashions and global elite tastes. This does not mean that locals lose complete agency in the process but instead that they articulate these transformations as far as they can, in an instrumental way so as to make a living in a context of historically created inextricable dependencies and a present of extended precariousness. Despite their subtle forms of resistance, none of these workers are in a position to transform history. On the contrary, they are stuck in time and space, confined in an "island of history," to paraphrase Marshall Sahlins (1987), and governed by Western imaginaries, tastes, temporalities, and casino capitalism spatialities. Through tourism development, they have become trapped in a historically uneven relationship and enclave, in which they must perform site-specific indigeneity as a service for the affluent classes.

This precariousness was vivid the last time I visited Temozón Sur, in March 2017. The community felt like it was under siege, but not due to any international summit or visits by important guests. There was an epidemic of *chikungunya* in the region, a dangerous viral disease transmitted by infected mosquitos that generates severe joint pains and fever. Every hut and building in the village was covered with makeshift mosquito nets. Black, green, and grey, these nets obscured the otherwise exposed interiors, and they gave a more than usually eerie vibe to the village. The streets were empty. At her house, Elena complained that the hacienda hotel's fumigation efforts ended right at its doors, and that the city council's efforts to eradicate mosquitos were not enough to protect her family. With only two fumigation machines, the city council had not even started prevention at Temozón's public areas or the school. The mayor was asking the hacienda hotel to do it, but to no avail. Villagers were overtly unhappy about the *chikungunya* epidemic, since those who become infected can be out of work for over a year. This discontent spurred many villagers to complain more openly about the hotel, although they still did so in private. As Elena put it, "They only look towards themselves [*hacia dentro*] but do not really look at the village. . . . With dogs with scabies, so many mosquitoes, and girls pregnant at thirteen, this is no place to live."

Although the hacienda hotel has been in business for more than ten years, Temozón Sur and the nearby towns, like Abalá, still have among the highest numbers of people living in extreme poverty in inland Yucatán. Fifty-seven percent of Abalá's population live in poverty and an additional 20 percent live in extreme poverty, according to official data (CONEVAL 2019a). Almost 90 percent of the town lacks access to basic services at home and nearly 60 percent of the population earns less than the national well-being standards and lacks access to state social security benefits (SEDESOL 2017). These blatant numbers call into question luxury tourism as a sustainable development strategy. If anything, as this chapter shows, luxury tourism reorganizes and re-spatializes inequalities and privileges, colonizing imagined regional geographies of the past and re-creating them for value extraction even as it entraps people in a sacrificial logic that jeopardizes their futures, if only because it has dispossessed them from their lands.

The next chapter travels to Tekit, an inland village just a few kilometers south of Temozón Sur and immediately north of Mayapan, the least frequented archeological site of the Ruta Puuc. There, outside of tourism's major circuits, I show how tourism's predatory practices pervade household and family organizations, the body, and the senses, sticking everyday life and imaginaries to urban dynamics in a still largely rural setting. The result is the production of a novel social and geographical space ruled by tourism's vivid ambivalences.

FOUR

City-Village

DOMESTIC MAQUILA IN THE TOURIST OFFSTAGE

OUT OF PLACE

Federal Highway 184 is a modern road that connects Mérida to inland Yucatán. Well transited, flat, narrow, and bumpy, Highway 184 is sketched through an endless expanse of dry tropical forest punctuated every now and then by tree snags, 7-Elevens, OXXO mini-marts, and a couple of Pemex gas stations. The road passes by the well-known tourist hotel and restaurant Hacienda Teya and the archeological site of Mayapan, comes close to the UNESCO World Heritage site of Uxmal, and goes by the recently restored indigenous luxury hotel Hacienda Santa Rosa, now managed by Marriott. Highway 184 also traverses an assortment of towns and villages with empty plazas and streets. These are the ghost villages of inland Yucatán, places stricken by poverty, settled listlessly under the layers of silence and stillness brought about by the collapse of the region's henequen agro-industrial business and by decades of migration to urban Mérida, the coasts, and the United States.

Kilometer 65, where Federal Highway 184 meets Yucatán's State Road 18, marks the entrance to Tekit. It is an entrance like many others: a sharp left, a long road plagued by unannounced speed bumps *(topes)* that reaches a main plaza, which features a church and the typical Spanish-style city council building. At first sight, this is a familiar landscape in inland Yucatán, but somehow, everything else seems to be utterly out of place.

The calm that characterizes the neighboring, mostly deserted villages is replaced here by a buoyant urban scene brimming with activity. Streets are crowded with people. Large pickups, polished Nissan Tsurus, and taxi tricycles zip by. Transit policemen make a symphony of whistles and corporeal gesticulations to try to avert collisions. On one side of the main plaza, there is a busy market with stalls selling vegetables, fruits, clothes, and toys. On the other side, there are two internet cafés, a gym (with separate entrances for men and women), two pawn shops, a clothing store, and a large Elektra store selling home appliances, loans, and consumer credit.

Judging by this intensely urban scene one would think that the road had led back to downtown Mérida, instead of to rural Yucatán. Like Mérida, Tekit has rush hour traffic, with peaks between six and eight in the morning, during the hour around noon, and after seven in the evening. Buses, *combis,* and *colectivos* (minibuses and vans) depart to and from Mérida every half hour. To secure a ride it is sometimes necessary to arrive an hour earlier and queue. On one side of the plaza a fleet of dozens of motor- and pedal-powered taxi tricycles await passengers. In 2015, the number of mototaxis in Tekit more than quadrupled, from one hundred to over five hundred, making "competition so hard that is difficult to keep regular clients [because] people want novelties, the latest," said Pepin, a young driver.

Conversations are ruled by the clock and are frequently interrupted with "I don't have time right now" *(ahorita no tengo tiempo)* or "I am in a rush" *(voy con prisa)*. Calendars and clocks are omnipresent on living room walls, and people check the time on their mobile devices almost as often as they take breaths. There is cellphone reception almost everywhere and electrical cables, black and red, thick and thin, crisscross the streets, connecting posts to homes. No one seems disconnected. The town has its own television station, Canal 19, which is exclusively dedicated to local news. Additionally, there are five soccer teams that regularly play evening games, and a popular soccer team at the state level, La Favorita de Tekit, is frequently featured in the region's *El Diario de Yucatán* and *Por Esto!* newspapers' sports sections. Elders and children can be spotted glued to their digital devices and many are active on social media. YouTube videos and Spotify are as ubiquitous here as in any large urban city center.

Newer concrete houses and vernacular huts mingle on the sides of paved streets. This architectural mixture of old and new is not uncommon in inland Yucatán. But there is something different about their juxtaposition here. In larger inland towns, like Oxkutzcab, many of the concrete houses are empty and typically feature half-built second floors, which signal stagnant dreams of prosperity created by international migration and remittances. In Tekit, a town half the size, concrete houses are modest in comparison, but they are packed with people, manufactured goods, and music, and they undergo continuous remodeling throughout the year. Side by side, there are also many

FIGURE 16. Urban hustle during school drop-off on a regular weekday, Tekit, 2015. Photo by author.

vernacular huts and the lively combination suggests a present that amalgamates smoothly with the past.

Furthermore, and unlike other inland villages and towns, Tekit does not suffer from the problems of an aging population, high unemployment, and migration. Ninety percent of Tekit's active population is employed, and the town has a nearly nonexistent emigration rate. There are eleven registered businesses offering financial services, mostly credit unions and cooperative banks. As its inhabitants put it, "Tekit is a magnet for work for the surrounding villages *(pueblitos).*" The result is that Tekit has an unusually young and gender-balanced population pyramid. Its 10,000 residents are distributed across 2,600 overcrowded households with an average of 4.5 persons each—well above the state's average of 3.5 (INEGI 2017; SEDESOL 2016b).

The unusual, out-of-place urban tableau that Tekit offers is at odds with not only neighboring towns and villages but also with stereotypical and statist tourist representations of inland Yucatán as the "space for Maya heritage and colonial history," as the space of a "vanishing culture" that I explored in chapter 3. Despite being only two hours away from Mérida and just a few kilometers away from the well-known Ruta Puuc archeological tourist itinerary, Tekit is absent from official or alternative tourism maps or narratives.[1] It is not talked about in travel blogs, and it is not, so far, part of any regional or state-driven tourism development plans. In fact, hardly any tourists visit there at all. Tekit seems to be trapped in a blind spot of the tourist imagination that has carved out the Yucatán Peninsula as "a world to escape to" organized around a collection of staged tourist places: paradisiac beaches, natural enclaves, and archeologically significant Maya ruins.

And yet, people in Tekit are stuck to tourism as much as, if not more than, those in Cancún, Celestún, or the luxury indigenous hacienda hotels that I have explored so far in this book. To understand how this is the case, this chapter shifts its attention from the tourist front stages toward the tourist backstage. It does so by examining how tourism's predatory and sticky orderings work at a distance, pulling places, transforming local architectures, and entrapping individuals in ambivalent shared sacrificial logics that are similar to those in consolidated regional tourism destinations.

As we will see, this is evident in Tekit: while it has not been directly planned for tourism, this town has nonetheless been deeply transformed by it. In this case, these transformations have not been fueled by the turquoise waters of the Caribbean Sea, the appeal of a spectacular nature setting or animal species such as the pink flamingo, or the enticing luxury of a nostalgic and exotic colonial past. In Tekit, it is textile manufacturing of a shirt, the guayabera—the favorite cultural souvenir for tourists visiting Yucatán and the de facto uniform for workers in the tourist industry in the region—that has generated these transformations. As Manuel, a colleague of mine from the Center for Research and Advanced Studies of the National Polytechnic Institute of Mexico (CINVESTAV) and the first person from Tekit to pursue a doctorate, explained to me in one of my visits there:

> Sewing for tourism has made Tekit a pulverized/scattered maquila [*maquila pulverizada*].[2] People in families sew for a whole range of people, for wealthy people of Mérida and Cancun, for guayabera factories in Mérida, for tourists, for hotels, to export to the States. . . . They just sew whenever there is an order [*un encargo*]. . . . Most people don't even know for whom. They just do the *encargos* that they are told to do . . . and this leaves them with pocket money at the end of the week. . . . Tekit, and not Mérida, is the guayabera capital of the world. . . . Here is where most guayaberas that you see in markets and downtown tourist stores are made, although nobody knows.

Manuel's words are backed up by numbers. Official economic data shows that Tekit has indeed become a giant pulverized maquila, distributed over 219 square kilometers and 1,034 productive economic units (see map 5). The vast majority, 98.2 percent, of these units are households registered as economic units that specialize in different aspects of the production of the

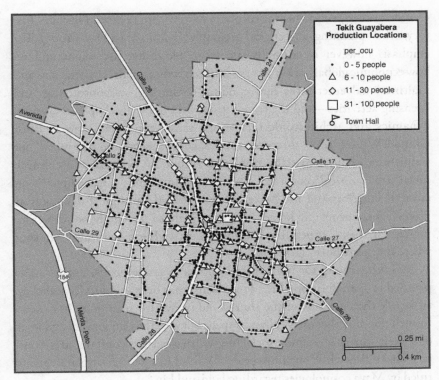

MAP 5. Households and workshops formally linked to guayabera production, Tekit. Map by author.

guayabera, such as unraveling *(deshilado)*, assembling *(armado)*, pleating *(alforzado)*, embroidering *(bordado)*, and seaming *(costura)*.

Not only has sewing for tourism transformed Tekit into a gigantic, spatially dispersed maquila dependent on tourism, but it has also created, rather organically, a new syncretic geographical formation: a city-village, an in-between space that is neither rural nor urban. I refer to this emergent space as a Mexican *desakota*. This is a term coined by geographer Terry McGee (1991) to refer to twentieth-century economic and geographical transformations in Indonesia. The term combines the Malay and Indonesian words *desa* (village) and *kota* (town). According to his definition, desakotas are geographical "regions linked to major urban centers by cheap transport axes where much more intense commercial agricultural and non-agricultural economic activities take place than in purely rural areas" (Moench and Gyawali 2008, 13). While McGee does not pay attention to cultural practices in his conceptualization of desakotas, these have been taken into consideration by subsequent users of the term within the social sciences, history, urban planning, and critical geography (Kusno 2013; Davis 2007). The emphasis however is normally on urban planning discussions and on how economic globalization actors—like the transnational corporations and multinational enterprises that conduct offshoring, subcontracting, and licensing activities—and the state actively and unevenly shape urban-rural dynamics and architectonic formations across the world. Yet, as Ruth Gilmore Wilson (2008, 36) writes, the desakota concept should be taken "not simply as a peculiar spatialization of the economic but also as a cultural, social, and political" construct. In this chapter, I follow her emphasis on cultural practices and use Mike Davis's broad definition of desakotas as places "where people no longer have to migrate to the city because the city migrates to them . . . their lives overturned, even while remaining on the spot where they were born" (2007, 9).[3]

In Tekit, sewing for tourism has implied a spontaneous, not formally planned re-spatialization of the town, which has been organically scaled up to satisfy the demands of the tourist industry. This scaling-up has transformed not only the town's physical space but also the temporality and logic of the relations that organize social life, which is entirely coproduced by tourist global pulses while remaining spatially fixed in a historically rural setting ruled by Maya cosmologies regarding land and kin.[4]

In what follows, I first discuss the re-spatialization of Tekit as a Mexican desakota. To do so, I historicize the emergence of the scattered or pulverized maquilas in which the guayabera is produced. I do so by analyzing local accounts of the origins of the industry in Tekit after the demise of henequen and by situating these local accounts within the wider contexts of the institutional impulse to develop textile maquiladoras in Mexico and the global discourses promoting cultural tourism as a sustainable development tool.

Then I show how the production of guayaberas for tourism works in practice, by looking at different modes of sewing guayaberas for the tourism market through the everyday practices of two families at the bottom and middle steps of the production chain: Luis and Lucía's household, and the Chan's medium-sized textile workshop. Through these examples, I discuss the sacrifices, kinship contradictions, and entrapments that sewing for tourism from home has had on Tekit's inhabitants, their bodies and health, their family life, and their imaginations of the future.

What I argue here is that, as with the previous examples in this book, these transformations have caught Tekit's inhabitants in a contradictory moral regime. On the one hand, sewing for tourism is generally described as a "true, true job" in which "one is in control of labor and timetables," "benefits stay in the family," and "life unfolds as it used to be." It is "thanks to tourism" that many, such as Manuel's father, Don Ben Xool, believe "there is life in Tekit," "and that life is good *(la buena vida)* in Tekit," because it has enabled people to keep extended families together, to maintain milpas with their rituals and tempos, and to care for infants and elders as "tradition commands" *(como manda la tradición)*, while also being able to enjoy the services, commodities, and amenities reserved for urban and tourism destinations.[5] Examples of such amenities include a post office that is open seven days a week, ten *tortillerias* with active mills, eight bakeries, over seventy restaurants and bars, one hotel, a travel agency, and several internet cafés, gyms, and small clothing stores. In 2016, the town also had a day care center and three preschools—both of which are rare in inland Yucatán—three elementary schools, one secondary school, and one high school, which opened in 2007; two outpatient health centers *(centros de salud de consulta externa)* and one health center for multiple consultations *(centro de atención multiple)* that attends to an unusually large number of kids with disabilities. Sewing for tourism has enabled Tekit's inhabitants, in short, to "keep both cash and corn" without leaving home, something that for most inland indigenous communities in Yucatán is only achieved by migrating to work in the service industry in Cancún or the Riviera Maya (Re Cruz 1996).

Yet, on the other hand, sewing for tourism is both physically and mentally exhausting work. It exhausts and devours the body. It subsumes everyday rhythms to tourism and market tempos by creating a financial stickiness that urges individuals to engage in just-in-time production logics and to incur both monetary and social debt from their own homes and kin. This new financial stickiness has reorganized forms of kinship obligations and reciprocity with varying intensity according to a family's position in the production chain. Marycarmen Chan, one of the youngest textile entrepreneurs in Tekit, offers a vivid insight into these contradictions in the next sections.

"GROWING THE GUAYABERA SEED": THE RISE AND DECLINE OF MAQUILAS IN INLAND YUCATÁN

People in Tekit use a gardening metaphor to explain the origins of sewing guayaberas for tourism in their town. The story goes like this:

There was land, productive but abandoned, where the henequen seed used to bloom. Until it died. Then, many other "seeds" were planted by the government—pigs, *mezclilla* (blue jeans). But they all failed to grow. Tekit was then "abandoned" by the state. Then, one of their own, Don Ramón Alonzo, "planted a new seed" (textiles), and "with his entrepreneurial vision" *(vision emprendedora)* and "care for all" *(cuidado de todos)* that seed sprouted, flourished, and brought "the good life" *(la buena vida)* to *el pueblo*. "It all started with Don Ramón," Manuel's niece Marycarmen Chan put it in an interview, "a real local entrepreneur and businessman who cared for his own."

This story, repeated over and over again, unites Tekit's inhabitants in a single overarching narrative of local success after the henequen crisis circa the mid-1970s. It is a story of entrepreneurialism, family impulse, and community strength in a context of economic crisis and state abandonment. This narrative of success is generally compared to the fates of nearby villages, such as Sotuta de Peon, which has been depleted due to seasonal migration to Cancún, or villages like Mama, "where silence is so big that you can hear your own steps walking." In Tekit, "families stayed together."

What this local story does not tell, however, is the context of old and contemporary forms of resource and labor extraction that made this "success" possible in the first place. To understand this story, we need to zoom out of the local to the regional, national, and international scales.

Don Ramón Alonzo's planting of the "guayabera seed" did not happen in a void. It took place in a ground that had been readied by social injustice and misery (Rubio Herrera 2017, 80). This is a memory that still lives on for many of the town's elders, like Don Ramón himself and Don Ben Xool, Manuel's father. Like most children of their generation, Don Ben and Don Ramón were Maya indigenous peasants who started working as henequen peones when they were around twelve years old. They worked for Hacienda Xmuyil, a few miles away from Tekit. With other workers from Tekit and neighboring villages, they lined up at two in the morning waiting for a truck to pick them up. They cut henequen spear-spine leaves *(pencas)* and were driven back once the sun "was too hot to work," around midday. Then they tended the milpa and the fields *(el monte)*. The work, Don Ben recalls, "was slaving" *(esclavo)*.

Then, in 1960, after almost a century of operation, Hacienda Xmuyil closed its doors after nylon was introduced in the global market. "We knew the hacienda was dead," Don Ramón recounts, "because one day they stopped coming to pick us up to go to work." At almost ninety-eight years old, his imperfect memory is plagued by geographical jumps and lacunae, and punctuated by imprecise but vivid moments in his trajectory of learning how to sew. In his accounts, he situates the need to support his newly created family as the leading cause for his migration to Mérida once the henequen collapsed. As he recalls it, his involvement in the city's textile business and his encounter with guayaberas were the results of a combination of fate, family trust, and financial support from his wife's kin.

Initially, Don Ramón was hired "under the table" by an established guayabera house in Mérida that specialized in tailor-made designs. He worked there for eight years, first cleaning, then as a delivery boy carrying clothes and threads from stores to factories. He learned to sew in the evenings with the help of Xito, his wife's cousin, who also worked at the factory. It was then that he landed a formal job at the factory. But his earnings were not enough, and the workdays were strenuous. "I did not see my kids or my wife," Don Ramón remembers, "It was not a good life."

Encouraged by Xito, he bought a discarded sewing machine from the factory's stock and brought it home. After work, he practiced sewing with the factory's leftover pieces. With some capital earned from small-scale sales of guayaberas in Mérida's markets, and with an agreement in place with the Abraham family's stores—owned by a consolidated merchant Lebanese family in Yucatán—he borrowed his first roll of cloth and he taught his wife to sew.

In 1965, he opened his own textile sweatshop or workshop *(taller)* in Mérida. He needed workers, so he brought six young people from Tekit, who were jobless after the henequen hacienda closed, to work for him in exchange for shelter and food. He kept working at the textile factory while Violeta, his wife, ran the workshop from home, cooking, attending to workers, and dispatching orders. They stayed in Mérida until 1972 when electricity came to Tekit and the highway connecting Mérida to Tekit was constructed. Moved by their workers' demands to go back "home" and their "too stressful" urban family life in Mérida, it was then that the Alonzo-Worbis family moved their textile workshop to Tekit. And they have stayed ever since, expanding the family business.

Although the labor conditions working in textiles were not much better in Tekit than in Mérida, the commute was shorter, and the work seemed less arduous. As Don Ben put it to me one day, the work in textile factories was much better than the work of henequen times, "since it did not mean working under the sun but under a fan." Others, like Don Luis Chan and Don Santos describe the work as "good work," since it was done "seated" and enabled people "access [*agarrar*] to labor," engaging "freely" as wage workers rather than as "slaves" as they had when they worked as peones for the hacienda (see Rubio Herrera 2017). Importantly, for many, domestic maquila textile labor enabled them to keep their traditional livelihoods: the milpa was kept alive and extended families stayed together.

Don Ramón's story must be understood within the context of Mexico's state-led attempt to consolidate the textile industry as a model for development through import substitution industrialization in the 1970s. Maquiladoras, along with seasonal migration to tourist Cancún, became the most widespread labor alternatives for farming and agriculture [*a trabajar el campo*] in Yucatán during the late 1970s. However, by the end of that decade, Tekit's inhabitants had learned from their neighbors in Sotuta, one of the largest migrant nodes in inland Yucatán, about the miseries that those migrating to Cancún suffered. In 1976 the opening of the Cantarell Oil Complex offshore of the Bay of Campeche and the ongoing efforts of the regional government to move inland populations to the Gulf of Mexico coast for fishing, as I discuss in chapter 2, created more pressure to migrate, though neither of these were options for many in Tekit, whose people described themselves as "people of the land and fearful of the sea."[6]

By the mid-1980s, therefore, the henequen zone in inland Yucatán was already a landscape primed for extraction, as its resilient workforce was ready to absorb the labor requirements of the first Mexican maquiladoras. Aided by the neoliberal gospel spreading throughout Latin America, maquiladoras in inland Yucatán followed modernization strategies that were part of the ideals of national growth, and which reflected the objective of "rationalizing the agro-export monoculture production and promoting the economic diversification of the state of Yucatán" (Torres 2003). In this decade, small textile workshops like Don Ramón's received state support, and the *maquilization* of inland Yucatán started in earnest.[7]

In 1985, Jabin opened its doors in Tekit. A factory that made casual clothing for export to the United States, it was the first textile maquiladora in Yucatán. Owned by Renato and Mario Menéndez, who also owned the popular newspaper *Por Esto!*, Jabin started with ten workers who were native to Tekit. By the mid-1990s, it employed half of the town's inhabitants. Many in Tekit remember the factory as the first air-conditioned building in town and the first enterprise that, after the demise of henequen, offered "real jobs." Some of its former workers, like Don Santos, Conception, and Lucía, who worked for Jabin as a shop-floor manager, seamstress, and ironer, respectively, referred to the textile factory as a "political project of the PRI," with close connections to Victor Cervera Pacheco, governor of Yucatán (1984–88 and 1995–2001).

According to their accounts, labor and production in Jabin followed a "Japanese model." Production was labor-intensive and standardized, and it featured part-time temporary jobs, a clear-cut gender division of labor, and no rotation in task assignments.[8] Don Santos and Conception recalled that foreign managers observed strict control of workers, and they hired more workers than necessary, as a strategy to pressure all workers to work efficiently and arrive on time, or risk being replaced. "We [Jabin] exported to the USA and a Japanese manager came to explain how to make more work," Santos explained. "He moved us from lines into modules where six or seven people worked. We were doing 150 garments a day and had a total of twelve modules. Work was hard and productive goals were not always met. There was retaliation and also bonuses for workers." Concepcion elaborated that "the engineers would come—they were from outside and supervised all the work. They told me how much to pay according to the bonuses and sanctions. People came late to work. They did not show up and they were fired. Then someone else would come and take his/her job."

In 1992, the state's Programa de Desarrollo Regional de la Zona Henequenera provided the legal framework for moving all maquiladoras to the most impoverished rural communities in Yucatán's henequen zone, where Tekit was located. The objective was to generate jobs, in order to counteract the massive migration underway to urban areas and combat extreme poverty (Castilla Ramos and Torres 2013). The relocation was also a direct response to the Mexican state's preference for export-oriented manufacturing as a way to revitalize rural areas and reincorporate indigenous populations to wage labor around the country.[9] It was at this point that Jabin quadrupled the number of workers in its textile maquiladora.

However, Jabin's buoyancy did not last for long. The maquiladora officially closed its doors in 1998, although it continued to make clothes for export by irregularly subcontracting with workers who sewed from home until 2000, when Jabin stopped all production. According to Don Santos, NAFTA forced Jabin to close. And he was right. In response to the United States, Mexico, and Canada signing NAFTA in 1994, textile maquiladoras in Mexico shifted to "in bond" production, which meant that they would focus on creating products almost exclusively for the United States and Canada at the expense of national and regional ones.[10] Jabin, like many other medium and small textile factories in Mexico, began to lay off workers on a daily basis. They could not compete with the large maquilas on the US-Mexico northern border, which centralized production for export at much cheaper costs. "There was no capital," Conception remembered, "its owners just dismissed us.... Work stopped coming."

Using an irregular semi-maquila setting to manufacture products at home—a practice that was often kept clandestine in order to avoid labor and health regulations—and sell the goods in regional open-air markets, or *tianguis*, held in urban and tourist centers became a way to make ends meet and to absorb the labor forces and resources that became redundant after NAFTA. While in other parts of Mexico this reorientation from export production to national and regional production did not entirely work, in the Yucatán Peninsula, planned state-led tourism development on the coasts and the ongoing impulse to promote cultural tourism inland paved the way for its success.[11]

Crucial here was the reorientation of the tourist policies formulated by the UN World Tourism Organization (UNWTO), which encouraged a move away from the "sea, sand, and sun" model—also referred to as the 3 S's—toward alternative or responsible forms of travel. By the end of the 1990s, the UNWTO was looking to support a new tourism model based on a novel trend: that of the 4 H's: "history, heritage, handicrafts, and habitat" (Smith 1996). As one of the most indebted countries in Latin America at that time, Mexico was eager to listen. It did so first through the implementation of ecotourism as a sustainable development strategy in natural protected areas along the Gulf of Mexico coast (chapter 2) and the promotion of cultural tourism in archeological sites and restored haciendas as community development experiments (chapter 3). These new tourist stages required not only the in situ transformations that I explore in the preceding chapters, but also the production of portable, "authentic" Maya cultural objects that could serve as symbols and mementos of Mexican heritage in the global market. This is when indigenous arts and crafts like hammocks, and traditional garments such as women's *huipils*, and above all, guayaberas entered the tourist popular imaginary of Yucatán in the world.[12]

"MADE IN YUCATÁN": THE MAKING OF A SANITIZED INDIGENOUS TRADITION

Guayaberas were introduced in Yucatán at the end of the nineteenth century following the henequen hacendados' frequent trips to Cuba and the United

States. They soon became symbols of fashion, power, and prestige linked to the hacendados' international mobility and agricultural and cultural capital. During the 1970s, President Luis Echeverría Álvarez (1970–76) popularized the garment in the rest of Mexico and beyond; as Cancún's main advocate, he wore them during official trips and public appearances. The garment has since become ubiquitous as professional attire among state officials, politicians, and businessmen, as a "wedding shirt," and as an everyday uniform worn by tourist workers.

Today, the guayabera is routinely featured in official tourism marketing campaigns as a "typical" and "locally produced" symbol of "a vanishing culture" that is still "alive" inland (en el interior). These tourist representations feed on and contribute to portrayals of inland Yucatán that fix it as the space for Maya heritage and colonial history, where indigenous Yucatec Maya people are represented as brown bodies bound to agricultural lifestyles and to an anachronistic, pre-Columbian past materialized in folk traditions and archeological ruins. In this sense the Yucatán becomes a distant yet proximate space that tourists can access by taking part in daily prepackaged "cultural" excursions. A popular state tourist slogan from the 1990s, "Yucatán es la Puerta al Mundo Maya y Mérida es la Capital Mundial de la guayabera" (Yucatán is the door to the Mayan world and Mérida is the guayabera capital of the world), informed the state tourism campaign of 2012, "Así es la Guayabera, así es Yucatán" (This is the guayabera, this is Yucatán), led, not by chance, by the Alonzo-Worbis family from Tekit. Their marketing efforts culminated that same year when March 21 was declared International Guayabera Day.

The declaration of an international day for guayaberas is far from tangential in the account of Tekit's transformation into a Mexican desakota. It is in fact one of the multiscalar, institutional, orchestrated efforts to strengthen global tourist circuits to Mexico by connecting Cancún with Mérida, as the "cultural capital of Yucatán."

Textile production in Tekit has directly benefited from this global turn to cultural tourism and the state-led strategy to promote the guayabera as a cultural souvenir. A key player in this process has been Yucatán's delegation to the Cámara Nacional de la Industria del Vestido (CANAIVE), led by Renan Worbis Meyers, Don Alonzo's nephew and the owner of Las Margaritas, the largest factory for guayaberas in Tekit. CANAIVE is a public institution in charge of promoting the region's textile industry at national and international levels and it is responsible for marketing guayaberas with that patina of cultural authenticity for tourist audiences. One of CANAIVE's major struggles in recent years has been to minimize foreign competition with the region's textiles (mostly from China). To do so, they have focused on professionalizing sewing and absorbing the market for guayabera tourism consumption by branding Mérida as the "guayabera capital of the world." One of the key elements in this process is a proposed certification label for guayaberas, "Manufacture 100% Yucatecan with materials of the highest quality," which would validate the clothing's authenticity.

To obtain a certification seal, Worbis Meyers explained in an interview with me in the air-conditioned office of his maquiladora, guayaberas would have to be "made by a legally established company," and the "design [would have to] meet the standards of the typical guayabera or be inspired by it." Although the certification label has yet to be created, the effort has spurred the state-sponsored presence of the garment in cultural events like regional, national, and international fairs. Word of the garment certification has also created fellowships and labor workshops in the region to train workers in what they consider appropriate traditional designs—which are generally only those envisioned by the Alonzo-Worbis kin. CANAIVE is also crafting a network and directory of local businesses that meet the criteria for the certification seal, and is encouraging medium-sized textile workshops in Tekit to join efforts to make Mérida the capital of the guayabera by promising both financial assistance and marketing for their garments and designs. However, only twenty-nine workshops out of the thousands of living-room households involved in sewing for tourism in Tekit are formally associated with CANAIVE. In my fieldwork, only eight of these said that they had benefited from the initiative so far. Many of these small proprietors, like Marycarmen Chan, while they celebrate the declaration of an international guayabera day, believe the certification seal is a step toward consolidating the Alonzo-Worbis family monopoly on tourist demand for the garment, and they are not willing to support the certification seal as it is.

The guayabera international day and the certification seal are part of a bigger national and state-led tourist project, the so-called Train Maya, which I discuss in the conclusion of this book. The Train Maya is an ambitious mega-infrastructural tourism project that aims to connect Quintana Roo, Yucatán, Campeche, Chiapas, and Tabasco through their "Maya cultural roots." In the Yucatán Peninsula, the Train Maya is a direct effort to "alleviate the saturated tourist route Cancún-Riviera Maya-Chichén Itzá-Xcaret" by moving tourists to alternative cultural destinations.[13] Not surprisingly, Worbis Meyers and CANAIVE have been among its most enthusiastic advocates. They have campaigned to revitalize the old henequen infrastructure in order to connect Cancún not just to Chichén Itzá but also to Valladolid and Mérida. In CANAIVE's plans, there is a stop at the outskirts of Tekit where tourists can buy guayaberas that have the certification seal. With this purpose in mind, and with the support of the state and local governments, Worbis Meyers has started to plan for a tourist *parador* to house vendors from Tekit. CANAIVE also plans to petition UNESCO to recognize the guayabera as a protected form of traditional craftsmanship.

Branding Mérida as the guayabera capital of the world veils the fact that most of these garments are in fact made in Tekit through a clandestine and pulverized domestic maquila system of production. In what follows, I elaborate on the labor, social, and kinship frictions that shape and sustain this system of domestic maquila production of guayaberas for tourism consumption and how it has completely, and rather organically, re-spatialized Tekit.

MAKING GUAYABERAS, INCURRING DEBT AND STRAINED KINSHIP RELATIONS

Guayaberas are the epicenter of contemporary social life in Tekit. They pervade conversations and are omnipresent in living rooms. Once there is "an order" *(encargo)* for guayaberas, people, objects, labor, and capital are mobilized inside and outside the town's boundaries. The garment's backs, fronts, and sleeves, organized in separate bundles of fabric, circulate in motor- and pedal-powered bikes, vans, and cars from house to house. They are protected from the dirt and dust of unpaved streets by large black plastic trash bags or fabric sacks. Imported fabrics, threads, hangers, and plastic covers from Costa Rica, the United States, Ireland, and China are either shipped to Tekit through the postal service or international carriers like UPS, DHL, or FedEx or bought in Mérida in national and multinational retail stores like San Francisco de Asís or Walmart.

There are many tasks involved in the production of a single guayabera. They do not generally happen in the same place nor are they performed by the same hands. Since Jabin closed its doors and Don Ramón started to distribute garments for assembly in town, guayaberas are made in a fragmented system of production in which parts of a single garment circulate across different family households (the dots and triangles in map 5), which function as domestic enterprises.[14] In each household, members specialize in

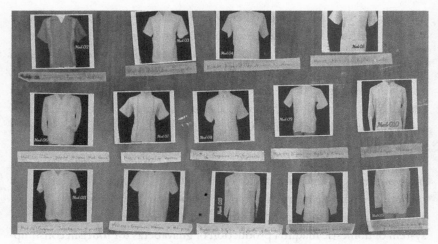

FIGURE 17. Models for finished guayaberas in a medium-sized workshop, Tekit, 2015. Photo by author.

particular production steps: drawing the patterns, cutting, sewing backs and fronts, unraveling, sewing bottoms, attaching necks and pockets, embroidering, ironing, packaging, and/or distributing. The production follows a gendered labor specialization. Men are normally involved in cutting, sewing the pieces together, and embroidering, while women do the unraveling, sew the buttons, and iron. Both men and women care for and maintain the sewing machines and equipment; although a range of mechanics from Mérida visit Tekit regularly, they are called in only when there are major malfunctions.

Spread all over town, the guayabera business is organized around a just-in-time system of production in which every house is a site of production. Also, kinship dictates what kind of labor takes places across and in each household. Crucially, participating (and moving up) in this system requires investing in increasingly expensive machinery—like sewing machines or industrial irons. These machines cost anywhere from four thousand to fifty thousand Mexican pesos, depending on if they are secondhand or thirdhand machines and if they can accomplish one or more tasks. To access these means of production, extended families become indebted. They participate in *tandas,* or solidarity and trust networks *(círculos de confianza).*[15] When kinship ties are broken, households ask for credit from financial institutions like Elektra, from Banco Azteca. These *tandas* provide families with enough liquidity to rent machines per hour, weekly, or to buy them. Generally speaking, the more debt a family has, the more machines, hands, and diversification of specialized knowledge it has. As the expertise required to operate these machines becomes more spatially concentrated, households are able to fill orders more quickly because their members are able to complete more of the guayabera production tasks, making their business more efficient.

One morning, as I sat in Marycarmen's office while she went over the bills for her family guayabera business, she said, "You know, one is ultimately stuck to what your machines can do." Marycarmen was referring to not only technologies, but also the kind of sticky attachments that reconfigure kinship and family sociality and that reconfigure family members as subjects of social, moral, and financial debt. As she explained:

> 'Doing maquila,' for everybody here, means to put together the garment, all together or just one part.... We say that the maquila is pulverized because everyone does part of the process at their homes.... Some can do it all, others can only do one part and then they bring the rest to a workshop to complete.... It all depends on the capital a family has ... but most people here in Tekit can only do assembling *(hacer el armado)* because they only have the capital for a *cerradora*.... This is why bits and pieces of the same garment are moving from one place to another.... If you want your business to prosper you have to get along with your family so you can get together the capital.

During fieldwork I learned that people in Tekit recognize different "forms of 'doing maquila,'" or sewing guayaberas for tourism, depending on where the sewing takes place, the kind of kin relationships among the workers, and the quality of the garments produced. Attending to location, for example, inhabitants recognize three different ways of making guayaberas or as they say, of "doing maquila" *(hacer maquila)* or "working the maquila" ("trabajar la maquila"). The first is to sew in one's living room *(en la sala)*, like Luis and Lucía, in which case only the nuclear family and consanguineous kin participate in the activity. This is perceived as a "decent" and "respectable" way to "do maquila," but it is also conceived as being "risky" and "experienced with suffering" *(sufrido)*, because it is physically demanding labor that is dependent on middlemen delivering garments.

The second form of "doing maquila" is to sew in a family workshop like that of Marycarmen Chan. Here, nuclear and extended, consanguineous and ritual (godparents and godchildren) kin work alongside others to whom they are related either through political or religious affiliations or as fictive kin. This is the most common way to do maquila in Tekit and the one perceived as the way to "a family's prosperity."

FIGURE 18. Morning shift in a medium-sized workshop, Tekit, 2015. Photo by author.

FIGURE 19. Sewing at home, Tekit, 2015. Photo by author.

The third modality is to sew in a place like Las Margaritas, which is considered to be "a proper maquiladora." This is the least desirable option, since workers are monitored and disciplined. The majority of the factory's shop-floor workers are young, "still without responsibilities" (i.e., not married), widows, and migrants from other towns.

People in Tekit also recognize three different ways of working the garment depending on its quality. The first one is to create high-quality guayaberas or "presidential" guayaberas. There are only two family workshops involved in this high-end market. One is Diego Avila, who owns a medium-sized family factory, employs nine workers, and works for established houses in Mérida like Gil Candila, as well as regional and national elites. These workshops do not sew at home, but in so-called design workshops. They import all their fabrics and travel to meet their clients at their houses. The Avila family is highly regarded in Tekit and its members are considered as "the real handcrafters" of guayaberas that tourism promotions talk about. The second way to work guayaberas, and the most common in Tekit, is to produce garments of medium quality, mostly for the tourism and hospitality industries as souvenirs or as uniforms for service workers. Medium-quality guayabera production is done both in medium-sized workshops like the Chans' and in "living rooms." The third modality is to produce poor-quality guayaberas out of textile leftovers and to peddle them in Mérida's markets and at local fairs. This third type of work is not always talked about, and is a practice relegated to the most marginalized families in town.

Debt and kinship are required not only to get into the production of the guayabera but also to remain in it. Keeping the garment in circulation requires circuits of social and economic debt that have spontaneously reorganized Tekit around novel social hierarchies and *kinship frictions*. I use the phrase kinship frictions here with two intentions in mind. First, to highlight the familial discords that occur in any family-led business. And second, to emphasize the embeddedness of these different ways of working the garment in larger patterns of global, regional, and local mediations informed by tourism development (Tsing 2005). These discords and embedded mediations are not contingent. Kinship frictions are an expression of historical contradictions that result from the unfolding dialectical oppositions (between the rural and the urban, the economic and the social, hacendados and peones, men and women) that inform the creation of these workshops in the first place. Understanding them in and from their ethnographic specificities is a condition for understanding the blurring between the productive and the reproductive spheres that animate capitalism.[16]

In tourism's re-spatialization of Tekit as a neither urban nor rural space, that is, as a desakota, those individuals with weaker or smaller kinship networks—or with broken ones—are more prone to liquidity constraints and therefore more likely to remain in the lowest steps of the production chain. Those with extended families and households that are capable of pooling labor and resources, like the Chans or the Alonzo-Worbis family, are more likely to perform better. In all cases, financial debt and a family's level of labor efficiency reconfigure internal forms of kinship obligations, dependencies, and reciprocities—as well as gender ideologies

In what follows, I zoom in on two families' histories and labor routines: Luis and Lucía's living room and the Chans' medium-sized workshop. In their two ways of sewing for tourism, these families and the organization of their domestic enterprises provide illustrative examples of the paradoxes of tourism and how it reconfigures socio-cultural, familial, and spatial life in the region.

Luis and Lucía's Living Room

Sewing for tourism at home in Tekit has many similarities to the domestic factories or "living room factories" that Hsiung (1996) describes in her analysis of satellite factories in Taiwan, in which married women create wooden jewelry boxes for export in their front yards and living rooms. These women, like domestic sewing workers in Tekit, are part of the larger contingent of "non-craft-based flexible workers" typical of the global garment industry of the last decades (Rothstein 2007). It is important to note that in Tekit both men and women from the same nuclear family work together in one-room houses. This is the case with Luis and Lucía's household.

After many years of selling fish "under the counter" in a stall in Mérida's downtown market, Luis, a native of Tekit, decided in 1998 that it was time to learn how to sew. After learning that Jabin was distributing guayaberas to be produced from home (maquiladas), for three months Luis observed the workers in the small workshop of a close friend who had been working for Jabin's factory. After this time, he was allowed to do the smallest and simplest tasks, such as sticking necks into the main garment, sewing buttonholes, or attaching buttons and pockets. In six months, as he recalls, "I was already able to use the machine and assemble a complete piece." He then worked at the workshop as an *armador* (garment assembler) for eight years.

There he met and married Lucía, who was also working there, ironing completed pieces. But Luis did not like the small factory: the "pay was not good" and he could "not spend time at home." He quit his job as an assembler and worked at his great-uncle's medium-sized factory for two years with eighteen other workers native to Tekit. They sewed for Los Angeles Rams NFL Cotton Fabrics, an American label linked to a sports team and well known in Tekit. Luis recalls the labor routines there as similar to those in the smaller workshop but "more structured" and "more stressful."

That workshop closed due to some of its workers becoming unable to pay family *tandas* on time. As a consequence, many families lost their sewing machines and had to migrate to find work in construction or to start working at Las Margaritas. Some of the workers, among them Luis's great-uncle, got into deep financial debt and news of the failure of the workshop fueled mistrust that kept Luis from being able to join other *tandas* in town. During those years, Lucía had kept ironing at another small workshop, but was eventually laid off due to her health-related absences. "I could not breathe properly," she recalled, sitting on her house's porch one day. "I had asthma and even brought a doctor's note from Mérida, but they did not do accommodations. . . . I was not family, after all." After being laid off, she worked sporadically at a friend's house, unraveling *(deshilado)* and ironing. But her health was weakening and she and her friend hardly made more than eight hundred Mexican pesos in a week (US$43).

With the skills to complete a garment on his own, Luis entered a family *tanda* with his brother's wife's family to buy a secondhand flatbed machine from the workshop he had worked for in 1998. "They were renovating their machineries and put some on sale. . . . I got a [good] price because I was in good-standing relations with the people I worked for and they sold it to me for two thousand pesos." The machine allowed him to put together pockets *(bibos)* and sleeves, and close the backs and fronts of guayaberas and uniform trousers. Since then, Luis says, he has been an assembler: "to assemble is the only part I can do with the capital and the machine that I can afford." Their purchase of the machine allowed Lucía to quit working for others and spend more time with him while at the same time "still make some money." By participating in another *tanda* with Lucía's family, they were able to buy a second machine. In 2006, coinciding with the federal and regional push for guayaberas as a distinctive cultural symbol of Yucatán and Maya heritage, Lucía started to sew from home. They now both work from home on their own and define themselves as *independientes* (autonomous/independent workers).

Luis and Lucía have mixed feelings about becoming *independientes*. On the one hand, they see it as progress toward "a good life," an achievement that has freed them from unfair labor conditions imposed by others. Being an *independiente* has also helped Lucía to recover her health, as well as her place in the house according to valued Maya household and marriage ideologies. But on the other hand, they acknowledge that being *independientes* in the guayabera business comes, as Luis put it many times in our conversations, "with big sacrifices." They talk about these sacrifices in terms of daily stress, Luis's deteriorating health, and the unpredictability of getting orders *(encargos)* or being paid for their work.

Part of this unpredictability has to do with broken family ties that impede their entry into the circuit of investment and debt required to participate and move up in the production system. Luis and Lucía's parents both passed away when they were young. Luis has a brother with whom he used to pool *encargos,* but this ended when his brother married and entered his wife's larger sewing networks. As a result, Luis and Lucía heavily depend on Mérida's textile factories' surplus production, which itself depends on national and international orders for the garment, which fluctuate depending on the volatility of the fashion industry and the stability of financial markets. Their household relies on the only surviving consanguineous kin line, which is provided by Lucía's uncle, Don Santos, a middleman who brings them orders to complete from Mérida. However, relying on a middleman is risky and volatile. It regularly results in late payments and sometimes in no payments at all. But, as Lucía put it one afternoon as she was doing dishes after lunch, "being kin [*parientes*] bonds us to my uncle. . . . He might not pay once because maybe they do not pay him but overall he brings work to do and we have to accept work [*agarrar*] from him to show trust [*confianza*], so he thinks about us when there is work to do."

These financialized kinship ties work as forms of entrapments that tie Luis and Lucía's household and its daily routines to physical territory under precarious and vulnerable conditions beyond their control. And yet, as they assert, their living conditions are "much better than those of migrants" because, despite its shortcomings, "sewing for tourism" has at least allowed them to have a relatively "easy and good life" in a context of economic crisis and frequent migration.

In 2008, when I first met them, Luis and Lucía lived in a remodeled Maya house with a thatched roof and a cement floor. The hut had wooden doors with metal bars. They had a queen bed that was immaculately covered with a white embroidered quilt, two matching side-tables, and a matching wooden wardrobe with a full mirror on one of its doors. There was a small TV with speakers on its own cabinet. The house had several power outlets. Their two flatbed Singer sewing machines sat below a window with metal bars right in front of their bed.

Each time I have visited them over last six years, the room has been arranged in the same way with the same furniture. While sewing from their living room has not enabled them to renovate their house or buy new furniture, it has enabled them to stay put in their home with their belongings and to avoid migration. It has also enabled them to spend time together—and this time, and health, are what they needed, they say, to conceive, after fifteen years of marriage, their first and only child, Jesús, who was born, healthy and big, in 2017.

With a newborn in the house, sewing dynamics have changed slightly. Lucía does all the household chores (washing, cooking, cleaning) and cares for the baby, while Luis sews full time, sometimes twelve or more hours a day. When there is nothing to sew, he tends to the child, their chickens, and the backyard patio where they grow vegetables to consume. They sew their own clothes. They hardly buy processed foods, except for baby formula, or Coke or Sprite when the heat is extreme. When Don Santos brings them a large order, they both sew day and night. In those periods, "the house is not cleaned," "meals are skipped," and baby Jesús stays with Sofia, their neighbor. So far, Sofia has been able to take care of the baby at these times, since her guayabera orders have not coincided with theirs, but Lucía thinks about this often. If Sofia has an "order" at the same time that they do, then, she says with resignation, "we will have to save money and put him in the daycare." Since Jesús's birth, labor routines have become stressful especially given the absence of extended family support. And this stress has fueled health complications.

During my last visit, Luis's eyes were watery and redder than usual. I asked about his vision and he told me he has cataracts and was about to receive treatment in a private eye clinic in Mérida, "so I do not go entirely blind." Cataracts are common in Tekit: sewing burns the eyes. Like many in Tekit, Luis planned a visit to Spark Therapeutics—a US organization that recently opened a franchise in Mérida under the name Mejora Vision MD—whose clientele mostly includes people from Tekit with large retinal dystrophies.

Since 2018, Luis has also had gastrointestinal distress. In a telephone conversation, Luis told me that things were "not looking good" and that he had visited the doctor because his stomach pains were constant. The money they had gathered (*juntado*) for the optometrist they instead used for a colonoscopy at Mérida's Centro de Especialidades, which revealed that he had a large malignant tumor.

Luis and Lucía represent an extreme case of vulnerability, one that speaks to the stickiness and predatory nature of tourism even when it happens somewhere else, away from the tourist front stages. Their case reveals how families who are not able to collectivize debt as fast as demands for the garment might require are subjected to a triple exploitation: the one resulting from tourism demands, the one established by regional maquiladoras, and the one exercised by their kinship-related limitations on participating fully in the guayabera business.

And yet, Luis and Lucía's living room labor dynamics are also representative of the ambivalent nature of tourism's contemporary orderings of space and social life. Both find that sewing at home has brought them "peace." It has enabled a desirable "quiet life" and the chance to attend to their backyard economy and subsist without needing to migrate. It has also enabled them to imagine a future that, however unrealistic, gives sense to their struggle. One day, back in 2012 and dreaming aloud, Luis told me that if someday they earned enough to save "big money," they would build a second room and a gas kitchen. Then they would buy one more chicken and raise at least two guinea pigs. For now, they celebrate that, day to day, Don Santos trusts them enough to continue to bring them *encargos* to complete.

The Chans' Family Workshop: Entrepreneurial Extended Kin

The Chans' family workshop is representative of medium-sized family workshops in Tekit that are similar in organization to the "sewing sweatshops" of the early 1970s in Mexico and other Latin American countries.[17] Medium-sized family workshops in Tekit employ between five and twelve workers on the shop floor, and they also subcontract living rooms to complete their orders. The majority of these workshops started as living room factories, like Luis and Lucía's, and were aided in their consolidation by state promotion of the guayabera as a cultural souvenir and heritage expression of a touristified Maya-ness in the late 1990s and 2000s.

Most of the families I interviewed in 2008 and 2012 who were organized into medium-sized workshops produced, per workshop, between two hundred and one thousand garments weekly. Workshops have regular timetables (from eight in the morning to six in the evening with a lunch break at noon of an hour and a half) and unlike living room factories, they are regulated by Mexican labor law. The Chans, for example, pay taxes on revenues as well as shares on workers' wages and machines, and their factory needs to meet national standards for sanitation and health. Textile workshops generally respect the minimum wage for those on the shop floor, although they regularly base their hiring on consanguineous and fictive kinship obligations.

Textile workshops like the Chans' are dependent on tourism's seasonality. They experience intense work peaks in July and December and sharp decreases in May and June, with a slight uptick in September and October. Beach destinations like Cancún and Puerto Vallarta, as well as cultural destinations such as Oaxaca and Veracruz, are leading distribution centers for the products of these workshops.

As already noted, many in Tekit perceive working in a family-run workshop as the main path toward a "family's prosperity" and "the good life." Many believe this prosperity is linked to the "entrepreneurial" dispositions of men such as Don Ramón Alonzo, who decades ago had the "courage to travel" outside of town in search of clients and tourist markets. This is also what Don Luis Chan, the head of the family, did. In one of our encounters, Marycarmen, his daughter, recounted their family's early stages as follows:

> We always worked as a family. We started working at my house sewing trousers, then my father started his visits in Cancún and found his clients.... In the earlier days, we had all the machines, the table for cutting, everything in the kitchen. When the workers left, my sister and I swept the floors, cleaned all around and put the tables and machines away to hang our hammocks to sleep. Every day was the same. Working, cleaning the kitchen.... We mostly did trousers,... uniforms and casual garments,... but sewing these pieces was what led us to the guayabera once these were in demand in Cancún.... Jeans were on the market and our selling went really down in 2007 so we could not compete and we had to look for other options to stay on the market. Tourism saved us.... I started doing *filipinas* [casual shirts] ... and then only guayaberas [formal shirts].... Now we mostly produce guayaberas.... My father and brothers distribute and I and one of my sisters are in charge of overseeing production in the *taller* ... while my father is traveling to Cancún.... We can now live the good life and celebrate in the fiesta because we took risks.

The Chans' guayabera business offers a good example of both the benefits and the contradictions that sewing for tourism has brought to the town. Don

Luis became a seasonal migrant to Cancún when the construction of the first hotels started. He commuted weekly to work in construction until he met the Sanchez family at a stand in Cancún's downtown Mercado 28, an open-air market catering to locals and some tourists who venture out of the Hotel Zone. Upon learning that he came from inland Yucatán, they asked him if he knew any merchants selling guayaberas. Don Luis seized the opportunity and agreed to bring them a batch of guayaberas to sell. Participating in *tandas* with his brothers and his wife's family, he pulled a batch together and since then the Chans have cooperated to enlarge the family business.

Don Luis manages the core of the family decisions and he is in charge of distribution. But Marycarmen handles production and she supervises workers. Since Marycarmen had had a "disposition to study" since she was little, Don Luis decided that she, rather than one of her two elder brothers, should be in charge of the family business. Thirty-two years old, single, and living in a room at her parents' house with the rest of the extended family, Marycarmen is referred to in her house as "the one who studies," and by her two brothers as "the boss" *(la jefa, la patrona)*. She says her father's trust in her originated in the early 2000s, when there were significant economic and technological changes as well as a higher-than-usual demand for guayaberas:

> I have been supervisor for five years.... I make all decisions.... My father started with the process of sewing. He worked for ten to fifteen years. But when technology and computers started, and we saw that most guayaberas were ordered though computers and emails, my father did not want to pursue that. He gave it to me to do because I had studied. I had studied informatics and it was all very helpful.... I could connect online and learn about who wanted guayaberas .... We started to do online orders and prospered this way.... Our stronger clients are in Cancún but also in Oaxaca and Veracruz, where they sell for tourists.

Marycarmen walks with a cell attached to her hand and a GPS device attached to her waist. She is an avid internet user and she actively promotes her family's business on Facebook. She not only supervises her two brothers but also controls much of the extended family dynamics in terms of who becomes part of the guayabera family business and how. The way she does this is by collectivizing debt. As she explains, her family has been able to move up in the guayabera business by investing as a family, through debt, in the increasingly expensive machinery needed to perform all the tasks required to complete a single garment. During our conversations,

Marycarmen further explained the interconnections between kinship and debt by using a reciprocity principle based on trust, solidarity, and blood,

> You can't trust someone that is not your kin, that is not your blood . . . because when you employ your kin you know they will never stop paying. They want work and if they are employed with me and they know I pay them, they can't be late in their payments. . . . I know if they are struggling and help them if they can't pay, changing the order of who needs to do the monthly payment, but since they work for me we all get along. . . . It is in our mutual interest.

Like other medium-sized workshops, Marycarmen's workshop is in a building of its own that the family self-constructed in 2008. The building has three rooms and an office that also functions as a small warehouse of sorts. The place is only ten minutes away from the home of Doña Ucha, her mother, where the extended family live.

During the past eleven years, the Chans' workshop has employed ten workers, most of them young and married and tied to Marycarmen by kinship. In the last six years, the Chans have developed three labels (Marcel, Chan, and MaryCar) and they own all their means of production, including eight machines and two irons. With this machinery, and hiring a cutter on demand, the workshop is able to complete in one location all the tasks required to create a single guayabera: cutting the cloth, putting the pieces together, making holes, sewing buttons, ironing, labeling, packaging, and distributing.

When orders back up or when they are larger than what the workshop can handle, Marycarmen distributes work to different households in the town, all extended kin, which "do maquila" for her. Using this scattered and subcontracted system of domestic production, she is able to irregularly employ an additional ten families. She estimates that with these arrangements, she is able to produce well over four hundred guayaberas weekly. Lately, they have diversified their production to sew uniform trousers for schools, hospitals, and hotels. In 2016, she estimated that while the bulk of their income came from guayabera production and distribution, they were also making over one thousand uniform trousers weekly and selling them to Cancún's warehouses, which in turn sold them to institutional buyers, such as hotels, hospitals, schools, and the government.

To meet production, Marycarmen also loans money to her extended kin for investments in machinery. These loans are based on an assumption of reciprocity, which ensures that her orders will be dispatched on time, and the clients will be satisfied. As she put it in an interview with me: "I don't mind if they can't pay for the machine up front. I lend it to them, and they can *agarrar* work from others when they need it, but when I have an order and I need them, then they need to do my work first."

These practices—pooling resources and maintaining family reciprocity—also allow Marycarmen to both monitor and control those working for her from their homes and to be physically proximate in case they need help with or further instructions about the subcontracted work orders.

The households in the Chan network operate like satellites organized by the transnational demand of the garment. With these provisional, under-the-counter, and more flexible agreements, the Chan family is able to contain competition, even among their own kin. Stuck together through financial debt, extended family members know that they must be 100 percent responsive to Marycarmen, or else they risk compromising the stability of the extended family business and hence, the promise of regular labor.

Sewing for tourism has in this case strengthened intrafamilial cooperation but it has also generated new contradictions. Medium-sized factories are subjected to internal contradictions, since the person who sews is at the same time a worker with a wage salary and also a *patron*, owner of the factory and machines.[18] Among the Chans, there are additional contradictions since Marycarmen is a single woman who manages youngsters, elders, men, and women from her kin, a practice that contradicts traditional indigenous Maya kinship and gender ideologies.

Despite Marycarmen's role as the manager of the family business in Tekit, her father does not allow her to travel alone to Cancún or Veracruz. These places are still considered "dangerous places," "cities of vice," and "not for decent women." Marycarmen relies on her brothers to "manage her business" in terms of the interactions with clients. The reason for this is that since the Alonzos started the guayabera business in Tekit, "sewing" has generally been conceived as a man's work, and has contributed to redefining contemporary indigenous masculinity in town.[19] For Marycarmen, this creates both personal and professional difficulties. As she explained to me, for small- and medium-sized workshops like theirs, which do not have the political connections of bigger workshops, the guayabera business is largely dependent on personal and face-to-face relations. The fact that she is unable to make face-to-face contact with some clients in Cancún, she says, "slows down production." Clients, she says, "want to trust, but in Cancún, no one trusts each other," and less so when you talk to one person over the phone but engage with someone else in person.

Marycarmen points to other difficulties of being a woman in charge of others in a male-dominated labor environment. As one example, she cites how difficult it is to give orders to elders. She also often disagrees with her brothers about when or what machinery to buy. Investing in new technology and machinery has become a symbol of social distinction and prestige in Tekit, and Marycarmen generally needs to mediate between her brothers' ambitions and the realities of a business that does not easily accommodate new technologies. Her case stands in contrast with the majority of workshops in Tekit, in which men are the decision-makers. Still, it is representative of the major internal conflicts these tourism-formed family businesses face.

The Chans, like most indigenous families in Tekit, follow patrilineal rules of descent, succession, and housing according to "old" Yucatec Maya organization (Wilk 1997). What this means in practice is that an unmarried woman like Marycarmen is not only under strict patriarchal control but also must follow the milpa cycles when making business decisions. Like most traditional Mayan families in Tekit, the Chans maintain a diversified backyard economy with chickens, turkeys, and pigs behind the house, along with citrus trees, avocados, chiles, and herbs. Cooking over an open fire rather than on a stove (even when they have one, as the Chans do) is privileged, and most women are expected to do the laundry by hand on the patio and to care for their younger siblings at home until they are around nine years old, when the unfolding of their characteristics in life, according to Maya cosmologies, is completed (Cervera Montejano 2011). Being able to wait for a younger sibling to develop his or her personality and labor fulfillments is considered part of having "a good life," and is not available to less fortunate families, like Luis and Lucía's. This waiting, the Chans say, is possible thanks to sewing for tourism from home.

Being dependent upon the milpa in a tourism-oriented economy creates additional contradictions. For the Chans, who have been able to make a decent living out of sewing for tourism and by establishing their own guayabera labels, the practices and spaces of the milpa are still ruled by the kinship organization typical of the colonial period. This is an itinerant system of production in which the agricultural practices of the members of a family are circumscribed to a specific geographical space called the *rumbo familiar,* or family location (Ortiz Yam 2013). For families like the Chans, the seasonality of the milpa dictates when, how, and who accesses sewing and wage labor, or, as happened to Manuel, Marycarmen's uncle, when, how, and who can study. As he explained to me, "My study schedules are timed with my father's milpa

. . . . I have to be here for the milpa to help him and I try to explain to my professors. I don't feel good about it but there is nothing I can change. I have to be here [in Tekit]."

This dependency on the milpa leads to increased unpredictability and deepened vulnerability, as agricultural production is entirely dependent on rainfall. In the face of climate change, work in and harvests from the milpa have become more difficult to predict and this unpredictability has contributed "to Yucatán *milperos* struggling to keep their farms alive," which, Marycarmen predicts, may ultimately lead to "making sewing and milpa probably irreconcilable" in the long term.[20]

The Chan family exemplifies the syncretism and ambivalences that tourism has created in inland Yucatán. For those families who are doing well in the guayabera business, gender roles and stereotypes have shifted to improve access to education and labor decisions, which has generated friction with traditional Maya upbringing and cosmologies. While gender ideologies persist—and there is still much to do regarding indigenous women's everyday physical and social mobility—paradoxically it has been the increased influence of the financial sector in the organization of social life, brought about by tourism, that has also created the space for some more equality within the family and in the workplace.

CONCLUSION: *LA BUENA VIDA?*

While apparently living beyond the tourism representation and reality of Yucatán as a "world to escape to," people in Tekit still are tied to the region's tourism whims and predatory and sticky logics. Sewing guayaberas has entrapped them in the vehement logic through which tourism appropriates bodies and extracts labor. It has forced urban rhythms in a historically rural space ruled by agricultural dynamics. It has subjected family and kinship relations to financial debt and bodies to health concerns and illnesses. "Sewing for tourism," Luis once put it, is "very tiring [*muy cansado*]. . . . We are vulnerable to labor abuses and the body permanently aches." As Marycarmen explained, sewing for tourism is an "uncertain" and, often, "slave business."

Workers like Luis and Lucía suffer from chronic back pains created by long hours spent bent over sewing machines. Many workers suffer from skin and pulmonary infections caused by manipulating textile garments and inhaling cotton toxins in poorly ventilated rooms. Lucía, like many other women who iron guayaberas in tropical weather, has asthma and bone pain. Early cataracts and blindness, caused by sewing under poor lightning conditions for hours on end, have become a new normal. Luis is almost blind, and he is only thirty-three years old. Don Santos, who works from his living room and commutes weekly to Mérida's factories, has cataracts, skin rashes, and chest congestion. He does not travel when he is sick, and all the families that depend on his orders suffer too.

According to official data, over 40 percent of Tekit's employed population does not have health care and 80 percent of employed people lack social security benefits. Seventy percent of the population still lacks access to basic household services, such as drainage and potable water. In 2015, 43 percent of households did not have a refrigerator, 41 percent did not have a washing machine, and 40 percent of the population was food insecure (CONEVAL 2019a). Additionally, a regional study recently estimated that Tekit's workshops produced close to nine tons of solid waste per month, and close to one hundred thousand kilograms per year. Thirty percent of this waste is burnt in the outskirts of the town, over 60 percent of it goes directly to landfills, and less than 10 percent is sold (Parra Argüello, Martin Calderon, and Navarrete Cante 2016, 14). Not far from the city center, piles of discarded materials are strewn about. These are toxic and nonbiodegradable supplies—like needles, oils, and synthetic fibers from garments and threads—that pollute sinkholes, contaminate the landscape, and end up in landfills as solid waste. These piles are some of the less obvious, but pernicious, effects of tourism's predatory environmental footprints in the region.

Tekit also reveals the power that tourism has to organize individual lives by sticking them to a present that might be undermining their own futures. In 2017, for example, 79 percent of Tekit's population had not completed elementary education, and the town had one of the largest high school dropout rates (60 percent) in the region. Commenting on this high dropout rate, Don Xito, an elementary school teacher in his sixties who has been working in Tekit for the last twelve years, said, "Since sewing guayaberas started to be big in Tekit's homes, it is almost impossible to keep students motivated in school. . . . Kids go home, sew for a few hours, do some *encargos,* and at the end of the week they can buy cell phones and designer clothes. . . . At fifteen years old, that is what they want and they can have it." Don Xito said, and Manuel agreed, that the weekly availability of cash that the guayabera business provides is "blinding Tekit's younger generations in the imagination of a sustainable future." His selection of the verb "blinding" was deliberate.

And yet, Tekit is almost unanimously described by its inhabitants as a place where "life is good" and where "everything" still unfolds according to traditional ideas of land, household organization, and family life. This good life they refer to happens amid a predatory system of production that both demands financial indebtedness and ravages their bodies. In contrast to the dispossession, violence, depression, and alienation *(desarraigo)* that characterize the lives of migrants who work in tourist cities such as Cancún, and their families, Tekit is perceived as "a good place to live" because young people do not need to migrate to the United States or to Cancún, mothers can stay at home to look after children, elders have their families around, backyard patios are planted, the milpa is productive, "nobody is gone," and food is served daily in the market stalls "even when the sun sets."[21] Sewing for tourism as part of domestic enterprises organized through kinship has enabled most families to access "corn and cash" on a daily basis, something that for other inland indigenous villages still only happens through migration to Cancún (Re Cruz 1996). Sewing for tourism has kept people in a town where they feel they belong and, importantly, that they care about. For most, sewing for tourism has ameliorated their material existence among otherwise underprivileged conditions of living. Most households have both beds and hammocks. Clothes are stored in wooden wardrobes with mirrors, and although refrigerators are still scarce, other appliances and electronics like air-conditioning systems, electric fans, and large plasma televisions abound. Mobile devices are ubiquitous as are designer clothes and other elements of Western fashion. For a few, sewing for tourism has even generated disposable income and the possibility of engaging in various forms of conspicuous consumption weekly or monthly. Of course, these are consumer goods that signal the increased financialization of everyday life, and yet, in Tekit, they also serve to make the present more bearable and meaningful.

This conspicuous consumption is evident at the town's religious fiesta, San Antonio de Padua, "the best in all Yucatán," but it is also conveyed through leisure and tourism. Those who prosper from the guayabera business take vacations and day trips to the region's most frequented tourism spots as well as to shopping malls. They have become tourists themselves. Last year for example, the Chans vacationed in Veracruz, visited the Biosphere Reserve Ria Celestún and San Felipe, and traveled, as an extended family, to Oaxaca. They are among the few families in the region who have enough money to purchase tickets for their extended family to tour archeological remains—an expense that has been prohibitive for most extended families in the region since the state implementation of international heritage conservation policies in the late 1990s, discussed in chapters 2 and 3.

Sewing for tourism at home is perceived as a worthwhile livelihood despite the sacrificial logic that it entails. In Tekit, one rarely hears the expression common among maquila workers on the US-Mexico border: *la maquila te mata* (the maquila kills you). Regardless of the step they represent in the production chain, most inhabitants express their satisfaction at "not having to travel or spend on lunches," "having flexible timetables," "respecting Saint Monday," and being able "to stay put with the family."[22] While working at home or in a family workshop can be stressful and demanding, people do not deal with retributions and can take brief respites from routine tasks to eat bread and drink, as workers in Marycarmen Chans' workshop regularly do. They can listen to their choice of music while they work. They can chitchat with and about people they care about while they sew. They can have their children around, or the freedom to drop them off and pick them up from school, and if they are busy with *encargos* then they can pay a moto taxi to ferry their children. By keeping families together, sewing for tourism has also enabled most to refrain from the "vices" that affect labor migrants in larger urban centers or locals in Celestún due to the spatial articulation of ecotours in town (chapter 2). Tekit has relatively low rates of alcoholism and drug abuse compared to similarly sized locations in inland Yucatán. As Don Santos points out, staying put and sewing at home in times of economic uncertainty helps to "keep your elder sons at home" so that they don't "become addicted to the wrong stuff," as has happened with younger migrants from Tekit's neighbor, Sotuta, to Cancún.

This is the ambivalence that people in Tekit are stuck with. However predatory and demanding, sewing for tourism has ameliorated otherwise precarious conditions of living, at least in the short term. For these reasons, sewing for tourism is the region's lesser of two evils. After centuries of slave work at the haciendas, most of Tekit's inhabitants have embraced the maquila of guayaberas for tourism because it has made them "free" to choose if and when they work or until how late in the day. For these reasons, Tekit's inhabitants, like Marycarmen, Luis and Lucía, Don Ramón and Doña Violeta, are proud of having stayed put in a context of regional diaspora and seasonal migration. They all point at their material belongings and ways of doing things "as they always have" as proof of their success. Sewing, as Don Luis Chan put it, is considered a "true job," "a good job," and a "job one aspires to." And the change is being nurtured, with the evolution of new rituals and symbolisms that cherish sewing guayaberas for tourism. For example, sewing implements have found a place in traditional ceremonies like the *jéets méek*, babies are today blessed by their godparents with pencil and paper, scissors and tape, with the hope that they will become good and expert guayabera sewers one day.[23] And scissors are now depicted in the village coat of arms, where they are placed side by side a henequen plant.

This good life, while real, is fragile and vulnerable. In one of our conversations, Don Ben stressed, "do not forget that because of the guayabera business, people know better how to sew than how to read. . . . But what will happen when guayabera work stops coming, as labor for the haciendas once stopped? . . . What will all those who sew and only know how to sew do then?" In the urgency of everyday life and with *encargos* coming through, this is not a question that still worries many.

Manuel and his wife, Ana, are an exception. Conscious of the likelihood that this system of maquila production will fail due to the fragility of international trade agreements, they are starting, slowly but steadily, to convince both of their extended kin to devote part of their surplus capital to apiculture and tourism. In particular, to the development of independent, "solidarity" and agro-ecological tours intended for alternative tourists who want to experience "the real Maya way of life by living it," but who have been put off by the increasingly scripted and packaged nature of tourism in the region.

In 2017, Manuel and Ana hosted their first group of four people in Tekit. The group was composed of two young French couples backpacking in the region, who learned about them through a common friend at the Universidad Autónoma de Yucatán (UADY). The couples stayed for one night in Ana's mother's traditional hut and worked with Ana tending to their native Melipona bee hives and bird watching. Then Manuel took them to Don Ben's milpa and to his niece Marycarmen's guayabera workshop, where each of them bought, in situ, a locally crafted guayabera. These tourists were part of the new state-funded organization Co'ox Mayab, which brings tourists to off-the-radar spots in Yucatán. In a brief survey they completed upon their departure, the French couples praised the experience but also complained about "the lack of sanitation," about "a large number of mosquitoes at night," and the "uncomfortable" night in the "hammocks without mosquito nets" and with mice. Manuel and Ana plan to build a separate toilet just for tourists in Ana's mother's hut and to invest in nets and new hammocks for their potential guests.

What the future holds for their new tourism initiative is still unknown, but their venture exemplifies, from another angle, the pervasiveness and predatory character of tourism's orderings of space and social life in contemporary Yucatán. When there are glimpses of change on the horizon, desires to move forward, or urgent needs to tackle uncertainty in the present, tourism is always the default choice.

Conclusion

TOURISM FIXATION AND DISCIPLINARY RETOOLINGS

IN JULY 2018, MEXICO ELECTED as president the left-wing politician Andrés Manuel López Obrador (best known by the acronym AMLO). His election was a double anomaly. It was an anomaly in a country that had endured the firm grip of one-party rule for almost a century, followed by almost two decades of right-wing governments. And it was also an anomaly within a global context of rising right-wing populism. The result of the Mexican election filled many parts of the country, including the Yucatán Peninsula, with hope for more socially inclusive and environmentally just futures.

On December 1, 2018, AMLO delivered his inaugural speech in Mexico City's zócalo, surrounded by tens of thousands of citizens. His speech was preceded by an indigenous ceremony to deliver him the wooden staff or *bastón de mando,* a ritual that had been absent from Mexican politics for over two centuries. Under the banner "Poor People Come First," a clear gesture toward indigenous and marginalized populations, AMLO promised a "radical change" and voiced sharp criticism of Mexico's neoliberal turn, which he described as "a calamity" and "a disaster." He blamed free market and pro-trade policies for Mexico's income inequality, international migration, and widespread poverty. He promised to fight corruption and to "purify public life" through an increase in public investments. He also reasserted his campaign's commitment to ban fracking and his opposition to genetically modified organisms, and he assured a thorough revision of NAFTA. Among the flagship undertakings of his presidency, AMLO cited two megaprojects: Mexico City's airport expansion, which he later rejected, and the Train Maya, which he embraced after a public referendum in December 2019.

AMLO's reference to Train Maya in his inaugural address to the nation was intentional. Starting in the early 2010s as a proposal by powerful regional businessmen in Quintana Roo and Yucatán, Train Maya had become a central emblem in the narrative of socioeconomic transformation of the newly elected president. Spanning five hundred kilometers, Train Maya promised to revitalize Mexico's southeast and to "promote economic development in and around tourism centers" in five states (Quintana Roo, Yucatán, Campeche, Tabasco, and Chiapas). These would be connected through their shared "Maya cultural heritage" alongside three thematic routes: the Caribbean Route, the Gulf Route, and the Forest Route, each organized around a series of stops integrating already established tourism destinations with natural protected areas and other less trafficked population centers. In three official promotional videos, AMLO described Train Maya as a "modern tourist and cultural train." Publicly, he has promoted the initiative as "progress" and "development," and has referred to it as "a train moved by respect for nature," and as a "a social project" that would generate better jobs, increase the circulation of people and commodities, and shorten commutes for thousands of service workers in the region. All of this while bringing "appreciation for a culture and a region that have been long forgotten."

Train Maya is still a project, but the ghosts and promises that it awakens are well known to many in the Yucatán Peninsula and beyond. AMLO's discourses reproduce, word for word, the old adage of the Yucatán Peninsula as "a world apart" and the contemporary tourist narrative of the region as "world to escape to." This is a world where, as one of the official promotional videos of the Train Maya puts it, Quintana Roo emerges as "Mexico's emblem of sun and the beach" and as the "gateway to national and international tourism," where Yucatán stands for the "fusion of Maya culture and the New World ... with a gastronomy that displays the nuances of a land rich in nature and cultural traditions," and where Campeche is "a magnet for adventurers seeking pirate stories."

In many ways, Train Maya illustrates how the idea of tourism as a positive tool for development has become deeply ingrained in public political discourse and public imaginaries. It shows how tourism captures the political imagination of the future by presenting itself, once again, as the agent that will (finally) deliver much-needed social change and economic development, combat poverty, and increase cultural inclusivity. In so doing, Train Maya illustrates tourism's almost unparalleled capacity to generate a promise that transcends entrenched political divisions, a promise that attracts equally those on the right as well as those on the left, those in favor of market-oriented societies as well as those who fiercely oppose them, those who are

TREN MAYA
Moderno, turístico y cultural

El plan de crecimiento para el sur de la Península de Yucatán, proyectado por el gobierno federal que encabeza el presidente Andrés Manuel López Obrador, y que está previsto para desarrollarse en cuatro años, potenciará la oferta turística del mundo maya y la economía de la región. Conoce algunos detalles de su construcción.

Ruta costa oeste

Cancún
Mérida
Valladolid
Tulum
Campeche
Escárcega
Bacalar
Xpujil
Candelaria
Palenque

Atravesará los estados de
Tabasco, Campeche, Chiapas, Yucatán y Quintana Roo.

Hasta
150 mil mdp
de inversión mixta (pública* y privada) costará su construcción.

16 mil mdp
El primer recurso con el que se contará en 2019.

20 mil
empleos locales generará en su primera etapa de construcción.

Recorrerá
1,500 km.

17
posibles estaciones.

TRES MODALIDADES
Sus usos serán: traslado de carga, transporte local y regional (que tendrá un precio más accesible) y turístico (con un costo mayor).

*Se utilizarán fondos recaudados del turismo: cerca de 7 mil mdp por año durante seis años.
Actualización: Julia Castillo. Fuentes: NTX México, lopezobrador.org.mx. Diseño y Arte Digital: Angie Guerrero.

NTX NOTIMEX

FIGURE 20. Official promotional poster for the "modern, cultural, and touristic" Tren Maya, Yucatán Peninsula, 2019. Source: Notimex Agencia de Noticias del Estado Mexicano.

willing to sacrifice natural environments at the altar of profit-making as well as those who want to protect those same environments.

The faith in initiatives like Train Maya can be seen as an expression of what Christo Sims (2017) calls "disruptive fixation," which is the relentless investment in repeatedly idealized sets of narratives, practices, or, in this case, infrastructure interventions, even when they "predictably fail to fulfill their professed aims" (171). The Yucatán Peninsula's forty-year infatuation with tourism is a textbook example of this type of disruptive fixation. Despite the obvious shortcomings of tourism-based developments in the region, despite their evident failure to deliver on the promise of inclusive growth, sustainable ecological development, or the empowerment of local indigenous populations, tourism somehow manages to reemerge—now in the form of a mega-infrastructural rail project publicly sanctioned by indigenous knowledge and practice—as the promise that will finally deliver a better and more just future. But how, exactly, is this possible? How can tourism continually reemerge unscathed from every failure in order to present itself as a panacea?

The answer that I would like to venture in this conclusion is that if tourism has this capacity to endlessly renew itself despite its failures, this is largely because we—as citizens, workers, tourists, researchers, and politicians—have contributed to emptying tourism of any political meaning or praxis. We do so, wittingly or unwittingly, when, as tourists, we treat tourism as just a set of recreational activities that we casually engage with in our free time, or when, as citizens, we allow politicians to treat tourism as if it were just another sector in the economy, or when, as researchers, we analyze tourism as if it were just a unique type of host-guest encounter. And also, when, as workers, we "play the tourist game" to make a living, to earn some more cash, to get ahead by accepting the terms of a contract that we probably had no part in creating. When we adopt and play by these rules, tourism is reduced to a leisure-specific activity that becomes detached from urgent geopolitical matters such as statecraft and nationalism, global inequality, land dispossession, indigenous oppression, climate change, or nuclear testing (Teaiwa 2001; Sheller 2007). Yet what I show in this book is that many of these phenomena have become deeply entangled with tourism, and are impossible to understand without considering it. Because, at the dawn of the twenty-first century, tourism is much *more* than a set of social practices associated to leisure, it is much *more* than an economic sector, and it is much *more* than a set of host-guest encounters. Or to borrow Marisol de la Cadena's (2019) words, yes, tourism is all these things—industry, social practice, encounter—but *not only* them.

Tourism today is fundamentally about power and space. It is about moral and ethical questions as much as it is about political, ecological, and spatial ones. What this means is that when we talk about tourism, when we do tourism, we are not just talking about or engaging in a set of practices localized in a particular space that produces "regional development." We are talking about relations with the past and about the social and geographical forces generating the uneven orderings of contemporary capitalism in both the global North and South. A force that works across geographic space, institutional levels, and bodies by redrawing the contemporary maps of social, cultural, economic, and ecological life at both the global and the most intimate scales. An organizing force that works by scaling-up places, bodies, culture, and nature for global consumption, crafting commodity-centered landscapes, and reconfiguring and normalizing the relations of humanity-in-nature as predatory and sacrificial. In so doing, tourism is sucking entire territories, ways of life, and ecosystems into a logic that is both predatory and sticky.

All of this is palpable in the Yucatán Peninsula, one of the regions of the world that tourism development has voraciously transformed since the mid-1970s. Since the founding of Cancún in 1974, tourism has become the new monocrop: a powerful extractive industry that has advanced by preying on the region's coasts, enclosing its beaches, ravaging its marine life, transforming its reefs, mangrove forests, and pink flamingos into commodities, and altering its built environments to accommodate global aesthetics of tourism consumption. Tourism has preyed on the region's inland and rural landscapes, reformatting vernacular architectures as architectures of escape (chapters 1 and 2). It has preyed on the region's past, fostering sedentarist narratives of indigeneity, reappropriating and selectively resignifying Maya cultural spaces, buildings, and practices to narrate the nation and foster global consumption (chapters 3 and 4). Tourist narratives have tied populations to "heritage" readings of the present that freeze them in nostalgic accounts of place and global Maya-ness, in a *here-ness* that is for consumption (chapter 3), as well as in exoticized wilderness (chapter 2) and in subservient face-to-face relations (chapter 1). In these places, we have seen how tourism has created and reactivated new and old patronages and client-patron relations that reconfigure local and regional dynamics of power and economy (chapter 2, 3, and 4).

Tourism has also created new forms of waiting and servitude, new illnesses and forms of financial and moral indebtedness (chapters 2 and 4). It has generated novel forms of place-based violence (chapter 2) and imposed new forms of entrepreneurial civic association that utterly dispossess peasants from land

and the benefits of their labor (chapter 4). Tourism development has generalized flexible forms of just-in-time production and regimes of corporeal discipline, all of which service workers endure even as they largely acknowledge that these practices are oppressive and wrong. These entrapments are recognized and dealt with in a sacrificial way that sometimes involves staying still in spaces scaled up by tourism in order to get physically proximate to tourism dollars (chapters 2 and 3) or remaining invisible to tourists in order to participate in the economic benefits of the industry from home (chapter 4). All of this amounts to a silencing, cancelling, and destruction of other possible alternatives.

These processes have involved massive material interventions in the landscape as well as symbolic interventions in the fabric of cultural life. These interventions have been legitimated by the state through modern, scientific, and internationalized discourses about economic growth, natural conservation, cultural heritage preservation, and indigenous empowerment, and they have been carried out through public and private alliances that span international, national, regional, and local scales involving the United Nations, the Mexican state, and regional and local governments, as well as citizens, including local, nonlocal, and indigenous populations. The result of this forty-year history of tourist interventions is a region whose physical geographies, sociocultural imaginaries, and everyday spatiotemporal practices have morphed to fit the kinds of market-driven representations of beach and nature paradises and authentic indigeneity that have allowed Yucatán to acquire its current position in the global tourist market. This position, as I show in this book, has been secured at the expense of further opening up the entire region to a predatory logic in which almost everything—from ecosystems to history, buildings, indigenous cultural practices, condiments, plants, birds, and labor—is suitable for tourism extraction.

It is essential to pay attention to the specifics of tourism's predatory logics in order to understand how tourism works in practice as an extractive industry. But that is not enough. In places like Yucatán, *tourism makes sense.* It makes sense at individual and collective levels because tourism-based developments—such as beach resorts, ecotours, restored haciendas, or veiled village factories—do not simply engender landscapes of desolation or ruination, as other extractive industries, such as oil, uranium, or diamond mining, have done in Latin America, Africa, and elsewhere (Büscher and Davidov 2013; Godoy 1985; Hilson and Clifford 2010). Tourism's predatory geographies extract labor, culture, and natural resources. Yes. But they do it while also opening up, enabling, and providing infrastructural development (roads, airports, housing, schools), tangible assets that make inhabitants feel more secure about precarious presents and suggest opportunities to imagine the future otherwise. In a place like the Yucatán Peninsula, ravaged by economic crises since the 1970s, these possibilities and prospects are palpable for those who have managed to get closer to tourism, such as real estate investors in Cancún, the boatmen and craftswomen in Celestún, those working for the hacienda in Temozón Sur, or those in Tekit with large extended kin networks who sew souvenirs and uniforms for the tourist industry at home. While tourism labor practices are not exempt from frictions, conflicts, and in some cases, violence, the sacrifices that workers make in the name of tourism make sense to them because tourism enables spaces of hope that, however precarious and fragile, still give meaning to the present and enable them to dream about and engage with the prospect of a future that the crises stole.

When compared with options like harsh agricultural labor, offshore oil mining, or migration to the United States, working for tourism still allows people like Luis and Lucía to sew at home in Tekit, to imagine that the end of their days will be in *el pueblo* and not as homeless or dispossessed workers in some foreign metropolis doing equally servile jobs away from their people. Sewing for tourism at home makes sense for families like the Chans, because it allows them to care for the milpa and live in accordance with and celebrate valued traditions while enjoying the benefits of the "good life" in a revitalized town in the midst of a rural landscape ravaged by state neglect, poverty, and migration. Tourism also makes sense for people like Miguel, Celestún's hostel owner, or Ana and Manuel, the proponents of indigenous solidarity tourism ventures in Tekit, because it has enabled them to rearrange traditional livelihoods and family networks through the development of business initiatives, and hence incomes, that would otherwise not exist. In the same way, tourism has also enabled the boatmen of Celestún to control their labor and to exert relative control over the distribution of resources in an overregulated community that is trapped within a UNESCO natural protected area. In these cases, tourism has activated dormant forms of reciprocity and labor activism that are put to work for the present by strategically entangling with the past— such as in the activation of collective forgetfulness as a mechanism to protest unfair labor decisions within the hacienda hotel's grounds (chapter 3).

In light of some of tourism's material affordances, advocates of tourism development argue that tourism has brought economic growth, stability, and hope to a region that was devastated and hopeless after the demise of the henequen industry. It is, they say, beneficial, a privileged tool of cultural adaptation, and hence resiliency. And, to an extent, this is true. Tourism development in Yucatán has indeed generated national and regional economic growth and has allowed an incipient urban middle class to form and consolidate in Mérida and Cancún. Tourism has brought income and work opportunities to young indigenous people living in abandoned inland towns and villages. It has brought back an appreciation for Maya cultural practices, it has cared for their preservation and curated a general awareness for global affairs. Tourism, in short, has put an impoverished and disconnected region back onto the map. From this perspective, initiatives like Train Maya are a continuation of these imaginaries of hope, cultural adaptation to a global order, economic development, and opportunity.

What I argue in this book is that rather than interpreting these examples as "benefits" created by tourism, we must see them as examples of the sticky emplacements created by tourism's predatory ways. Reducing tourism to discussions about its benefits and disadvantages loses sight of both the predation that makes these benefits possible and the forms of entrapment that they in turn create. Conceptualizing tourism as just a tool for development or a vehicle for adaptation loses sight of the tension between giving while depriving, opening while entrapping, that characterizes tourism's inner workings. As a result, we end up creating a misleading, and potentially dangerous narrative that blurs tourism's direct responsibility in larger processes of ecological neglect, international migration, labor, race and gender inequality, commodification of resources, and the financialization of land and everyday life.

It is only insofar as we approach tourism from this tension, acknowledging that it gives while depriving, that we can capture what, I argue, is one of the most consequential effects of tourism's contemporary orderings of space and ecological and sociocultural life. Tourism entraps people in contradictory moral regimes that become expressed as sacrificial practices. These sacrifices are most evident in the trajectory of the many indigenous workers in Cancún who work to beautify and fumigate the city's hotel zone and its beaches after a hurricane strikes, while their families and houses remain unattended (chapter 1). These contradictory moral regimes are salient in the adolescent children of Celestún's beach craftswomen, who sacrifice their education in order to get physically proximate to tourists so that they can enjoy some of the small benefits that ecotourism provides their families (chapter 2). Moral contradictions are evident for the workers at inland hacienda hotels, whose livelihoods allow them to avoid migration but depend on their performance of old forms of gendered and racialized labor relations that their parents fought against (chapter 3). And contradictions are evident for those in Tekit who endure work-related health problems and moral and financial indebtedness in order to get a chance to sew for tourism and avoid migration (chapter 4).

Ethnographically illuminating tourism's predatory ways and entrapments helps to repoliticize tourism and highlight its centrality in patterns of spatial production. All around the world, states, regional and local governments, institutional agencies, NGOs, and private actors continue to use tourism as a development strategy. And, as in the Yucatán Peninsula, they do so despite its failures and obvious shortcomings, and despite empirical evidence about its complicity in reproducing and extending patterns of social inequality, privatization of public resources, and ecological neglect. In the Peruvian Andes, for example, the state, development institutions, NGOs, researchers, and locals embrace tourism as a road to development despite the fact that it accelerates the melting of glaciers (Carey 2010). In many postdisaster or post-crisis scenarios, tourism reemerges as the leading path for moving forward. We have seen evidence of this after Hurricanes Gilbert (1989), Isidore (2002), and Wilma (2005) in Yucatán, but the same applies to New Orleans after Hurricane Katrina (2005), Thailand after the 2004 tsunami, Haiti after the 2010 earthquake, Nepal after the 2015 earthquake, or in the Dominican Republic and Puerto Rico after Hurricane Maria (2018).[1] Tourism's regenerative power has also been championed by states, private corporations, development agents, citizens, and tourists themselves as the way forward after crisis situations, like the 2002 bombing in Bali, the 2017 Barcelona attacks, the 2017 Las Vegas shootings, and the 2019 Notre-Dame Cathedral fire in Paris. In these places, international, national, regional, and local authorities as well as public opinion have promoted tourism as the best way to "bounce back," given tourism's capacity to fight fear through joy and play (Korstanje 2017).

The same logic of predation and entrapment that I use to describe the Yucatán Peninsula is applicable to parts of the Caribbean, such as Vieques, an island that the US military has used for years as a testing ground and whose population now lives amid a destroyed ecosystem. Here, too, local and US governments are looking at tourism as the opportunity for progress, while reproducing old modes of colonial domination and abuse (Sheller 2007). This logic is also visible in Cuba, where the government, researchers, and tourists anchor the island's tourist present to a romanticized revolutionary past (Jayawardena 2003; Dominguez 1975). These entrapments are also at work in many parts of rural Europe, like northern Spain or Sweden, where "back to nature" and "rural tourism" initiatives often become the sole source of labor in communities decimated by decades of governmental neglect and migration to urban centers (García García 1998; Svensson 2009). These entrapments are also evident in other areas, like New Zealand, Morocco, or Tanzania, where while many indigenous groups continue their traditions irrespective of tourism, others have become increasingly trapped in and bound to reviving nostalgic imaginations of primitivism (Stasch 2014).

This list could go on and on.

The dyad of predation-as-extraction and stickiness-as-entrapment is par- ticularly relevant in the developing world, where disadvantaged populations cannot resist the intrusion of economic and cultural globalization through tourism, and where tourism often becomes the only alternative, or the least- bad possible alternative, to make a living. In these places, it is easier for tour- ism to exclude, or limit, the possibility of other orderings and ways of being (Ek and Hultman 2008, 224). It may well be that this dyad becomes more pronounced and salient in landscapes as Yucatán, which have been histori- cally opened to resource extraction, where populations have endured land loss, and where states have learned to navigate corporate control. Perhaps the entrapments generated by tourism's predatory orderings may be less powerful in economically advantaged regions of the world, where the scale of exploita- tion and sacrifice demanded by the tourist industry may be weaker since there are sometimes other viable economic alternatives within reach, such as industry or retail. Yet, in these places, my analysis is still of use as a way to acknowledge the ambivalent attachments toward consumption that tourist practices and spaces create, and how they encroach upon our ability to plan for, or imagine, futures outside capitalism. Because whether we want to or not, we are forced to live within the representations that tourism creates of the places in which we live or where we visit. Increasingly, our cities, towns, and villages are planned *for* tourism. We have to navigate the infrastructure, roads, and paths carved out for tourism, from hotels, beaches, museums, and malls, to scenic routes, heritage areas, and must-see attractions. In some cases, cities run the risk of becoming spectacles of consumption, as some scholars believe has already happened in New York City (Wynn 2011), Barcelona (Garcés 2018), and Palma de Majorca (Franquesa 2013). In places like Colombia or California, urban planning, transportation, and housing revolve around shopping malls that are re-created as tourist resorts in order to keep consumers captive longer (Dávila 2016). In other places, tourism and tourists are weaponized by states, adapted for use as vehicles for surveillance, territorial control, and nationalist propaganda. This is for example the case in China's recent turn to mega-theme-park tourism developments in areas within its Belt and Road Initiative, in which tourism is openly used as a tool for assimilation of the Uyghur ethnic minority (Mostafanezhad, Córdoba Azcárate, and Norum, forthcoming 2021).

This acritical embrace of tourism as a promise of development needs revisiting. Doing so demands a disciplinary retooling (Larkin 2013), one that recognizes tourism's agency in the production of space and asserts and communicates its rapacious and sticky nature. For this to happen, we need first to question scholarly language around tourism research itself, as feminist postcolonial critics Jamaica Kinkaid (1988) and Haunani-Kay Trask (1991), Aikau and Gonzalez (2019), Teresia Teaiwa (2001) and Rebecca Stein (2008) have done. In particular, they argue for moving away from language that describes tourism as hospitality and abandoning, once and for all, the vocabulary about host-guest encounters through which Valene Smith (1977) vindicated and established tourism as a legitimate object of study in anthropology and the social sciences. The language of hospitality and encounters, while useful to understanding the situated micro-dynamics that comprise tourism, risks reducing the study of tourism to a subspecialty that remains disconnected from the study of how contemporary capitalism—of whatever variety, be it state, disaster, finance, or philanthropic—works.

Moving beyond the encounters trope might be a first step toward rescuing tourism from the subdisciplinary corner to which it has been confined and claiming its centrality as a major contemporary geographical force that shapes how capitalism, globalization, ecological deterioration, and indigenous oppression take place today. This is important not only because it addresses what tourism is and how it works, but also because tourism is, to this day, still largely missing from larger public discussions and knowledge production about capitalism, extraction, and climate change. In a context of ecological crisis and increasing global inequality, there is an urgent need to publicly short-circuit the eternal renewal of the promise of tourism that is embedded in the blind embrace of megatourism projects such as Train Maya.

Discussions in this direction are already happening. Over the last five years, critical tourism scholars, Western media outlets, and public opinion have begun to criticize "overtourism," the observable and palpable predation of physical and ecological spaces, as well as of imaginaries about otherness and the future. Scholars use this term to call attention to the fact that too much tourism can negatively affect the livelihoods of local communities, in particular through its impact on the environment and natural resources (Dodds and Butler 2019). Discussions about overtourism have mostly focused on Western cities like Venice and Barcelona, where citizens, outnumbered by tourists, have started to publicly protest tourism's rapacious ways. In these cities, residents have demanded that tourists go home. Posters and graffiti on the streets, on museum walls, at beaches, and on buses read: "Your tourism ruins my neighborhood" and "This is not tourism, it is an invasion." In these fights against tourism, citizens call for better regulation, better tourist education, reduced tourist numbers, fewer licenses for tourism rentals, and controls on what they consider to be tourists' intrusive meanderings. These citizens are not seeking an end to tourism as such, but to limit how crowds of tourists limit their access to fair housing, congest their work commutes, or prevent them from enjoying a walk in a public space. Their social movements are also an invitation to further question the UN proclamation of a right to tourism. When tourists' rights prevail over citizenship rights then tourism helps to reproduce privilege and exacerbate inequality.

At the same time, others are harnessing tourism for critical and emancipatory projects. For example, communities of fishermen in places like Cabo Pulmo National Park in Baja California and Grenada in the Caribbean are successfully recovering coral reefs damaged by excessive tourism and implementing disaster mitigation programs that work for both tourists and the population. Likewise, in New York City, new walking tours are questioning and challenging mainstream representations of the city and, in doing so, expanding alternative imaginations of what New York could be and is for visitors and locals alike (Wynn 2011). In Cuba, Simoni (2018) urges us to consider transnational processes of identity formation in challenging the island's representation of revolution for mainstream tourists. In Hawai'i, initiatives like DeTours have recently emerged out of anger toward tourism's excesses and abuses in relation to indigenous women's bodies. They aim to decolonize tourism by educating tourists about how the United States used the islands as a strategic linchpin "to extend American empire across the Pacific" (Aikau and Gonzalez 2019; Gonzalez, forthcoming 2021). In the Caribbean, Sheller (2012, 2020) has called for the epistemic restructuring of tourist metaphors to sensitize tourists to mobility injustice and island futures in the face of climate change. And in Mediterranean Spain and some islands in Thailand, local governments have put limits to tourism's hunger by demolishing resorts and closing down beaches that do not meet environmental regulations or where tourist crowds negatively impact residents' use of leisure spaces. All are examples that call for and set social and environmental limits when tourism has gone too far.

As scholars, citizens, and prospective tourists, we need to think further about the power that tourism has to shape geographical and social space, to model behavior, to cancel stories, *and* to build alternative habits of mind and practice. In the late 1980s Lash and Urry argued that tourism had taken over and organized much of contemporary cultural experience. People, they argued, are tourists all the time, everywhere, "whether they are literally mobile or only experience simulated mobility through the incredible fluidity of multiple signs and electronic images" (Lash and Urry 1987, 10). In this book, I have shown that one does not necessarily need to be a tourist or to encounter tourists face-to-face to be overtaken by the industry. Sometimes it is those farther away from tourists, like Luis and Lucía, who become more deeply entangled in tourism's predatory transformations of space, body, and mind. At some point in reading this book, you may have thought, "Well, tourism does more harm than good, and we should put an end to it." In many ways, this is true. There are numerous examples of destructive tourism that should not be perpetuated, such as those that exacerbate imperialist, racist, and sexist attitudes, those that utterly displace locals in the name of gentrification, and those that blatantly contribute to ecological ruination. But I do not intend for this book to be a manifesto against all forms of tourism. What my research in the Yucatán Peninsula shows, rather, is that in becoming tourists and/or workers for tourism, we have become anesthetized to tourism's predatory logics, which in many places in the world, including in the Yucatán, are physically carving up the Earth's crust with little regard for its renewal. It is urgent that we understand how this conundrum between extracting and entrapping works and that we think further about tourism as an object of scholarly and political concern. Only by doing so it will be possible to repoliticize tourism and bring it to the table as a structural force and matter of vital concern in the age of climate crisis and deepening global inequalities. My ethnographic analysis has attempted to do just that: to recenter tourism's importance in discussions about how we make sense, imagine, and act in the world. Moreover, my goal has been to call attention to the need to reevaluate the unevenness and contradictions that make tourism what it is.

. . .

On December 16, 2018, Train Maya was officially launched. Its supervision and land management, as had happened in the founding of Cancún, were in the hands of FONATUR. Despite a lack of any public environmental or social assessments, in March 2019 the first rail tracks were placed, with the goal of eventually connecting Palenque in Chiapas with Mérida in Yucatán. In the first months of 2020, ground was broken for the two other stretches. Prior to the 2019 project's launching and the initial construction, communities performed indigenous ceremonies "to seek Mother Earth's blessings" at Chichén Itzá and Palenque. Governors of the five states involved in the initiative attended these public ceremonies as did representatives of the states' indigenous inhabitants, who conceive these ceremonies as a necessary gesture toward political recognition. Yet, while making room for the performance of indigenous difference, AMLO has made several public calls to invite private investors to participate in the construction process, repeating his commitment to offer federal subsidies for every kilometer built by the private sector. In February 2020, AMLO announced that Train Maya's tracks would be constructed and supervised by the Mexican Defense Ministry starting in 2022, a move which signals not only the project's centrality for the Mexican state, but also a renewed nexus between tourism and militarism in the country.

The opposition to the train has been growing. Detractors of the initiative include national, regional, and local researchers, the Zapatista Army of National Liberation (EZLN), environmental groups, and indigenous collectives from Chiapas and Tabasco as well as from Guatemala. In their public appearances, still small and scattered, protestors highlight that nearly a third of Train Maya's rail tracks are to be laid through tropical forests in which native species and features such as jaguars and bees, mangrove forests and cenotes are endangered and quickly disappearing.[2] Under the banner "Resistance in Defense of the Territory," Train Maya's detractors highlight the dangers of the public-private mixed partnerships that finance the train, which are further opening the land to state and corporate control by construction firms from Korea, China, and the United States. In the Yucatán Peninsula, many inhabitants are concerned about Train Maya's plan to reactivate the rail system that once transported and distributed henequen because doing so would awaken old forms of servitude and gendered and racialized mobilities, which tourism has already done. Train Maya, they say, is just another "big capitalist mega-project that means destruction," and they assert that it will further erode and usurp land from already marginalized indigenous peoples and put their cultures, once again, up for sale. And yet, detractors also know that tourism is a fundamental way to get ahead without migrating, and they know that tourism works best if sanctioned by the state. For this reason, while indigenous ceremonies are seen by detractors as an example of the political cooptation of indigeneity by the state, they also understand that these ceremonies might also be doing something more than that. For once, they could be publicly performing a shared recognition of the stickiness of tourism *as* development, and gesturing to the need to include other voices in its reconceptualization moving forward. It is unavoidable, they might be saying, that train tracks built in and around tourism destinations will erase and destroy as they have in the past. But as they have in the past, they will also create and enable new life to unfold. This time, however, recognizing indigenous worldviews and making them visible in and through political performance in advance of extraction might also be creating the possibilities for better, more equal redistribution.

With construction under way and opposition gaining momentum at regional, national, and international scales, many in Yucatán still feel overtly ambivalent about Train Maya. In a recent interview for a local newspaper, a regional sociologist supported the project by saying:

> Train Maya is the biggest work to be done in the Peninsula since Cancún was funded. I am alarmed . . . that so many central Mexicans are concerned about the environmental damage that the project may create because they have exchanged mangrove forests for dollars for decades and they have never cared about it. On the contrary, many of them have been predators in their summer holidays here. . . . Do not be hypocrites—let us have a railroad track that will run across the forests and alongside our roads. Let us have what you have always had.[3]

A tourism researcher from a regional university and a leading scholar in the opposition to Cancún's excesses expressed similar ambivalence about the project in an interview with me: "On the one hand, I see that this can be the new Cancún, and I see all the abuse coming back again. But on the other hand, I also see that if it is well done, this can improve the living conditions of many families living from tourism in the region." Luis in Tekit, unable to sew anymore due to his rapidly deteriorating health, also agrees with them. "The train," he said in a weakened voice one afternoon at his thatched house, "might bring more opportunities for *el pueblo*. If they [the government, businesspeople, construction corporations] do not ruin it, it can make life a bit easier for us when tourists start to arrive here."

Their words, once again, point to the tension between predation and provision that characterizes tourism today, and they also explain why, once more, we remain stuck with it.

NOTES

INTRODUCTION

1. The names given for most persons in this book are pseudonyms except in the cases were they explicitly asked me to be referred to with their real names. Bracketed ellipses indicate omissions, not faltering speech.

2. See Germann Molz (2017) and Mostafanezhad (2014) for a discussion on recent discourses and geographies of voluntourism as an example of a tourism niche predicated upon "giving back." See MacCannell (2011) and Fennell (2015) for discussions of tourism and ethics.

3. These quotes are from Erika Karp, speaking on behalf of the World Travel and Tourism Council (World Travel and Tourism Council 2016). For an institutional description of tourism as an export sector, see International Trade Centre and UN World Tourism Organization (2017).

4. On the varying definitions of development as a concept in development theory, policy, and practice, see Pieterse (2009). On the relationship between tourism and development policy see Mowforth and Munt (2015); Duffy and Smith (2003); Sharpley (2009); Telfer and Sharpley (2015); Stronza and Hunt (2012).

5. Charles Taylor (2003) has defined *imaginaries* as ways in which people imagine and act in the worlds they inhabit. Imaginaries bring together "a sense of the normal expectations that we have of one another, the kind of common understanding which enables us to carry out the collective practices that make up our social life" (106–7). As a concept, imaginaries has been widely and variously used in tourism research (e.g., Leite 2017, Simpson 2017; Salazar 2012; Urry 2011). My use of the concept of imaginaries in its relationship with tourism aligns best with John Urry's (2011) and Coleman and Crang's (2002) understanding of tourism imaginaries as embodied and performative practices that generate meaning *and* spatiality. Another way to refer to imaginaries as produced by the tourism industry would be through the term "mindscapes," used by Löfgren (2002) in *On Holiday*. Here he explores the relations between mindscapes and landscapes in a historical study of vacationing in California: "It is by moving in physical terrain and fantasylands or mediaworlds,"

he writes, "that we create vacationscapes. Personal memories mix with collective images" (2).

6. Sorkin (1992) and Dávila's (2016) research on urban built environments and class and identity formation in North American and Latin American cities, and in particular, on the proliferation of themed environments and shopping malls since the late 1980s, directly points at leisure consumption as a driving force in patterns of land transformation, identity, and class formation. See Crawford (1992) and Mac-Cannell (2011) for the effects on consumers. According to Vogel (2016), malls in the twenty-first century deserve the same or even more serious consideration than mountains have traditionally had in the theorization of nature.

7. Tourism conjures up Boltanksi and Chiapello's (2018) "spirit of capitalism" with great success. It brings forth individual and collective commitments to capitalist ideology in the name of both individual and collective benefits. The 2017 Fyre Festival and its collapse is perhaps an extreme example of how far this commitment goes when pushed by social media and how disastrous the failure to meet tourist expectations can be for local economies and environments. See Joe Coscarelli, Melena Ryzik, and Ben Sisario "In Wreckage of the Fyre Festival, Fury, Lawsuits and an Inquiry," *New York Times,* May 21, 2017, https://www.nytimes.com/2017/05/21 /arts/music/fyre-festival-billy-mcfarland-ja-rule-criminal-investigation.html.

8. In 1999, the UNWTO Global Code of Ethics for Tourism ratified tourism as a vital force in "economic development, international understanding, peace, prosperity and universal respect for, and observance of, human rights and foundational freedoms for all without distinction as to race, sex, language or religion" (UNWTO 2007, preamble). Article 7 defines the "right to tourism," asserting that "1. The prospect of direct and personal access to the discovery and enjoyment of the planet's resources constitutes a right equally open to all the world's inhabitants. . . . 2. The universal right to tourism must be regarded as the corollary of the right to rest and leisure . . . . 3. Social tourism . . . should be developed with the support of the public authorities" (UNWTO 2007). See Fennell (2014) and Bianchi, Stephenson, and Hannam (2020) for a discussion on the contradictions of tourism's ethics and the right to travel.

9. Veijola et al. (2014) offer a fascinating account of tourism, disruption, and untidiness. On the role of tourism in heritage preservation, see Barbara Kirshenblatt-Gimblett (1998). She addresses how tourism has staged the world as a museum and explores heritage as a new and contested mode of cultural production. See Smith (2006), Collins (2015), Herzfeld (2010, 2016), and Prentice (1993) for critical engagement with heritage studies and the impact of tourism upon heritage policies. Di Giovine (2008), Mota Santos (2016), Bourdeau and Gravari-Barbas (2016), and Franquesa (2013) offer wonderful empirical examinations of the contending uses of cultural and natural heritage for tourism purposes across the globe. See Walker (2009) and Wallace (2005) for accounts of what counts as heritage among Maya peoples in Guatemala and Yucatán and the dangers of oversimplification imposed by tourism development. See Gordillo (2014) for an ethnographic account of the transformation of rubble and debris into ruin and heritage in the Argentine Andes with fascinating connections to the Yucatán Peninsula.

10. Recent efforts to decolonize tourism (Gonzalez 2013; Stein 2008) are demanding deeper attention to the role of tourism "in shaping images and imaginative geographies of conflict" (Vanden Boer 2016, 9). This latter work mostly addresses existing conflicts and denounces the continuities in colonial modes of domination (in space and of indigenous women's bodies) by tracing the interplay between militarism and tourism (Gonzalez 2013; Teaiwa 1994). See Aikau and Gonzalez (2019) for a recent exercise in decolonizing travel and tourism.

11. See Becklake (2019) for a discussion on tourism and securitization with evidence from Guatemala, and see Garcés (2018) for an essay on tourism's role in Barcelona's urban gentrification and contemporary political action.

12. The top ten tourist destinations in the world according to 2017 data were France (86.9 million annual visitors), Spain (81.8 million), the United States (76.9 million), China (60.7 million), Italy (58.3 million), Mexico (39.3 million), the United Kingdom (37.7 million), Turkey (37.6 million), Germany (37.5 million), and Thailand (35.4 million). These countries have economies that are highly reliant on tourism, for which tourism represents 7 percent or more of their GDP. According to UNWTO (2018b), there are over fifty-one destinations where tourists outnumber residents. Among them are Andorra, which is home to less than seventy thousand inhabitants and received 2.36 million tourists in 2015, Barcelona, which has less than two million residents and receives nine million tourists annually and Macao, the Seychelles, Barbados, the Bahamas, and Hong Kong.

13. Debates on too much tourism and overtourism began to emerge as I finished this book. I will come back to them in the conclusion; for reference see Shankman (2017), Dodds (2019), and Milano, Cheer, and Novelli (2019).

14. The 2017 Global Terrorism Index by the Institute for Economics and Peace has named popular destinations as Thailand, India, Philippines, Turkey, and Egypt among the top twenty countries at highest risk for attack (see Institute for Economic and Peace 2017). For a historical analysis of the relationship between tourism and terrorism, see Richter and Waugh (1986) and Pizam and Smith (2000). For a contemporary analysis on the situation of tourism, terrorism, and religion, see for example Clarke et al. (2017).

15. For ethnographical insights into the Anthropocene, tourism, and climate change, see Carey (2010) and Moore (2016). For a broader discussion on tourism and climate change, see Hall and Higham (2005) and Reddy and Wilkes (2012).

16. Adrian Franklin (2004) says that tourism should be better understood as "an active ordering of modernity" (279). Tourism, as he puts it, "orders both the spaces of tourism, including the sites that are visited and the spaces of mobility that get them there but also, the tourists themselves. They become self-ordering, self-directed tourists constantly *interpellated* by, and curious for the places that have been opened up in their name and which become relevant to them" (280). This, he argues is a vastly nationalist project imbued with high-culture institutional and state ideals and born with the generalization and democratization of travel after the Second World War. *Orderings* (plural) has been a central term in the mobilities paradigm, used to call attention to the generative character of spatial organizations and the role of

movement in organizing social practice (Sheller and Urry 2004; Büscher, Urry, and Witchger 2010). I use the term *tourism as an ordering* of late capitalism to refer to the overarching and generalized way in which tourism dictates material and symbolic landscape transformations as well as labor. I also use the term *tourism orderings* (plural) to acknowledge that this ordering might have different expressions according to localized histories.

17. John Urry (2011) coined the term "the tourist gaze" in the 1990s to emphasize the social organization of tourism and its systematic nature. He defined the tourist gaze as that systematically organized principle which structures the world for visual consumption. As he puts it, "The tourist gaze suggests that tourist experience involves a particular way of seeing. Images and myths about what to see tend to be distinctive, striking, unusual, and extraordinary. Such visual and narrative depictions of tourist destinations are strategically promoted by the marketing industry to contrast with people's daily routine and work schedules at home. These imaginaries are captured through signs which signify a particular fantasy" (Urry 2011, 184).

18. Spatialization is the English translation of the French concept *l'espace,* used by Henri Lefebvre (1992) to refer to the social aspects of processes of space production. Shields (1992) uses the concept to talk about "place-images" and to reclaim the processes according to which cultural values and social meanings are fixed in geographical space. Low (2016) uses the concept to talk about spatializing culture and defines it as the process of "locating both physically and conceptually, social relations and social practice in social space" (61). In another context, Zilberg (2011) offers an ethnographically powerful example of spatialization at work in her research on the so-called "transnational gang crisis" fostered between El Salvador and Los Angeles. Directly addressing tourism, Sheller (2003, 2007, 2009) uses the concept of spatial rescaling in her analysis of the Caribbean region's transformations in the face of contemporary urban restructuring brought about by, among other forces, luxury property developments and the cruise ship industry. She points out how these developments contribute to weakening islands' state sovereignty, territorial integrity, and democratic citizenship. Building on empirical evidence from Vieques in Puerto Rico, Sheller shows how tourism in particular has been a crucial force in the spatialization of the Caribbean. I am informed by these uses of the concept here.

19. According to Brenner and Theodore (2002, 2003), Brenner, Marcuse, and Mayer (2011), and Peck (2013), tourism is a neoliberal project insofar as it inscribes market logics in the landscape and contributes to enlarging the presence of markets.

20. See Holston (1989) for an ethnographic account on the centrality of architecture and design in the construction of modernist cities. I am following here Herman and Chomsky's (2002) idea of manufacturing consent in their definition of mass communication media as "effective and powerful ideological institutions that carry out a system-supportive propaganda function, by reliance on market forces, internalized assumptions, and self-censorship, and without overt coercion" (306). In many ways, tourism in Yucatán works in a similar fashion. Tourism also participates in capitalism's economy of enrichment, as Boltanski and Chiapello

(2018) put it, drawing "its substance from exploitation of the *past* (. . .) *of things that are already there*" (xii).

21. Pointing at tourism's ritualized nature, Graburn (1977) defined it as a sacred journey. See Stasch (2009) on primitivism, tourism, and place.

22. International tourism and its associated mobilities have also become a political sacred objective, and in places such as Guatemala (Becklake 2019), Macedonia (Mattioli 2014), Hawai'i (Desmond 1999; Gonzalez 2013), and Israel (Kelly 2016; Stein 2008), providing security for tourists' bodies and movements seems more important than providing services for citizens.

23. Important research has been conducted on ecotourism as a form of extractivist tourism. Duffy (2002, 2008), Brockington, Duffy, and Igoe (2008), and Sharpley (2009) have critically discussed the use of ecotourism and conservationism as avenues for the neoliberalization of nature. Along these lines, Büscher and Davidov (2013) have coined the term "ecotourism-extraction nexus" to address the similarities in how gas extraction and ecotourism operate in Ecuador. Loperena (2017) studies the relations between sustainable tourism and extractivism in Honduras following Hurricane Mitch in 1998. My discussion (in particular chapter 2) is informed by this body of work, but I expand the conceptualization of tourism as an extractive industry beyond nature tourism modalities to refer to all forms of tourism. Prior to these debates, Hoskins (2002) used the term "predatory voyeurs" to refer to adventure tourists' visual consumption of primitivism among the Sumba in Bali. She uses the term "predatory" to highlight the blood and violence involved in this uneven form of consumption and places the emphasis on tourists' experiences. From another angle, Miller (2017) has also exposed the interrelation between the cultural industries and the classic extractive industries and companies, showing how greenwashing in the cultural industries has become an enabler of our current ecological crisis. I take this exploration further to argue that tourism, as part of the cultural industries, is itself extractive. In a similar vein, Sheller (2003) has argued that tourism demands a process of "eating bodies" that was also characteristic of colonial relations in the Caribbean. Sheller (2014) has also recently explored how the centrality of aluminum has played a crucial role in the aesthetics of modernity, and taking tourism as a main driver of modernity, she shows that aluminum is inextricably linked to a politics of mining and smelting that has directly contributed to ecological deterioration. Redclift (2006) has compared tourism development in the Caribbean coast of the Yucatán Peninsula with the extraction of chicle in earlier decades. I find inspiration in this body of work for the arguments developed here.

24. On the multiscalar nature of extractive industries, also see Finn (1998) and Sawyer (2004).

25. On extractivism and enclave economies in the Latin American context, see Gudynas (2015) and Svampa (2015). In tourism research, there has been a great deal of discussion about virtual tourism as a way to reduce congestion in physical places that are saturated with visitors (such as Venice), but even virtual tours require the material and physical transformation of place.

26. See de la Cadena (2019) on the processes of "uncommoning" nature and the cancellation of excess inherent to extractivism in Latin America and beyond. The

documentaries *Jamaica for Sale* by Esther Figueroa and Diana McCaulay (2006) and *Gringo Trails* by Pegi Vail (2015) serve as good pedagogical examples of the unintended consequences of shaping geographies for tourism. See MacCannell (1992) for an analysis of the processes of staging in tourism.

27. *Starchitecture* refers to a type of architecture designed by celebrity architects (à la Frank Gehry).

28. Recent debates among Latin American scholars prefer the term *neoextractivism* over *extractivism,* as it emphasizes both the active role of the state in negotiating shares of profit as well as the extent of the exploitation of nonrenewable natural resources. See Gudynas (2015) and Farthing and Fabricant (2018) for other examples, although none dealing with the tourism industry. In the Yucatán Peninsula, tourism's extractive practices have been deeply ingrained in national and regional development plans, making it a proper example of Latin American neoextractivism in practice.

29. The so-called last-chance tourism or doomed tourism was the 2018 trend in international travel and consists of visiting "endangered" places before they disappear due to anthropogenic climate change. Favorite destinations of this form of traveling are the Arctic, parts of New Zealand, and Venice. For a discussion see Lemelin et al. (2010).

30. It could be said that tourism's predatory orderings are "not just a capitalist practice, but a central practice through which capitalism sustains itself" (Büscher and Fletcher 2017, 651). In fact, tourism does not only parallel the predatory model of the oil and gas industries; it is also one of its biggest customers. See Miller (2017) for a discussion.

31. On territorial and identity struggles linked to extraction and on the violence of extractive practices to indigenous and local communities, see Gómez-Barris (2017), McNeish (2013), Sawyer (2004), and Sawyer and Gómez (2012). See also Neil Smith (1997) for an account of the different forms of violence implied in processes of geographical uneven development.

32. See Harvey, Krohn-Hansen, and Nustad (2019) for a recent discussion of ecological amputations and the Anthropocene.

33. I am thankful to Chandra Mukerji for putting it this way (personal communication, October 2018)

34. Stickiness has been approached as an anthropological, sociological, and geographical concept to describe the power of colonial grids and modern state formations upon the organization of social and economic life (Scott 1999); to describe the perseverance of industrial districts in a context of increased globalization (Markusen 1996); to describe the frictions or "sticky grips" of global connections (Tsing 2005); and to account for global infrastructures and splintering urbanism (Graham and Marvin 2001). Mobility scholars have also used the term to reflect on the power of tourism *mediascapes* in the organization of material and virtual space for tourism consumption (Ek and Hultman 2008). Although he engages with it in a different way than I do in this book, Sharkey (2013) has used the phrase "stuck in place" to theorize the pervasive ongoing racial inequality observed in urban black

neighborhoods in America. I am inspired by his analysis because it urges us to consider the spatiality of contemporary forms of urban poverty and inequality in a historical and intergenerational light. In archeology, Ian Hodder (2012) describes the actor network concept of "entanglement" as a form of stickiness that describes how societies are entrapped into maintaining and sustaining material worlds. In feminist and postcolonial studies, Haraway (2018) refers to "sticky threads" to describe the webs of technoscience; Ahmed (2014) uses the term to address the circulation of emotion through objects and relations that become sticky because they are saturated with affect.

35. I am inspired by Bonilla's (2015) use of the term "strategic entanglements" to describe the contemporary labor activism of political activists in Guadeloupe, who make use of maroon tactics in a present context in which they are trapped as they were when enslaved. Strategic entanglements with past forms of slave resistance practices, she says, allow "political actors to temporarily break, circumvent, and contest the norms of a system from which they are unable to fully disentangle" (42). Chapter 3 addresses how these strategic entanglements with past forms of labor resistance are performed by workers at hacienda hotels in inland Yucatán. A contemporary account of the ways in which particular indigenous persons are swayed by tourism and the long-lasting impacts upon their world views can be found in de la Cadena (2015). On moral encounters in tourism, see Mostafanezhad and Hannam (2016) and Simoni (2018).

36. I build on Wendy Brown's (2016) conceptualization of sacrificial citizenship: individuals governed by a discourse of a moralized shared sacrifice. I choose the plural form, *sacrificial logics*, to point out that there are a multiplicity of ways in which people buy into tourism's predatory logics and that while overall these could be described as sacrificial, their expressions and manifestations in the everyday vary across places and peoples and their positionalities within the industry.

37. Milpa is a traditional intercropping system. In the Yucatán Peninsula it refers to both the plot of land, and the agricultural and religious practices of caring for that land (Terán and Rasmussen 1994). Chapter 4 engages ethnographically with this practice.

38. Some scholars view the Caste Wars as an embryonic form of the 1994 Zapatista uprising in Chiapas and other subsequent indigenous demands regarding land and labor in Latin America (Stephens 2018; Reed 2001).

39. Mexican *ejido* is a land tenure system resulting from the Mexican Revolution (1910) and aimed at abolishing large estates or *latifundios* and restoring land to indigenous populations and the dispossessed. For a historical discussion of Mexican *ejidos,* see (B. W. Fallaw 1995, 2001; Joseph and Nugent 1994). For a contemporary study of *ejido* reforms in Mexico following the 1992 Mexican Agrarian Reform, see Vázquez Castillo (2004). On the historical specificities of *ejidos* and haciendas in Yucatán, see Chardon (1963).

40. Prior to the henequen boom, parts of the region, in particular Campeche and Quintana Roo, had already been connected to global markets through the extraction of dyewood *(palo de Campeche* or *palo de tinte)*, mahogany, and, notably, chicle (gum) (Redclift 2004; Forero and Redclift 2006). Between 1910 and the

1950s, Quintana Roo was a global epicenter in the production of manufactured gum, a product that could be obtained only from a substance extracted from the wild *zapote* or *chicozapote* tree (Redclift 2004) that grew in the eastern and southern areas of the region—areas that would later be part of state tourism development plans. *Palo de tinte*, mahogany, and chicle production practices had long-lasting consequences in changing tropical forests (Steen and Tucker 1991). Their trade greatly suffered from the introduction of synthetic dyes and materials, and the dismantling of production was followed by extensive unemployment and social unrest.

41. At a regional level, up until the mid-1990s, air traffic at Mérida's airport was robust and affordable but the rerouting of flights to Cancún's airport shifted the focus and flow of people to Cancún, making what had been a periphery the epicenter of international travel. In 2007, Cancún registered regular flight connections with twelve Mexican cities (including over twenty daily flights to Mexico City), forty-five US cities (including eight daily flights to Miami, and three to Atlanta, Dallas, Houston, New York, and Philadelphia), as well as regular connections with four Canadian, eight European, and seven other Latin American cities, including three daily flights to La Habana, Cuba (Córdoba Ordóñez and Córdoba Azcárate 2007).

42. "New 7 Wonders Of the World: 2007," available at https://world.new7wonders.com/, accessed May 2020.

43. See Susan Vincil, "10Best Day Trip: Visit Tiny Tulum's Ancient Mayan Ruins," *USA Today*, March 1, 2012, https://www.10best.com/interests/food-travel/how-tulum-became-Mexicos-hottest-culinary-destination/.

44. Contemporary ethnographies and travel essays about the region have intended to cover this gap in historical research (Breglia 2006, 2014; Castellanos 2010b; Castañeda 1996; Loewe 2010; Guardado 2012; García de Fuentes 1979; Re Cruz 1996; Everton 2012). These ethnographies explore how the deployment of tourism as a state-planned development strategy has affected the region. They point to Cancún's planned creation as the turning point in the regional shift from henequen to tourism. They show the ubiquity of top-down, state-led tourist developments, and they reveal how planned tourism development has created a strong process of regionalization by thickening national and transnational exchanges between coastal and urban areas, like Cancún and Mérida, and partially widening demographic, labor, and commodity flows to inland areas, like Valladolid or Hunucmá, where the *touristification* of "the Maya" is now rampant (Castellanos 2010b, 2015; Loewe 2010). These ethnographies agree that tourism has brought a return to servitude for many, "contributing little to nothing to the public good" (Loewe 2010, 35). For example, Castellanos (2015) argues in her ethnography of Maya indigenous migrant workers in Cancún that tourism development of the city has brought forth a "history of colonial exploitation and nationalistic projects intended to assimilate and erase indigenous practices" (69). Similarly, Breglia (2006) and Castañeda (1996) highlight how this form of exploitation reflects a tendency for local communities to become dispossessed from land and resources through cultural heritage management practices planned for tourist purposes.

45. The region is an ideal unit of analysis in political economy and human geography. I am informed here by relational and action-centered approaches to the region and regionalization processes (Thrift 1994, 1996; Meusburger, Werlen, and Suarsana 2018; Gregory 1994; Anderson 2016). Attention to geographical regional scales figures prominently in development and tourism studies research, most notably among those working on tourism planning and governance in Europe and developing countries (Jenkins 1982; Pattullo 2005; Williams and Montanari 1995). On the regional scale in Mexico, see Berger and Wood (2010). GIS technology has recently resuscitated the importance of scale in tourism analysis, mostly via quantitative and managerial approaches to tourism and their relations with both the environment and the physical movements of tourism (Lee et al. 2013; Grêt-Regamey et al. 2008; Fox, n.d.). Tourism's active role in processes of scale reorganization has received attention by Sheller (2003, 2009), Duffy (2002), Williams and Lew (2014), and Williams and Montanari (1995). More generally, I am following here the privilege of the everyday in the theorization of the production of space enunciated by De Certeau (2011), Lefevbre (1994), and Massey (1994).

46. The works of LaBrecque (2005), LaBrecque and Bretton (1982), and more recently Taylor (2018) in the region are exceptions to this rule. The main area of interest for these authors is understanding the gendered nature and lived experiences of global phenomena on an everyday basis.

47. Regional approaches to the study of ecological and biological patterns in the region are, however, more common (see Urquiza-Haas, Dolman, and Peres 2007; Carte et al. 2010; Whitmore et al. 1996). Michael R. Redclift (2006) in *Frontiers* offers a comparative account of the development of chicle and tourism in the state of Quintana Roo, where Cancún is located, and his analysis is both an exception and an inspiration for my work.

48. The work of Gavin Smith (1991; 2019) and Narotzky and Smith (2006) advances the reconceptualization of social reproduction's role in patterns of capital accumulation through an ethnography of the specifics of different forms of labor (in Spain and Peru), and has also served as an inspiration for my ethnography.

49. On mobile methods, also see Candea (2007), Haldrup and Larsen (2009), and Elliot, Norum, and Salazar (2018).

CHAPTER 1. BEACH ENCLOSURES

1. "Excellence Riveria Cancun," Trip Advisor, last retrieved June 2017, https://www.tripadvisor.com/ShowUserReviews-g240327-d499896-r84207327-Excellence_Riviera_Cancun-Puerto_Morelos_Yucatan_Peninsula.html#); this particular comment is no longer available but comments of this kind reoccur frequently.

2. In 2017, Euromonitor placed Cancún among the strongest growing cities in the Americas; see Euromonitor Research, "Cancun Expected to Be the Strongest Growing City in the Americas," *Euromonitor International* (blog), Nov. 21, 2017 https://blog.euromonitor.com/Cancún-strongest-growing-city-2017-americas/.

Also see Mastercard, "Global Destination Cities Index 2019," https://newsroom.mastercard.com/wp-content/uploads/2019/09/GDCI-Global-Report-FINAL-1.pdf.

3. Enclosure is a concept widely used in the geographical and sociological literature to refer to the English process of cordoning off land and resources, that is, the commons, in favor of private interests (see Harvey 2011). In the special issue "Enclosures: Fences, Walls and Contested Spaces" in *Radical History Review,* there are examples of contemporary enclosures that proceed in a similar fashion to Cancún (see Chazkel and Serlin 2010). Recently, Fields (2017) has used the concept of enclosure to make sense of the "deliberately fractured landscape" (2) of Palestine.

4. I have elaborated an earlier version of this argument in Córdoba Azcárate, Baptista, and Domínguez Rubio (2014), with specific details on the respective post-hurricane reconstruction processes.

5. Maquiladoras were first created in 1965 at the US-Mexico border, and first expanded to nonborder areas in 1971. These manufacturing facilities were conceived in Mexican legislation as a means of both integrating Mexico's economy with the world economy and creating a main source of foreign investment (Kopinak 1996, 5).

6. According to Whitfield (2006) marketization is characterized by five key elements: "the commodification of services and infrastructure; the commodification of labor such as the reorganization of work and jobs to maximise productivity and assist transfer to another employer; restructuring the state competition and market mechanisms; restructuring democratic accountability and user involvement; embedding business interests and promoting liberalization internationally" (3). Also see Birch and Siemiatycki (2016) for an account of neoliberalism and the geographies of marketization.

7. The other planned tourist cities conceived and created after Cancún in Mexico were: Ixtapa-Zihuatanejo (Guerrero), also in 1974; Loreto and San José del Cabo (Baja California), planned in 1976; and Bahias de Huatulco (Oaxaca), in 1984. See Dávila López (2014), Monterrubio, Osorio, and Benítez (2018), and Wilson (2008) for a comparative analysis of Mexico's CIPs. For insights on Bahias de Huatulco, see Brenner (2005). Cancún's tourism model has also been replicated across Latin America, Africa, South East Asia, and the Middle East (see Torres and Momsen 2005a; Wallace 2005).

8. For an academic discussion on the origins of Cancún, see Hoffman, Fainstein, and Judd (2003), Redclift (2006), and Pelas (2011). For a detailed official narrative and historical images from FONATUR, see Vega Campos (2010)

9. See more at Córdoba Azcárate, Baptista, and Domínguez Rubio (2014), Pelas (2011), and Manuel-Navarrete (2012).

10. I am using the term *multiscalar* to highlight the combined geographical and institutional character of these efforts and alliances, which involve simultaneous interplay among international, national, regional, and local levels and institutions. FONATUR was the result of the coupling of two of the most important tourism development agencies, Tourism Infrastructure Trust Fund (INFRATUR) and

Tourism Guarantee and Promotion (FOGATUR). For a discussion of FONATUR's tasks, see Torres and Momsen (2005a and 2005b) and Pelas (2011).

11. On the *ejido* crisis and indigenous livelihood strategies in Yucatán and Quintana Roo, see Warman (2001(and Castellanos (2010a and 2010b).

12. Madrid's presidency also saw the first attempts to replicate Cancún's segregated planning for tourism in other areas of Mexico, in particular in Bahías de Huatulco, in Oaxaca.

13. I use the term *disaster capitalism*, informed by Naomi Klein's (2008) *Shock Doctrine,* to show that governments and corporations use moments of crisis or catastrophes to generate economic profit. These insights come from broader Marxist readings of disasters as both creative and destructive occasions, among them Harvey (2007).

14. Since 1970, official recordings of weather events have accounted for only seasonal tropical storms and low-intensity hurricanes or tropical cyclones (category 3 or less, according to the Safire–Simpson Hurricane Scale). Cancún's Protección Civil has only a record of Hurricane Allen in 1980 prior to Hurricane Gilbert.

15. Susan Taylor Martin, "Gilbert Left Damage throughout All of Caribbean," *St. Petersburg Times,* September 16, 1988, https://www.newspapers.com/clip/20583592 /we-survived-hurricane-gilbert/.

16. See Escudero-Castillo et al. (2018) for a quantitative and visual analysis of sand loss in Cancún in the aftermath of Gilbert and Wilma. The authors point at posthurricane unfettered urbanization as the main reason for the destination's sand loss.

17. Since 1983, the water supply (drinking water and sewage) in most of Mexico had been the responsibility of municipal governments. This privatization process was accelerated under the new Law of National Waters by which different municipalities contract their water management to subsidiaries of transnational corporations, such as Vivendi. For a discussion see Ruiz Marrero (2005).

18. This process of immaterial segregation and privatization of space is representative of many contemporary enclosed cities in North America and Latin America, as has been explored by Low and Lawrence-Zúñiga (2003) and Low (1999, 2004).

19. Material losses related to the tourism sector alone were estimated at US$2.9 billion, with about US$11 million being claimed from insurance companies for personal damages in Cancún and the Riviera Maya (Alvarez 2015).

20. Castellanos (2010b) defines Cancún post-Wilma as a "phantom city" and documents the use of Wilma as a creative and destructive occasion from the perspective and experiences of indigenous migrant workers. Guardado and López Santillán (2010) have studied the cultural logics of the privatization of space along the Riviera Maya coast, which followed Cancún's example.

21. I have elaborated on this story at length in Córdoba Azcárate, Baptista, and Domínguez Rubio (2014).

22. Naomi Klein (2008) shows how the destructive effects of Sri Lanka's 2004 tsunami in fishing communities along the shoreline were used by the country's

government, the US government, and tourism corporations to establish new buffer zones that would regulate the beaches as off-limits for tourism development. This practice paved the way for islands like Phuket to reemerge as boutique luxury destinations at the expense of the displacement of already relocated and vulnerable populations. She describes this process as a "second tsunami" or the "wider wave." Also see Johnson (2011) for an analysis of public policy restructuring after Katrina in New Orleans.

23. Castellanos (2020) has recently identified a form of social resistance among indigenous migrant workers, motivated by their access to housing in Cancún City, that she describes as a process of "waiting out" the state.

24. Wilson (2012) offers a description of Mexico's beach vendors. Although her research does not include Cancún, similar practices to those described in her work are also observable here.

25. I am using here the term *emotional labor* to refer to the mental and physical work routines that workers must undergo to evoke and suppress particular feelings in order to generate and manage feelings of happiness and escape in tourists. Emotional labor implies that workers are monitored and surveilled in their capacities to create those feelings for tourists. See Hochschild (2012) for a discussion of the term.

26. As Castellanos (2010b, 2015) has demonstrated, indigenous stereotypes inform Maya indigenous family migratory patterns to Cancún and the United States. A typical example of these practices is that of the Maya maid, in which indigenous women's sexuality is used as a marketing strategy to attract Western consumers. This is also evident in other tourist destinations, in particular Hawai'i where women's bodies in movement are the main tourist attraction, as studied by Desmond (1999) and Enloe (2000).

27. Similar experiences were reported by Castellanos (2010b) in her encounters with hotel maids in Cancún's Hotel Zone. In her ethnography, she describes, for example, how she stayed for hours in her hotel room in order to speak with hotel maids, who were always looking at the door so as not to be caught in conversation with a guest.

28. Castellanos, personal communication, February 2018. Also see Fraga and Doyon (2008).

29. An interesting comparison could be drawn with the tourist city of Acapulco, where tourism development has historically faced significant opposition, with a strong civic mobilization staking a claim for better redistribution of resources and services from the city and the state (Anduiza 2019). For a discussion of Cancún's civic and community associations and the ongoing rise of ecological organizations, see Velasco Ruiz (2018).

30. Similar accounts regarding wages could be found in Trip Advisor forums as of June 2017.

31. TenCate Geotube, "Geotube Shoreline Protection and Breakwater Construction Bring Cancun Beaches Back to Life," FYI News Bulletin G2007-07, accessed October 2018, https://gowatersolve.com/uploads/20100623105600Tencate%20NB_Geotube_CancunBeaches-20110923083616.pdf.

32. I have elaborated on this ethnographic vignette and worked extensively on the appropriation of disaster mapping and environmental art as a tool for urban governance in Cancún; see Córdoba Azcárate (2019).

33. See Koerner (2016) for an account on how geotextile tubes work on Cancún's beaches. Most geotextile tubes in Cancún are from TenCate Corporate, a multinational company focused, as they put it, "on the growing demand for protection of people and their living and working environments." See "The Company: About TenCate," TenCate.com, accessed April 2020, https://www.tencate.com/en/About-TenCate/The-company.

34. Sand dredging in Cancún is performed by two of the largest sand dredging companies in the world, the multinationals TenCate Geosynthetics, https://www.tencatego.eu/en/markets/water-infrastructure, and Jan de Nuul Multinational, https://www.jandenul.com/en/about-jdn/company-profile/history, both accessed April 2020.

35. MUSA website, accessed April 2020, https://musamexico.org/.

CHAPTER 2. WILD HOTSPOTS

1. Edensor (2001) uses the terms *enclavic tourist space* and *heterogeneous tourist space* to define, respectively, those "single purpose destinations" that are "carefully planned and managed," where "tourists are subject to soft control" and where there is minimal ambiguity and contradiction, as, for example, in theme parks or museums; and those more "weakly classified tourist spaces," with "no clear boundaries," "multi-purposed spaces in which a wide range of activities and people co-exist." While Cancún, the Riviera Maya, and Chichén Itzá were clearly enclavic tourist spaces, in the mid-1990s Celestún was a heterogenous tourist space.

2. Academic research on frontiers is important here as a referent mobilized to address human and social geography changes in contexts of resource extraction as well as the development of racialized capitalism (Petras and Veltmeyer 2016; Saldaña-Portillo 2016; Redclift 2006; Larsen 2015).

3. Scholarly discussions of local populations directly negotiating with international interlocutors—effectively bypassing regional and national levels—identify this as an example of "scale bending" (Smith 2008). Examples of this process abound, particularly in Latin American debates on indigeneity, extractivism, development, and autonomy. Bolivia and the Ecuadorian Andes are good examples of this. See for example Anthias (2017), Fabricant (2012), McNeish (2013), and Postero (2017). See Fortun (2001) and Tsing (2005) for ethnographic discussions of the role of the global environmental movement, ecological disasters, and the rise of advocacy. Thus far, the literature has not examined tourism in depth, nor has it considered how these international-to-local negotiations are generative of geographical space themselves. My work is a contribution in these directions.

4. An analogy to protecting animal species rather than people could be established with the processes of protecting the environment over people, as Park and

Pellow (2013) have noted for Aspen, Colorado, one of the West's most elite ski resorts. Here, the desire to protect particular imaginations of nature-as-environment mask forms of white nationalism and anti-immigrant sentiment and is a direct trigger to reinforce racial ideologies.

5. According to the World Wildlife Fund, an ecoregion is a "large unit of land or water containing a geographically distinct assemblage of species, natural communities, and environmental conditions"; see "Ecoregions," World Wildlife Fund, accessed April 2020, https://www.worldwildlife.org/biomes.

6. For a discussion on Celestún's inclusion in the MAB program, see García-Frapolli et al. (2009).

7. La Marcha al Mar was the name for a series of national policies led by president Adolfo Ruiz Cortines (1952–58) to support fishing in the country's coasts in an effort to decentralize urban pressures in inland areas, incorporate ports into a national network of fishing ports, and make use of marine resources for the economy. In Yucatán, these policies were adopted in the 1980s by Governor Cervera Pacheco (see Quezada 2011).

8. See also the Celestún City Council's Facebook page, H. Ayuntamiento de Celestún 2018–2021, Facebook, https://www.facebook.com/H-Ayuntamiento-de-Celest%C3%BAn-2018-2021-258963214950957/?eid=ARC1E5BVoVRNraPEdpjg_xiTEdJIfbAbRRCF1QzqbaQ10IHHJxi_RYvt8eDcyNUJnf_yU1ApBykdREcw&hc_ref=ARTfpotZO7zFXr7P2Q441AUfbRAaO49nRzFZTg5yV9j_Lqiqfpi1bbhVg3vXC30mlOg&fref=nf.

9. Violence in natural protected areas has been a common concern and area of research, particularly when indigenous populations are involved. Ethnographic works for reference on tourism in these areas include Duffy (2002) in Belize; Arnold (2018) in the Brazilian Amazon; Gonzalez (2013) in Hawai'i and the Philippines, and Loperena (2017) in Honduras. These ethnographies, as well as my own work in Celestún, exemplify larger arguments on extractive industries and the way in which natural extraction struggles are always also social struggles (see Sawyer and Gómez 2012).

10. Lisa Coleman, "Thinking Pink in Celestún," *Mexico Premiere*, Feb. 13, 2012, accessed April 2020, www.mexicopremiere.com/thinking-pink-in-celestun/.

11. I elaborated on this concept in Córdoba Azcárate (2011)

12. "Crónica de un conflicto anunciado: Estalla la violencia en Celestún," *La Revista Peninsular*, 2002; the article is no longer available on the *Revista Peninsular* website, having been replaced by tourist promotion: http://www.larevista.com.mx/yucatan/redescubre-y-aventurate-con-celestun-12057.

13. It is worth noting that in other Mexican places, such as Oaxaca and Chiapas, as well as in countries like Guatemala and Bolivia, conflicts within indigenous communities and against the state have been longstanding, leading to long histories of military and police intervention and of indigenous communities claiming their own forms of governance (Stephen 2013; Sadlier 2019; Sullivan 1989; Saldaña-Portillo 2016; Nájera 2009). This has not been the case in Yucatán as a whole, and is even less so in communities such as Celestún where indigenous populations are not the majority.

14. A video of the protest was published by *El Diario de Yucatán* and is available at "Vecinos de Celestún casi linchan a su alcalde," video, 1:23, posted May 20, 2017 by Yucatán Ahora, https://www.youtube.com/watch?v=GjISMVZoDtc.

15. "Intentan linchar al alcalde de Celestún (videos)," *De Peso Yucatán*, May 20, 2017, https://depesoyucatan.com/policia/en-medio-de-balas-polis-rescatan-a-edil-de-celestun/. The article is explicitly referring to a local species of red ants. In so doing the author is playing with contrasts in the behaviors as well as the colors of wildlife: the soft pink of easily frightened flamingos and the vital red of aggressive ants.

16. Similar frictions are observable in Tulum, where the push towards ecotourism within the resort industry has also advanced through intense privatization and land appropriation (Guardado 2012).

17. See the websites for Playa Maya Resorts Yucatán, http://playamayayucatan .com, and Eco-Paraiso Xixim Celestun, https://hotelxixim.com. Both offer drone views and pictures of the beach that are worth watching to have a sense of the powerful ways in which Celestún is branded as a natural paradise as well as the scope of the hotels' land holdings.

18. The last Demographic and Health Service (DHS) health survey for Celestún dates from 1987. https://dhsprogram.com/publications/publication-fr24-dhs-final-reports.cfm. Since then, estimates have been made by the student interns at the health clinic but these are not published and are accessible only for in situ consultation.

19. In her ethnography about women garbage collectors in Celestún, Hanson (2017) observes: "Up to 15 tons of additional trash is produced per day by tourists in December and March–April, and between 2–10 tons in the summer months (June–August)" (5).

20. Celestún is no different than other natural protected areas facing similar contradictions. Feminist scholars have pointed to the consequences of ignoring gendered and sociocultural practices in the understanding and management of nature in conservation areas. See Agarwal (2001) and Elmhirst (2011). For further discussion on Celestún, see Hanson's work on women garbage collectors (Hanson 2016, 2017; Buechler and Hanson 2016).

CHAPTER 3. COLONIAL ENCLAVES

1. "Un bunker, la hacienda Temozón Sur, sede de la reunión Calderón-Bush," *Proceso*, March 7, 2007, https://www.proceso.com.mx/206084/un-bunker-la-hacienda-Temozón-sur-sede-de-la-reunion-calderon-bush.

2. Al Giordano, "Accused Narco Banker to Host Bush-Calderón Meeting in Yucatán," *Narco News Bulletin*, March 11, 2007, accessed October 2018, https://narconews.com/Issue45/article2584.html.

3. "The World's Billionaires: Number 828 Roberto Hernandez," Forbes, accessed April 2020, https://www.forbes.com/profile/roberto-hernandez-ramirez /#145b910f504d. The Haciendas venture includes Hacienda Santa Rosa, Hacienda San

José, Hacienda Uayamon, Hacienda Temozón Sur, and Hacienda Puerta Campeche. See http://thehaciendas.com/.

4. See website for Hacienda Temozón Sur, Marriot Luxury Collection, https:// www.marriott.com/hotels/travel/midtl-hacienda-temozon-a-luxury-collection-hotel-temozon-sur/, and Geoff Whitmore, "Details Surrounding the Marriott and Starwood Merger," *Forbes*, April 18, 2018, https://www.forbes.com/sites /geoffwhitmore/2018/04/18/details-surrounding-the-marriott-starwood-merger /#17871e285c07.

5. "Misión y Visión," Fundación Haciendas Mundo Maya, www .haciendasmundomaya.org/mision-vision-valores.html.

6. An interesting comparison could be drawn with some Western cities, where, according to Edensor (2005), material concern with the creation of manicured landscapes for tourism out of industrial sites demands the neglect of other ruins. This intentional neglect informs the creation of voids within the fabric of everyday life.

7. I am following here Breglia's (2009) definition of re-patronage in hacienda hotels in Yucatán as the historical permanence of a set of values, imaginaries, and social relations that find their origins in the hacienda system and that are now expressed in a new social context in which international managers act as the patrons and Maya indigenous persons as peones. An interesting comparison could be drawn with the implementation of heritage tourism on Southern plantations in the United States and the way these sites are refurbished to sanitize a history of oppression, enslavement, and insurrection (Adams 2007; Miles 2017).

8. The use of precolonial nostalgia and authenticity of indigenous cultures for tourism purposes has been particularly relevant in Mexico (e.g., Berghe 1994; Ayora-Díaz 2000; Castañeda 2004). We can find a historical precedent in the way indigenous peoples and spaces were represented as inhabiting "sedentarist indigenous pasts" in Mexico's first cartographic representations from 1858; see Craib (2004) for a fascinating account of this matter and how it helped to advance Mexico's centralizing governmental tendencies (37). In these sedentarist representations, haciendas are asserted as pivotal places for the narration of the Mexican nation. Precolonial nostalgia and the performance of authenticity should also be contextualized as responding to the larger contemporary momentum of nationalist struggles and of efforts by indigenous communities to assert control over land, resources, and forms of government. This is particularly relevant in Latin America, where the Bolivian case is representative of the contestation of neoliberalism (Godale and Postero 2013; Canessa 2012; Postero 2017). Berliner (2014) has recently coined the term "exonostalgia" to refer to the fascination of anthropology—and we can extend here, of the tourism and heritage industries—with the exotic and nostalgia, and with the political implications of that fascination.

9. Carstensen and Roazen-Parrillo (1983) offer a critical historical insight into the relations between these harvesting machines and technologies and Yucatán's companies and elites.

10. See Evans (2013) for a discussion of these interlocking dependencies and their shared expressions in the agriculture, politics, and ecology of these three regions. The gardening practices that I explore later in the chapter offer an example.

11. For a detailed history of the ownership of Hacienda Temozón Sur, the Peón family, and their links to Yucatán's revolutionary past, see Menéndez Rodríguez (1992) and Savarino Roggero (1992). I am grateful to Ben Fallaw for pointing me in their direction.

12. In *Destination Culture*, Barbara Kirshenblatt-Gimblett (1998) argues that re-creation of virtual worlds into which visitors enter is a common aspect of in situ displays. "In situ displays," she says in her ethnography of Plimoth Plantation, "are immersive and environmental. They privilege 'experience' and tend to thematize rather than set their subject forth. At their most fully realized . . . they recreate a virtual world into which the visitor enters. This effect is modeled on the experience of travel and the pleasures of engaging the life world as the ultimate exhibition of itself" (4).

13. Fallaw (2001) writes about this moment as follows: "the symbolically charged signature of the first land grant of the crusade at Temozón was prefaced by peasant speakers and an elaborately choreographed agrarian tableaux that lasted several hours under the blazing August sun. . . . One unidentified Maya speaker at Temozón was photographed addressing the president. . . . 'The Mayas have not opened their mouths to explain their situation in a long time,' implying that Cardenas' presence opened up a genuine dialogue between the people and their government" (89).

14. The PNR Femenine Sector (PNRSF) created chapters of the Liga Femenina across the nation. In Yucatán, research by Buck Kachaluba (2018) reports eleven leagues, including one in Temozón with 107 members and activities such as combating alcoholism, fostering hygiene, and providing prenatal care and education for women. Buck Kachaluba describes how recruitment for the leagues took place: "All willing women of 14 years or older, 'living honestly' in the town in which the league was formed, were invited to become members, which gave them the right to use cooperative resources and take advantage of medical service. They were obliged, in return, to attend meetings punctually, fill commissions, make sure their children attended school and received vaccinations, and participate in league projects to improve their homes and their communities and to combat alcoholism and general vice." This form of organizing is similar to the one FHMM expects workers to adhere to.

15. Within these new globalized elites, local scholar Ramírez (personal communication, October 2012, Mérida) differentiates three major groups: a group composed of no more than ten businessmen who managed to gain control of the three major economic sectors at a regional level (tourism, construction, and commerce); a second group whose members hold influential positions in major international and national corporations with regional interests as well as in service-oriented and automobile industries; and a third, broader group composed of politicians closely associated to land speculation and real estate development corporations at

regional, national, and international levels. The reconstruction of henequen haciendas into luxury hotels and the development of a hybrid public-private partnership to manage them is closely associated with this last group.

16. See "The World Heritage Convention," UNESCO, https://whc.unesco.org/en/convention/.

17. Visitors to Chichén Itzá during the 1980s amounted to a few thousand and were mostly concentrated around the spring equinox and summer solstice. In 2017, Chichén Itzá was the most visited archeological destination in México, with over 2.6 million visitors annually. According to Yucatán's government statistics, over five thousand tourists visited the site daily during the 2016 peak seasons (SECTUR 2017). According to Castañeda (1996, 2004) the place has become such an attraction that it is performing almost the same central role it did for Maya religiosity, economy, and politics centuries ago.

18. It is not by chance that Mexico and Spain, with economies overtly dependent on tourism, are among the countries with the most UN designations of natural and cultural heritage sites. See the UNESCO World Heritage List, available at https://whc.unesco.org/en/list/).

19. In the tourism industry this form of cultural tourism is often also referred to as New Age tourism, for its appeal to the desire for spiritual connection (Dallen and Olsen 2006).

20. Greg Benchwick, "The Forgotten Ruins of Mexico's Ruta Puuc," *BBC Travel*, October 25, 2011, http://www.bbc.com/travel/story/20111024-the-forgotten-ruins-of-mexicos-ruta-puuc.

21. See "Historical City of Izamal (Izamal, Mayan Continuity in an Historical City)," UNESCO, accessed April 2020, https://whc.unesco.org/en/tentativelists/5394/.

22. In the context of globalization, luxury and taste are still considered in this fashion as part of economic exchange and consumption practices. In "creative economies" (Flew 2011), for example, the goods and services derived from cultural or artistic production are uncritically seen as repositories of taste and as a main resource in the achievement of economic development (UNCTAD Creative Economy Report 2010).

23. In tourism studies, Wang (1999) argues that the tourism industry has displaced attention from an objective form of authenticity to an existential one. According to this move, both tourists and the tourist industry are moved toward the creation and consumption of unique experiences rather than of particular objects or monuments per se. Luxury tourism in former henequen haciendas, like other forms of indigenous luxury tourism, can be seen, however, as a rebirth of a combination of both forms of searching for authenticity while traveling. The indigenous luxury tourism that haciendas produce and engage with fosters a unique experience that must happen in and within particular architectural milieus—buildings and settings that have been previously recognized and sanctioned, mostly by UNESCO, for their global representation as "meaningful culture."

24. See Besky (2013) for a fascinating account of Darjeeling tea, taste, and the landscapes of distinction that its cultivation and circulation forged in postcolonial India.

25. Wendy Perrin, "Luxury 10 New Rules," *Condé Nast Traveler* (blog), December 1, 2010, https://www.cntraveler.com/stories/2010-12-01/luxury-s-10-new-rules.

26. See the website for Hacienda Temozón Sur, Marriot Luxury Collection, https://www.marriott.com/hotels/travel/midtl-hacienda-temozon-a-luxury-collection-hotel-temozon-sur/, accessed May 2020.

27. "Voluntourism," slum tourism and favela tourism are related examples of this global turn in tourism practices. Mostly they imply the movement from North to South and from urban to rural areas, and they work by capitalizing on discourses of poverty and racial inequality. See Mostafanezha (2014) and Freire-Medeiros (2014) for ethnographic accounts of these forms of tourism in Southeast Asia and Latin America, respectively.

28. See Johnson (2011) for an account of what he calls "the consumer-criminal mentality" in New Orleans after Hurricane Katrina and the proliferation of malls, themed spaces, and also, Starwood hotels.

29. Hacienda Temozón Sur, Marriot Luxury Collection, https://www.marriott.com/hotels/travel/midtl-hacienda-temozon-a-luxury-collection-hotel-temozon-sur/, accessed May 2020.

30. Sarah Buck Kachaluba, personal communication, November 2018 and published at "Temozón: La Hacienda-Hotel (Estudio de Casa)," Pueblos Yucatecos: Una exploración de experiencias históricas y contemporáneas de comunidades rurales en Yucatán, México, online collection, https://library.ucsd.edu/pueblos-yucatecos/exhibits/show/pueblosyucatecos/pueblos-yucatecos-pueblos/Temozón/Temozón-hacienda-hotel.

31. Hacienda Temozón Sur, Marriot Luxury Collection, https://www.marriott.com/hotels/travel/midtl-hacienda-temozon-a-luxury-collection-hotel-temozon-sur/, accessed May 2020.

32. In their study of the reconversion of New Orleans's Rising Sun Hotel, anthropologists Dawdy and Weyhing (2008) note how food practices in colonial times "enunciated a hierarchy of taste where native resources were positively valued while showing how easily they could be 'civilized' by French cooking practices and hence, absorb the native into the colonial body and protect against a constant assault on the senses" (390). See Ayora Díaz (2012) for a contemporary approach to culinary practices in Yucatán. See Germann Molz (2007) for a broader discussion on the sensuous mobilities implied in culinary tourism.

33. For a historical approach on the prevalence of diabetes in rural Yucatán, see Loria et al. (2018).

34. For an account on ritual uses of cenotes in henequen haciendas, see Savarino Roggero (1992).

35. In recent years, the number of registered civic organizations in the service sector in México has grown dramatically. In 2009 there were 10,704 civic

organizations, and in 2014 this number had increased to 23,469. Yucatán has followed the national trend, registering 245 organizations in 2009 and almost 500 in 2014 (Fierro Reyes 2015).

36. See the website for Fundación Haciendas Mundo Maya, http://www .haciendasmundomaya.org/, accessed May 2020.

37. The FHMM and Hacienda Temozón Sur have received numerous global awards, including the "Investor in People Award" by the World Travel and Tourism Council (2005) and the World's Servers Award, given by Condé Nast Traveler (2007). These international recognitions signal that the hacienda hotels are legitimate private-public partnerships in tourism development, portraying them as the new global benefactors of indigenous communities, while positioning inland Yucatán as a sanctioned landscape of responsible forms of leisure. In 2019, Taller Maya launched an online store with an exclusive catalogue and products that span from hammocks and cushion covers to exclusive jewelry and accessories for the home and for babies. See https://www.tallermaya.org/.

38. I have recently historicized the different uses of indigeneity in state-led tourism branding of the region; see Castellanos and Córdoba Azcárate (forthcoming, 2021).

39. Castellanos (2007) describes similar tensions for Kuchmil migrant indigenous women working as domestic servants in Cancún, where they are described as "Guadalupes," an allusion to Guadalupe, the protagonist of a Televisa soap opera of that name, first aired in 1984, that follows the story of a peasant girl who has migrated to the city to work as a maid and her love affair with one of her employers. For in-depth ethnographies on traditional gender roles in Yucatán, see Elmendorf (1983), Re Cruz, (1996), Kintz (1990), and Juárez (2002). These studies show similar continuities in the way gender roles are performed in Yucatán but also call attention to the fact that most of the time these roles are aspirational, since in reality they are lived differently depending on individual communities.

CHAPTER 4. CITY-VILLAGE

1. See chapter 3 for some contextualization of the archeological Ruta Puuc.

2. In Tekit, *maquila* refers to the process of working, that is, to "doing maquila" *(hacer maquila)*, independently of where the work is done (at home or in a factory). In general, the term *maquiladora* is reserved for the place of work; it is generally used to refer to medium and large factories and not to household workshops. The subtitle of this chapter, "Domestic Maquila in the Tourist Offstage," aims to accommodate to this local definition. In his interview, Manuel uses the term "pulverized maquila" to refer to both transformations in labor and transformations in the physical, material, and social landscape. Lefebvre (1992) used the term *pulverized* to reflect on the attempts by state and capital to fragment and segment space into manageable units of control. See Brenner and Elden (2009) for a discussion.

3. In some aspects, Tekit's contemporary urban transformations also resemble King's (2007) "colonial third culture" in his description of the rather organic cross-

cultural amalgamation of British and Indian forms of urban expression in British India of the nineteenth and twentieth centuries, in particular, military spaces (cantonments), residential spaces (bungalow-compounds), and social spaces (hill stations).

4. Carswell and De Neve (2014) have explored the various ways in which rural Indian villages have become articulated to urban centers through textile manufacture and according to perceptions of caste, debt bondage, and availability of free labor. Although they do not use the term desakota to define the emerging rural-urban configurations that result, their arguments resonate with my research in Tekit. In the villages they studied, textile manufacture is also done through Singer sewing machines and access to machinery is also enabled through credit and tangled in caste social organization. In Yucatán, other inland towns involved in textile manufacture include Chocholá, Tecoh, Teabo, and Kimbilá. Their residents produce uniforms, guayaberas, and huipils at home. The label Mexican desakotas could also be applied to these inland towns, though further ethnographic research would be needed.

5. Milpa is the traditional agricultural system of production used by Maya populations in inland Yucatán. It consists of intercropping maize, beans, and squash in cycles of slash-and-burn (two years of cultivation, eight years of rest). See Terán and Rasmussen (1994) and LaBrecque and Breton (1982) for discussions of the Maya rituals, cosmologies, and gender division of labor associated with this agricultural system.

6. See Breglia (2014) for insight into the oil industry in Campeche, and Fraga and Cervera (2004) for insight into the migration of inland Yucatán populations to the Gulf of Mexico coast.

7. *Maquilization* is a concept used by sociologists to describe the generalization of the working process of maquila factories in the US-Mexico border regions to the southern part of Mexico according to four main characteristics: a largely feminized labor force, extreme segmentation of skill categories, lowering of real wages, and nonunion orientation (Kopinak 1996, 219). For a historical and geographical account of maquilas in Yucatán, see García de Fuentes et al. (2000) and Biles (2004).

8. See Kenney and Florida (1994) for an analysis of Japanese models of production in Mexican maquiladoras.

9. According to the Organization for Economic Co-operation and Development (OECD) "Territorial Reviews: Yucatán" (2007), at the end of 1999 there were over 130 maquiladoras in operation in the state, employing over thirty-five thousand people. The vast majority of these factories, like Jabin, were export-oriented firms that produced clothing and apparel for markets in the United States. In 2001, the state of Yucatán accounted for almost 10 percent of the total number of Mexicans employed in clothing and apparel maquiladoras. "Apparel maquiladoras accounted for one third of the total manufacturing employment and more than two-thirds of total exports in the state" (OECD 2007). During the first half of the year 2000, over 40 percent of maquiladoras in Yucatán had closed or moved out of the state, leaving inland Yucatán in a profound abandonment yet again.

10. NAFTA extended permission to produce "in bond" (using imported materials to create manufactured goods for duty-free export), previously restricted to

maquilas, to all Mexican industries. In 1994 Mónica Gambrill, quoted in Kopinak (1996), predicted that "Mexican business will have to completely reconvert traditional production adopting the maquila formula consisting of US technology, capital and components and administration, Mexican labor and overhead and huge economies of scale ... the balance could be unfavorable for business and workers" (17). Tekit is an example of this prediction coming to pass.

11. See Selby, Murphy, and Lorenzen (2014) on strategies that Mexican households used to face this reorientation of production; González Salazar (2012) for a discussion of the reorientation of textile maquilas and women's work in Mexico; and Kopinak (2003) for a contemporary analysis of the maquilization of the Tijuana–San Diego border.

12. The making and marketing of cultural objects for tourism is not unique to Yucatán and has been studied in other areas of Mexico and beyond as part of global commodity supply chain analysis and an attention to material culture. Relevant to my analysis are for example Chibnik (2003) on Oaxacan wood carvings, Sylvanus (2016) on wax cloth in West Africa, and the edited volume by Little and McAnany (2011), which gives global examples of textile production and circulation. See Mansvelt (2005) for a more general approach to the geographies of consumption and commercial culture.

13. Train Maya has received priority support from President Andrés Manuel López Obrador (AMLO), who has extended the train's original plans to include connections within tourist towns in the state of Yucatán, following Meyers and CANAIVE's proposal to use existing train infrastructure; see "Tren Maya, Opción Viable y Económica para Envoi de Mercancia a la Riviera Maya: CANAIVE Yucatán," *Sureste Informa*, November 12, 2018, http://suresteinforma.com/noticias /tren-maya-opcion-viable-y-economica-para-envio-de-mercancia-a-la-rivera-maya-canaive-yucatan-134487/. For more on Train Maya, see the conclusion.

14. Gavin Smith (1991), in his research of livelihood and resistance in Peru, refers to domestic enterprises organized by kinship as "ghostly figures outside the domain of political economy" that all the same fully dictate the course of economic and political life. Tekit's domestic maquila workshops can also be understood as an expression of ghostly enterprises insofar as they work through flexible formal and informal arrangements organized through kinship and yet are not recognized by the state as fundamental pieces of the economy.

15. Biles (2005) describes *tandas* in Yucatán as follows: "*Tandas* are usually formed by a small group of people who know each other through their work or residence. Members deposit money regularly, which is distributed to participants following a cyclical schedule. This form of credit is particularly effective in that it creates not only liquidity, but also reciprocity.... *tandas* are an efficient form of financial mediation that distributes risk and economizes on transaction costs" (165). For an extended discussion on *tandas* and reciprocity in Mexico, see Mansell-Carstens (1996). Han (2012) describes the dependence on these informal credit associations in Chile and their significance in the advancement of neoliberal policies among the poor.

16. See Smith (2019) for an extended discussion of the need to attend to ethnographic specificities when studying social reproduction.

17. In particular, they recall the domestic textile workshops in Neza, in the metropolis of Mexico City (Alonso Herrero 1991).

18. These internal contradictions are similar to the ones described by Alonso Herrero (1988, 1991) in domestic textile factories in Neza.

19. See Rubio Herrera (2017) on sewing and masculinity in Tekit.

20. The U.S. Agency for International Development (USAID), private donors, and the environmental group Nature Conservancy are providing technical and financial support to get farmers in inland Yucatán to adopt the Milpa Maya Mejorada (or improved milpa) program, in which care for the milpa would include using irrigation and adding organic nutrients to feed the soil. As an NPR documentary on the topic highlighted, "At a larger scale, the project aims to help México receive payments from private companies and the governments of developed countries to combat climate change." Gabriel Popkin, "Mayans Have Farmed the Same Way for Millennia. Climate Change Means They Can't," *NPR,* February 3, 2017, https://www.npr.org/sections/thesalt/2017/02/03/510272265/mayans-have-farmed-the-same-way-for-millennia-climate-change-means-they-cant.

21. The good life that people refer to in Tekit could be a form of "cruel optimism" (Berlant 2011), when forms of inhabiting and desiring the present become obstacles to further flourishing. However, here I argue that this combination of scattered maquila production with tending to the milpa might actually be creating more resilient spaces for these inland communities in the face of catastrophic futures. Families such as the Chans remain in control of their land and they succeed in the guayabera business, which results in having a relatively diversified, if still small, income. Kusno (2013) work on *kampongs* (irregular settlements) as forms of semi-urbanism and their resiliency in flood-prone Jakarta is an interesting comparison.

22. "Saint Monday" *(San Lunes)* is a colloquial way to refer to the need to rest, or to the inability to go to work that follows after a Sunday of excessive alcohol drinking. Having Mondays off is a culturally acceptable practice in Tekit's workshops as long as worker catches up on his or her work during the week. Not doing so is considered an offense to the work of others and gaining a reputation as someone who takes Mondays off and does not catch up makes it very difficult for a worker to receive *encargos,* even within a family.

23. *Jéets méek* is a traditional Maya ritual intended to define an infant's future. See Villanueva Villanueva and Prieto (2007) and Rubio Herrera (2017) for ethnographic elaborations of these rituals.

CONCLUSION

1. For ethnographic evidence in New Orleans and Katrina, see Johnson (2011); for Thailand and Puerto Rico, see Klein (2008, 2018); for Haiti's 2010 earthquake, see Sheller (2013); for Nepal's earthquake see Beirman et al. (2018).

2. Victor Lichtinger and Homero Aridjis, "The Mayan Trainwreck," *Washington Post,* December 4, 2018, https://www.washingtonpost.com/news/theworldpost/wp/2018/12/04/amlo/.

3. Miguel Aguilar, "Breve Historia de un Tren Peninsular" *Regeneración,* no. 14, November 2018, https://regeneracion.mx/breve-historia-de-un-tren-peninsular/. For insight into indigenous voices and Train Maya, see Laura Castellanos, "La Guerra de los pueblos indígenas ya comenzó en Mexico," *Washington Post,* December 16, 2019, https://www.washingtonpost.com/es/post-opinion/2019/12/16/la-guerra-de-los-pueblos-indigenas-contra-el-tren-maya-ya-comenzo-en-mexico/.

REFERENCES

Adams, Jessica. 2007. *Wounds of Returning: Race, Memory, and Property on the Post-slavery Plantation*. New ed. Chapel Hill: The University of North Carolina Press.

Agarwal, Bina. 2001. "Participatory Exclusions, Community Forestry, and Gender: An Analysis for South Asia and a Conceptual Framework." *World Development* 29 (10): 1623–48. https://doi.org/10.1016/S0305-750X(01)00066-3.

Aguirre, Benigno E. 1989. *The Effects of Hurricane Gilbert in Cancun*. College Station, TX: Hazard Reduction Recovery Center, College of Architecture, Texas A & M University.

Ahmed, Sarah. 2014. *The Cultural Politics of Emotion*. Edinburgh: Edinburgh University Press.

Aikau, Hokulani K., and Vernadette Vicuña Gonzalez, eds. 2019. *Detours: A Decolonial Guide to Hawai'i*. Durham, NC: Duke University Press.

Alonso Herrero, Jose Antonio. 1988. "La maquila industrial domiciliaria en la metrópoli mexicana." *Estudios Sociológicos* 6 (18): 517–33.

———. 1991. *Mujeres maquiladoras y microindustria doméstica*. Mexico City: Distribuciones Fontamara.

Alston, Lee J., Shannan Mattiace, and Tomas Nonnenmacher. 2009. "Coercion, Culture, and Contracts: Labor and Debt on Henequen Haciendas in Yucatán, Mexico, 1870–1915." *The Journal of Economic History* 69 (1): 104–37.

Alvarez, Ricardo A. 2015. *Hurricane Mitigation for the Built Environment*. Boca Raton, FL: CRC Press.

Ancona Riestra, Roberto. 1996. *Arquitectura de las Haciendas Henequeneras*. Mérida: Universidad Autónoma de Yucatán.

Anderson, Benedict. 2016. *Imagined Communities: Reflections on the Origin and Spread of Nationalism*. Rev. ed. London: Verso.

Anduiza, Marcel. 2019. "Acapulco, Historical Perspective." PhD thesis, University of Chicago.

Anthias, Penelope. 2017. "Ch'ixi Landscapes: Indigeneity and Capitalism in the Bolivian Chaco." *Geoforum* 82:268–75. https://doi.org/10.1016/j.geoforum.2016.09.013.

Arnold, Chris Feliciano. 2018. *The Third Bank of the River: Power and Survival in the Twenty-First-Century Amazon*. New York: Picador.Ayora Díaz, Steffan Igor. 2000. "Imagining Authenticity in the Local Medicines of Chiapas, Mexico." *Critique of Anthropology* 20 (2): 173–90. https://doi.org/10.1177/0308275X0002000205.

———. 2012. *Foodscapes, Foodfields, and Identities in Yucatán*. CEDLA Latin America Studies, 99. New York: Berghahn Books.

Baklanoff, Eric N., and Edward H. Moseley, eds. 2008. *Yucatán in an Era of Globalization*. Tuscaloosa: University of Alabama Press.

Baldacchino, Godfrey. 2012. "The Lure of the Island: A Spatial Analysis of Power Relations." *Journal of Marine and Island Cultures* 1 (2): 55–62. https://doi.org/10.1016/j.imic.2012.11.003.

Baños Ramírez, Othón. 2003. *Modernidad, Imaginario e Identidad Rurales: El Caso de Yucatán*. México: Centro de Estudios Sociológicos, Colegio de México.

———. 2014. "Inés Ortiz Yam, De milperos a henequeneros en Yucatán 1870–1937." *Nuevo Mundo Mundos Nuevos*. December. http://journals.openedition.org/nuevomundo/67571.

Baranowski, Shelley, Christopher Endy, Waleed Hazbun, Stephanie Malia Hom, Gordon Pirie, Trevor Simmons, and Eric G. E. Zuelow. 2015. "Tourism and Empire." *Journal of Tourism History* 7 (1–2): 100–30. https://doi.org/10.1080/1755182X.2015.1063709.

Batllori Sampedro, Eduardo, José Luis Febles Patrón, Julio Iván González Piedra, and Julio Díaz Sosa. 2006. "Caracterización Hidrológica de La Región Costera Noroccidental Del Estado de Yucatán, México." *Investigaciones Geográficas*. 59:74–92.

Baud, Michiel, and Annelou Ypeij. 2009. *Cultural Tourism in Latin America: The Politics of Space and Imagery*. CEDLA Latin American Studies, 96. Leiden: Brill.

Becklake, Sarah. 2019. "The Role of NGOs in Touristic Securitization: The Case of La Antigua Guatemala." *Space and Culture* 23 (1): 34–47 https://doi.org/10.1177/1206331219871888.

Beirman, David, Pranil Kumar Upadhayaya, Pankaj Pradhananga, and Simon Darcy. 2018. "Nepal Tourism in the Aftermath of the April/May 2015 Earthquake and Aftershocks: Repercussions, Recovery and the Rise of New Tourism Sectors." *Tourism Recreation Research* 43 (4): 544–54. https://doi.org/10.1080/02508281.2018.1501534.

Benchwick, Greg. 2011. *Lonely Planet Cancun and the Yucatan Encounter*. Oakland, CA: Lonely Planet.

Berger, Dina. 2006. *The Development of Mexico's Tourism Industry: Pyramids by Day, Martinis by Night*. New York: Palgrave Macmillan Press.

Berger, Dina, and Andrew Grant Wood, eds. 2010. *Holiday in Mexico: Critical Reflections on Tourism and Tourist Encounters*. Durham, NC: Duke University Press.

Berghe, P. L. van den. 1994. *The Quest for the Other: Ethnic Tourism in San Cristóbal, Mexico*. Seattle: University of Washington Press.

Berlant, Lauren. 2011. *Cruel Optimism*. Durham, NC: Duke University Press.

Berliner, David. 2014. "On Exonostalgia." *Anthropological Theory* 14 (4): 373–86. https://doi.org/10.1177/1463499614554150.

Besky, Sarah. 2013. *The Darjeeling Distinction: Labor and Justice on Fair-Trade Tea Plantations in India.* Berkeley: University of California Press.

Bianchi, Raoul. 2003. "Place and Power in Tourism Development: Tracing the Complex Articulations of Community and Locality." *PASOS Revista de Turismo y Patrimonio Cultural* 2003 (1): 13–32. https://doi.org/10.25145/j.pasos.2003.01.002.

Bianchi, Raoul V., Marcus L. Stephenson, and Kevin Hannam. 2020. "The Contradictory Politics of the Right to Travel: Mobilities, Borders and Tourism. *Mobilities* 15 (2): 290–306. DOI: 10.1080/17450101.2020.1723251.

Biles, James J. 2004. "Export-Oriented Industrialization and Regional Development: A Case Study of Maquiladora Production in Yucatán, Mexico." *Regional Studies* 38 (5): 517–32. https://doi.org/10.1080/0143116042000229294.

———. 2005. "Globalization of Banking and Local Access to Financial Resources: A Case Study from Southeastern Yucatan." *The Industrial Geographer* 2 (2): 159–73.

Birch, Kean, and Matti Siemiatycki. 2016. "Neoliberalism and the Geographies of Marketization: The Entangling of State and Markets." *Progress in Human Geography* 40 (2): 177–98. https://doi.org/10.1177/0309132515570512.

Bissell, David, and Gillian Fuller, eds. 2013. *Stillness in a Mobile World.* London: Routledge.

Boissevain, Jeremy, ed. 1996. *Coping with Tourists: European Reactions to Mass Tourism.* Providence, RI: Berghahn Books.

Boltanski, Luc, and Eve Chiapello. 2018. *The New Spirit of Capitalism.* Translated by Gregory Elliott. Repr. ed. London: Verso.

Bonilla, Yarimar. 2015. *Non-Sovereign Futures: French Caribbean Politics in the Wake of Disenchantment.* Chicago: University of Chicago Press.

Bourdeau, Laurent, and Maria Gravari-Barbas. 2016. *World Heritage, Tourism and Identity: Inscription and Co-Production.* London: Routledge.

Brannon, Jeffrey T., and Eric N. Baklanoff. 1987. *Agrarian Reform and Public Enterprise in Mexico: The Political Economy of Yucatan's Henequen Industry.* Tuscaloosa: University of Alabama Press.

Brannon, Jeffrey T., and Gilbert M. Joseph, eds. 2002. *Land, Labor, and Capital in Modern Yucatan: Essays in Regional History and Political Economy.* Tuscaloosa: University of Alabama Press.

Breglia, Lisa. 2005. "Keeping World Heritage in the Family: A Genealogy of Maya Labour at Chichén Itzá." *International Journal of Heritage Studies* 11 (5): 385–98. https://doi.org/10.1080/13527250500337421.

———. 2006. *Monumental Ambivalence: The Politics of Heritage.* Joe R. and Teresa Lozano Long Series in Latin American and Latino Art and Culture. Austin: University of Texas Press.

———. 2009. "Hacienda Hotels And Other Ironies Of Luxury In Yucatán, Mexico." In *Cultural Tourism in Latin America: The Politics of Space and Imagery,* edited by Michiel Baud and Annelou Ypeij, 245–61. CEDLA Latin American Studies, 96. Leiden: Brill.

————. 2014. *Living with Oil: Promises, Peaks, and Declines on Mexico's Gulf Coast.* Repr. ed. Austin: University of Texas Press.

Brenner, Ludger. 2005. "State-Planned Tourism Destinations: The Case of Huatulco, Mexico." *Tourism Geographies* 7 (2): 138–64. https://doi.org/10.1080 /14616680500072349.

Brenner, Neil, and Stuart Elden. 2009. "Henri Lefebvre on State, Space, Territory." *International Political Sociology* 3 (4): 353–77. https://doi.org/10.1111/j.1749-5687 .2009.00081.x.

Brenner, Neil, Peter Marcuse, and Margit Mayer, eds. 2011. *Cities for People, Not for Profit: Critical Urban Theory and the Right to the City.* London: Routledge.

Brenner, Neil, and Nik Theodore. 2002. "Cities and the Geographies of 'Actually Existing Neoliberalism.'" *Antipode* 34 (3): 349–79. https://doi.org/10.1111 /1467–8330.00246.

————, eds. 2003. *Spaces of Neoliberalism: Urban Restructuring in North America and Western Europe.* Malden, MA: Wiley-Blackwell.

Brewer, Anthony. 1998. "Luxury and Economic Development: David Hume and Adam Smith." *Scottish Journal of Political Economy* 45 (1): 78–98. https://doi .org/10.1111/1467–9485.00082.Britton, Stephen G. 1982. "The Political Economy of Tourism in the Third World." *Annals of Tourism Research* 9 (3): 331–58. https:// doi.org/10.1016/0160–7383(82)90018–4.

————. 1991. "Tourism, Capital, and Place: Towards a Critical Geography of Tourism." *Society and Space* 9 (4): 451–78. https://doi.org/10.1068/d090451.

Brockington, Dan, Rosaleen Duffy, and Jim Igoe. 2008. *Nature Unbound: Conservation, Capitalism and the Future of Protected Areas.* London: Routledge.

Brown, Wendy. 2016. "Sacrificial Citizenship: Neoliberalism, Human Capital, and Austerity Politics." *Constellations* 23 (1): 3–14. https://doi.org/10.1111 /1467–8675.12166.

Bruner, Edward M. 2001. "The Maasai and the Lion King: Authenticity, Nationalism, and Globalization in African Tourism." *American Ethnologist* 28 (4): 881–908. https://doi.org/10.1525/ae.2001.28.4.881.

————. 2004. *Culture on Tour: Ethnographies of Travel.* Chicago: University of Chicago Press.

Buck Kachaluba, Sarah. 2018. *Pueblos Yucatecos.* Digital collection. https://library. ucsd.edu/dc/collection/bb3484668h.

Buechler, Stephanie, and Anne-Marie Hanson, eds. 2016. *A Political Ecology of Women, Water and Global Environmental Change.* London: Routledge.

Bunten, Alexis Celeste. 2008. "Sharing Culture or Selling out? Developing the Commodified Persona in the Heritage Industry." *American Ethnologist* 35 (3): 380–95. https://doi.org/10.1111/j.1548–1425.2008.00041.x.

Burawoy, Michael, Joseph A. Blum, Sheba George, Millie Thayer, Zsuzsa Gille, Teresa Gowan, Lynne Haney, Maren Klawiter, Steve H. Lopez, and Sean Riain. 2000. *Global Ethnography: Forces, Connections, and Imaginations in a Postmodern World.* Berkeley: University of California Press.

Büscher, Bram, and Veronica Davidov, eds. 2013. *The Ecotourism-Extraction Nexus: Political Economies and Rural Realities of (Un)Comfortable Bedfellows*. London: Routledge.

Büscher, Bram, and Robert Fletcher. 2017. "Destructive Creation: Capital Accumulation and the Structural Violence of Tourism." *Journal of Sustainable Tourism* 25 (5): 651–67. https://doi.org/10.1080/09669582.2016.1159214.

Büscher, Monika, John Urry, and Katian Witchger, eds. 2010. *Mobile Methods*. Abingdon, UK: Routledge.

Butler, R. W. 1990. "Alternative Tourism: Pious Hope or Trojan Horse?" *Journal of Travel Research* 28 (3): 40–45. https://doi.org/10.1177/004728759002800310.

Byrne, Denis. 2014. *Counterheritage: Critical Perspectives on Heritage Conservation in Asia*. New York: Routledge.

Caldeira, Teresa P. R. 1996. "Fortified Enclaves: The New Urban Segregation." *Public Culture* 8 (2): 303–328. https://doi.org/10.1215/08992363-8-2-303.

———. 2000. *City of Walls: Crime, Segregation and Citizenship in Sao Paulo*. Berkeley: University of California.

Candea, Matei. 2007. "Arbitrary Locations: In Defence of the Bounded Field-Site." *Journal of the Royal Anthropological Institute* 13 (1): 167–84. https://doi.org/10.1111/j.1467-9655.2007.00419.x.

Canessa, Andrew. 2012. "Gender, Indigeneity, and the Performance of Authenticity in Latin American Tourism." *Latin American Perspectives* 39 (6): 109–15. https://doi.org/10.1177/0094582X12456681.

Carey, Mark. 2010. *In the Shadow of Melting Glaciers: Climate Change and Andean Society*. New York: Oxford University Press.

Caribbean Tourism Organization. 2015. Historical Data (1970–2015). https://www.onecaribbean.org/statistics/historical-data-1970-2015/.

Carstensen, Fred V., and Diane Roazen-Parrillo. 1983. "International Harvester, Molina y Compania, and the Henequen Market: A Comment." *Latin American Research Review* 18 (3): 197–203.

Carswell, Grace, and Geert De Neve. 2014. "T-Shirts and Tumblers: Caste, Dependency and Work under Neoliberalisation in South India." *Contributions to Indian Sociology* 48 (1): 103–31. https://doi.org/10.1177/0069966713502423.

Carte, Lindsey, Mason McWatters, Erin Daley, and Rebecca Torres. 2010. "Experiencing Agricultural Failure: Internal Migration, Tourism and Local Perceptions of Regional Change in the Yucatan." *Geoforum* 41 (5): 700–10. https://doi.org/10.1016/j.geoforum.2010.03.002.

Castañeda, Quetzil. 1996. *In the Museum of Maya Culture: Touring Chichén Itzá*. Minneapolis: University of Minnesota Press.

———. 2004. "'We Are Not Indigenous!': An Introduction to the Maya Identity of Yucatan." *Journal of Latin American Anthropology* 9 (1): 36–63. https://doi.org/10.1525/jlca.2004.9.1.36.

Castellanos, M. Bianet. 2007. "Adolescent Migration to Cancún: Reconfiguring Maya Households and Gender Relations in Mexico's Yucatán Peninsula." *Frontiers: A Journal of Women Studies* 28 (3): 1–27.

————. 2010a. "Cancun and the Campo: Indigenous Migration and Tourism Development in the Yucatán Peninsula." In *Holiday in Mexico: Critical Reflections on Tourism and Tourist Encounters,* edited by Dina Berger and Andrew Grant Wood, 241–64. Durham, NC: Duke University Press.

————. 2010b. *A Return to Servitude: Maya Migration and the Tourist Trade in Cancún.* First Peoples, New Directions in Indigenous Studies. Minneapolis: University of Minnesota Press.

————. 2015. "Idealizing Maya Culture: The Politics of Race, Indigeneity, and Immigration among Maya Restaurant Owners in Southern California." *Diálogo* 18 (2): 67–78. https://doi.org/10.1353/dlg.2015.0041.

————. 2020. *Indigenous Dispossession: Housing and Maya Indebtedness in Mexico.* Stanford, CA: Stanford University Press.

Castellanos, M. Bianet, and Matilde Córdoba Azcárate. Forthcoming 2021. "Guardians of Tradition: Yucatec Maya Women, Tourism Media and Popular Geopolitics." In *Tourism Geopolitics,* edited by Mary Mostafanezhad, Matilde Córdoba Azcárate, and and Roger Norum, 312–40. Tucson: University of Arizona Press.

Castilla Ramos, Beatriz, and Beatriz Torres. 2013. *Tras las huellas del trabajo: De la firma red a los 'otros trabajos.'* Mérida: Universidad Autónoma de Yucatán.

Castro Alvarez, Ulises. 2007. "El turismo como política central de desarrollo y sus repercuciones en el ámbito local: Algunas consideraciones referentes al desarrollo de enclaves turísticos en méxico." *TURyDES: Revista de Investigacion en Turismo y Desarrollo Local.* October. http://dspace.uan.mx:8080/xmlui/handle /123456789/133.

Cater, Erlet. 2006. "Ecotourism as a Western Construct." *Journal of Ecotourism* 5 (1–2): 23–39. https://doi.org/10.1080/14724040608668445.

Cervera Montejano, Maria Dolores. 2011. "¿Quién me cuida?: Características de las interacciones entre los niños mayas yucatecos y sus cuidadores." *Estudios de Antropología Biológica* 14 (2). http://revistas.unam.mx/index.php/eab/article /view/27275.

Chambers, Erve. 2009. *Native Tours: The Anthropology of Travel and Tourism.* 2nd ed. Long Grove, IL: Waveland Press.

Chardon, Roland E. 1963. "Hacienda and Ejido in Yucatán: The Example of Santa Ana Cucá." *Annals of the Association of American Geographers* 53 (2): 174–93. https://doi.org/10.1111/j.1467-8306.1963.tb00440.x.

Chazkel, Amy, and David Serlin. 2010. "Editors' Introduction." *Radical History Review* 2010 (108): 1–10. https://doi.org/10.1215/01636545-2010-001.

Chibnik, Michael. 2003. *Crafting Tradition: The Making and Marketing of Oaxacan Wood Carvings.* Austin: University of Texas Press.

Chronis, Athinodoros, and Ronald D. Hampton. 2008. "Consuming the Authentic Gettysburg: How a Tourist Landscape Becomes an Authentic Experience." *Journal of Consumer Behaviour* 7 (2): 111–26. https://doi.org/10.1002/cb.241.

Clancy, Michael. 2001. *Exporting Paradise: Tourism and Development in Mexico.* Tourism Social Science Series. New York: Pergamon.

Clarke, Alan, Ayesha Chowdhury, Kevin Griffin, and Razaq Raj. 2017. "Terrorism, Tourism and Religious Travellers." *International Journal of Religious Tourism and Pilgrimage* 5 (1). https://doi.org/10.21427/d7bd8g.

Clayton, Anthony, and Maximiliano E. Korstanje. 2012. "Tourism and Terrorism: Conflicts and Commonalities." *Worldwide Hospitality and Tourism Themes* 4 (1): 8–25. https://doi.org/10.1108/17554211211198552.

Clifford, James. 1997. *Routes: Travel and Translation in the Late Twentieth Century.* Cambridge, MA: Harvard University Press.

Clifton, Dixon. 1991. "Yucatan after the Wind: Human and Environmental Impact of Hurricane Gilbert in the Central and Eastern Yucatan Peninsula." *GeoJournal* 23 (4): 337–45.

Cohen, Erik. 1987. "'Alternative Tourism': A Critique." *Tourism Recreation Research* 12 (2): 13–18. https://doi.org/10.1080/02508281.1987.11014508.

Coleman, Simon, and Mike Crang. 2002. *Tourism: Between Place and Performance.* New York: Berghahn Books.

Collins, John F. 2015. *Revolt of the Saints: Memory and Redemption in the Twilight of Brazilian Racial Democracy.* Durham, NC: Duke University Press.

Comaroff, Jean, and John Comaroff. 2003. "Ethnography on an Awkward Scale: Postcolonial Anthropology and the Violence of Abstraction." *Ethnography* 4 (2): 147–79.

CONANP (Comisión Nacional de Áreas Naturales Protegidas). 2018. "Marco Estratégico de Turismo Sustentable en Áreas Naturales Progeidas." Secretaría de Medio Ambiente y Recursos Naturales, Mexico. https://www.conanp.gob.mx /acciones/advc/MarcoEstrategico.pdf.

CONEVAL (Consejo Nacional de Evaluación de la Política de Desarrollo Social). 2019a. *Monitoreo por entidades federativas Yucatán 2019.* https://www.coneval .org.mx/coordinacion/entidades/Yucatan/Paginas/pob_municipal.aspx.

———. 2019b. *Monitoreo por entidades federativas Quintana Roo 2019.* https:// www.coneval.org.mx/coordinacion/entidades/QuintanaRoo/Paginas/principal .aspx.

Córdoba Azcárate, Matilde. 2011. "Contentious Hotspots: Ecotourism and the Restructuring of Place at the Biosphere Reserve Ria Celestun (Yucatan, Mexico)." *Tourist Studies.* 10 (2): 99–116. https://doi.org/10.1177/1468797611403033.

———. 2014. "The Uneven Pragmatics of 'Affordable' Luxury Tourism in Inland Yucatan, Mexico." In *Elite Mobilities,* 149–75. London: Routledge, Taylor & Francis.

———. 2019. "Fueling Ecological Neglect in a Manufactured Tourist City: Planning, Disaster Mapping, and Environmental Art in Cancun, Mexico." *Journal of Sustainable Tourism* 27 (4): 503–21. https://doi.org/10.1080/09669582.2018.1478839.

Córdoba Azcárate, Matilde, Idalina Baptista, and Fernando Domínguez Rubio. 2014. "Enclosures within Enclosures and Hurricane Reconstruction in Cancún, Mexico." *City and Society* 26 (1): 96–119. https://doi.org/10.1111/ciso.12026.

Córdoba Ordóñez, Juan, and Matilde Córdoba Azcárate. 2007. "Turismo y Desarrollo Regional: Tres Modelos de Implementación Turística En Quintana Roo (Yucatán, Mexico)." In *Desarrollo Local y Medio Ambiente en América*

Latina: Instrumentos y Acciones, edited by Eduardo Muscar Benasayag and Henrique Bruno Schmitt, 355–68. Madrid: Universidad Complutense de Madrid.

Craib, Raymond. 2004. *Cartographic Mexico: A History of State Fixations and Fugitive Landscapes.* Durham, NC: Duke University Press.

Crawford, Margaret. 1992. "The World in a Shopping Mall." In *Variations on a Theme Park: Scenes from the New American City,* edited by Michael Sorkin, 3–30. New York: Hill and Wang.

Cunningham, Andrew S. 2005. "David Hume's Account of Luxury." *Journal of the History of Economic Thought* 27 (3): 231–50. https://doi.org/10.1080/09557570500183405.

Dallen, Timothy, and Daniel Olsen. 2006. *Tourism, Religion, and Spiritual Journeys.* New York: Routledge.

Datatour (Análisis Integral del Turismo, Gobierno de Mexico). 2018. *Reporte Personalizado de los Centros Turisticos DataTour.* https://www.datatur.sectur.gob.mx/SitePages/ActividadHotelera.aspx.

Dávila, Arlene. 2016. *El Mall: The Spatial and Class Politics of Shopping Malls in Latin America.* Oakland: University of California Press.

Dávila López, Arturo. 2014. "Centros integralmente planeados (CIPS) en México: Las piezas del proyecto turístico de FONATUR." Paper presented at VI Seminario Internacional de Investigación en Urbanismo, Barcelona-Bogotá, Junio 2014. Barcelona: DUOT. https://upcommons.upc.edu/handle/2099/15985.

Davis, Mike. 2007. *Planet of Slums.* London: Verso.

Dawdy, Shannon Lee, and Richard Weyhing. 2008. "Beneath the Rising Sun: 'Frenchness' and the Archaeology of Desire." *International Journal of Historical Archaeology* 12 (4): 370–87.

de Certeau, Michel. 2011. *The Practice of Everyday Life.* Berkeley: University of California Press.

de la Cadena, Marisol. 2015. *Earth Beings: Ecologies of Practice across Andean Worlds.* Durham, NC: Duke University Press.

———. 2019. "Uncommoning Nature: Stories from the Anthropo-Not-Seen." In *Anthropos and the Material,* edited by Penny Harvey and Christian Krohn-Hansen, 35–58. Durham, NC: Duke University Press.

Desmond, Jane. 1999. *Staging Tourism: Bodies on Display from Waikiki to Sea World.* Chicago: University of Chicago Press.

di Giovine, Michael A. 2008. *The Heritage-Scape: UNESCO, World Heritage, and Tourism.* Washington, DC: Lexington Books.

Dodds, Rachel, ed. 2019. *Overtourism: Issues, Realities and Solutions.* Boston: DeGruyter.

Dodds, Rachel, and Richard Butler. 2019. *Overtourism: Tourism at Its Breaking Point.* Berlin: Walter de Gruyter GmbH.

Dominguez, Virginia R. 1975. *From Neighbor to Stranger: The Dilemma of Caribbean Peoples in the United States.* New Haven, CT: Antilles Research Program, Yale University.

Duffy, Rosaleen. 2002. *A Trip Too Far: Ecotourism, Politics and Exploitation*. London: Earthscan Publications.

———. 2008. "Neoliberalising Nature: Global Networks and Ecotourism Development in Madagasgar." *Journal of Sustainable Tourism* 16 (3): 327–44. https://doi.org/10.1080/09669580802154124.

Duffy, Rosaleen, and Mick Smith. 2003. *The Ethics of Tourism Development*. London: Routledge.

Edensor, Tim. 1998. *Tourists at the Taj: Performance and Meaning at a Symbolic Site*. London: Routledge.

———. 2001. "Performing Tourism, Staging Tourism: (Re)Producing Tourist Space and Practice." *Tourist Studies* 1 (1): 59–81. https://doi.org/10.1177/146879760100100104.

———. 2005. *Industrial Ruins: Space, Aesthetics and Materiality*. Oxford: Berg Publishers.

Eiss, Paul K. 2010. *In the Name of El Pueblo: Place, Community, and the Politics of History in Yucatán*. Latin America Otherwise. Durham, NC: Duke University Press.

Ek, Richard, and Johan Hultman. 2008. "Sticky Landscapes and Smooth Experiences: The Biopower of Tourism Mobilities in the Öresund Region." *Mobilities* 3 (2): 223–42. https://doi.org/10.1080/17450100802095312.

Elliot, Alice, Roger Norum, and Noel B. Salazar, eds. 2018. *Methodologies of Mobility: Ethnography and Experiment*. New York: Berghahn Books.

Elliott, Anthony, and John Urry. 2010. *Mobile Lives*. London: Routledge.

Elmendorf, Mary Lindsay. 1983. *Nine Mayan Women*. New York: Schenkman Publishing.

Elmhirst, Rebecca. 2011. "Introducing New Feminist Political Ecologies." In "New Feminist Political Ecologies." Themed issue, *Geoforum* 42 (2): 129–32. https://doi.org/10.1016/j.geoforum.2011.01.006.

Enloe, Cynthia. 2000. *Bananas, Beaches and Bases: Making Feminist Sense of International Politics*. Updated ed. Berkeley: University of California Press.

Escudero-Castillo, Mireille, Angélica Felix-Delgado, Rodolfo Silva, Ismael Mariño-Tapia, and Edgar Mendoza. 2018. "Beach Erosion and Loss of Protection Environmental Services in Cancun, Mexico." *Ocean and Coastal Management* 156 (April): 183–97. https://doi.org/10.1016/j.ocecoaman.2017.06.015.

Evans, Sterling David. 2013. *Bound in Twine: The History and Ecology of the Henequen-Wheat Complex for Mexico and the American and Canadian Plains, 1880–1950*. Repr. ed. College Station, TX: Texas A&M University Press.

Everton, Macduff. 2012. *The Modern Maya: Incidents of Travel and Friendship in Yucatán*. Austin: University of Texas Press.

Fabricant, Nicole. 2012. *Mobilizing Bolivia's Displaced: Indigenous Politics and the Struggle over Land*. New ed. Chapel Hill: University of North Carolina Press.

Fallaw, Ben. 1995. "Peasants, Caciques, and Camarillas: Rural Politics and State Formation in Yucatán, 1924–1940." PhD dissertation, University of Chicago.

———. 2001. *Cárdenas Compromised: The Failure of Reform in Postrevolutionary Yucatán*. Durham, NC: Duke University Press.

Fallaw, Ben, and Terry Rugeley, eds. 2012. *Forced Marches: Soldiers and Military Caciques in Modern Mexico*. Tucson: University of Arizona Press.

Farthing, Linda, and Nicole Fabricant. 2018. "Open Veins Revisited: Charting the Social, Economic, and Political Contours of the New Extractivism in Latin America." *Latin American Perspectives* 45 (5): 4–17. https://doi.org/10.1177/0094582X18785882.

Fennell, David A. 2014. "Exploring the Boundaries of a New Moral Order for Tourism's Global Code of Ethics: An Opinion Piece on the Position of Animals in the Tourism Industry." *Journal of Sustainable Tourism* 22 (7): 983–96. https://doi.org/10.1080/09669582.2014.918137.

Fields, Gary. 2017. *Enclosure: Palestinian Landscapes in a Historical Mirror*. Oakland, California: University of California Press.

Fierro Reyes, Gabriela. 2015. "Turismo de Hacienda e Intervención Comunitaria En El Contexto Rural Yucateco: El Caso de La Fundación Haciendas Del Mundo Maya." *Desacatos*, no. 47 (April): 54–71.

Figueroa, Esther, and Diana McCaulay, dirs. 2006. *Jamaica for Sale*. Documentary. http://www.jamaicaforsale.net/Movie.html.

Finn, Janet L. 1998. *Tracing the Veins*. Berkeley: University of California Press.

Fletcher, Robert. 2014. *Romancing the Wild: Cultural Dimensions of Ecotourism*. Durham, NC: Duke University Press.

Flew, Terry. 2011. *The Creative Industries: Culture and Policy*. Los Angeles: SAGE Publications.

FONATUR (Fondo Nacional de Fomento al Turismo). 1982. *Un Desarrollo Turístico en la Costa Turquesa*. Cancún, Quintana Roo: Fondo Nacional de Fomento al Turismo.

———. 2006. *Planeación de Centros Turísticos: La Experiencia y Práctica de FONATUR*. Mexico City: Fondo Nacional de Fomento al Turismo.

Forero, Oscar A., and Michael R. Redclift. 2006. "The Role of the Mexican State in the Development of Chicle Extraction in Yucatán, and the Continuing Importance of Coyotaje." *Journal of Latin American Studies* 38 (1): 65–93. https://doi.org/10.1017/S0022216X05000295.

Fortun, Kim. 2001. *Advocacy after Bhopal: Environmentalism, Disaster, New Global Orders*. Chicago: University of Chicago Press.

Fox, David J. 1961. "Henequen in Yucatan: A Mexican Fibre Crop." *Transactions and Papers (Institute of British Geographers)* 29:215–29. https://doi.org/10.2307/621253.

Fox, Jefferson. 1992. "The Problem of Scale in Community Resource Management." *Environmental and Management* 16: 289–97.

Fraga, Julia, and Dolores Cervera. 2004. "Una Aproximación a La Construcción de Un Paisaje Costero En El Área Maya." In *Naturaleza y Sociedad En El Área Maya: Pasado, Presente y Futuro*, edited by M. P. Colunga-Garcia and A. Larque Saavedra, 175–88. Mérida: Academia Mexicana de Ciencias-CICY.

Fraga, Julia, and Sabrina Doyon. 2008. *Descentralizacion y manejo ambiental: Gobernanza Costera en Mexico.* Ottawa: Plaza y Valdes.

Franklin, Adrian. 2004. "Tourism as an Ordering: Towards a New Ontology of Tourism." *Tourist Studies* 4 (3): 277–301. https://doi.org/10.1177/1468797604057328.

Franquesa, Jaume. 2013. "On Keeping and Selling: The Political Economy of Heritage Making in Contemporary Spain." *Current Anthropology* 54 (3): 346–69. https://doi.org/10.1086/670620.

Freire-Medeiros, Bianca. 2014. *Touring Poverty.* London: Routledge.

Garcés, Marina. 2018. *Ciudad Princesa.* Barcelona: Galaxia Gutenberg.

García de Fuentes, Ana. 1979. *Cancún, Turismo y Subdesarrollo Regional.* Serie Cuadernos. México: Universidad Nacional Autónoma de México, Instituto de Geografía.

García de Fuentes, Ana, María Eugenia de la O Martínez, Cirila Quintero Ramírez, and Josefina Morales. 2000. *El Eslabón Industrial: Cuatro Imágenes de La Maquila En México.* Colección Los Grandes Problemas Nacionales. México City: Editorial Nuestro Tiempo.

García-Frapolli, Eduardo, Gabriel Ramos-Fernández, Eduardo Galicia, and Arturo Serrano. 2009. "The Complex Reality of Biodiversity Conservation through Natural Protected Area Policy: Three Cases from the Yucatan Peninsula, Mexico." *Land Use Policy* 26 (3): 715–22.

García García, José Luis. 1998. "De la cultura como patrimonio al patrimonio cultural." *Política y Sociedad* 27: 9–20. https://core.ac.uk/download/pdf/38819323.pdf.

Germann Molz, Jennie. 2007. "Eating Difference: The Cosmopolitan Mobilities of Culinary Tourism." *Space and Culture* 10 (1): 77–93. https://doi.org/10.1177/1206331206296383.

———. 2017. "Giving Back, Doing Good, Feeling Global: The Affective Flows of Family Voluntourism." *Journal of Contemporary Ethnography* 46 (3): 334–60. https://doi.org/10.1177/0891241615610382.

Godale, Mark, and Nancy Postero. 2013. *Neoliberalism Interrupted: Social Change and Contested Governance in Contemporary Latin America.* Stanford, CA: Stanford University Press.

Godoy, R. 1985. "Mining: Anthropological Perspectives." *Annual Review of Anthropology* 14 (1): 199–217. https://doi.org/10.1146/annurev.an.14.100185.001215.

Gómez-Barris, Macarena. 2017. *The Extractive Zone: Social Ecologies and Decolonial Perspectives.* Durham, NC: Duke University Press.

Gonzalez, Vernadette Vicuña. 2013. *Securing Paradise: Tourism and Militarism in Hawai'i and the Philippines.* Next Wave. Durham, NC: Duke University Press.

———. Forthcoming 2021. "Afterword: On the Rage of Women from Small Islands." In *Tourism Geopolitics,* edited by Mary Mostafanezhad, Matilde Córdoba Azcárate, and Roger Norum. Tucson: University of Arizona Press.

Gordillo, Gastón R. 2014. *Rubble: The Afterlife of Destruction.* Durham, NC: Duke University Press.

Goreau, Thomas J., and Wolf Hilbertz. 2005. "Marine Ecosystem Restoration: Costs and Benefits for Coral Reefs." *World Resource Review* 17 (3): 35. http://www.globalcoral.org/_oldgcra/WRR%20Goreau%20&%20Hilbertz%202005.pdf.

Graburn, Nelson. 1977. "Tourism: A Sacred Journey" in *Hosts and Guests: the Anthropology of Tourism,* edited by Valene Smith, 17–31. Philadelphia: University of Pennsylvania Press.

Graham, Steve, and Simon Marvin. 2001. *Splintering Urbanism: Networked Infrastructures, Technological Mobilities and the Urban Condition.* London: Routledge.

Gravari-Barbas, Maria, and Nelson Graburn, eds. 2016. *Tourism Imaginaries at the Disciplinary Crossroads: Place, Practice, Media.* Burlington, VT: Routledge.

Greenwood, Davydd. 1989. "Culture by the Pound: An Anthropological Perspective on Tourism as Cultural Commoditization." In *Host and Guests: The Anthropology of Tourism,* edited by Valene Smith, 171–86. Philadelphia: University of Pennsylvania Press.

Gregory, Derek. 1994. *Geographical Imaginations.* Cambridge: Wiley-Blackwell.

Grêt-Regamey, Adrienne, Peter Bebi, Ian D. Bishop, and Willy A. Schmid. 2008. "Linking GIS-Based Models to Value Ecosystem Services in an Alpine Region." *Journal of Environmental Management* 89 (3): 197–208. https://doi.org/10.1016/j.jenvman.2007.05.019.

Grupo Ciudad, Desarrollo y Conservación Consultora. 2007. *Estudio sobre el Impacto Urbano del Desarrollo Turístico en la Zona Hotelera de Cancún.* http://biblioteca.coqcyt.gob.mx/bvic/captura/upload/estudio-de-impacto-socioeco-proyin.pdf, accessed March 26, 2012.

Guardado, Gustavo Marín, and Angeles López Santillán. 2010. "Turismo, capitalismo y producción de lo exótico: Una perspectiva crítica para el estudio de la mercantilización del espacio y la cultura." *Relaciones: Estudios de Historia y Sociedad* 124 (31): 219–58.

———. 2015. "Sin Tierras No Hay Paraíso. Turismo, Organizaciones Agrarias y Apropiación Territorial En México." *Pasos: Revista de Turismo y Patrimonio Cultural* 15: 5–38.

Gudynas, Eduardo. 2015. *Extractivismos: Ecología, economía y política de un modo de entender el desarrollo y la naturaleza.* Cochabamba, Bolivia: CEDIB, Centro de Documentación e Información Bolivia.

Guerrero, José Manuel Crespo, and Araceli Jiménez Pelcastre. 2017. "Organización e impacto territorial de la actividad pesquera comercial ribereña en la Reserva de la biosfera Ría Celestún (México)." *Anales de Geografía de la Universidad Complutense* 37 (2): 297–324. https://doi.org/10.5209/AGUC.57727.

Guerrero Rodriguez, Rafael. 2012. "Planned Tourism Destinations, a Strategy for Development? The Case of Cancun, Mexico." *Review of Tourism Sciences* 4. http://jotr.eu/index.php/volume4/35-planned.

Haldrup, Michael, and Jonas Larsen. 2009. *Tourism, Performance and the Everyday: Consuming the Orient.* London: Routledge.

Hall, C. Michael, and James E. S. Higham, eds. 2005. *Tourism, Recreation and Climate Change*. Clevedon, UK: Channel View Publications.

Hall, Derek R. 2017. *Tourism and Geopolitics: Issues and Concepts from Central and Eastern Europe*. Wallingford: CABI.

Han, Clara. 2012. *Life in Debt: Times of Care and Violence in Neoliberal Chile*. Berkeley: University of California Press.

Hannam, Kevin, Mimi Sheller, and John Urry. 2006. "Editorial: Mobilities, Immobilities and Moorings." *Mobilities* 1 (1): 1–22. https://doi.org/10.1080/17450100500489189.

Hanson, Anne-Marie. 2016. "Women's Ecological Oral Histories of Recycling and Development in Coastal Yucatán." *Gender, Place and Culture* 23 (4): 467–83. https://doi.org/10.1080/0966369X.2015.1013445.

———. 2017. "Women's Environmental Health Activism around Waste and Plastic Pollution in the Coastal Wetlands of Yucatán." *Gender and Development* 25 (2): 221–34. https://doi.org/10.1080/13552074.2017.1335450.

Haraway, Donna. 2018. *Modest–Witness@Second_Millenium. FemaleMan_Meets_OncoMouse: Feminism and Technoscience*. New York: Routledge.

Harcourt, Wendy, and Ingrid L. Nelson, eds. 2015. *Practicing Feminist Political Ecologies: Moving Beyond the "Green Economy."* London: Zed Books.Harvey, David. 2005. *Spaces of Neoliberalization: Towards a Theory of Uneven Geographical Development*. Stuttgart: Franz Steiner Verlag.

———. 2007. "Neoliberalism as Creative Destruction." *Annals of the American Academy of Political and Social Science* 610: 22–44.

———. 2011. "The Future of the Commons." *Radical History Review* 2011 (109): 101–7. https://doi.org/10.1215/01636545-2010-017.

Harvey, Penny, Christian Krohn-Hansen, and Knut G. Nustad, eds. 2019. *Anthropos and the Material*. Durham, NC: Duke University Press.

Herman, Edward S., and Noam Chomsky. 2002. *Manufacturing Consent: The Political Economy of the Mass Media*. Repr. ed. New York: Pantheon.

Herzfeld, Michael. 2010. "Engagement, Gentrification, and the Neoliberal Hijacking of History." *Current Anthropology* 51 (S2): S259–67. https://doi.org/10.1086/653420.

———. 2016. "Spatial Cleansing: Monumental Vacuity and the Idea of the West." *Journal of Material Culture* 11 (12): 127–49. https://doi.org/10.1177/1359183506063016.

Hiernaux Nicolás, Daniel. 1989. *Teoría y praxis del espacio turístico*. México: UAM-Xochimilco, División de Ciencias y Artes para el Diseño, Departamento de Teoría y Análisis.

Hilson, Gavin, and Martin J. Clifford. 2010. "A 'Kimberley Protest': Diamond Mining, Export Sanctions, and Poverty in Akwatia, Ghana." *African Affairs* 109 (436): 431–50. https://doi.org/10.1093/afraf/adq020.

Hirsch, Fred. 1976. *Social Limits to Growth*. Cambridge, MA: Harvard University Press.

Hobsbawm, E. J., and T. O. Ranger, eds. 1992. *The Invention of Tradition*. Cambridge: Cambridge University Press.

Hochschild, Arlie Russell. 2012. *The Managed Heart: Commercialization of Human Feeling.* 3rd ed., Updated with a New Preface. Berkeley: University of California Press.

Hodder, Ian. 2012. *Entangled: An Archaeology of the Relationships between Humans and Things.* Malden, MA: Wiley-Blackwell.

Hoffman, Lily M., Susan S. Fainstein, and Dennis R. Judd, eds. 2003. *Cities and Visitors: Regulating People, Markets, and City Space.* Malden, MA: Wiley-Blackwell.

Holston, James. 1989. *The Modernist City: An Anthropological Critique of Brasília.* Chicago: University of Chicago Press.

Hoskins, Janet. 2002. "Predatory Voyeurs: Tourists and 'Tribal Violence' in Remote Indonesia." *American Ethnologist* 29 (4): 797–828. https://doi.org/10.1525/ae.2002.29.4.797.

Hsiung, Ping-Chun. 1996. *Living Rooms as Factories: Class, Gender, and the Satelite Factory System in Taiwan.* Philadelphia: Temple University Press.

Hume, David. 1985. *Essays: Moral, Political, and Literary.* Rev. ed. Indianapolis: Liberty Fund.

Igoe, Jim. 2017. *The Nature of Spectacle: On Images, Money, and Conserving Capitalism.* Tucson: University of Arizona Press.

IMPLAN (Instituto de Planeación de Desarrollo Urbano). 2009. *Plan estratégico de desarrollo sustentable Cancún 2030.* Cancún: Instituto de Planeación de Desarrollo.

INEGI (Instituto Nacional de Estadistica, Geografia e Informatica). 1995. *Celestún Cuaderno Estadístico Municipal 1995.* http://internet.contenidos.inegi.org.mx/contenidos/productos/prod_serv/contenidos/espanol/bvinegi/productos/historicos/1290/702825925437/702825925437.pdf.

——. 2000. *Anuario Estadistico y Geografico de Yucatan.* Aguascalientes: INEGI.

——. 2005. *Anuario Estadistico y Geográfico de Yucatan.* Aguascalientes: INEGI.

——. 2008. *Anuario Estadístico de Yucatán.* Aguascalientes: INEGI.

——. 2010. *Censos de población y vivienda.* http://www3.inegi.org.mx/sistemas/biinegi/?e=07&m=065&src=487.

——. 2014. *Anuario Estadistico y Geográfico de Yucatán.* http://internet.contenidos.inegi.org.mx/contenidos/productos/prod_serv/contenidos/espanol/bvinegi/productos/anuario_14/702825066581.pdf.

——. 2015a. *Cuéntame: Dinámica de la Población Quintana Roo 1900–2015.* http://cuentame.inegi.org.mx/monografias/informacion/qroo/poblacion/dinamica.aspx?tema=me&e=23.

——. 2015b. *Cuéntame: Dinámica de la Población, División municipal Yucatán 1900–2015.* http://cuentame.inegi.org.mx/mapas/pdf/entidades/div_municipal/yucmpios.pdf.

——. 2017. *Anuario Estadístico y Geográfico de Yucatán.* Aguascalientes: INEGI. https://www.datatur.sectur.gob.mx/ITxEF_Docs/YUC_ANUARIO_PDF.pdf.

——. 2018. *Anuario Estadístico y Geográfico de Yucatán: Microrregiones Temozón Sur.* http://www.microrregiones.gob.mx/zap/datGenerales.aspx?entra=nacion&ent=31&mun=085.

———. 2019. *Directorio Estadístico Nacional de Unidades Económicas*. https://en.www.inegi.org.mx/app/mapa/denue/.

Institute for Economics and Peace. 2017. "Global Terrorism Index 2017: Measuring and Understanding the Impact of Terrorism." START National Consortium for the Study of Terrorism and Reponses to Terrorism, US Department of Homeland Security and University of Maryland. http://visionofhumanity.org/app/uploads/2017/11/Global-Terrorism-Index-2017.pdf.

International Trade Centre and UN World Tourism Organization. 2017. "National Tourism Export Strategies." http://www.intracen.org/uploadedFiles/intracenorg/Content/Redesign/Audience/policy_makers/ITC-UNWTO%20Tourism%20Export%20Strategies%20-%20About2.pdf.

Issa, John J., and Chandana Jayawardena. 2003. "The 'All-inclusive' Concept in the Caribbean." *International Journal of Contemporary Hospitality Management* 15 (3): 167–71. https://doi.org/10.1108/09596110310470211.

Jamal, Tazim, and Amanda Stronza. 2009. "Collaboration Theory and Tourism Practice in Protected Areas: Stakeholders, Structuring and Sustainability." *Journal of Sustainable Tourism* 17 (2): 169–89. https://doi.org/10.1080/09669580802495741.

Jayawardena, Chandana. 2003. "Revolution to Revolution: Why Is Tourism Booming in Cuba?" *International Journal of Contemporary Hospitality Management* 15 (1): 52–58. https://doi.org/10.1108/09596110310458990.

Jenkins, C. L. 1982. "The Effects of Scale in Tourism Projects in Developing Countries." *Annals of Tourism Research* 9 (2): 229–49. https://doi.org/10.1016/0160-7383(82)90047-0.

Johnson, Cedric, ed. 2011. *The Neoliberal Deluge: Hurricane Katrina, Late Capitalism, and the Remaking of New Orleans*. Minneapolis: University of Minnesota Press.

Joseph, G. M., and Daniel Nugent, eds. 1994. *Everyday Forms of State Formation: Revolution and the Negotiation of Rule in Modern Mexico*. Durham, NC: Duke University Press.

Juárez, Ana M. 2002. "Ongoing Struggles: Mayas and Immigrants in Tourist Era Tulum." *Journal of Latin American Anthropology* 7 (1): 34–67. https://doi.org/10.1525/jlca.2002.7.1.34.

Karjanen, David J. 2016. *The Servant Class City: Urban Revitalization versus the Working Poor in San Diego*. Minneapolis: University of Minnesota Press.

Katz, Friedrich. 1974. "Labor Conditions on Haciendas in Porfirian Mexico: Some Trends and Tendencies." *The Hispanic American Historical Review* 54 (1): 1–47. https://doi.org/10.2307/2512838.

Kelly, Jennifer Lynn. 2016. "Asymmetrical Itineraries: Militarism, Tourism, and Solidarity in Occupied Palestine." *American Quarterly* 68 (3): 723–45. https://doi.org/10.1353/aq.2016.0060.

Kenney, Martin, and Richard Florida. 1994. "Japanese Maquiladoras: Production Organization and Global Commodity Chains." *World Development* 22 (1): 27–44. https://doi.org/10.1016/0305-750X(94)90166-X.

Kincaid, Jamaica. 1988. *A Small Place*. London: Penguin Books.

King, Anthony D. 2007. *Colonial Urban Development*. London: Routledge.

Kintz, Ellen R. 1990. *Life under the Tropical Canopy: Tradition and Change among the Yucatec Maya*. Fort Worth, TX: Harcourt College Publishers.

Kirshenblatt-Gimblett, Barbara. 1995. "Theorizing Heritage." *Ethnomusicology* 39 (3): 367. https://doi.org/10.2307/924627.

———. 1998. *Destination Culture: Tourism, Museums, and Heritage*. Berkeley: University of California Press.

Klein, Naomi. 2008. *The Shock Doctrine: The Rise of Disaster Capitalism*. London: Penguin Books.

———. 2018. *The Battle For Paradise: Puerto Rico Takes on the Disaster Capitalists*. Chicago: Haymarket Books.

Koerner, Robert. 2016. *Geotextiles: From Design to Applications*. Waltham, MA: Woodhead Publishing.

Kopinak, Kathryn. 1996. *Desert Capitalism: Maquiladoras in North America's Western Industrial Corridor*. Tucson: University of Arizona Press.

———. 2003. "Globalization in Tijuana Maquiladoras: Using Historical Antecedents and Migration to Test Globalization Models," *Papeles de Población* 9 (37): 219–242.

Korstanje, Maximiliano E. 2017. *Terrorism, Tourism and the End of Hospitality in the "West."* London: Palgrave Macmillan.

Kusno, Abidin. 2013. *After the New Order: Space, Politics, and Jakarta*. Honolulu: University of Hawaiʻi Press.

LaBrecque, Marie-France. 2005. "Cultural Appreciation and Economic Depreciation of the Mayas of Northern Yucatán, Mexico." *Latin American Perspectives* 32 (4): 87–105.

LaBrecque, Marie-France, and Yvan Breton, eds. 1982. *La organización de la producción de los mayas de Yucatán*. México City: Instituto Nacional Indigenista.

Larkin, Brian. 2013. "The Politics and Poetics of Infrastructure." *Annual Review of Anthropology* 42:327–43. https://doi.org/10.1146/annurev-anthro-092412-155522.

Larsen, P. 2015. *Post-frontier Resource Governance: Indigenous Rights, Extraction and Conservation in the Peruvian Amazon*. Houndmills, UK: Palgrave Macmillan.

Lash, Scott, and John Urry. 1987. *The End of Organized Capitalism*. London: Wiley Blackwell.

Leatherman, Thomas L., and Alan Goodman. 2005. "Coca-Colonization of Diets in the Yucatan." *Social Science and Medicine*. The Social Production of Health: Critical Contributions from Evolutionary, Biological and Cultural Anthropology: Papers in Memory of Arthur J. Rubel, 61 (4): 833–46. https://doi.org/10.1016/j.socscimed.2004.08.047.

Lee, Sang-Hyun, Jin-Yong Choi, Seung-Hwan Yoo, and Yun-Gyeong Oh. 2013. "Evaluating Spatial Centrality for Integrated Tourism Management in Rural Areas Using GIS and Network Analysis." *Tourism Management* 34 (February): 14–24. https://doi.org/10.1016/j.tourman.2012.03.005.

Lefebvre, Henri. 1994. *The Production of Space*. Translated by Donald Nicholson-Smith. Oxford: Wiley-Blackwell.

Leite, Naomi. 2017. *Unorthodox Kin: Portuguese Marranos and the Global Search for Belonging*. Oakland: University of California Press.

Lemelin, Harvey, Jackie Dawson, Emma J. Stewart, Pat Maher, and Michael Lueck. 2010. "Last-Chance Tourism: The Boom, Doom, and Gloom of Visiting Vanishing Destinations." *Current Issues in Tourism* 13 (5): 477–93. https://doi.org/10.1080/13683500903406367.

Lenzen, Manfred, Ya-Yen Sun, Futu Faturay, Yuan-Peng Ting, Arne Geschke, and Arunima Malik. 2018. "The Carbon Footprint of Global Tourism." *Nature Climate Change* 8 (6): 522–28. https://doi.org/10.1038/s41558-018-0141-x.

Lew, Alan A. 2001. "Tourism and Geography Space." *Tourism Geographies* 3 (1): 1–1. https://doi.org/10.1080/14616680010008676.

Lisle, Debbie. 2016. *Holidays in the Danger Zone*. Minneapolis: University of Minnesota Press.

Little, Walter E., and Patricia A. McAnany, eds. 2011. *Textile Economies: Power and Value from the Local to the Transnational*. Lanham, MD: AltaMira Press.

Loewe, Ronald. 2010. *Maya or Mestizo? Nationalism, Modernity, and Its Discontents*. Teaching Culture: UTP Ethnographies for the Classroom. Toronto: University of Toronto Press.

Löfgren, Orvar. 2002. *On Holiday: A History of Vacationing*. Berkeley: University of California Press.

Loperena, Christopher A. 2017. "Honduras Is Open for Business: Extractivist Tourism as Sustainable Development in the Wake of Disaster?" *Journal of Sustainable Tourism* 25 (5): 618–33. https://doi.org/10.1080/09669582.2016.1231808.

Loria, Alvar, Pedro Arroyo, Victoria Fernandez, Jeanette Pardio, and Hugo Laviada. 2018. "Prevalence of Obesity and Diabetes in the Socioeconomic Transition of Rural Mayas of Yucatan from 1962 to 2000." *Ethnicity and Health*. (February): 1–7. https://doi.org/10.1080/13557858.2018.1442560.

Low, Setha M., ed. 1999. *Theorizing the City: The New Urban Anthropology Reader*. New Brunswick, NJ: Rutgers University Press.

———. 2004. *Behind the Gates: Life, Security, and the Pursuit of Happiness in Fortress America*. New York: Routledge.

———. 2016. *Spatializing Culture: The Ethnography of Space and Place*. New York: Routledge.

Low, Setha M., and Denise Lawrence-Zúñiga, eds. 2003. *The Anthropology of Space and Place: Locating Culture*. Malden, MA: Wiley-Blackwell.

Low, Setha, Dana Taplin, and Suzanne Scheld. 2005. *Rethinking Urban Parks: Public Space and Cultural Diversity*. Austin: University of Texas Press.

Lutz, Wolfang, Leonel Priet, and Warren Sanderson. 2000. *Population, Development and Environment on the Yucatán Peninsula: From Ancient Maya to 2030*. Luxenburg: International Institute for Applied Systems Analysis.

MacCannell, Dean. 1973. "Staged Authenticity: Arrangements of Social Space in Tourist Settings." *American Journal of Sociology* 79 (3): 589–603.

————. 1992. *Empty Meeting Grounds.* London: Taylor and Francis.

————. 2011. *The Ethics of Sightseeing.* Berkeley: University of California Press.

Macnaghten, Phil, and John Urry. 1998. *Contested Natures.* Thousand Oaks, CA: SAGE Publications.

Mansell-Carstens, C. 1996. "Popular Financial Culture in Mexico: The Case of the Tanda." In *Changing Structure of Mexico: Political, Social, and Economic Prospects,* edited by Laura Randall, 77–81. New York: Armonk.

Mansvelt, Juliana. 2005. *Geographies of Consumption.* Thousand Oaks, CA: Sage Publications.

Manuel-Navarrete, David. 2012. "Entanglements of Power and Spatial Inequalities in Tourism in the Mexican Caribbean," *DesiguALdades.net: International Research Network on Interdependent Inequalities in Latin America.* Working paper 17. Available https://www.desigualdades.net/Working_Papers/Search-Working-Papers/Working-Paper-17-_Entanglements-of-Power-and-Spatial-Inequalities-in-Tourism-in-the-Mexican-Caribbean_/index.html.

Marcus, George E. 1995. "Ethnography in/of the World System: The Emergence of Multi-Sited Ethnography." *Annual Review of Anthropology* 24:95–117.

Markusen, Ann. 1996. "Sticky Places in Slippery Space: A Typology of Industrial Districts." *Economic Geography* 72 (3): 293–313. https://doi.org/10.2307/144402.

Mármol, Camila del, Joan Frigolé, and Susana Narotzky. 2010. *Los lindes del patrimonio: Consumo y valores del pasado.* Barcelona: Icaria.

Martí, Fernando. 1998. *Cancun, Paradise Invented: Notes on Landscape and Architecture.* Mexico City: Impresora Formal S.A. De CV.

Martínez, Claudia Inés. 2012. "Organización espacial del turismo de cruceros en México." *Études caribéennes* 18 (April). https://doi.org/10.4000/etudescaribeennes.5077.

Massey, Doreen B. 1994. *Space, Place, and Gender.* Minneapolis: University of Minnesota Press.

Mattiace, Shannan, and Tomas Nonnenmacher. 2014. "The Organization of Hacienda Labor during the Mexican Revolution: Evidence from Yucatán." *Mexican Studies/Estudios Mexicanos* 30 (2): 366–96. https://doi.org/10.1525/msem.2014.30.2.366.

Mattioli, Fabio. 2014. "Unchanging Boundaries: The Reconstruction of Skopje and the Politics of Heritage." *International Journal of Heritage Studies* 20 (6): 599–615. https://doi.org/10.1080/13527258.2013.818569.

McGee, Terry G. 1991. "The Emergence of Desakota Regions in Asia : Expanding a Hypothesis." In *The Extended Metropolis : Settlement Transition in Asia,* edited by Norton Sydney Ginsburg, Bruce Koppel, and T.G. McGee, –26. Honolulu: University of Hawai'i Press.

McNeish, John-Andrews. 2013. "Extraction, Protest and Indigeneity in Bolivia: The TIPNIS Effect." *Journal of Latin American and Caribean Ethnic Studies* 8 (2): 221–42. Doi: 10.1080/17442222.2013.808495.

Meehan, Katie, and Kendra Strauss, eds. 2015. *Precarious Worlds: Contested Geographies of Social Reproduction.* Athens: University of Georgia Press.

Menéndez Rodríguez, Hernán. 1992. "La Revolución Mexicana En Yucatán y Los Hacendados: Salvador Alvarado y Carlos Peón." *Unicornio* 64 (14 June): 3–11.

Méndez-Contreras, Jessica, Federico Dickinson, and Teresa Castillo-Burguete. 2008. "Community Member Viewpoints on the Ría Celestún Biosphere Reserve, Yucatan, Mexico: Suggestions for Improving the Community/Natural Protected Area Relationship." *Human Ecology* 31 (1): 111–13. http://agris.fao.org/agris-search/search.do?recordID=US201600017138.

Meusburger, Peter, Benno Werlen, and Laura Suarsana, eds. 2018. *Knowledge and Action*. New York: Springer International.

Milano, Claudio, Joseph Cheer, and Marina Novelli, eds. 2019. *Over Tourism: A Growing Global Phenomena*. Boston: CABI.

Miles, Tiya. 2017. *Tales from the Haunted South: Dark Tourism and Memories of Slavery from the Civil War Era*. Repr. ed. Chapel Hill: University of North Carolina Press.

Miller, Toby. 2017. *Greenwashing Culture*. Abingdon: Routledge.

Moench, Marcus, and Dipak Gyawali. 2008. "Desakota. Reinterpreting the Urban-Rural Continuum." Available at https://assets.publishing.service.gov.uk/media/57a08bc3ed915d3cfd000f14/Desakota-Part-II-A.pdf.

Monterrubio, Carlos, Maribel Osorio, and Jazmín Benítez. 2018. "Comparing Enclave Tourism's Socioeconomic Impacts: A Dependency Theory Approach to Three State-Planned Resorts in Mexico." *Journal of Destination Marketing and Management* 8 (June): 412–22. https://doi.org/10.1016/j.jdmm.2017.08.004.

Moore, Amelia. 2016. "Anthropocene Anthropology: Reconceptualizing Contemporary Global Change." *Journal of the Royal Anthropological Institute* 22 (1): 27–46.

Moore, Jason W. 2015. *Capitalism in the Web of Life: Ecology and the Accumulation of Capital*. New York: Verso.

Moseley, Edward H., and Edward Davis Terry, eds. 1980. *Yucatán, a World Apart*. Tuscaloosa: University of Alabama Press.

Mostafanezhad, Mary. 2014. *Volunteer Tourism: Popular Humanitarianism in Neoliberal Times*. Aldershot, UK: Ashgate.

Mostafanezhad, Mary, and Kevin Hannam. 2016. *Moral Encounters in Tourism*. London: Routledge.

Mostafanezhad, Mary, Matilde Córdoba Azcárate, and Roger Norum. Forthcoming 2021. *Tourism Geopolitics*. Tucson: University of Arizona Press.

Mota Santos, Paula. 2016. "Crossed Gazes over an Old City: Photography and the 'Experientiation' of a Heritage Place." *International Journal of Heritage Studies* 22 (2): 131–44. https://doi.org/10.1080/13527258.2015.1108925.

Mowforth, Martin, and Ian Munt. 2015. *Tourism and Sustainability: Development, Globalisation and New Tourism in the Third World*. 4th ed. Abingdon, UK: Routledge.

Mukerji, Chandra. 1997. *Territorial Ambitions and the Gardens of Versailles*. Cambridge Cultural Social Studies. Cambridge: Cambridge University Press.

Mukul, Eric Villanueva. 1990. *La formación de las regiones en la agricultura: el caso de Yucatán*. Mérida: Maldonado Editores.

Munt, Ian. 1994. "Eco-Tourism or Ego-Tourism?" *Race and Class* 36 (1): 49–60. https://journals.sagepub.com/doi/10.1177/030639689403600104.

Nájera, Lourdes Gutiérrez. 2009. "Transnational Migration, Conflict, and Divergent Ideologies of Progress." *Urban Anthropology and Studies of Cultural Systems and World Economic Development* 38 (2–4): 269–302.

Narotzky, Susana, and Gavin Smith. 2006. *Immediate Struggles: People, Power, and Place in Rural Spain.* Berkeley: University of California Press.

Nash, Dennison. 1977. "Tourism as a Form of Imperialism." In *Hosts and Guests: The Anthropology of Tourism,* edited by Valene L. Smith, 33–47. Philadelphia: University of Pennsylvania Press.

Nickel, Herbert J. 1997. *El peonaje en las haciendas mexicanas: Interpretaciones, fuentes, hallazgos.* México City: Universidad Iberoamericana.

Nixon, Angelique V. 2017. *Resisting Paradise: Tourism, Diaspora, and Sexuality in Caribbean Culture.* Repr. ed. Jackson: University Press of Mississippi.

Norman, Myers. 2003. "Biodiversity Hotspots Revisited." *BioScience* 53 (10): 916–17.

OECD (Organization for Economic Co-operation and Development). 2007. "Territorial Reviews: Yucatán, México." https://www.oecd.org/cfe/regional-policy/oecdterritorialreviewsyucatanmexico.htm.

———. 2017. *Tourism Policy Review of Mexico.* OECD Studies on Tourism. Paris: OECD Publishing.

Ortiz Yam, Inés. 2013. *De Milperos a Henequeneros En Yucatán, 1870–1937.* México City: El Colegio de México.

Osten, Sarah. 2018. *The Mexican Revolution's Wake: The Making of a Political System, 1920–1929.* Cambridge Latin American Studies. Cambridge: Cambridge University Press.

Page, Stephen J. 2009. "Current Issue in Tourism: The Evolution of Travel Medicine Research: A New Research Agenda for Tourism?" *Tourism Management* 30 (2): 149–57. https://doi.org/10.1016/j.tourman.2008.04.011.

Park, Lisa, and David Pellow. 2013. *The Slums of Aspen: Immigrants vs. the Enviornment in America's Eden.* New York: NYU Press.

Parra Argüello, Fanny Yolanda, Elsy Veronica Martin Calderon, and Angel Navarrete Cante. 2016. "Análisis del Comportamiento Ambiental y Social de la Industria de la Confección de Tekit, Yucatan." Paper presented at Asociación Mexicana de Ciencias para el Desarrollo Regional, A.C., Mexico. Available at http://ru.iiec.unam.mx/3233/.

Pastor, Manuel. 1989. "Latin America, the Debt Crisis, and the International Monetary Fund." *Latin American Perspectives* 16 (1): 79–110.

Patel, Raj, and Jason W. Moore. 2017. *A History of the World in Seven Cheap Things: A Guide to Capitalism, Nature, and the Future of the Planet.* Oakland: University of California Press.

Pattullo, Polly. 2005. *Last Resorts: The Cost of Tourism in the Caribbean.* 2nd ed. London: Monthly Review Press.

Peck, Jamie. 2013. *Constructions of Neoliberal Reason.* Repr. ed. Oxford: Oxford University Press.

Pelas, Holly Renee. 2011. "Tourism Development in Cancun, Mexico: An Analysis of State Directed Tourism Initiatives in a Developing Nation." MA thesis. Georgetown University.

Peniche Rivero, Piedad. 1999. "La Comunidad Doméstica de La Hacienda Henequenera de Yucatán, México, 1870–1915." *Mexican Studies/Estudios Mexicanos* 15 (1): 1–33. https://doi.org/10.2307/1051941.

Petras, James, and Henry Veltmeyer. 2016. *Extractive Imperialism in the Americas: Capitalism's New Frontier*. Repr. ed. Chicago: Haymarket Books.

Picard, David, and Mike Robinson. 2006. *Festivals, Tourism and Social Change: Remaking Worlds*. Bristol: Channel View Publications.

Picard, Michel, and Robert Everett Wood. 1997. *Tourism, Ethnicity, and the State in Asian and Pacific Societies*. Honolulu: University of Hawai'i Press.

Pieterse, Jan Nederveen. 2009. *Development Theory*. 2nd ed. Los Angeles: SAGE Publications.

Pinkus Rendón, Manuel Jesús, and Miguel Ángel Pinkus Rendón. 2015. "El ecoturismo: Quimera o realidad de desarrollo en la Reserva de la Biosfera Ría Celestún, México." *LiminaR. Estudios Sociales y Humanísticos* 13 (1): 69–80. https://doi.org/10.29043/liminar.v13i1.367.

Pi-Sunyer, Oriol, and Brooke Thomas. 1997. "Tourism, Environmentalism and Cultural Survival in Quintana Roo." In *Environmental Sociology: From Analysis to Action,* edited by Leslie King and Deborah McCarthy Auriffeille, 43–61. Lanham, MD: Rowman and Littlefield.

Pizam, Abraham, and Ginger Smith. 2000. "Tourism and Terrorism: A Quantitative Analysis of Major Terrorist Acts and Their Impact on Tourism Destinations." *Tourism Economics* 6 (2): 123–38. https://doi.org/10.5367/000000000101297523.

Postero, Nancy. 2017. *The Indigenous State: Race, Politics, and Performance in Plurinational Bolivia*. Oakland: University of California Press.

Pradilla Cobos, Emilio. 1997. "Fragmentación y exclusión en la megalópolis mexicana." *Nueva Sociedad* 156:180–93.

Prats, Llorenc. 2004. *Antropologia y Patrimonio*. Granada: Ariel.

Pratt, Mary Louise. 2007. *Imperial Eyes: Travel Writing and Transculturation*. 2nd ed. London: Routledge.

Prentice, Richard. 1993. *Tourism and Heritage Attractions*. New York: Routledge.

Quezada, Sergio. 2011. *Yucatán: Historia breve*. 2nd ed. Mexico City: Fondo de Cultura Económica.

Ramírez, Gloria Luz Alejandre, and Eduardo Torres Alonso. 2016. "El Primer Congreso Feminista de Yucatán 1916: El Camino a La Legislación Del Sufragio y Reconocimiento de Ciudadanía a Las Mujeres. Construcción y Tropiezos." *Estudios Políticos* 39 (September): 59–89. https://doi.org/10.1016/j.espol.2016.10.003.

Ramsar Convention on Wetlands. 2004. "From the Mountains to the Sea: Wetlands that work for us." World Wetlands Day, Mexico. Accessible at https://www.ramsar.org/activity/world-wetlands-day-2004.

Re Cruz, Alicia. 1996. *The Two Milpas of Chan Kom: Scenarios of a Maya Village Life*. SUNY Series in Anthropology of Work. Albany: State University of New York Press.

Redclift, Michael. 2004. *Chewing Gum: The Fortunes of Taste*. New York: Routledge.

———. 2006. *Frontiers: Histories of Civil Society and Nature*. Cambridge, MA: MIT Press.

Reddy, Maharaj Vijay, and Keith Wilkes. 2012. *Tourism, Climate Change and Sustainability*. London: Routledge.

Redfield, Robert. 1968. *The Folk Culture of Yucatan*. University of Chicago Publications in Anthropology, Social Anthropology Series. Chicago: The University of Chicago Press.

Reed, Nelson A. 2001. *The Caste War of Yucatán*. Rev. ed. Stanford, CA: Stanford University Press.

Richter, Linda K., and William L. Waugh. 1986. "Terrorism and Tourism as Logical Companions." *Tourism Management* 7 (4): 230–38. https://doi.org/10.1016/0261-5177(86)90033-6.

Rocheleau, Dianne, Barbara Thomas-Slayter, and Esther Wangari, eds. 1996. *Feminist Political Ecology: Global Issues and Local Experience*. London: Routledge.

Rodriguez Viqueira, Manuel, and Victor Fuentes Freixanet. 2006. "Traditional Mayan Architecture According to Latitude and Altitude." Paper presented at PLEA2006: The 23rd Conference on Passive and Low Energy Architecture, Géneve, September 6–8, 2006. https://www.researchgate.net/publication/268383050_Traditional_Mayan_Architecture_According_to_Latitude_and_Altitude.

Rojek, Chris, and John Urry, eds. 1997. *Touring Cultures: Transformations of Travel and Theory*. London: Routledge.

Rothstein, Frances Abrahamer. 2007. *Globalization in Rural Mexico: Three Decades of Change*. Austin: University of Texas Press.

Rottenberg, Robert. 1995. *Landscape and Power in Vienna*. Baltimore, MD: John Hopkins University Press.

Rubio Herrera, Amada. 2017. "La costura como 'verdadero trabajo' masculino en Tekit, Yucatán." *Península* 12 (1). http://www.revistas.unam.mx/index.php/peninsula/article/view/58269.

Ruiz Marrero, Carmelo. 2005. "Water Privatization in Latin America." *Global Policy Forum*. https://www.globalpolicy.org/social-and-economic-policy/global-public-goods-1-101/46063-water-privatization-in-latin-america.html.

Ruz, Mario Humberto. 2006. *De la mano de lo sacro: Santos y demonios en el mundo Maya*. Mexico City: Universidad Nacional Autónoma de Mexico.

Sadlier, Stephen. 2019. *Movements on the Streets and in Schools: State Repression, Neoliberal Reforms, and Oaxaca Teacher Counter-Pedagogies*. New ed. New York: Peter Lang, International Academic Publishers.

Sahlins, Marshall. 1987. *Islands of History*. Chicago: University of Chicago Press.

Salazar, Noel B. 2012. *Envisioning Eden: Mobilizing Imaginaries in Tourism and Beyond*. New York: Berghahn Books.

Salazar, Noel B., and Nelson H. H. Graburn, eds. 2016. *Tourism Imaginaries: Anthropological Approaches*. New York: Berghahn Books.

Saldaña-Portillo, María Josefina. 2016. *Indian Given: Racial Geographies across Mexico and the United States*. Durham, NC: Duke University Press.

Savarino Roggero, Franco. 1992. "Pueblos, Élites y Dinámica Local En El Proceso Revolucionario: El Caso de Abalá, Yucatán 1815–1924." *Historias* 30 (abril-septiembre): 61–77.

Sawyer, Suzana. 2004. *Crude Chronicles: Indigenous Politics, Multinational Oil, and Neoliberalism in Ecuador*. Durham, NC: Duke University Press.

Sawyer, Suzana, and Edmund Terence Gómez. 2012. *The Politics of Resource Extraction: Indigenous Peoples, Corporations and the State*. London: Palgrave.

Schwenkel, Christina. 2014. "Socialist Palimpsests in Urban Vietnam." *Architecture beyond Europe*, no. 6. https://doi.org/10.4000/abe.909.

Scott, James C. 1999. *Seeing like a State: How Certain Schemes to Improve the Human Condition Have Failed*. New Haven, CT: Yale University Press.

SECTUR (Secretaría de Turismo). 1996. *Programa de Desarrollo del Sector Turismo 1995–2000*. México City: Secretaría de Turismo.

———. 2006. *Compendio Estadístico del Turismo en Mexico*. México City: Secretaria de Turismo.

———. 2011. *Estadísticas Más Recientes de la Actividad Sector Turismo*. http://datatur.sectur.gob.mx/work/docs/5_reporte_semana/sem082011.pdf.

———. 2017. *Compendio Estadístico del Turismo en México: Llegadas a Museos y Zonas Arqueológicas*. México City: Secretaría de Turismo. https://www.datatur.sectur.gob.mx/SitePages/ActividadesCulturales.aspx.

SEDESMA (Secretaría de Medio Ambiente y Pesca). 1996. *Programa Áreas Naturales Protegidas de Mexico 1995–2000*. http://legismex.mty.itesm.mx/progs/panpm.pdf

SEDESOL (Secretaría de Desarrollo Social). 2010. *Información Urbana Ciudad de Cancún, 2010*. México City: Secretaria de Desarrollo Social, Delegación Quintana Roo, Subdelegación de Desarrollo Urbano y Ordenación del Territorio, Gobierno Federal de México.

———. 2016a. *Informe Anual sobre la Situación de Pobreza y Rezago Celestún*. http://inderm.yucatan.gob.mx/files-content/general/off974bad76fdbca969c354a549874a8.pdf.

———. 2016b. *Informe Anual sobre la Situación de Pobreza y Rezago Tekit, Yucatán*. http://inderm.yucatan.gob.mx/files-content/general/3258c9b78260af548fb91824edcd7573.pdf.

———. 2017. *Informe Anual sobre la Situación de Pobreza y Rezago Abalá*. http://diariooficial.gob.mx/SEDESOL/2017/Yucatan_001.pdf.

———. 2019. *Informe Anual sobre la Situación de Pobreza y Rezago Tekit, Yucatán*. https://extranet.bienestar.gob.mx/pnt/Informe/inf_municipal_31080.pdf.

Selby, Henry A., Arthur D. Murphy, and Stephen A. Lorenzen. 2014. *The Mexican Urban Household: Organizing for Self-Defense*. Austin: University of Texas Press.

SEMARNAT (Secretaría de Medio Ambiente y Recursos Naturales). 2000. *Programa de Manejo de la Reserva de la Biosfera Ria Celestún*. México City: Comisión Nacional de Áreas Protegidas.

———. 2009. *Programa Nacional para la Prevención y Gestión de Residuos*. Mexico City: Secretaría del Medio Ambiente y Recursos Naturales.

Shankman, Samantha, dir. 2017. *Documentary: Barcelona and the Trials of Twenty-First Century Overtourism*. https://skift.com/2017/08/01/video-barcelona-and-the-trials-of-21st-century-overtourism/.

Sharkey, Patrick. 2013. *Stuck in Place: Urban Neighborhoods and the End of Progress toward Racial Equality*. Chicago: University of Chicago Press.

Sharpley, Richard. 2009. *Tourism Development and the Environment: Beyond Sustainability?* London: Routledge.

Sheller, Mimi. 2003. *Consuming the Caribbean: From Arawaks to Zombies*. London: Routledge.

———. 2007. "Retouching the 'Untouched Island': Post-military Tourism in Vieques, Puerto Rico." *Téoros. Revue de recherche en tourisme* 26 (1). http://journals.openedition.org/teoros/2823.

———. 2009. "The New Caribbean Complexity: Mobility Systems, Tourism and Spatial Rescaling." *Singapore Journal of Tropical Geography* 30 (2): 189–203. https://doi.org/10.1111/j.1467-9493.2009.00365.x.

———. 2013. "The Islanding Effect: Post-disaster Mobility Systems and Humanitarian Logistics in Haiti." *Cultural Geographies* 20 (2): 185–204. https://doi.org/10.1177/1474474012438828.

———. 2014. *Aluminum Dreams*. Boston: MIT Press.

———. 2020. *Island Futures. Caribbean Survival in the Anthropocene*. Durham, NC: Duke University Press.

Sheller, Mimi, and John Urry. 2004. *Tourism Mobilities: Places to Play, Places in Play*. London: Routledge.

Shields, Rob. 1992. *Places on the Margin: Alternative Geographies of Modernity*. London: Routledge.

Shoval, Noam. 2018. "Urban Planning and Tourism in European Cities." *Tourism Geographies* 20 (3): 371–76. https://doi.org/10.1080/14616688.2018.1457078.

Simoni, Valerio. 2018. *Tourism and Informal Encounters in Cuba*. New York: Berghahn Books.

Simpson, Timothy, ed. 2017. *Tourist Utopias: Offshore Islands, Enclave Spaces, and Mobile Imaginaries*. Amsterdam: Amsterdam University Press.

Sims, Christo. 2017. *Disruptive Fixation: School Reform and the Pitfalls of Techno-Idealism*. Princeton Studies in Culture and Technology. Princeton, NJ: Princeton University Press.

Sinn, Hans-Werner. 2012. *Casino Capitalism: How the Financial Crisis Came about and What Needs to Be Done Now*. Repr. ed. Oxford: Oxford University Press.

Smith, Adam. [1776] 1925. *An Inquiry into the Nature and Causes of the Wealth of Nations*. Edited by E. Cannan. London: King.

Smith, Gavin. 1991. *Livelihood and Resistance.* Berkeley: University of California Press.

———. 2019. "Reflections on the Changing Sphere of Social Reproduction and Class Struggle: Cases from Peru and Spain." Unpublished manuscript.

Smith, Laurajane. 2006. *Uses of Heritage.* London: Routledge.

Smith, Neil. 2008. "Scale Bending and the Fate of the National." In *Scale and Geographic Inquiry,* edited by Eric Sheppard and Robert B. McMaster, 192–212. Hoboken, NJ: John Wiley and Sons.

Smith, Neil. 2008. *Uneven Development: Nature, Capital, and the Production of Space.* 3rd ed. Athens: University of Georgia Press.

Smith, Valene L., ed. 1977. *Hosts and Guests: The Anthropology of Tourism.* Philadelphia: University of Pennsylvania Press.

———. 1996. "The Four Hs of Tribal Tourism: Acoma: A Pueblo Case Study." *Progress in Tourism and Hospitality Research* 2 (3–4): 295–306. https://doi.org/10.1002/pth.6070020310.

Sorkin, Michael, ed. 1992. *Variations on a Theme Park: The New American City and the End of Public Space.* New York: Hill and Wang.

Stasch, Rupert. 2009. *Society of Others.* Berkeley: University of California Press.

———. 2014. "Primitivist Tourism and Romantic Individualism: On the Values in Exotic Stereotypy about Cultural Others." *Anthropological Theory* 14 (2): 191–214. https://doi.org/10.1177/1463499614534114.

Steen, Harold K., and Richard P. Tucker, eds. 1991. *Changing Tropical Forests: Historical Perspectives on Today's Challenges in Central and South America.* Durham, NC: Duke University Press.

Stein, Rebecca L. 2008. *Itineraries in Conflict: Israelis, Palestinians, and the Political Lives of Tourism.* Durham, NC: Duke University Press.

Stephen, Lynn. 2013. *We Are the Face of Oaxaca: Testimony and Social Movements.* Durham, NC: Duke University Press.

Stephens, Michele McArdle. 2018. *In the Lands of Fire and Sun: Resistance and Accommodation in the Huichol Sierra, 1723–1930.* Lincoln: University of Nebraska Press.

Stone, Andrea J. 2010. *Images from the Underworld: Naj Tunich and the Tradition of Maya Cave Painting.* Austin: University of Texas Press.

Stronza, Amanda, and Carter Hunt. 2012. "Visions of Tourism: From Modernization to Sustainability." *Practicing Anthropology* 34 (3): 19–22. https://doi.org/10.17730/praa.34.3.0203vv87563xt730.

Sullivan, Paul. 1989. *Unfinished Conversations: Mayas and Foreigners Between Two Wars.* New York: Knopf.

Svampa, Maristella. 2015. "Commodities Consensus: Neoextractivism and Enclosure of the Commons in Latin America." *South Atlantic Quarterly* 114 (1): 65–82. https://doi.org/10.1215/00382876-2831290.

Svensson, Eva. 2009. "Consuming Nature–Producing Heritage: Aspects on Conservation, Economic Growth and Community Participation in a Forested, Sparsely Populated Area in Sweden." *International Journal of Heritage Studies* 15 (6): 540–59. https://doi.org/10.1080/13527250903210837.

Sylvanus, Nina. 2016. *Patterns in Circulation: Cloth, Gender, and Materiality in West Africa*. Chicago: University of Chicago Press.

Talledos Sánchez, Édgar. 2012. "La imposición de un espacio: De La Crucecita a Bahías de Huatulco." *Revista Mexicana de Ciencias Políticas y Sociales* 57 (216). http://dx.doi.org/10.22201/fcpys.2448492xe.2012.216.34842.

Taylor, Charles. 2003. *Modern Social Imaginaries*. Durham, NC: Duke University Press.

Taylor, Sarah. 2018. *On Being Maya and Getting By: Heritage Politics and Community Development in Yucatán*. Boulder: University Press of Colorado.

Teaiwa, Teresia. 1994. "Bikinis and Other s/Pacific n/Oceans." *The Contemporary Pacific* 6 (1): 87–109. http://scholarspace.manoa.hawaii.edu/handle/10125 /12958.

———. 2001. "Militarism, Tourism and the Native: Articulations in Oceania." PhD dissertation. University of California, Santa Cruz.

Telfer, David J., and Richard Sharpley. 2015. *Tourism and Development in the Developing World*. 2nd ed. London: Routledge.

Terán, Silvia, and Christian H. Rasmussen. 1994. *La Milpa de Los Mayas: La agricultura de los mayas prehispánicos y actuales en el noreste de Yucatán*. Mérida: Danida.

Terry, Edward Davis, ed. 2010. *Peripheral Visions: Politics, Society, and the Challenges of Modernity in Yucatan*. Tuscaloosa: University of Alabama Press.

Thrift, Nigel. 1994. "Taking Aim at the Heart of the Region." In *Human Geography: Society, Space and Social Science,* edited by Derek Gregory, Ron Martin, and Graham Smith, 200–31. London: Macmillan Education UK.

———. 1996. *Spatial Formations*. Thousand Oaks, CA: SAGE Publications.

TIES (International Ecotourism Society). 1990. "What Is Ecotourism?" Available at https://ecotourism.org/what-is-ecotourism/.

Torres, Rebecca. 2003. "Linkages between Tourism and Agriculture in Mexico." *Annals of Tourism Research* 30 (3): 546–66. https://doi.org/10.1016/S0160-7383 (02)00103-2.

Torres, Rebecca, and Janet D. Momsen. 2004. "Challenges and Potential for Linking Tourism and Agriculture to Achieve Pro-Poor Tourism Objectives." *Progress in Development Studies* 4 (4): 244–318. DOI: 10.1191/1464993404ps0920a.

———. 2005a. "Gringolandia: The Construction of a New Tourist Space in Mexico." *Annals of the Association of American Geographers* 95 (2): 314–35. https:// doi.org/10.1111/j.1467-8306.2005.00462.x.

———. 2005b. "Planned Tourism Development in Quintana Roo, Mexico: Engine for Regional Development or Prescription for Inequitable Growth?" *Current Issues in Tourism* 8 (4): 259–85. https://doi.org/10.1080/13683500508668218.

Trask, Haunani-Kay. 1991. "Lovely Hula Lands: Corporate Tourism and the Prostitution of Hawaiian Culture." *Border/Lines,* no. 23. https://journals.lib.unb.ca /index.php/bl/article/view/24958.

Tsing, Anna Lowenhaupt. 2005. *Friction: An Ethnography of Global Connection*. Princeton, NJ: Princeton University Press.

Turner, Louis, and John Ash. 1975. *The Golden Hordes: International Tourism and the Pleasure Periphery*. London: Constable and Robinson.

Uc Espadas, Martha Concepción. 2007. "Estrategias de Vida en Hogares Costeros, Estudio de Caso en Celestún, Yucatán." Master's thesis, Department of Human Ecology, Centro de Estudios Avanzados del IPN de Merida.

UNCTAD (United Nations Conference on Trade and Development). 2010. *Creative Economy Report*. https://unctad.org/en/Docs/ditctab20103_en.pdf.

UNESCO. 1979. "Man and the Biosphere (MAB) Programme." https://en.unesco.org/mab.

———. 2009. "Biosphere Reserves." https://en.unesco.org/node/314143.

———. 2017. "A New Roadmap for the Man and the Biosphere (MAB) Programme and Its World Network of Biosphere Reserves 2009–2017." https://unesdoc.unesco.org/ark:/48223/pf0000247418.

UNFCCC (United Nations Framework Convention on Climate Change). 2010. *Cancun Agreements*. https://unfccc.int/process/conferences/pastconferences/cancun-climate-change-conference-november-2010/statements-and-resources/Agreements.

United Nations. 2015. "Resolution adopted by the General Assembly on 22 December 2015: International Year of Sustainable Tourism for Development, 2017." http://www.un.org/en/ga/search/view_doc.asp?symbol=A/RES/70/193&referer=/english/&Lang=E.

UNWTO (United Nations World Tourism Organization). 1980. "Manila Declaration on World Tourism." https://www.e-unwto.org/doi/abs/10.18111/unwtodeclarations.1980.01.01.

———. 1985. "Tourism Bill of Rights and Tourism Code." Available at https://www.univeur.org/cuebc/downloads/PDF%20carte/67.%20Sofia.PDF.

———. 2004. "Indicators of Sustainable Development for Tourism Destinations: A Guidebook." https://www.e-unwto.org/doi/book/10.18111/9789284407262.

———. 2007. "United Nations World Tourism Organization Global Code of Ethics for Tourism." https://www.unwto.org/global-code-of-ethics-for-tourism.

———. 2017a. "Manila Call for Action on Measuring Sustainable Development." https://www.e-unwto.org/doi/abs/10.18111/unwtodeclarations.2017.26.01.

———. 2017b. "Tourism for Sustainable Development in Least Developed Countries: Leveraging Resources For Sustainable Tourism with the Enhanced Integrated Framework." https://www.e-unwto.org/doi/pdf/10.18111/9789284418848.

———. 2018a. Tourism and Poverty Alleviation." https://www.e-unwto.org/doi/book/10.18111/9789284405497.

———. 2018b. "UNWTO Tourism Highlights: 2018 Edition." https://www.e-unwto.org/doi/pdf/10.18111/9789284419876.

———. 2019a. *Compendium of Tourism Statistics, Data 2013–2017*. Madrid: UNWTO.

———. 2019b. "International Tourism Highlights: 2019 Edition." https://www.e-unwto.org/doi/pdf/10.18111/9789284421152.

Urquiza-Haas, Tania, Paul M. Dolman, and Carlos A. Peres. 2007. "Regional Scale Variation in Forest Structure and Biomass in the Yucatan Peninsula, Mexico: Effects of Forest Disturbance." *Forest Ecology and Management* 247 (1): 80–90. https://doi.org/10.1016/j.foreco.2007.04.015.

Urry, John. 1995. *Consuming Places*. London: Routledge.

———. 2007. *Mobilities*. Cambridge: Polity Press.

———. 2011. *The Tourist Gaze 3.0*. 3rd ed. Los Angeles: SAGE Publications.

Vail, Pegi, dir. 2015. *Gringo Trails*. Icarus Films.

Vainikka, Vilhelmiina. 2013. "Rethinking Mass Tourism." *Tourist Studies* 13 (3): 268–86. https://doi.org/10.1177/1468797613498163.

———. 2015. "Stereotypes and Professional Reflections on Mass Tourism: Focusing on Tour Operators, Mass Tourism Destinations, and Mass Tourists." *Études Caribéennes*, no. 31–32. https://doi.org/10.4000/etudescaribeennes.7609.

Vanden Boer, Dorien. 2016. "Toward Decolonization in Tourism: Engaged Tourism and the Jerusalem Tourism Cluster." *Jerusalem Quarterly* 65:9–21.

Vázquez Castillo, María Teresa. 2004. *Land Privatization in Mexico: Urbanization, Formation of Regions, and Globalization in Ejidos*. Latin American Studies, Social Sciences and Law. New York: Routledge.

Vega Campos, Marielena. 2010. *FONATUR 35 Años. Única Historia Narrada Por Sus Fundadores y Protagonistas*. México City: Fondo Nacional de Fomento al Turismo, FONATUR.

Veijola, S., J. Germann Molz, Olli Pyyhtinen, E. Hockert, Alexander Grit, Jennie Germann Molz, and Emily Höckert. 2014. *Disruptive Tourism and Its Untidy Guests: Alternative Ontologies for Future Hospitalities*. London: Palgrave Macmillan.

Velasco Ruiz, Enrique. 2017. "Ambientalismo Ciudadano Como Política de La Historia En El Caribe Mexicano Norte ¡Cancún, Despierta! ¿El Manglar Está Vivo?" Paper presented at Seminario Permanente de Turismo, Mérida, Yucatán, March 30, 2017.

Villanueva Villanueva, Nancy Beatriz, and Virginia Prieto. 2007. "Rituales de Hetzmek En Yucatán." *Estudios de Cultura Maya* 33:73–88. https://doi.org/DOI:10.19130/iifl.ecm.2009.33.41.

Vogel, Steven. 2016. *Thinking like a Mall: Environmental Philosophy after the End of Nature*. Repr. ed. Cambridge, MA: MIT Press.

Walker, Cameron Jean. 2009. *Heritage or Heresy: Archaeology and Culture on the Maya Riviera*. Tuscaloosa: University Alabama Press.

Wallace, James M. Tim, ed. 2005. *Tourism and Applied Anthropologists: Linking Theory and Practice*. Arlington, VA: Wiley-Blackwell.

Wang, Ning. 1999. "Rethinking Authenticity in Tourism Experience." *Annals of Tourism Research* 26 (2): 349–70. https://doi.org/10.1016/S0160–7383 (98)00103–0.

Warman, Arturo. 2001. *El Campo Mexicano en el Siglo XX*. Mexico City: Fondo de Cultura Económica.

Warnken, Jan, and Chris Guilding. 2009. "Multi-Ownership of Tourism Accommodation Complexes: A Critique of Types, Relative Merits, and Challenges

Arising." *Tourism Management* 30 (5): 704–14. https://doi.org/10.1016/j.tourman.2008.10.023.

Weaver, David B., and Laura J. Lawton. 2007. "Twenty Years On: The State of Contemporary Ecotourism Research." *Tourism Management* 28 (5): 1168–79. https://doi.org/10.1016/j.tourman.2007.03.004.

Wells, Allen. 1982. "Family Elites in a Boom-and-Bust Economy: The Molinas and Peóns of Porfirian Yucatán." *Hispanic American Historical Review* 62 (2): 224–53. https://doi.org/10.2307/2514979.

———. 1985. *Yucatan's Gilded Age: Haciendas, Henequen, and International Harvester, 1860–1915.* Albuquerque: University of New Mexico Press.

———. 1991. "From Hacienda to Plantation: The Transformation of Santo Domingo Xcuyum." In *Land, Labor and Capital in Modern Yucatan: Essays in Regional History and Political Economy,* edited by Jeffrey T. Brannon and Gilbert M. Joseph, 112–42. Tuscaloosa: University of Alabama Press.

Wells, Allen, and Gilbert M. Joseph. 1996. *Summer of Discontent, Seasons of Upheaval: Elite Politics and Rural Insurgency in Yucatán, 1876–1915.* Stanford, CA: Stanford University Press.

Whitfield, Dexter. 2006. "A Typology of Privatisation and Marketisation." European Services Strategy Unit, ESSU Research Report 1: 1–12. https://www.european-services-strategy.org.uk/wp-content/uploads/2006/11/essu-research-paper-1-2.pdf..

Whitmore, Thomas J., Mark Brenner, Jason H. Curtis, Bruce H. Dahlin, and Barbara W. Leyden. 1996. "Holocene Climatic and Human Influences on Lakes of the Yucatan Peninsula, Mexico: An Interdisciplinary, Palaeolimnological Approach." *The Holocene* 6 (3): 273–87. https://doi.org/10.1177/095968369600600303.

Wilk, Richard R. 1997. *Household Ecology: Economic Change and Domestic Life among the Kekchi Maya in Belize.* DeKalb: Northern Illinois University Press.

Williams, Allan M., and Armando Montanari. 1995. "Tourism Regions and Spaces in a Changing Social Framework." *Tijdschrift Voor Economische En Sociale Geografie* 86 (1): 3–12. https://doi.org/10.1111/j.1467-9663.1995.tb01823.x..

Williams, Stephen, and Alan A. Lew. 2014. *Tourism Geography: Critical Understandings of Place, Space and Experience.* 3rd ed. London: Routledge.

Wilson, Tamar Diana. 2008. "Economic and Social Impacts of Tourism in Mexico." *Latin American Perspectives* 35 (3): 37–52. https://doi.org/10.1177/0094582X08315758.

———. 2012. *Economic Life of Mexican Beach Vendors: Acapulco, Puerto Vallarta, and Cabo San Lucas.* Lanham, MD: Lexington Books.

Wilson Gilmore, Ruth. 2008. "Forgotten Places and the Seeds of Grassroots Planning." In *Engaging Contradictions: Theory, Politics, and Methods of Activist Scholarship,* edited by Charles R. Hale, 31–61. Berkeley: University of California Press.

Witynski, Karen, and Joe P. Carr. 2008. *Hacienda Style.* Layton, UT: Gibbs Smith.

Wolf, Eric R., and Sidney W. Mintz. 1957. "Haciendas and Plantations in Middle America and the Antilles." *Social and Economic Studies* 6 (3): 380–412.

Wong, Alfred. 2015. "Caribbean Island Tourism: Pathway to Continued Colonial Servitude." *Études Caribéennes,* no. 31–32. https://doi.org/10.4000/etudescaribeennes.7524.

World Travel and Tourism Council. 2016. "At the Intersection of Tourism and Capitalism Lies Global Prosperity." *Medium* (blog). April 1, 2016. Accessed April 2020. https://medium.com/@WTTC/at-the-intersection-of-tourism-and-capitalism-lies-global-prosperity-ac1f324e6e64.

———. 2019. "Travel and Tourism Economic Impact, 2019." https://wttc.org/Research/Economic-Impact.

Wynn, Jonathan R. 2011. *The Tour Guide: Walking and Talking New York*. Chicago: University of Chicago Press.

Young, Eric Van. 2006. *Hacienda and Market in Eighteenth-Century Mexico*. Lanham, MD: Rowman and Littlefield.

Zilberg, Elana. 2011. *Space of Detention: The Making of a Transnational Gang Crisis between Los Angeles and San Salvador*. Durham, NC: Duke University Press.

Zizek, Slavoj. 2009. *First as Tragedy, Then as Farce*. London: Verso.

INDEX

Page numbers in italics denote illustrations.

alternative tourism *(continued)*
119, 144, 158; environmental sustainability discourse and rise of, 73–74, 103; Tekit and new forms for, 180–81; Tekit/sewing for tourism as invisible to, 149–50. *See also* cultural tourism; ecotourism

Alvarez, Ricardo A., 49, 209n19
AMLO. *See* López Obrador, Andrés Manuel
Ancona Riestra, Roberto, 114, 115, 123, 125, 126
Anderson, Benedict, 207n45
Andorra, 201n12
animal species: commodification of charismatic species, 84; preservation of single, 75–76
Antarctic, 11
Anthias, Penelope, 211n3
Anthropocene/Capitalocene, 9. *See also* capitalism; climate change; environmental crisis
anthropology: disciplinary retooling about tourism, 193–96; exonostalgia, 214n8
apiculture, 180
appropriation of space: hotspots and, 88. *See also* enclosure; enclosures within enclosures (Cancún); land dispossession; privatization
archeological tourism, 26, 110, 178–79
architecture: and de facto privatization of beaches, 46; and hacienda luxury tourism, 106, 110, 112, 216n23; of henequen haciendas, as reinforcing racialized social and economic distance, 115–16; starchitecture, 13, 204n27; urban planning and push for tourism growth through, 6; vernacular, 187. *See also* Maya vernacular huts
architectures of escape, 32, 187. *See also* all-inclusive resorts; enclosure; high-rise condominiums
Arctic, 204n29
Aspen, Colorado, 211–12n4
Atlantic City, 6, 73
authenticity: and cultural objects as souvenirs, 158, 159–61, 220n12; hacienda luxury tourism and, 119, 214n8, 216n19,

216n23; indigenous tourism and, 121, 216n23; predatory logic of tourism and, 188; taste and, 121

Bahamas, 201n12
Bahias de Huatulco (Oaxaca), 208n7, 209n12
Baja California, 194
Baklanoff, Eric N., 21, 114
Bali, 191, 203n23
Banco Nacional de Comercio Exterior (BNCE), 134
Bank of Mexico, 36
Baños Ramírez, Othón, 21
Barbados, 34, 201n12
Barcelona, 6, 8–9, 191, 192, 194, 201n12
Batllori Sampedro, Eduardo, 78, 79
beaches: in ecotourism, 85, 92–94, 95–96, 97, 102. *See also* beaches, de facto privatization of; beaches, production and maintenance of
beaches, de facto privatization of: architecture and, 46; beach guards and, 55, 102; disaster capitalism and, 42, 50; ecotourism and, 102; public access, shrinkage of, 53; public access under the law, 46, 53, 55; and racialized/class-based surveillance and profiling, 46–48, 55–56; selective maintenance of, 62–63; and sensorial experience of the beach, loss of, 53. *See also* enclosures within enclosures (Cancún)
beaches, production and maintenance of: climate change and increasing damage, 64–65; and coastal erosion, 15, 62–64; coral-reef destruction and, 15, 62, 64; geotextile tubes, 62–64, *63*, 65, 211n33; high-rise condominiums and lack of contributions to, 52–53; hurricane damage, 31–32, 43, 49; mitigation of receding beaches, sacrificial logic of researchers, 18; sand dredging and pumping, 11, 15, 64, 65, 211n34; seaweed *(sargazo)* removal, 31, *57*, 64; untreated sewage discharge into the ocean, 62
beach resort tourism: all-inclusive resorts compared with traditional, 45; critiques of, and rise of alternative tourism, 66,

Castellanos, M. Bianet, 218nn38–39
Caste Wars (1847–1901), 21, 35, 39, 205n38
Castilla Ramos, Beatriz, 157
Castillo-Burguete, Teresa, 215n11
Celestún: changes over time in, 67–70;
     ecological neglect of, 85–86; fishing as
     livelihood in, 79–81, 92, 97–98, 212n7;
     fish meal industry, and destruction of,
     75, 79, 85, 89–90; as frontier, 71, 211n2;
     health and health care and, 104, 105,
     213n18; independent regional tourists,
     73, 100, 101–3, 178–79; inland labor
     migration to, 79–81, 212n7; irregular
     settlements in, 81, 85–86, 102, 104; map
     of, 77; Mexican state agencies in, 82–83;
     patronage system in (patron/cacique),
     80, 89–90, 100, 102; population of, 75,
     76, 80; research institutions in, 82;
     sensory landscape of, 89; as site for
     research, 25–27; urbanization of, 80–81;
     waste management and sanitation,
     85–86, 102, 103, 104, 105
—conflict and violence in: overview, 1–2, 8,
     70–71, 72–73, 104, 105; appropriation
     of geographical space by labor, 94,
     95–96, 97; appropriation of land by
     politicians, 99–100; burning down of
     tourist infrastructure, 92; burning of
     boats, 98; ecotourism's contradictions as
     source of, 71, 83; fishing limits and, 76,
     97–98, 105; identity and territory and,
     97; with Isla Arena (neighboring vil-
     lage), 76, 79, 81; location of tourist
     infrastructure, 92–93, 94; militariza-
     tion and, 71, 97–98, 99, 104; as notori-
     ous, 71; privatization and, 100; regula-
     tions/overregulation, 76, 92, 97–98, 105;
     and "the technicians" and "the govern-
     ment people," 81–83, 98–99, 212n9;
     urbanization and, 81, 104
—as ecotourism destination: overview,
     103–5; access to benefits of, as highly
     restricted, 86–87, 89, 92, 94, 103–4; and
     the beach, 85, 92–94, 95–96, 97; and the
     beach, de facto privatization of, 102;
     and the estuary/pink flamingo nesting
     and eating, 85; as heterogenous tourist
     space, 211n1; as hotspot (extractive pit),

72, 73, 87–89, 96, 103; local lack of
     knowledge of extent of the biosphere,
     78–79; marketing of, 70–71; Mexican
     state, designation of biosphere, 74,
     75–78; Mexican state, regulations to
     maximize profits, 90–92; the pink
     flamingo as icon of, 84; and the pink
     flamingo, commodification of, 110; and
     the pink flamingo, impacts on and
     protections for, 90, 91, 98; scaling-up of,
     71–72, 103–4; tourist infrastructure, 90,
     100, 102, 105, 213n17; tourist infrastruc-
     ture (paradores), 85, 86, 90–91; tours,
     regulation of, 86, 90–91. See also Bio-
     sphere Reserve Ria Celestún;
     Celestún—conflicts and violence in
—labor and: overview, 72; boatmen (lanch-
     eros), 72, 89–90; boatmen (lancheros),
     Federacion de Lancheros Unidos de
     Celestún, 90–91, 92; boatmen (lanch-
     eros), trained as nature guides, 91–92;
     boatmen from the beach (lancheros de la
     playa), 92–94; boatmen from the estu-
     ary (lancheros de la ria), monopoly of,
     92, 94, 97; craftswomen (artesanas), 72,
     94–96, 95, 97; and direct appeals to
     global expert discourses, 72, 96–97, 98,
     105, 211n3; flexible labor and, 94;
     immobility of, 94–96; plastic-
     gatherers (pepenadoras), 102; sacrificial
     logic of, 96; wages/income, 91, 97,
     104. See also Celestún—conflict and
     violence in
cenotes: definition of, 20; endangered, 196;
     geological conditions that create, 20;
     open-air, 85; privatization of, hacienda
     tourism and, 15, 133, 142; as sacred space,
     133, 217n34; as working space, 134–35,
     140
Centre of Research and Advanced Studies
     of Mérida (CINVESTAV), 71, 78, 82,
     150
Cervera, Dolores, 79, 219n6
Cervera Montejano, Maria Dolores, 175
Cervera Pacheco, Victor, 84, 156–57, 212n7
Chambers, Erve, 8
Chazkel, Amy, 208n3
Cheer, Joseph, 201n13

Chiapas, 97, 121n13, 133; Train Maya and, 160, 184, 196; Zapatistas, 196, 205n38

Chiapello, Eve, 202–3n20

Chibnik, Michael, 220n12

Chichén Itzá: among "new Seven Wonders of the World," 23; as enclavic tourist space, 211n1; and nostalgic representations of Maya culture, 110; number of visitors per year, 23, 216n17; scripted rituals of, 68; Train Maya and, 160–61, 196; on World Heritage list, 118

chicle (gum) production, 203n23, 205–6n40

Chicxulub crater, 20

chikungunya disease, 145–46

childcare/daycare, 153, 169, 175, 179

children: in Maya cosmology, 175, 180, 221n23. *See also* education

China, 161, 193, 196, 201n12

Chocholá, 219n4

Chomsky, Noam, 202–3n20

citizenship, tourism as vector of, 7, 200n7

civic organizations: Acapulco and, 210n29; Cancún and lack of, 60; Celestún's *lancheros* and, 90–91, 92, 134; hacienda tourism and women's, 134–36; henequen industry and women's, 117, 215n14; state mandated as condition of alternative tourism support, 90, 134. *See also tandas* (solidarity and trust networks), sewing for tourism and

Clancy, Michael, 34, 36

class: de facto privatization of beaches and profiling based on, 46–48, 55–56; henequen industry and social organization, 114–15; upward mobility and tourism, 6–7. *See also* hacienda luxury tourism; labor; luxury indigenous tourism; middle class; poverty

Clayton, Anthony, 9

Clifford, James, 26, 188

Clifton, Dixon, 43

climate change: overview, 9, 15; as disregarded in urban governance, 33, 65–66; glacial melting caused by tourism, 191; and increasing deterioration of beaches, 64–65; increasingly recurrent and virulent storms and, 32; international summits on, 65–66; and the milpa (traditional agriculture), dependence on, 176, 221n20; percentage of greenhouse gas emissions created by tourism, 9. *See also* disaster capitalism; environmental crisis; hurricanes

Clinton, Bill, 106

coasts. *See* Biosphere Reserve Ria Celestún; Cancún; Caribbean beach resorts; Celestún

Cohen, Erik, 8

Coleman, Simon, 199n5

Collins, John F., 200n9

Colombia, 192

colonialism: coca-colonization of diet, 132; decolonization of tourism, 194, 201n10; food practices and the hierarchy of taste, 217n32; hacienda luxury tourism and colonization of the agro-industrial past, 110–11, 112, 122, 122–23, 126–27, 143–46, 214nn6–7; milpa practices and, 175; tourism as development and reproduction of, 191, 206n44. *See also* architecture; labor servitudes

colonial third culture, 218–19n3

community participation discourse, expansion of tourism through, 5, 27

CONANP (Comisión Nacional de Áreas Naturales Protegidas), 75, 82

CONEVAL (Consejo Nacional de Evaluación de la Política de Desarrollo Social), 61, 146, 177

consumption: built environments as fostering, 6, 200n6; capitalist, 12, 14–15, 27; cities as spectacles of, 192; conspicuous, 114–15, 121, 178–79; ethical luxury consumption, 121–22; global, 10, 14–15, 24, 32, 33, 40–41, 48, 64, 88–89, 112, 144, 187; the good life for indigenous workers and, 19, 153, 177, 178–79; political ideologies of, 11–12; production and, 12, 14–15. *See also* tourism orderings

Co'ox Mayab, 180

coral reefs: artificial, as museum (MUSA), 66; deterioration of, 15, 62, 64; disaster mitigation programs for, 194

cosmopolitanism, and the extractive logic of tourism, 13

Ecuador, 203n23, 211n3
Edensor, Tim, 8, 88, 130, 211n1, 214n6
education: in Celestún, 104; as component of ecotourism, 74; milpa cycles and ability to attend college, 175–76; in Tekit, 153, 175–76, 177
Eiss, Paul K., 24
ejido system, 21, 39, 100, 116–17, 205n39, 215n13
Ek, Richard, 192, 204–5n34
Elden, Stuart, 218n2
electricity. *See* housing and infrastructure
Elliott, Anthony, 111
Elmendorf, Mary Lindsay, 218n39
Elmhirst, Rebecca, 213n20
El Palmar State Reserve, 76
emotional labor, 56, 210n25
empowerment. *See* indigenous empowerment discourse
enclavic tourist spaces, 211n1
enclosure: definition of, 208n3; and ecological deterioration, 15–16; and global postdisaster opportunism, 16–17, 53–54, 209–10nn22; hacienda luxury tourism and, 142; orderings of tourism and, 11; sacrificial logic and, 18–19, 33, 54, 55–56. *See also* architecture; capitalism; enclosures within enclosures (Cancún); environmental crisis; flexible labor; land dispossession; privatization
enclosures within enclosures (Cancún): overview, 32–33; and curtailment of tourist economic and social interactions outside the resort, 45–46, 54–55; defined as nested instruments of flexible privatization, 32, 40–41; dependency of the region on, 33, 48; as environmentally unsustainable, 42; as exclusionary, 42, 46; and friction between representations of Cancún and reality, 54–55; high-rise condominiums and, 51; and labor, 33; post-hurricane opportunism and development of, 15–16, 32–33, 41, 42–43; as predatory geography, 48; sacrificial logic and, 33, 54, 61; segregated design of Cancún and, 36–37. *See also* beaches, de facto privatization of
encounters trope, 186, 193

Enloe, Cynthia, 4–5, 7–8, 210n26
Enríquez Savignac, Antonio, 34
environmental crisis: extractive logic of tourism as contributing to, 15–16, 191; greenwashing of extractive industries and, 203n23; and last-chance/doomed tourism, 204n29; and seasonality of tourism, 17; and violence of tourism, 15. *See also* capitalism; climate change; environmental damage; environmental regulations; environmental sustainability discourse; hurricanes
environmental damage: dyewood, mahogany, and chicle production and, 205–6n40; ecotourism as coupled with faith in market solutions to, 74; illegal/unregulated waste dumping, 129, 177; of mass tourism, and rise of ecotourism, 66, 72; UN-inspired coastal assessment reports, as disregarded, 65. *See also* sewage; waste and waste management
environmental disasters. *See* capitalism; hurricanes
environmental regulations: Cancún and avoidance of, as hampering tourism ventures, 65; cutting, and ecotourism, 75
environmental sustainability discourse: expansion of tourism through, 5, 188; hacienda tourism and, 129; rise of ecotourism and, 27, 73–74
Escudero-Castillo, Mireille, 62, 209n16
ethical spending/mindful travel discourses, expansion of tourism and, 5, 121–22
etiquette, 131–32
Europe: Cancún airport flights to, 206n41; destinations in which tourists outnumber residents, 8–9, 201n12; and entrapments of tourism as development, 191–92; hacienda tourism and relation to, 126–27, 128, 143–44; the henequen haciendas and relation to, 126–27, 158–59; and urban planning as inseparable from tourism, 6
Evans, Sterling David, 113, 215n10
exclusion: and predatory logic of tourism, 30; the tourist gaze and, 11
exonostalgia, 214n8

extraction as logic of tourism: overview, 187; definition of, 12–13, 203n23; ecotourism as form of, 71–72, 73, 74–75, 203n23; and the endless creation of new zones of commodification, 14–15, 188; historical basis of, 22–23; and hope, spaces of, 188–90; hotspots as contentious sites of, 72, 73, 87–89, 96, 103; industrial extraction and, 13, 203n23; and the landscape, transformation of, 13; maintenance of tourist spaces and, 15–16; neoextractivism, 204n28; predatory geography and, 40–41, 45, 188; territorial enclaves and, 13. *See also* labor; predatory logic of tourism; sacrificial logic; stickiness-as-entrapment; tourism orderings

extractivismo in Latin America. *See* extraction as logic of tourism

Fabricant, Nicole, 204n28, 211n3
Fainstein, Susan S., 208n8
fair trade, 136
Fallaw, Ben, 22–24, 116, 205n39, 215nn11,13
Farthing, Linda, 204n28
favela tourism, 217n27
FHMM. *See* Fundacio Haciendas del Mundo Maya
Fierro Reyes, Gabriela, 217–18n35
Figueroa, Esther, 203–4n26
Finn, Janet L., 203n24
fishing: Celestún and limits on, 76, 97–98, 105; labor migration and, 79–81, 156, 212n7; lack of state response to hurricane damage to, 44–45; promoted by the state in response to the henequen crisis, 79–80, 156
Fletcher, Robert, 74, 204n30
flexible labor: overview, 10; and the come-and-go city, 60; maquiladoras and, 33; sacrificial logic and, 18, 188; sewing for tourism (Tekit) and, 166, 174, 220n14
Fomento Cultural Banamex, 118
FONATUR (Fondo Nacional de Fomento al Turismo): beach maintenance and, 62–63; establishment of, 208–9n10; National Fund for Tourism Promotion, 36; and privatization of Cancún, 44, 51;

state management of Cancún via, 37; and Train Maya, 196
food: coca-colonization of the Mayan diet, 132; colonial practices and hierarchy of taste, 217n32; importation of, for Cancún's Hotel Zone, 45–46; indigenous, in hacienda tourism's fusion cuisine, 132; insecurity statistics, 177. *See also* milpa (traditional Maya agricultural system); poverty
Forero, Oscar A., 22, 205–6n40
Fortun, Kim, 211n3
Fox, Vincente, 49, 51
Fraga, Julia, 79, 85, 210n28, 219n6
France, 11, 191, 201n12
Franklin, Adrian, 201–2n16
Franquesa, Jaume, 6, 112, 192, 200n9
Freire-Medeiros, Bianca, 217n27
Frigolé, Joan, 127
frontier enclave developments, 35–36
Fundacio Haciendas del Mundo Maya (FHMM), 109–10, 125, 129, 134, 135–36, 137–38, 140, 142, 215n14, 218n37
Fyre Festival (2017), 200n7

Gambrill, Mónica, 219–20n10
Garcés, Marina, 192, 201n11
García de Fuentes, Ana, 36, 37, 206n44, 219n7 ·
gaze, tourist, 9–10, 14, 202n17
gendered labor: indigenous stereotypes and, 56, 130–31, 210n26, 218n39; sewing for tourism and labor specialization, 162, 174. *See also* race—gendered labor and hierarchies of
gender ideologies: sewing for tourism (Tekit) and indigenous traditions, 174–75, 176; the tourist gaze and patterns of, 11
gender violence, 104
gentrification, 6
geotextile tubes, 62–64, *63*, 65, 211n33
Germann Molz, Jennie, 199n2, 217n32
Germany, 201n12
"giving back" discourse, 5, 136
global ethnography, 25
Godale, Mark, 214n8
Gómez-Barris, Macarena, 13, 204n31

Gómez, Edmund Terence, 204n32, 212n9
Gonzalez, Vernadette Vicuña, 6, 8, 10, 193, 194, 201n10, 203n22, 212n9
the good life: and child care, 153, 179; child development and, 175; and consumer goods and services, access to, 153, 177, 178–79; as cruel optimism, 221n20; and extended family, maintenance of, 153, 156, 178, 179; fragility of, 180; and hope, spaces of, 170, 189; labor conditions better than henequen production, 155–56, 179; labor conditions better than maquiladoras, 179; and the land, holding onto, 178; and the milpa (agricultural system), maintenance of, 153, 156, 178, 189, 221n21; and origin story of sewing for tourism (Tekit), 154; and resiliency, 221n21; and "Saint Monday," respect for, 179, 221n22; and traditions, 153, 156, 168, 175, 178–80, 221n23; and "vice," avoidance of, 179. See also labor migration, the good life and avoidance of
Goodman, Alan, 132
Gordillo, Gastón R., 200n9
Goreau, Thomas J., 62, 64, 66
Graburn, Nelson, 5–6, 203n21
Graham, Steve, 48, 204n34
grand tours, 11
Gravari-Barbas, Maria, 5–6, 200n9
Greenwood, Davydd, 14
Gregory, Derek, 207n45
Grenada, 194
Guadeloupe, 205n35
Guardado, Gustavo Marín, 40, 133, 206n44, 209n20, 213n16
Guatemala, 35, 133, 196, 203n22, 212n13
guayaberas: certification seal for, 160, 161; as cultural souvenir, 158, 159–61, 165, 170, 220n12; International Guayabera Day, 159; origins and popularization of, 158–59; as professional ("presidential") attire, 159, 165; quality levels of, 165; and representations of the Maya people as vanishing but still alive, 159; in tourism marketing campaigns, 159; and Train Maya project, 160–61; as uniform worn by tourism workers, 131, 159, 165; as

wedding shirt, 159. See also sewing for tourism—guayaberas as focus of
Gudynas, Eduardo, 15, 203n25, 204n28
Gulf of Mexico coast: expansion of high-rise condominiums to, 100, 102, 105; rebranded as "the Pink Coast," 105. See also Biosphere Reserve Ria Celestún; Celestún
Gyawali, Dipak, 151

haciendas (henequen): overview, 113–14; architecture of, as reinforcing racialized social and economic distance, 115–16; and boom/bust of the henequen industry, 113, 117, 120; casas grandes, 115, 116, 126; civic organizations, 117, 215n14; collapse of the henequen industry and closure of, 117; conspicuous consumption and, 114–15; debt-peonage labor system of, 115, 134; and Europe/the international, relation to, 126–27, 158–59; labor organizing, 116–17; labor resistance, 137, 138; land reform and, 116–17, 215n13; and the rise of global elites, 117, 215–16n15; sewing for tourism labor conditions as preferable to, 155–56, 179; social organization of, 114–15; vernacular Maya houses, 116; violence and, 116–17. See also hacienda luxury tourism; henequen (sisal) industry
hacienda luxury tourism: appropriation of Maya healing traditions by, 132–33; architecture and, 106, 110, 112, 216n23; authenticity and, 119, 214n8, 216n19, 216n23; casas grandes as focus of, 116, 126–27, 128; and conflict-free representation of Maya Otherness, 136; critique of mass tourism and rise of, 119, 144; cuisine of, as fusion with indigenous foods, 132; environmental neglect as fueled by, 129; and Europe, relation to, 126–27, 128, 143–44; everyday objects, display of, 126–27; and gardens as political and economic resource, 128–30, 137, 138; gated entrances, 123; as guilt-free experience, 127, 129, 136, 144; and heritage preservation discourse, 110, 112, 118–19, 144; and imaginaries of the

agro-industrial past, colonization of, 110–11, 112, 122, 122–23, 126–27, 143–46, 214nn6–7; and indigenous empowerment discourse, 109–10, 112, 121–22, 144; and luxury as mobilized for economic development, 112, 119, 121–22, 131–32, 216n22; the manager as embodying the old foreman's role, 130–31, 138; and militarization, 106–7; nostalgia and, 13, 110–11, 112, 122, 125, 126, 136, 214n8; postdisaster opportunism and, 109, 112, 125–26; and privatization, 125–26, 133, 140, 142, 144; and production of site-specific forms of being indigenous, 111, 112, 145; and public-private partnerships, 109, 110, 118, 215–16n15, 218n37; and sedentarist representations of indigenous pasts, 111, 187, 214n8; and service, guest expectations of, 131–32; and social responsibility discourse, 109–10, 218n37; staged enactments in surrounding village, 106, 123–26. *See also* Hacienda Temozón Sur; luxury indigenous tourism; Temozón (village)

—labor and: avoidance of migration as factor for, 108–9, 137, 139, 140–42; civic societies (cooperatives) of, and practices of dispossession, 134–36; English speaking, 131; etiquette and, 131–32; garden workers, 128–30, 137, 138; immobility of, 2, 135; naturalization of the indigenous self as uniformed and servile, 132; patronage (*patrones/peones*) system of henequen hacienda as re-created in, 112, 116, 122, 125, 130–32, 138, 141, 144–45, 215n12; and the re-creation of racialized and gendered labor servitude, 107–9, 111, 122, 130–31; resistance by, strategic entanglement with past forms of, 111, 137–40, 205n35; sacrificial logic of, 112–13, 136–37, 139, 140–43, 146; surveillance of, 128, 131; suspicion of impurity of workers in, by indigenous elders, 142–43, 218n39; uniforms/required garments, 106, 131, 142; wages/income, 135, 138, 146; women giving massages (*sobadas*), 2, 132–33, 134–35, 140, 142;

women making handicrafts, 124–25, 134, 135–36, 218n37

The Haciendas, 109–10, 118. *See also* Hacienda Temozón Sur

Hacienda Santa Rosa, 147

Hacienda Temozón Sur, *120*; awards received by, 218n37; and ethical luxury consumption, 121–22; gardens of, 128–30, 137, 138; gated access, 123; in the henequen-production era, 116–17; immobility of labor and, 2, 135; Mexico-US presidential summits at, 106–9; and re-creation of the hacendado/peon labor regime, 122, 130–32; restoration of, 118; as site for research, 25–27; staged enactment of Temozón village as contrasted with the actual landscape, 106, 123–26; women's labor giving massages (*sobadas*), 2, 132–33, 134–35, 140, 142; women's labor making handicrafts, 124–25, 134, 135–36, 218n37. *See also* hacienda luxury tourism

Hacienda Xmuyil, 154–55

Haiti, 191

Haldrup, Michael, 11, 207n48

Hall, C. Michael, 201n15

Hall, Derek R., 12

Han, Clara, 220n15

Hannam, Kevin, 10, 88, 200n8, 205n35

Hanson, Anne-Marie, 81, 86, 213n20, 213nn19–20

Haraway, Donna, 204–5n34

Harcourt, Wendy, 25

Harvey, Penny, 42, 88, 208n3, 209n13

Hawai'i, 194, 203n22, 210n26

health and health care: cancer, 170; cataracts and blindness, 169, 177; in Celestún, 104, 105, 213n18; coca-colonization of the Mayan diet and, 132; diabetes and obesity, 132; hacienda tourism workers and villagers and, 140, 145–46; illegal waste dumping and, 129; indigenous medicine, 129; sewing for tourism and standards for sanitation and, 171; Tekit health care, 153, 169, 177; Tekit health problems from sewing for tourism, 3, 167, 169–70, 176–77 henequen (sisal) industry: overview, 21; collapse of, 117; collapse of, and labor migration to Cancún, 38–39, 134, 156; collapse of, and rise of tourism, 21–22, 39–40, 206n44; collapse of, and sewing for tourism, 154–55; collapse of, and turn to maquiladoras, 134, 156; economic importance of, 113–14; fishing promoted by the state to replace, 79–80, 156; and global markets, connection of the Yucatán to, 21; labor conditions of, as slaving (*esclavo*), 113, 115, 127, 154, 155–56; and racial divide, 21; Train Maya and infrastructure of, 160–61, 196, 220n13. *See also* haciendas (henequen); Mexican state; tourism as development

heritage, as industry, 118

heritage preservation discourse: conflicts of, 7, 200n9; expansion of tourism through, 5, 188; hacienda luxury tourism and, 110, 112, 118–19, 144; imaginary of tourism built through, 5; "imperial eyes" and, 110, 121; and objectification of places, 127–28

heritage, theory of, 112

Herman, Edward S., 202–3n20

Hernández, Roberto, 109, 118, 125, 129, 136–37, 141

Herzfeld, Michael, 200n9

heterogeneous tourist spaces, 211n1

Hiernaux Nicolás, Daniel, 43–44

Higham, James E. S., 201n15

high-rise condominiums: overview, 29–30; attempts to regulate, 53; conversion of all-inclusive resorts to, after Hurricane Wilma, 50–51; and de facto privatization of beaches, 53, 55; expansion to the Gulf of Mexico coast, 100, 102, 105; investment risk transferred to tourists via, 50, 52–53; multiownership of, and lack of accountability, 51–53; social displacement created by, 30, 102. *See also* all-inclusive resorts; enclosure

Hirsch, Fred, 14

Hobsbawm, E. J., 8

Hochschild, Arlie Russell, 210n25

Hodder, Ian, 204–5n34

Hoffman, Lily M., 208n8

Holbox, 39–40

Holston, James, 6, 202–3n20

Honduras, 203n23

Hong Kong, 201n12

hope, spaces of, 3, 18, 112–13, 188–90

Hoskins, Janet, 203n23

hospitality, language of, 193

household: dynamics of, 3; family life and, 16, 104, 149–52; and family organization, 146, 161–78; scale of, 8. *See also* sewing for tourism (Tekit)—kinship and; social reproduction

housing and infrastructure: Cancún laborers required to live on site, 58; privatization of infrastructure, 44, 100, 209n17; in Tekit, 148–49, 155, 169, 177; in Temozón (village), 125–26, 141, 143. *See also* Cancún City; irregular settlements; Maya vernacular huts; waste and waste management

Hsiung, Ping-Chun, 166

huipil garment, 158, 219n4

Hultman, Johan, 192, 204–5n34

human right, tourism as, 7, 194, 200n8

Hume, David, 121

Hunt, Carter, 199n4

Hunucma, 85, 206n44

Hurricane Allen (1980), 209n14

Hurricane Gilbert (1989): and Cancún, 32–33, 41–42, 43–48, 50, 51, 191; and Celestún, 75, 80, 85

Hurricane Isidore (2002), 109, 112, 125, 134, 141, 191

Hurricane Ivan (2004), 65

Hurricane Katrina (2005), 54, 191

Hurricane Maria (2018), 191

Hurricane Paula (2010), 30–31, 53, 60, *63*

hurricanes: Celestún and damage to fish meal industry, 75, 85; expansion of tourism in the wake of, 15–16. *See also* Cancún—hurricanes and; climate change; disaster capitalism

Hurricane Wilma (2005), 1, 32–33, 42, 48–51, 59, 62, 105, 191

Hurtado, Fernandez, 34–35

Igoe, Jim, 11, 72, 74, 84, 203n23

imaginaries of tourism: overview, 5–6; Cancún development and, 36, 54–55;

Marine Protected Area of Cozumel, 66
marketization of urban governance, 33, 39, 208n6
Markusen, Ann, 204n34
Mármol, Camila del, 127
Marriot Hotels and Resorts, Luxury Collection, 109, 118, 131. *See also* hacienda luxury tourism
Martí, Fernando, 36, 38
Marvin, Simon, 48, 204n34
Marxism, and disaster capitalism, 209n13
Massey, Doreen B., 207n45
mass tourism, 19, 26, 34, 45, 66; social differences and, 72–73; standardized mass consumerism, 4, 144. *See also* beach resort tourism
Mattiace, Shannan, 114, 115
Mattioli, Fabio, 6, 203n22
Mayapan, 118–19, 147
Maya people: hotels targeting entire village as labor source, 58; popularity of the Yucatán Peninsula as "the land of," 23; touristification of, 206n44. *See also* good life, the; indigeneity; indigenous empowerment discourse; indigenous peoples; labor; Maya traditions; Maya vernacular huts; milpa (traditional Maya agricultural system); stereotypical representations of Maya Otherness
Maya traditions: baby blessing (jéets méek), 180, 221n23; child development, 175; gender ideologies, 174–75, 176; the good life and evolution of, 179–80, 221n23; the good life and maintenance of, 153, 156, 168, 175, 178; healing, hacienda luxury tourism and appropriation of, 132–33; sewing for tourism and new developments in, 179–80; and tourism as imaginary of hope, 190. *See also* Maya vernacular huts; milpa (traditional Maya agricultural system)
Maya vernacular huts: and the henequen industry, 116; as staged enactment in hacienda tourism, 106, 123, 135; in urban-village mix of Tekit, 148–49
Mayer, Margit, 202n19
Meehan, Katie, 25
Mena, Ignacio de, 116–17

Méndez-Contreras, Jessica, 215n11
Mérida: airport of, and rerouting of flights to Cancún, 206n41; as excluded from sites of research, 26; as "guayabera capital of the world," 159, 160–61; and guayabera production, 155, 161, 162, 165; middle-class formed due to tourism, 190; as "the White City," henequen production and, 21; Train Maya and, 160–61, 196
methodology: combined approach to, 25, 207n48; exclusions, 26–27; literature review, 23–24, 25, 206n44; positionality of the researcher, 83; pseudonyms, 199n1; and the regional scale as unit of analysis, 24–25, 207n45; the Yucatán Peninsula as site of research, 19–20, 25–27
Mexican–American War (1846–47), 21
Mexican Revolution (1910), 21, 137, 205n39; and land reform (*ejido* system), 21, 39, 100, 116–17, 205n39, 215n13
Mexican state: declaration of the Biosphere Reserve Ria Celestún, 74, 75–78; deregulation of foreign investment, 44; ecotourism pushed by, 70, 75, 84, 90–92; "La Marcha al Mar" policy, 79–80, 212n7; minimum wage and other labor laws, 135, 171; nostalgia and formation of, 214n8; relocation of maquiladoras in the Yucatán to henequen zone, 157, 219n19; and the Yucatán Peninsula, struggle to control, 20–21, 35. *See also* indigeneity; indigenous peoples; labor; landscapes of tourism; Mexico, National Development Plans; militarization; nationalism; neoliberalism; public-private partnerships; tourism as development
Mexico, National Development Plans: 1983, 39; 1989–1994, 44; 2001–2006, 5; CIP (*centros integralmente planeados*) tourism plans, 34, 208n7; First National Tourism Plan (1962), 33; National Plan for the Development of the Tourist Sector, 75; Planned Tourism Destination Policy, 33–34
middle class: incipient, tourism and formation of, 190; as marketing target for

Cancún City, 37; as regional tourists from Tekit (sewing for tourists), 178–79; as regional tourists in Celestún, 101–2

Milano, Claudio, 201n13

militarization: of Cancún after Hurricane Wilma, 49; and conflict and violence in Celestún, 71, 97–98, *99*, 104; hacienda luxury tourism and, 106–7; and long-standing conflicts, generally, 212n13; tourist-site development of infrastructures of, 8; and Train Maya, 196

milpa (traditional Maya agricultural system): abandoned henequen fields reclaimed for, 129; climate change and, 176, 221n20; definition of, 205n37, 219n5; the good life and ability to maintain, 153, 156, 178, 189, 221n21; improved milpa project, 221n20; and sacrificial logic, 19; sewing for tourism (Tekit) and cycles of, 175–76. *See also* good life, the

mining, 11, 13, 188, 203n23

Mintz, Sidney W., 113

mobilities paradigm: labor immobilities, 2, 94–96, 135; orderings as term in, 25, 201–2n16

modernization discourses, tourism promoted through: overview, 4, 22, 27; and Cancún, creation of, 35–36

Moench, Marcus, 151

Momsen, Janet D., 40, 44, 46, 208–9nn7,10

Moore, Amelia, 201n15

Moore, Jason W., 9, 14, 15

Morocco, 192

Moseley, Edward H., 20, 21, 23

Mostafanezhad, Mary, 12, 193, 199n2, 205n35

Mota Santos, Paula, 200n9

Mowforth, Martin, 4, 73, 74, 199n4

Mukerji, Chandra, 128, 204n33

Mukul, Eric Villanueva, 114

multiscalar: agreements, 125; alliance, 36; definition, 208–9n10; effort, 36, 49, 159; logistics, 13; nature, 203n24. *See also* scale; scaling-up; tourism orderings

multisited research, 25

Munt, Ian, 4, 73, 74, 199n4

MUSA (underwater contemporary museum of art), 66

NAFTA, 157–58, 183, 219–20n10

Nájera, Lourdes Gutiérrez, 212n13

Narotzky, Susana, 127, 207n48

Nash, Dennison, 7

National Fund for Tourism Promotion (FONATUR), 36

nationalism: heritage preservation discourse and, 119; orderings of tourism as project of, 201–2n16; and sedentarist representations of indigenous peoples, 214n8; tourism as advancing, 8, 192–93, 206n44; and tourist-site development of military infrastructure, 8. *See also* tourism as development

natural protected areas: exclusion of humans from, 213n20; violence in, as common concern, 212nn9,13. *See also* biospheres; neoliberalism

nature tourism, as extractive industry, 203n23

nature, Western-centric definition of, 74

Nelson, Ingrid L., 25

neoextractivism, 204n28

neoliberalism: AMLO and criticism of, 183; contestation of, 214n8; ecotourism and the neoliberalization of nature, 203n23; and expansion of tourism industry, 4–5; labor hierarchies in Cancún and, 56; manufactured consent and, 10, 202–3n20; maquiladoras and, 156; marketization of urban governance, 33, 39, 208n6; tourism as project of, 10, 202n19. *See also* capitalism; disaster capitalism; flexible labor; labor servitudes; privatization

New Age (spiritual) tourism, 26, 133, 216n19

New Orleans, 53–54, 191, 217n32

New York City, 192, 194

New Zealand, 192, 204n29

Neza (Mexico City), 221n17

Nichupte lacunar system, 36–37

Niños y Crias, 82

Nixon, Angelique V., 7, 8, 36

Nonnenmacher, Tomas, 114, 115

Norum, Roger, 12, 193

nostalgia: archeological tourism and, 110;
exonostalgia, 214n8; hacienda luxury
tourism and, 13, 110–11, 112, 122, 125,
126, 136, 214n8; and Mexican state
formation, 214n8
Notre-Dame Cathedral fire, 191
Novelli, Marina, 201n13
Nugent, Daniel, 205n39

Oaxaca, 171, 172, 208n7, 209n12, 212n13
OECD (Organization for Economic Co-
operation and Development), 22, 219n9
oil industry, 13, 39, 156, 188
Olsen, Daniel, 216n19
orderings. *See* tourism orderings
Ortiz Caso, Daniel, 35
Ortiz Yam, Inés, 175
Osten, Sarah, 23
the Other, tourism's symbolic orderings
and, 10–11
overtourism, 8–9, 193–94, 201n12
Oxkutzcab, 148

Palenque, 196
Palma de Majorca, 6, 192
Paris, 9
Park, Lisa, 211–12n4
Partido Nacional Revolucionario (PNR),
117
Partido Socialista del Sureste (PSS), 134
Patel, Raj, 14
patronage: Celestún system of (*cacique*), 80,
89–90, 100, 102; the hacienda/
henequen industry and social organiza-
tion of, 114–15; hacienda luxury tourism
and re-creation of henequen system of,
112, 116, 122, 125, 130–32, 138, 141, 144–
45, 215n12
Patronato de las Unidades Culturales y
Turísticas del Estado de Yucatán (CUL-
TUR), 82, 90–91, 94
Patrón Laviada, Alejandro, 118
Patrón Laviada, Patricio, 118
Pattullo, Polly, 6, 34, 72, 74, 207n45
Paz Paredes, Sigfrido, 35–36
Peeck, Jamie, 202n19
Pelas, Holly Renee, 208–9nn8–10
Pellow, David, 211–12n4

Peón, Carlos, 114
Peón Suárez, Humberto, 114
Peru, 191
philanthropic capitalism, 111. *See also*
capitalism
Phuket, 209–10n22
pink shrimp, fishing for, 79, 81, 97–98
plastic collection for resale, 100, 102
Playa del Carmen, 39–40
policing, tourist police, 31
politics, tourism orderings and, 11–12
positionality of the researcher, 83
Postero, Nancy, 214n8
poverty: Cancún and, 61; Celestún and,
104; expansion of tourism via
discourse of, 5; and ghost villages,
147; Tekit and, 177; of Temozón village,
and lack of opportunity, 123–26, 133,
145–46
predatory geography: commodification
and, 48, 55, 72, 111, 188; extraction
and, 40–41, 45, 188; and financial
capitalism, 14, 54, 61, 144, 178; and
racial and socioeconomic profiling,
55. *See also* capitalism; neoliberalism;
predatory and sticky tourism geography; predatory logic of tourism;
stickiness-as-entrapment; tourism
orderings
predatory and sticky tourism geography, 1,
12, 19, 54, 71, 103, 122, 150, 170, 179, 187,
191. *See also* predatory logic of tourism;
re-spatializing; scaling-up; stickiness-as-
entrapment; tourism orderings
predatory logic of tourism, 16–18, 27, 60,
72, 88, 96, 105, 146, 181, 187–88, 190–92;
definition of, 12–13; displacement of risk
and, 52; enclosures within enclosures
and, 48; and environmental unsustainability, 15–16, 177, 191; financial capitalism and, 14, 61; global nature of, 191–93;
and historical practices of exclusion, 30;
land appropriation and, 100; "positional
goods," places and people as, 14; as
practice of capital accumulation, 54,
144, 204n30; reengineering of the
Earth and, 13; splintered nature of, 48;
as system of production, 178. *See also*

Rojek, Chris, 4, 121
Rothstein, Frances Abrahamer, 166
Rottenberg, Robert, 128
Rubio Herrera, Amada, 154, 155–56,
208nn4,9, 221nn19,23
Ruiz Cortines, Adolfo, 212n7
rural space, 166, 176; back to nature/rural
tourism, 191–92. *See also* desakotas
Ruta Puuc, 110, 118–19, 149

sacrificial logic: overview, 188; and ambiva-
lent/contradictory moral regimes,
17–18, 58–59, 152–53; Cancún workers
and, 33, 54, 55–56, 59–60; Celestún
workers and, 96; definition of, 18–19,
205n36; detachment and disengagement
resulting from, 59–60; flexible labor
and, 18, 88; hacienda tourism and,
112–13, 136–37, 139, 140–43, 146; of land
through enclosures, 18–19, 33, 54, 55–56,
61; misinterpretation of indigenous
culture, 136; and progress, tourism as,
19; and researchers working to mitigate
receding beaches, 18; sewing for tourism
and, 150, 152–53, 168, 170, 176–81; and
stereotypical indigenous Maya representations, 18–19. *See also* flexible labor;
labor; predatory logic of tourism; stickiness-as-entrapment; tourism orderings
safety. *See* security
Sahlins, Marshall, 145
Salazar, Noel B., 5–6, 199n5
Saldaña-Portillo, María Josefina, 211n2,
212n13
Salinas, Carlos, 44
sand dredging and pumping, 11, 15, 64, 65,
211n34
Sanderson, Warren, 129
San Francisco, 6
San José del Cabo (Baja California), 208n7
Savarino Roggero, Franco, 215n11, 217n34
Sawyer, Suzana, 97, 203n24, 204n32, 212n9
scale: across scales, 27; economies of,
220n10; of exploitation and sacrifice,
192; international, national, regional,
and local, 8, 13, 19, 27, 79, 144, 154, 168,
184, 188, 197; intimate, 187; national, 98;
politics of, 25; regional, 22–25, 98,

207n45; scale-bending, 211n3; small-
scale, 37, 51, 59, 74, 113, 155; up-scale
global, 52, 72. *See also* multiscalar;
scaling-up
scaling-up: definition of, 10; on the ecological level, 11; ecotourism and, 71–72,
103–4; hacienda tourism and, 143–45;
on the material level, 10; on the political
level, 11–12, 203n22; and production
and maintenance of "a world to escape
to," 27; and the regional as ethnographic
unit of analysis, 24; sewing for tourism
(Tekit) and, 152; on the symbolic level,
10–11. *See also* extraction as logic of
tourism; predatory logic of tourism;
re-spatializing; tourism orderings
Scheld, Suzanne, 8, 144
Schwenkel, Christina, 111
Scott, James, 204n34
seasonality of tourism, 17, 171
seasonal migration. *See* labor migration—
seasonal indigenous workers
sea turtles, 85
SECTUR (Secretaría de Turismo), 44, 74,
216n17
security: beach guards, 55, 102; and hurricane damage in Cancún City, 31; implications about lack of, and curtailment
of tourist interaction with locals, 54–55;
of tourists, as priority, 203n22. *See also*
militarization; policing
SEDESMA (Secretaría de Medio Ambiente
y Pesca), 75
SEDESOL (Secretaría de Desarrollo
Social), 49, 51, 146, 149
SEMARNAT (Secretaría de Medio Ambiente y Recursos Naturales), 70, 78, 79,
82, 83, 85, 91, 104
Serlin, David, 208n3
service economy: and servant class cities, 61;
shift to, 4, 17. *See also* consumption;
labor servitudes
sewage: and destruction of coral reefs, 62,
64; privatization of services, 209n17;
size of treatment system in Cancún, 62.
See also waste and waste management
sewing for tourism (Tekit): alternative to,
agro-ecological/indigenous solidarity

Taplin, Dana, 8, 144

taste: and authenticity, 121; colonial food practices and hierarchy of, 217n32; and luxury, 112, 121, 216n22

Taylor, Charles, 199–200n5

Taylor, Sarah, 207n46

Teabo, 219n4

Teaiwa, Teresia, 186, 193, 201n10

Tecoh, 219n4

Tekit: overview, 146, 147–52; abandonment by the state, 154; alcohol/drug abuse rates as lower in, 179; amenities and services offered by, 147–49, 153; bustling urban-style scene of, in contrast to surrounding countryside, 147–49, *149*, 154; childcare and, 153, 169, 175; clocks and calendars as ruling, 148; as colonial third culture, 218–19n3; and cultural Otherness as primitivism, 13; as desa-kota (city-village), 151–52, 153–58, 159, 166, 219n4; education and, 153, 175–76, 177; entrapment and, 150, 153; financial services in, 149, 162; health care and, 153, 169, 177; health problems and, 3, 167, 169–70, 176–77; and the henequen industry, collapse of, 154–55; highway connecting to Mérida, 147, 155; housing and infrastructure, 148–49, 155, 169, 177; labor migration as avoided in, 149, 152, 153, 168–69, 170, 178, 179; maquiladoras and, 156–58, 219–20nn7,9,10; population and demographics of, 149; poverty and, 177; as pulverized/scattered maquila, 150–51, *151*, 161, 163, 218n2; scaling-up of, 152; as site for research, 25–27; tourism as absent from, 149–50; tourism infrastructure proposed for, 160–61; and tourism, new alternatives in, 180–81, 189; Train Maya and, 160–61, 197–98; transportation and traffic in, 148, *149*; unemployment rate as low in, 149; waste management and, 177. *See also* good life, the; milpa (traditional Maya agricultural system); sewing for tourism (Tekit)

Telfer, David J., 5, 32, 34, 53, 199n4

Temozón (village): artisanal workshops of, 106, 124–25, 134, 135–36, 218n37;

chikungunya disease and lack of help from the hotel, 145–46; deforestation and, 129; housing and infrastructure, 125–26, 141, 143; Maya vernacular huts as staged enactment, 106, 123, 135; Mexico-US presidential summits and, 106; and postdisaster opportunism, 112, 125–26; poverty and lack of opportunity as reality of, 123–26, 133, 145–46; waste management and, 129, 141; white *ternos* garments as symbol of the Maya, 106, 142. *See also* hacienda luxury tourism; Hacienda Temozón Sur

Terán, Silvia, 219n5

Terry, Edward Davis, 20, 23–24

textile industry, state-led consolidation as development model, 156. *See also* guayaberas; maquiladoras; sewing for tourism (Tekit)

Thailand, 191, 194–95, 201n12

Thames Town, 6

Theodore, Nik, 202n19

the past, hacienda luxury tourism and colonization of the agro-industrial, 110–11, 112, 122, 122–23, 126–27, 143–46, 214nn6-7

Thomas-Slayer, Barbara, 25

Thrift, Nigel, 207n45

time-share resorts: villas, 50, 51. *See also* high-rise condominiums

Torres, Beatriz, 157

Torres, Rebecca, 40, 44, 46, 156, 208–9nn7,10

tourism: global rise of, 22; as hospitality industry, 186, 193; as human right vs. privilege, 7, 194, 200n8; overtourism, 8–9, 193–94, 201n12; regional, by locals, 73, 100, 101–3, 178–79; rethinking, 193–95; as sacred journey, 203n21; size and growth of global industry, 5; the tourist gaze, 9–10, 14, 202n17. *See also* imaginaries of tourism; landscapes of tourism; predatory logic of tourism; sacrificial logic; stickiness-as-entrapment; tourism as development; tourism orderings; tourism, types of tourism as development: overview, 5, 11, 39; as assimilation project, 8, 35, 193, 206n44; Caribbean resort economies as import substitution industrial strategy, 34; and cities as spectacles of consumption, 192; continued faith in, despite failures of, 186, 191–93; and the debt crisis of 1982, 39; as disruptive fixation, 186; economic multiplier effect as focus of, 34, 39–40; employment opportunities as focus of, 34; and the energy crisis (late 1970s), 39; environmental unsustainability of beach resort tourism and rise of ecotourism, 66; foreign currency generation as focus of, 34, 35–36, 44; and historical forms of extraction, 22–23; and hope, imaginaries of, 3, 18, 112–13, 188–90; Lopez Portillo and, 39; de la Madrid and, 39; as modernization strategy, 35–36, 39–40; political divisions as transcended by promise of, 184, 186; political meaning of tourism as vacated to enable, 186–87, 190, 193; as strategy of state control, 35. *See also* capitalism; extraction as logic of tourism; Mexican state; Mexico, National Development Plans; modernization discourses; predatory logic of tourism; stickiness-as-entrapment; Train Maya

tourism orderings, 9–12, 201–2n16; of space, 27, 96, 111, 170, 181, 190; the tourist gaze as, 9–10, 14, 202n17. *See also* capitalism; consumption; predatory logic of tourism; production of space; re-spatializing; scaling-up; stickiness-as-entrapment

tourism, types of: adventure tourism, 203n23; archeological tourism, 26, 110, 178–79; last-chance/doomed, 204n29; virtual tourism, 203n25; voluntourism/slum tourism/favela tourism, 217n27. *See also* alternative tourism; beach resort tourism; cultural tourism; ecotourism; nature tourism

tourist-host relationship: ambivalence of, 7–8, 200n9; as encounters trope, 186, 193

traditions. *See* Maya traditions

Train Maya: overview, 27, 183–84; ambivalence toward, 197–98; AMLO as supporting, 27, 183–84, 196, 220n13; henequen industry infrastructure and, 160–61, 196, 220n13; indigenous ceremonies blessing, 196, 197; launch of, 196; marketing of, 184, *185*; the military and, 196; opposition to, 196–97; and Tekit guayabera production, 160–61, 197–98; and "tourism as development," 184, 186, 190

Trask, Haunani-Kay, 193

Tsing, Anna Lowenhaupt, 165, 204–5n34, 211n3

tsunami (2004), 53–54, 191, 209–10n22

Tulum: as destination, 23; ecotourism and, 26, 213n16; and nostalgic representations of Maya culture, 110; tourist boom of, 39–40

Turkey, 201n12

Uc Espadas, Martha Concepción, 85

UN (United Nations): and the forty-year history of tourist interventions, 188; Global Code of Ethics for Tourism, 7, 200n8; International Year of Sustainable Tourism for Development (2017), 5; tourism as human right, 7, 194, 200n8

UN Climate Change Conference (2010), 65–66

UN Global Platform for Disaster Risk Reduction (2017), 65–66

UN Man and the Biosphere Program (MAB), 77–78

UN Small Island State Conference (2018), 66

UNCTAD (United Nations Conference on Trade and Development), 216n22

UNESCO (United Nations Educational Scientific and Cultural Organization): on Biosphere Reserve Ria Celestún, 78; on management of biosphere reserves, 77–78; and Uxmal, 110; World Heritage sites, 76, 110, 118–19, 216nn18,23

UNISDR (United Nations International Office for Disaster and Risk Reduction), 65

UNWTO (United Nations World Tourism Organization): Bill of Rights and

Tourism Code, 7; on cultural exchange, 6; on destinations where tourists outnumber residents, 201n12; International Trade Centre and, 199n3; Manila Declaration on World Tourism, 7; support for transition from beach resort tourism to alternative tourism, 158

UN World Heritage Convention (1972), 118

UN World Network of Biosphere Reserves, 78

uniforms for workers: the guayabera as, 131, 159, 165; in hacienda tourism, 106, 131, 142; naturalization of the indigenous self as uniformed and servile, 132; trousers, sewing for tourism (Tekit) and, 173

United Kingdom, 11, 201n12

United States: Cancún airport flights to, 206n41; economy of tourism in, 201n12; and the guayabera, 158–59, 161; and henequen (sisal) industry of Mexico, 113–14; heritage tourism on Southern plantations, 214n7; NAFTA, 157–58, 183, 219–20n10; post-9/11, 7; and urban planning as inseparable from tourism, 6; US Agency for International Development (USAID), 221n20. *See also* maquiladoras

urban governance: climate change as disregarded in, 33, 65–66; marketization of, 33, 39, 208n6

urbanization: desakotas (city-villages), 151–52, 159, 166, 219n4; and environmental deterioration, 9

urban planning: cities as spectacles of consumption, 192; lack of, for Cancún City, 44–45; and privatization in the wake of Hurricane Gilbert, 44; tourism as inseparable from, 6

Urry, John, 4, 10, 11, 15, 25, 74, 88, 111, 121, 195, 199–200n5, 201–2nn16–17

Uxmal, 68, 110, 118–19, 147

Uyghur people, 193

Vail, Pegi, 203–4n26

Vainikka, Vilhelmiina, 8, 66

Valladolid, 26, 160–61, 206n44

Vancouver, Canada, 6

Vázquez Castillo, María Teresa, 205n19

Vega Campos, Marielena, 34–35, 37, 208n8

Veijola, S., 200n9

Velasco Ruiz, Enrique, 210n29

Venice, 8–9, 194, 204n29

Veracruz, and guayaberas, 171, 172, 174

Vieques, 191

Villanueva Villanueva, Nancy Beatriz, 221n23

violence: ecological crisis as, 15; gender/domestic, 104; in natural protection areas, 212nn9,13; terrorist attacks on tourist sites and infrastructures, 9, 191. *See also* Celestún—conflict and violence in

virtual tourism, 203n25

Vogel, Steven, 6, 103, 200n6

voluntourism, 217n27

wages/income: in Cancún, 61; in Celestún, 91, 97, 104; in hacienda luxury tourism, 135, 138, 146; minimum wage law, 135, 171; and sewing for tourism (Tekit), 178–79

Wallace, James M. Tim, 200n9, 208n7

Wangari, Esther, 25

Wang, Ning, 216n23

Warman, Arturo, 209n11

waste and waste management: in Celestún, 85–86, 102, 103, 104, 105; illegal/unregulated dumping, 129, 177; in Tekit, 177; in Temozón (village), 129, 141. *See also* sewage

water services: lack of, 177; privatization of, 44, 100, 209n17. *See also* housing and infrastructure; sewage

Weaver, David B., 74

Wells, Allen, 20, 114–15, 116, 137

Wetlands Convention (Ramsar), 76–77

Weyhing, Richard, 217n32

Wilk, Richard R., 175

Williams, Stephen, 207n45

Wilson Gilmore, Ruth, 152

Wilson, Tamar Diana, 208n7, 210n24

Witchger, Katian, 25, 201–2n16

Witynski, Karen, 116

Wolf, Eric R., 113

women's sexuality, commodification of, 210n26

Founded in 1893,
UNIVERSITY OF CALIFORNIA PRESS
publishes bold, progressive books and journals
on topics in the arts, humanities, social sciences,
and natural sciences—with a focus on social
justice issues—that inspire thought and action
among readers worldwide.

The UC PRESS FOUNDATION
raises funds to uphold the press's vital role
as an independent, nonprofit publisher, and
receives philanthropic support from a wide
range of individuals and institutions—and from
committed readers like you. To learn more, visit
ucpress.edu/supportus.